graphic agitation

Liz McQuiston

Social and Political Graphics since the Sixties

Phaidon Press Limited
Regent's Wharf
All Saints Street
London N1 9PA

Phaidon Press Inc.
180 Varick Street
New York, NY 10014

www.phaidon.com

First published 1993
Reprinted in paperback,
1995, 1998, 2000,
2004, 2006
© 1993 Phaidon Press Ltd

ISBN
0 7148 3458 0

A CIP catalogue record for
this book is available from
the British Library

Printed in Hong Kong

Frontispiece
'Eat': anti-Vietnam War
poster by Tomi Ungerer,
1967.
*Cover photograph by
Julian Lee*

Acknowledgements
The author wishes to give
special thanks to the
following for consultation
and generous assistance
in the making of this book.

Rene Andrew
Joseph P. Ansell
Phil Bicker
Frances Bloomfield
John Campbell, ACT UP
   London
Estelle Carol, Barbara
   Bejna, Shirley Jensen and
   Julie Zolot of the Chicago
   Women's Graphics
   Collective
Julia Church
Dr Hazel Clark, Hong Kong
   Polytechnic
Yiannis Frangoulis
Jude Harris
Sue Herron
Steve Jeppesen, Course
   Director, and the
   students of the
   Commercial Art Dept of
   The American College in
   London (Eva Chiu, Gioia
   Francella, Andre Pang,
   Gabriella Pucsok and
   others)
Barry Kitts
Wolfgang Kreile

Mrs N. Levenstein
Tom and Tina Maxwell
Edward McDonald
John McKay, Ravensbourne
   College of Design
   and Communication
George E. McQuiston
Victor McQuiston
Chris Holmlund, Baldwin
   Lee, Susan Metros and
   the Art Dept, University of
   Tennessee/Knoxville
Mary V. Mullin, ICOGRADA
William Owen
Suzanne Perkins
Sue Plummer
David Reeson
Viv Reid, Newham Drugs
   Advice Project, London
Mike Sheedy
Michelle Thomas
Mrs Jacqueline Thompson
Teal Triggs
Professor Michael Twyman,
   Dept of Typography
   and Graphic
   Communication,
   University of Reading
Shelley van Rooyen
Dan Walsh, Liberation
   Graphics
Carol A. Wells, Center for
   the Study of Political
   Graphics.

Publishers' note
This work is intended as a résumé of the growth of political and social agitation
via graphics since the 1960s. The publishers wish to make it clear that the views
expressed in the images contained in this publication are not their own but those
of the individuals and organizations that created them. The publishers do not
consider that these views are necessarily justified, truthful or accurate.

   The materials included demonstrate the utilization of graphic art by individuals
and bodies with differing aims. Those employing graphic means to spread their
views are of varying repute, and range from governments through to terrorist
organizations and include, amongst others, various pressure groups and
commercial institutions. This book depicts the many graphic methods used and
portrays the lengths to which people will go in order to communicate their views to
the public. The inclusion of such work is for the purpose of criticism and review of
the use of the graphic medium and in no way indicates that the publishers agree
with the sentiments expressed therein, nor that the targets of any of the
illustrations are deserving of such treatment.

Contents

Introduction
Three decades of graphic agitation

The term 'political graphics' sets off a flood of images and impressions. Angry protest posters or banners for demonstrations may spring to mind, or the razzmatazz and hard-sell of political party campaigns. The 'newspeak' of war propaganda, subversion through the underground press, caricatures in daily newspapers, graffiti sprayed on walls and pavements or badges and t-shirts shouting slogans within a crowd: all represent the graphic 'voice' of propaganda, protest and agitation. And although the forms may be ephemeral, the effects are not. Press images and posters become icons of an era, marking turning points in past history, while media campaigns and billboards influence the present, bearing images and slogans that become engrained in our personal politics.

This book takes a broad look, over the past three decades, at the use of graphics for propaganda and protest. It deals with both the official graphic voice of the Establishment as well as the unofficial voice of dissenters and agitators. For both are part of the political landscape and exert an influence over society's attitudes and opinions both belong to an on-going context of power struggles; and both have generated graphic innovations over the decades.

The nature of the work contained here is extremely varied. The term 'graphics' is used to describe a wide range of graphic statements – from the crudest amateur t-shirt or wall graffiti to the most elaborate professional media campaign. 'Graphic design' in itself describes a broad-based field of activity, encompassing design for print, advertising, moving graphics for film and TV, and all manner of visual communication and design. Graphic designers often work across a variety of disciplines and media, and at the same time much interesting graphic work has emanated from artists in other areas of visual communication. To reflect this broad scenario, the net has been cast widely and freely to include projects from professional graphic designers (also fine artists, stylists, fashion designers and so on) as well as influential amateur contributions. All however will be discussed within a design-related context, looking at graphic roles, techniques and traditions.

Political and social issues are also assigned broad meaning here, for both have undergone substantial change and redefinition over the past decade, particularly in relation to the visual arts and design. Up to the mid-1980s, 'politics' usually inferred party politics. But with the build-up of 'awareness' activities – including charity rock events such as Live

Aid, pressure groups campaigning for new attitudes towards peace and the environment and style magazines promoting activism and human rights – the term politics has grown more and more to signify popular movements relating to social issues. This has evolved into the 1990s trend towards 'personal politics', an individual awareness and concern for world problems, and a sense of responsibility to self, friends and family, society and the planet as a whole – perhaps as a sign of growing disillusionment with governments and political parties unable to get to grips with today's global problems and crises. In the light of such developments, the many and varied forms of graphic design remain an important instrument for political – and personal – expression.

The 1960s provide a useful starting point for this collection, both socially and graphically. Many of the social revolutions that have moulded contemporary life were staged in the Sixties. A decade of turbulence and social change, the era lives on as one of our greatest modern-day myths. But it was equally a creative watershed. The energy of change also surged through the art and design worlds, bringing innovations in graphics, fashion, film and photography. In addition, many of the anti-establishment statements of that time were made through a graphic medium. The US poster boom, which reflected the mounting anti-war feeling, and the psychedelic graphics surrounding drugs and music, were all part of a communication link between the young, the protesters, the drop-outs. The ensuing visual language with its colours and fantasies was soon drawn into the mainstream and spread round the world, and the notion of graphics as a tool for popular expression – a means of speaking out and being heard – has been a vital facet of rebellion and youth culture ever since.

This is not however a history book; there is no attempt to provide a comprehensive historical survey of political events over 30 years – either in individual countries or within an international scenario. Neither is the intention to provide in-depth coverage on any particular issue, movement, group or individual. The interests and concerns of this book are design-led: chapter headings appear as broad themes, and the book's emphasis lies in the depiction of an on-going flux of struggles and concerns, and the part that graphics can play in expressing such struggles. For example, rather than concentrate campaigns and projects relating to anti-racism all in one place, they are in fact sited within sections relating to national politics, liberation movements, human rights and so on. Their reappearance throughout the book highlights the continuing and endemic nature of racial struggles, how they differ from country to country and culture to culture, and the different forms of graphic expression they have generated over the years.

Various themes recur throughout the book. First and foremost is the theme of power. Politics is essentially about power and control, and most of the graphic material in this collection is discussed as part of a struggle for, or against, power. Often the power struggles are between the Establishment or ruling party and the person in the street. The notion of 'the street' appears throughout as a symbol of the public domain, a forum or arena for the 'masses' and their graphic statements.

FREE SOUTH AFRICA

4

3

Social comment takes many graphic forms. 1 T-shirt design by fashion stylist Judy Blame, Britain 1992. 2 The NAMES Project quilt created in memory of people who have died of AIDS, photo by Marc Geller, USA 1987. 3 'Nobody's perfect', postcard by Klaus Staeck designed in the International Year of the Disabled, West Germany 1981. 4 Anti-apartheid poster by Keith Haring, USA 1985.

1

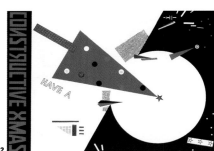

2

3

Censorship and levels of tolerance – whether by the ruling party or the public itself – are issues that vary greatly between the countries represented, and allow interesting visual comparisons to be made. Visual satire and other forms of graphic criticism and abuse tend to be most highly developed in those countries that have a long democratic tradition of freedom of speech and freedom of the press, such as America, Britain, Germany and France, although degrees of tolerance vary. (The billboard showing Margaret Thatcher hanging by a noose on page 49 lasted only a few days in Britain, but it is unlikely that its equivalent would ever have been displayed in America.) In the creative communities of these countries, freedom of expression is viewed as a basic right to be preserved and defended, with parameters that must be continually challenged and stretched. Censorship of any kind is consequently a matter of great debate, and a relatively sophisticated battle of policies and protests. It is a far cry from the death penalties and disappearances experienced in some areas of the world. In Ceausescu's Romania, for example, any critical comment against government or leader was confined to a scribble of graffiti on the wall (page 69), whilst many former Iron Curtain countries are only now beginning to understand and deal with the effects of many years of Communist state control and artistic censorship.

Visual language and graphic language are phrases often used when discussing work. These refer to a combination of elements – style, symbolism, typography, atmosphere or tone, historical and artistic references and so forth – which communicate a message in a particular way, or with particular emotion or force. Graphic symbolism plays an especially interesting role in communicating the ideals and aspirations of struggles, in that events or entire causes may be reduced to a simple graphic shape, or collection of objects, which embodies their essence or meaning. A favourite among graphic designers (and the subject of much pastiche, as shown here) is El Lissitzky's 1919 abstract composition 'Beat the Whites with the Red Wedge', a modernistic battlefield of shapes, and powerfully symbolic in its show of Bolshevik strength over the White Russians. More recently, in the 1989 uprising in Romania the emblem for the Popular Revolution was derived from cutting the centre out of the country's flag (removing the old regime's emblem), a gesture that was quickly crystallized into a graphic symbol of anger and suffering.

Media and technology can also have great effect on the meaning and resonance of the message. The more direct, or cruder, methods of image-making and duplicating (handwriting, stencilling, photocopying, hand-stamping) can provide immediacy and emotional impact. Silkscreen remains a favourite medium for low-run prints and is still difficult to rival for boldness and 'bite', as well as for economy and low-tech convenience. Offset litho liberated the 1960s underground from the constraints of silkscreen and letterpress and played a substantial role in the graphic revolutions of that era, whilst the new technology of the 1980s and 1990s possesses its own in-built visual language. Bitmap typefaces, electronic colours, pixellated textures, special screen

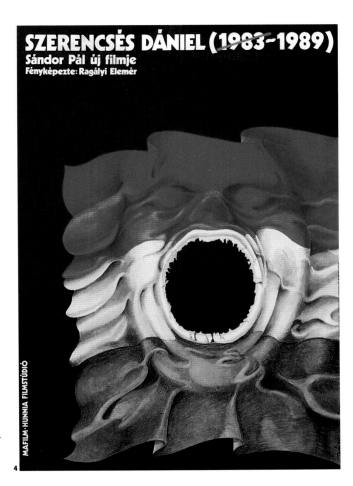

4

5

1 & 2 'Beat the Whites with the Red Wedge', poster by El Lissitzky, Soviet Russia 1919; Christmas card pastiche by South Atlantic Souvenirs, Britain 1980s.
3 'Attack!', poster by a group protesting against the World Bank and highlighting the cause of Third World aid and human rights, West Germany 1988.
4 'Lucky Daniel', poster by Péter Pócs for a Hungarian film concerned with the post-1956 emigration to the West. The image refers to the period of October/November 1956 when the insurgents cut the hated Russian-style herald out of the Hungarian flag. The poster was banned in 1983, then reprinted in 1989 (hence the two dates).
5 First Day Cover printed envelope and franking stamp (1990) commemorating the Romanian popular revolution of December 1989.

effects and various genres of icons conjure up high-tech societies, future worlds and real or imagined military operations, an issue exploited in the comment on the Gulf War shown on page 60.

Finally, the book examines important issues centring around the concept of 'format' – that is, the form that carries a graphic image or message. (The medium of print, for example, encompasses many different formats, such as books, billboards and magazines.) Format, media and visual language all work together to define the size and scope – and ultimately the impact – of the graphic statement.

The roles and functions of traditional formats such as posters or billboards can be traced throughout the different chapters. Posters, for example, function best when communicating a simple idea, in a way that is visually arresting. Along with film and radio they are highly suited to the role of propaganda, as they can travel fast and be changed frequently. Because of their instant impact, posters can function amidst a large amount of conflicting information and visual 'noise', or in a place where people must read quickly such as streets or busy stations; they can also communicate to a non-literate audience or an audience not happy or accustomed to reading. One of the poster's greatest roles

has been as a political tool in the revolution and reconstruction of socialist societies (such as the Soviet Union, China and Cuba); the poster also played an important role in solidarity and consciousness-raising in the liberation movements of the Sixties and remains to this day a crucial format for popular movements and educational organizations. The Center for the Study of Political Graphics in Los Angeles, for example, currently prepares exhibitions of its political poster collections for display in public places – such as university libraries, galleries, government buildings and theatres – with the educational aim of providing an alternative to interpretations of current events presented by the mainstream media. All exhibitions are fully annotated, and include interpretative essays, translations and contextual information. The Center therefore strives to continue the agitational tradition of the protest poster, while relating it to a current audience and context.

But at the same time traditions are being expanded and uprooted: formats and their roles are changing. The 1990s are about participation, interactivity and activism. Stars of the fashion and music industry contribute to causes ranging from AIDS to the rainforest; style

3

4

5

Examples of the many roles of posters.
1 Spontaneous street graphics: the Catalan Independence Movement lynches the Olympic games mascot Cobi in this poster, a sign of resentment towards the focus given to the 1992 summer games in Barcelona.
2 Keeping the memory of past tragedies alive: poster for a concert for the victims of Communism, designed by István Orosz, Hungary 1990.
3 & 4 The Center for the Study of Political Graphics promotes a modern educational role for protest posters. Two posters from the Center's collection are shown here, both opposed to the 1991 Gulf War: 'No Blood for Oil' by Keith R. Potter and Steven Lyons, USA 1990, and 'US Out of the Middle East', by Fireworks Graphics Collective, USA 1990.
5 'Rodeo', poster by Doug Minkler criticizing aspects of educational and social programming, USA 1992.

1

COLORS

a magazine about the rest of the world   una revista sobre el resto del mundo

las tribus en nueva york
cowboys en polonia
el rey de tonga y la reina del ajo
(Y UN PRÍNCIPE O DOS)
desayuno en el tibet
(EN EGIPTO, EN RUSIA Y EN LA COSTA DE MARFIL)
héroes en guatemala
(EN AFRICA DEL SUR Y EN TAILANDIA)
besos en todas partes

tribes in new york
cowboys in poland
breakfast in tibet
(AND EGYPT AND RUSSIA AND CÔTE D'IVOIRE)
king of tonga & queen of garlic
(AND A PRINCE OR TWO)
heroes in guatemala
(AND SOUTH AFRICA AND THAILAND)
kisses everywhere

2

3   4

5

magazines confront racism and fascism; corporate magazines and press campaigns ask young people to write in and say what's on their mind (see Benetton and Esprit on pages 204-5); fashion and style have become vehicles for self-awareness, cultural identity and pride. Street formats with traditional commercial roles – signs, billboards, stickers, fly-posters – have become platforms for questioning, moralizing or arguing in the public domain.

The roles of mainstream communication formats, traditionally based on distance and authority, are now breaking down and being redefined towards involvement and participation. The information industries have brought social dilemmas and global concerns within our reach. People are now in touch with the world, and have the technology and the means to confront the big issues such as poverty, homelessness, racism, right-wing extremism, the threat of AIDS and the destruction of natural resources – and in coming years, will no doubt find ever more imaginative and creative ways to deal with them. Political graphics look set to continue to be transformed through new media and technology, as people take their destiny into their own hands, unite against the world's problems, and make their voices heard.

Social and political issues expand into style and fashion.
1 'Keep Britain Tidy', t-shirt designed by fashion stylist Judy Blame, with a graphic inspired by the International Tidy Man symbol (model: Mark Lawrence; photographer: Pierre Rutschi). From a style essay in the Activism issue of *i-D* magazine, Britain, April 1992.
2 *Colors*, Benetton's combined youth magazine and clothes catalogue, 1991.
3 & 4 British style magazines *i-D* and *The Face* explore the themes of anti-racism and anti-fascism in 1992.
5 Malcolm X earrings, a small part of the large collection of clothes and accessories generated by the films of Spike Lee and sold through his shop Spike's Joint in New York City, 1992.

1 MONSTER SOUP commonly called THAMES WATER

2

Propaganda and protest graphics
A brief historical outline

Propaganda and protest through the graphic arts have a long and turbulent history that stretches far back over the centuries, and shadows developments in print technology. Social satire, political cartooning, pamphleting, graffiti and other types of agitation in current usage all have roots in the very distant past.

Street graphics date back to Roman times; early displays of a politicized graphic voice have been cited in the 'graffiti' of Pompeii, where political slogans and commentary were written, painted and carved onto city walls. Later, during the Renaissance, placards carrying political comments were hung on public statues; it was also possible for a dialogue to develop between a number of these 'talking statues' or *pasquinades*. Both examples mark the beginnings of a tradition of street debate – between the public, its parties and leaders – that still finds form in present-day activities such as graffiti, fly-posting and organized marches and rallies. Talking back and arguing (graphically) in the streets is evidently one of our longest traditions.

The spirit of agitation found its true form, however, in printed multiples. The invention of various print techniques during the mid- to late 1400s – most notably, Gutenberg's invention of movable type –

allowed early German prints to reflect public opinion and peasant life, while spreading new ideas. Enlisting the help of satire and humour, print quickly became the vehicle of the man in the street, with illustrations acting as the new mass language.

Martin Luther's Reformation movement (1520-21) was spread through print and particularly leaflets illustrated by German artists working in woodcut or wood engraving, including Albrecht Dürer, Lucas Cranach, Mathias Grünewald and Hans Holbein the Younger. In a wave of solidarity graphic artists also recorded the horrors of the Peasants' War, which ended in 1525. By the mid-1500s political prints and illustrated leaflets were widely available, sold by roving street sellers. Opposition to the church in Rome and nobility were two main themes.

For much of Europe the 1600s were years of constant armed struggle: religious wars, territorial wars, uprisings and revolutions were rife. Not surprisingly, this gave rise to a war artist tradition. Vast numbers of engravings were produced to document the battles, glorify the victors and justify the carnage, brutality and butchery. Jacques Callot, working in the early part of the century, was one of the most important chroniclers of the European wars, and exceptional for his concentration on horrors and destruction. He produced a large series of engraved prints entitled *The Miseries of War*, which depicted the mass hangings, sackings, pillaging and other brutalities of that gruesome era. The positive side of such devastation was that it sparked the rebellion of peasants and workers against the aristocracy. This atmosphere of growing criticism was to find vibrant form in the graphic satire of the next century.

The age of satire and social comment

The 1700s brought a new role for political graphics. No longer a recording device confined to lamenting on the sidelines, graphics were now charged with influencing and expressing public opinion. British satire led the way; its golden era began with the engraver William Hogarth (1697-1764), a pioneer of stinging social criticism and responsible for establishing the tradition of caricature in England.

Also from this period came the wealth of prints generated by the French Revolution and by the split between Britain and its American colonies. Furthermore, the invention of lithography by Aloys Senefelder in 1796 in Germany allowed greater freedom in drawing straight onto a surface, while also dramatically increasing the number of copies it was possible to produce.

The 1800s were essentially the years of visual satire, caricature and comic art. British satire flourished in the early 1800s through the work of Thomas Rowlandson, James Gillray, Isaac Cruikshank (and his sons Robert and George) and many others. In addition to scathing social and political satire, they found an extremely popular target in Napoleon, the first international figure in caricature. Caricaturists throughout Europe

made 'Boney' a legend in his own time, transferring his image and tales from country to country and revelling in his defeat and decline.

But away from the courts and the centre stage of world power-games, the massacres continued. Francisco Goya's series of etchings *The Disasters of War* depicted the horror and brutality taking place in the background of the battlelines, while Spain fought a war of independence against French-Napoleonic domination (1808-13). No battle scenes, glorious or otherwise, were shown; only a despairing realism and depiction of human suffering and waste.

By 1830, Britain's golden era of graphic satire was over, for public taste had grown more conservative and less tolerant of visual abuse. The focus immediately shifted to France, where the French newspapers began their spirited fight with censorship. The liberal revolution of 1830 brought the elected King Louis-Philippe to power and, by his own proclamation, freedom of the press. Three months later Charles Philipon founded the satirical weekly *La Caricature*, and almost immediately overshot the mark. His famous representation of the king as a pear-head (for which he was hauled to court in 1831, but then acquitted) was the first of many sensations. His daily paper *Le Charivari* was launched in 1832; by 1834 *La Caricature* was banned; by 1850 two more papers had been launched. Amid such enterprise and devilry, Philipon furthered the development of lithography and fostered a team of remarkable satirical artists that included Honoré Daumier, Paul Gavarni, Charles-Joseph Traviés, Jean-Ignace Grandville, and Henri Bonaventure Monnier – as well as a very young Gustave Doré.

The French golden era of political caricature lasted from 1830 until 1835, when general censorship was re-introduced. From thereon

1 *Monster Soup*, an etching by 'Paul Pry' William Heath, Britain 1828.
2 *The Hanging Tree*, an engraving from the series *The Miseries of War* by Jacques Callot, 1633.
3 *Maniac Ravings* or *Little Boney in a Strong Fit*, print by James Gillray, 1803.
4 Two pieces from Francisco Goya's series of etchings *The Disasters of War*, published in 1863 and depicting the Spanish resistance to Napoleonic domination. Shown here are (top) *Que valor!* (What courage) and (below) *No se puede mirar* (I can't bear to look).

French satire and caricature had to steer away from officials in government, and so instead targeted society and its mores. No one was safe – rich or poor, high or low – and the commentaries were produced in abundance for the daily deadlines of journals and newspapers. Well-known and widely copied in other countries, the artists involved were the undisputed leaders of sophisticated, graphic wit. (Doré for example grew to be famous in both England and France, producing book illustrations, paintings, and other works, as well as extraordinary social documentaries of the London poor.) Throughout the 1800s French comic papers would thrive in great numbers; *Le Rire* (1895) and *Le Sourire* (1899) count among the most famous.

Improvements in printing press design meant that mass-circulation illustrated newspapers were possible by the mid-1800s. In the latter half of the century both education and newspapers were entering their heyday. In both Europe and America, printing processes could now supply a growing literate readership and thus influence public opinion and votes. Cartoons appeared in newspapers and magazines, which were considered important vehicles for political debate and discussion.

Leading cartoonist and caricaturist Thomas Nast visualized the political forces of America as battles between good and evil, and also invented the party symbols of the Democrats (the donkey) and the Republicans (the elephant). Nast took political art into new investigative territory, and held considerable influence on the voting public. His greatest victory on this score came in 1871 when he used his visual skills to expose the corruption of the New York City administration and the Tammany Hall Ring, led by 'Boss' Tweed (William Marcy Tweed). Nast's relentless graphic campaign against Tweed, which ran in

Harper's Weekly magazine, portrayed Tweed in ever-worsening forms, and eventually turned the public against him. As a result, both the Ring and Tweed met their downfall, causing Tweed to make his famous lament about 'them damn pictures'.

America's satirical weekly *Puck*, which catered for a wide range of graphic humour, set off a deluge of periodicals that flooded America in graphic humour and cartooning. *Life* was one of the most influential, and home to Charles Dana Gibson's famous invention, the Gibson Girl. In the later part of the century, cartoons and comic strips were indeed the main carriers of political comment in America.

Also operating at that time was the great Mexican artist and printmaker José Guadalupe Posada. Considered to be the prime carrier of the spirit of the Mexican people, his prolific output – estimated to be over 15,000 prints – included numerous illustrations for the popular press: broadsheets, posters and street gazettes. Posada's graphics dealt with politics and social satire as well as providing a journalistic coverage of the latest news events. He was perhaps best known for his macabre and humourous *calaveras* – the dancing skeletons of Death, derived from folklore and ceremonies such as the Day of the Dead – which he used to represent his contemporaries, both friend and foe alike. But his work also provided an intense documentary of the period leading up to the Mexican Revolution of 1910.

Posada died in 1913, and was revered by other artists of that revolutionary period – particularly Diego Rivera, who became known for his public murals and political themes during the 1920s and 1930s. Both Rivera and his wife, the painter Frida Kahlo, were active members of the Mexican Communist Party and influential artists of the time.

2

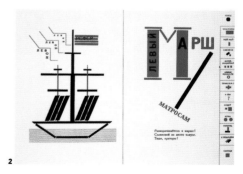

1

1 Poster promoting
the purchase of shares
in the state merchant
air service, designed by
Alexander Rodchenko,
1923.
2 Spread from *For the
Voice*, a book of poems
by Vladimir Mayakovsky,
designed by El Lissitzky,
1923.
3 Poster for Dziga
Vertov's film *Kino
Glaz* (Cinema Eye),
designed by Alexander
Rodchenko, 1924.
4 Railways
advertisement by
Vladimir Mayakovsky,
in the form of a
serialized window
poster as pioneered by
ROSTA, *c.*1920.

The avant-garde and World War One

On the other side of the Atlantic, meanwhile, the sharp edge of satire had gone soft. *Punch: The London Charivari*, founded in 1841, was influential throughout the second half of the 1800s but with a much less acidic form of graphic humour than its French counterpart; and the caricatures of the popular *Vanity Fair* were placid and pretty. But the Germans soon changed all that with the founding in 1896 of *Simplicissimus*, the sharpest and most influential satirical journal of them all (discussed on page 21).

The new century brought Europe advances in industrialization and new expectations for the union of art and industry. It also brought a rejection of the old traditions and social order, and an explosion of intellectually-based avant-garde art movements that embraced a new vision of an industrialized world. With the Futurist manifesto of 1909, the Modern Movement was born and spread like wildfire across countries as well as disciplines, involving writers, artists, designers and architects. In 1915 Kasimir Malevich invented Suprematism in Russia, which acted as the foundation for Constructivism. Dadaism, a protest against the First World War and all established values, followed in

Switzerland in 1916 and spread to New York, Paris and Berlin. Soon after, De Stijl was born in Holland, led by theorists Theo van Doesburg and Piet Mondrian. A new visual language grew out of the manifestos, journals, posters and other published works of these movements – created from 1910 to 1930 – which still has a strong influence on the visual arts today.

Constructivism is perhaps the best example of politics and revolution expressed directly through art and design, resulting in the creation of a new visual language. It was derived from Russian Suprematism, a purely abstract form of art utilizing simple geometric shapes. In the early 1920s the Constructivists rejected Suprematism's purely artistic and spiritual intentions and applied Suprematist forms across a broad range of applied arts and design including industrial design, furniture, textiles, theatre sets and graphics. Both movements worked in the service of the 1917 Bolshevik Revolution towards the 'construction' of a new society, creating everyday products and utility items for the new proletariat.

The painter and sculptor Alexander Rodchenko was one of Constructivism's leading artists. He produced a wide range of two- and three-dimensional work including graphic design for journals, film posters, advertisements (for state goods and services) and books – often working in collaboration with his friend, the poet Mayakovsky. Rodchenko's work most typifies the graphic language of Constructivism. His experiments with photomontage and his use of spatial dynamics, geometric forms and flat, bright colours produced a bold, utilitarian graphic style that encapsulated the sense of energy and optimism for the Soviet future.

El Lissitzky was another key artist in the Constructivist movement and the person most responsible for spreading its principles across Europe through lecturing, travelling and writing. In this way he also became one of the main links between the different avant-garde movements, for he collaborated on projects with many of their leading personalities and became involved in the important art publications of the time. He developed the concept of Constructivist typography, which soon became known as the New Typography and was then developed by László Moholy-Nagy and Herbert Bayer at the Bauhaus. Lissitzky's work equally embodies the spirit of the revolution, but with an underlying intellectualism and more delicately balanced sensitivity. Consequently Lissitzky produced the real landmarks of Constructivist graphics such as the propaganda poster 'Beat the Whites with the Red Wedge' in 1919, and the designs and illustrations for Mayakovsky's book of poems *For Reading Out Loud* (also known as *For the Voice*) in 1923.

The Constructivist movement had many remarkable qualities. The artists involved were in the extraordinary position of being able to turn their private abstract experiments into socially-orientated public art and design, as part of the Bolshevik revolutionary machine. Another

important aspect was the way in which the new visual language was played out in many different disciplines, including architectural work by Vladimir Tatlin, theatre sets by Alexander Vesnin and costume and textile designs by Varvara Stepanova and Ljubov Popova.

In addition, the propaganda tools of this period were highly innovative. ROSTA, the Russian Telegraph Agency, used a system of numbered posters to disseminate news and propaganda to a largely illiterate population. Each poster carried a group of pictures with captions arranged in a manner similar to a strip cartoon. Stencilled copies were made at great speed by families or small collectives, then forwarded to all the regions and placed in the windows of shops, railway stations or business premises – often replacing the old poster number and continuing the sequence. 'Agitprop' trains, painted with bright colours and political slogans and loaded down with printing presses, film newsreels, artists, film-makers and writers, ploughed their way to the distant corners of the country, spreading the word of revolution. Soviet cinema was also developing at this time in the hands of such directors as Dziga Vertov and Sergei Eisenstein, and played a crucial role in the political climate.

Perhaps most remarkable was the short time period in which these events occurred. By the end of the 1920s, roughly 12 years after the revolution, it was all over. Stalin outlawed abstract art and design in 1932, and Socialist Realism was introduced. But Constructivism was to cast a heavy influence through the years, and for many today it still embodies the spirit of revolution in visual form.

Avant-garde movements such as Constructivism naturally play a large part in any historical survey, in that they broke away from previous

graphic conventions and gave birth to the modern forms and concepts that we use today. But the significance of other graphic developments should not be overlooked.

At the turn of the century, the modern poster was established as a highly persuasive commercial advertising tool as well as an outstanding popular art form. The campaign for women's suffrage was probably the first to borrow the styles and techniques of commercial advertising posters to serve a distinct political cause or anti-establishment viewpoint. In the campaign's most militant years, from 1900 to 1920, advertising techniques were used to influence the electorate, and the stylized realism of art nouveau, so prevalent at the time, served to undermine the 'ugly suffragette' theory and keep the tone soft yet persuasive. Many of the suffrage posters avoided political confrontation, or the display of an antagonistic attitude to men; this was particularly the case with American posters, where persuasion often took the form of a 'civilized' appeal to men for reform and justice. The British movement, on the other hand, was highly publicized for its aggressive militancy, and consequently its posters were more assertive.

Suffrage posters were published privately or by local and national organizations such as the National Women's Suffrage Association (NAWSA) in New York, and the Women's Social and Political Union (WSPU) or Artists' Suffrage League in London. Banners and signs also played an important part in suffrage marches and meetings, and a mass of inventive popular ephemera and graphic imagery surrounded the movement. Women's suffrage and equality was also very much an international movement and consequently imagery was generated in many countries around the world.

The campaign for women's suffrage took different graphic forms on each side of the Atlantic. While American imagery stylishly swayed its audience, the British equivalent was generally more militant.

1 'Suffragettes', sheet music with illustration by Reginald Rigby, Britain 1913.
2 'Suffragists on the War Path', postcard, Britain c.1910.
3 'Votes for Women', poster by B.M. Boye, USA c.1913.

The use of a popular, commercial art form – the poster – for political purposes was developed in a much grander style in World War One. For governments faced with the problem of selling a war to their public – and sustaining it with the consequent drain on money, supplies and human life – the obvious solution was to approach the professionals who knew how to sell ideas and products: commercial artists. In this fashion the modern advertising poster became the main vehicle for sustaining one of the most devastating wars in history.

World War One posters, produced by participating countries, were characterized by a wide variety of talent and approach. The German war posters boasted master artists of world renown such as Ludwig Hohlwein and Lucian Bernhard, and conveyed the patriotic idealism of heroics and sacrifice. British posters had a much tougher psychological grip on their audience. Britain entered the war with no conscription and relied on volunteers, and consequently British posters often employed scare tactics (claiming atrocities committed by the enemy) or attempted to shame men into volunteering with implications of cowardice and loss of honour. A good example of the use of shaming and guilt was the poster by Saville Lumley that posed the question

'Daddy, what did YOU do in the Great War?', asked by a child sitting on her father's knee. The most successful British recruitment poster was Alfred Leete's famous depiction of Lord Kitchener, pointing an accusing finger at the viewer and demanding 'Your country needs YOU'.

The Americans rallied with a populist approach, derived from well-known magazine and book illustrators of the time. Names such as Charles Dana Gibson and Howard Chandler Christy were drawn into the war effort. Appeals were made through realistic representations of ordinary people or popular symbols such as Uncle Sam and the Statue of Liberty; images of women were often used to supply sex appeal and glamour. But the Americans also succumbed to scare tactics and accusatory pointing fingers, supplying their own version of 'I Want You' (with Uncle Sam) by James Montgomery Flagg in 1917. Most impressive were the numbers involved: posters printed in editions of 10,000 to one million copies each flooded the cities and towns.

With a wide variety of approaches extending across all the different countries, World War One saw the modern poster at the height of its power and influence, with all the strategies and tactics of modern advertising being put to the test.

Economic crisis and the rise of Fascism

Throughout the 1920s the American economy boomed, but the Wall Street Crash of 1929 set off a world economic crisis and America plunged into the Great Depression. During those painful years, federal programmes tried to revitalize the country. In the early 1930s, artists hard hit by the Depression were employed by the Federal Art Project as part of the Works Progress Administration or WPA. This fostered a variety of new directions in art, among them the move towards an expression of American identity which gradually developed into the Social Realist movement. Social Realism depicted the misery of the poor, particularly in the mid- and western rural regions of the country, and committed artists such as Ben Shahn worked to combat social injustice and prejudice. His memorial drawings of Sacco and Vanzetti (Italian emigrant workers wrongly sentenced to death) provided one of the best examples of his work's emotional power, as well as displaying Shahn's distinctive use of text and lettering.

World War One had also left in its wake a distressed and exhausted Europe. While the idealism of Constructivism was flourishing in Russia, the Weimar Republic was struggling to deal with reparation payments owed from the war. It spiralled into unemployment and inflation, which peaked in 1923 with the collapse of the currency. Thereafter the economy began to recover and industrial production was on the rise; but so was nationalism and Adolf Hitler. The US stock market crash of 1929 plunged Germany into economic crisis once more, and paved the way for takeover by Hitler's Nazi Party. In 1933 he took up office as German chancellor.

Chronicling this process was *Simplicissimus*, the tough satirical weekly with the distinctive bulldog symbol (drawn by Thomas Theodor Heine, co-founder and contributor to the magazine). It was launched in 1896, and over the next three decades *Simplicissimus* was the world leader in biting satire. The chief artists were Olaf Gulbransson and Karl Arnold, and their use of a sophisticated and at times decorative outline style, to make aggressive and often vicious comment, was revolutionary at the time and influenced generations of artists thereafter. The paper's favourite targets for ridicule were capitalism, the ruling classes, and (eventually) Hitler; and it was consequently forced to close in 1933.

There were others operating in the shadow of Fascism. John Heartfield's scathing photomontages denounced Hitler, Göring and other Nazi bosses with shocking and bloody imagery, often published as the front covers of the Communist magazine *AIZ* (*Arbeiter Illustrierte Zeitung*, meaning Workers' Illustrated Paper). Both Heartfield and *AIZ* were forced to leave Germany and continued working in Prague, where Heartfield produced his best and most disturbing imagery; he finally fled to England in 1938.

Other graphic artists whose drawings and prints depicted the reality that surrounded them also suffered: Otto Dix was barred from exhibiting and jailed; George Grosz, fearing for his life, fled to America. Käthe Kollwitz, whose graphic art had for years been dedicated to exposing the poverty and oppression of the German working class and the wider

1 & 2 World War One recruitment tactics: poster by James Montgomery Flagg, USA 1917, and poster by Saville Lumley, Britain c.1917.
3 Ben Shahn's 1931 commemoration of Sacco and Vanzetti, the Italian emigrant workers wrongly sentenced to death in 1929.

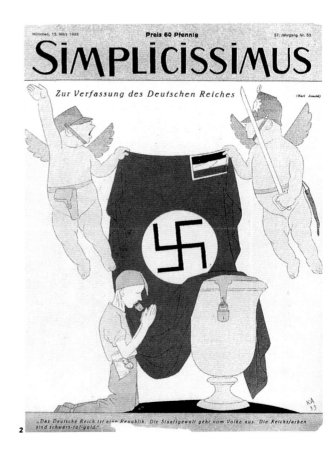

despair of war, was dismissed from teaching at the Berlin Academy in 1933. She remained working in Germany despite official persecution.

Further casualties included the Dutch jobbing printer Hendrik Werkman, now hailed as one of the great pioneers of modern typography. He produced experimental typographic compositions and his own periodical entitled *The Next Call*, which he sent to friends and colleagues in the avant-garde scene around the world. From 1940 to 1944 he also printed 40 issues of the clandestine publication *The Blue Barge* – which urged readers to keep up a 'spiritual resistance' to the German occupation – as well as other secret publications. In 1945 he was arrested and shot by the German secret police, only a few days before the liberation of Groningen. Much of his work was destroyed.

In Vienna, Otto Neurath and Marie Reidemeister (later, Marie Neurath) pioneered the Isotype system of pictorial symbols, a means of presenting vital social statistics on housing, health and other issues to the population of post-war Austria. They were forced to leave their base in Vienna in 1934, moving first to Holland and then to England. Meanwhile the Modern Movement's prime educational experiment, the Bauhaus – established in 1919 by Walter Gropius – had been forced to close. Having moved from Weimar to Dessau and finally to Berlin, it was shut down by the Nazis in 1933 and its staff and students scattered.

The radicalism of the avant-garde was considered anti-German and decadent. Its members were seen as supporters of Marxism or the Bolshevik Revolution (a severe threat to the Nazis' power grip), its institutions deemed to be occupied by foreigners and Jews. The products and concepts of Modernism were denounced as 'cultural Bolshevism', and the art movements derived from Cubism as 'degenerate art'. Ironically some unexpected good did come of the avant-garde's expulsion from Nazi Germany, for it served to spread their ideas and influence around the world.

Modern art and the avant-garde were at times extremely active in the fight against Fascism, most notably during the Spanish Civil War (1936-9). Picasso's painting *Guernica*, one of modern art's most powerful political statements, was an expression of outrage at the bombing of a Basque town in 1937. Exhibited that same year at the Paris World Exhibition as a memorial of the tragedy, it placed the standard of the modern art movements firmly on the Left. As political art, it marked the end of an era, for the political role of the war artist

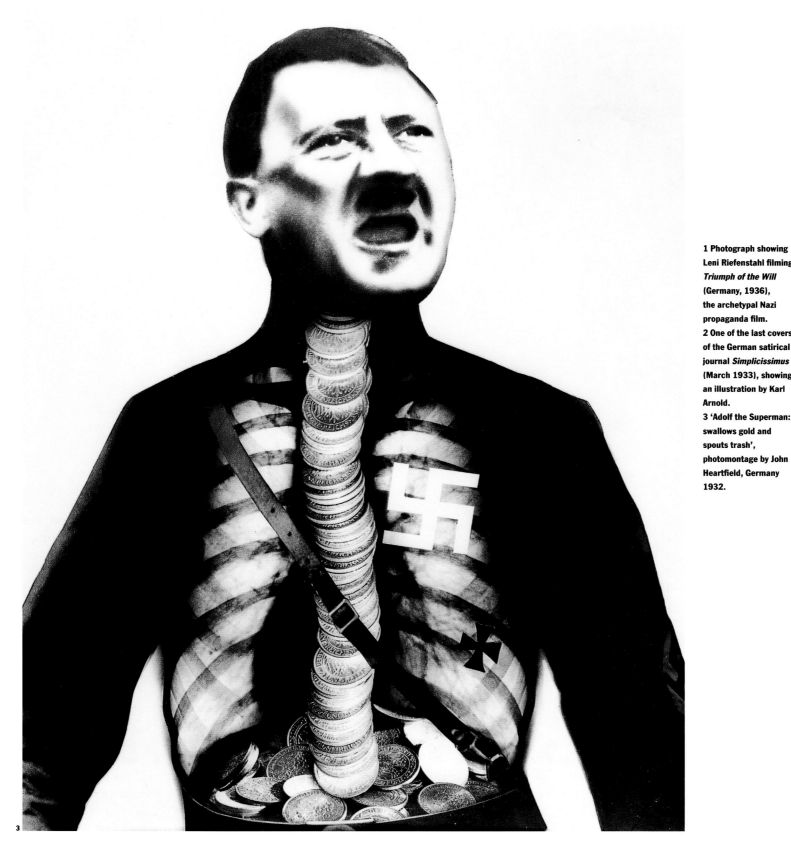

1 Photograph showing
Leni Riefenstahl filming
Triumph of the Will
(Germany, 1936),
the archetypal Nazi
propaganda film.
2 One of the last covers
of the German satirical
journal *Simplicissimus*
(March 1933), showing
an illustration by Karl
Arnold.
3 'Adolf the Superman:
swallows gold and
spouts trash',
photomontage by John
Heartfield, Germany
1932.

3

Dans la lutte actuelle, je vois du côté fasciste les forces
périmées, de l'autre côté le peuple dont les immenses ressources
créatrices donneront à l'Espagne un élan qui étonnera
le monde.   Miró.

was soon to be superseded by photography. From World War Two onwards it was photographs that were to affect people's politics, not paintings.

Fascist intervention in Spain also brought international aid and volunteers to back the Spanish Republican forces. Posters such as Joan Miró's 'Aidez l'Espagne' were produced to encourage international supplies and aid, and to condemn the fascist bombings in the eyes of the world. The posters of this struggle exploited the prevailing styles and influences of the time. Their use of symbolism and simplification of forms and figures was borrowed from Surrealism and the advertising art of Cassandre, Carlu, McKnight Kauffer and others. Symbolic objects were often grouped together; Cubist-influenced figures or forms were highly simplified and cropped to show dramatic detail, and images – often photographic – were juxtaposed and montaged to poignant effect. This use of graphic symbolism, as opposed to realistic representation, heralded a new form of modern political poster.

World War Two and the Cold War years

World War Two placed graphic design in some of its most challenging roles, working for both good and evil. It occupied a central place in Hitler's empire-building, and for the Allies generated solidarity and support in war effort projects and information design services aimed at the public good.

Hitler's design strategy for the Third Reich was one of the most powerful and threatening national identities the world has ever experienced, and benefited from the thoroughness applied to any tough corporate identity programme. He outlined his initial ideas on the art of propaganda in *Mein Kampf*, written while he was in prison; this included the use of stereotypes, strategies, and target audiences – as well as praise for the British, who, as Hitler noted, treated propaganda as a weapon in its own right. Once in power, the transformation was systematic: a new flag and emblem (the swastika) were employed immediately; non-serifed typefaces were replaced by traditional gothic black-letter typefaces known as Deutsche Schrift; and Goebbels was appointed State Minister for Propaganda and People's Entertainment, with the mission of co-ordinating the all-important media of film, broadcasting and print to promote a 'Greater Germany'.

From thereon followed a massive strategy of image and information manipulation: co-ordinated colours, slogans, emblems, and uniforms; vast and meticulously staged rallies and demonstrations; and an outpouring of anti-Semitic and racist material. Still photography, newsreels and documentaries, carefully edited to present the success of the Nazi 'New Europe', were a crucial part of Nazi indoctrination and an everlasting reminder of the ability of such media forms to distort reality. The design 'machinery' was difficult to fault; the content, aims and motives have remained among the greatest horrors of all time.

On the Allied side, government propaganda, in the form of public information and morale-boosting, was the main function of the graphic arts. Britain's Ministry of Information (MOI) issued morale posters that

2

3

1 'Aidez l'Espagne', design for a French anti-Fascist pamphlet by Joan Miró, 1937.
2 Front cover of the political parody 'Adolf in Blunderland' (the published script of a radio broadcast), illustrated by Norman Mansbridge, Britain 1939.
3 Poster from the British 'Dig for Victory' campaign (artist unknown).

1

1 Poster by the British
designer FHK Henrion
for the United States
Office of War
Information, 1944.
It was designed to
be shown on the
continent after the
D-Day liberation.
2 Poster supporting
the fight for the four
freedoms of Western
democracy, as
illustrated by Norman
Rockwell, USA 1939-45.

2

called for public help in aiding factory production and guarding national security. (Good examples were the 1940 'Careless Talk Costs Lives' and 'Dig for Victory' campaigns.) The MOI also made heavy use of public exhibitions created by well-known designers of the time such as FHK Henrion, Charles Hasler, George Him and Jan Le Witt. In addition, the War Office produced posters and educational/instructional material; much of their best work was created by graphic designer and poster artist Abram Games.

The end of the war brought a significant reconstruction problem for Britain. Efforts to encourage post-war recovery and keep the public going despite rationing of food and clothing led to the creation of events such as the 'Britain Can Make It' exhibition at the Victoria & Albert Museum in 1946, and culminated in the greatest morale-raising exercise of all: the Festival of Britain in 1951.

America once again relied on posters as the primary medium for war propaganda, and the United States Office of War Information (OWI) and other government departments drew the nation's best popular artists and illustrators into action. American war posters mainly aimed to encourage the purchase of war bonds, build public morale and keep up production. Their overriding characteristics were large production runs, high-quality printing and a diversity of graphic styles that ranged from home-town realism to modernist experimentation. They included posters by Norman Rockwell (whose paintings, reproduced in *The Saturday Evening Post*, championed America's values, freedoms and way of life); Social Realist painters such as Ben Shahn and Bernard Perlin; and refugee artists such as Jean Carlu, who was working for the Free French cause and supporting the American war effort.

The advent of the Cold War in the 1950s saw America rise to its highest levels of world power and consumer power. But the deepening divisions between Eastern socialism and Western capitalism were reflected in waves of conformism on both sides of the line. For the West, the heroic peasant-worker imagery of Communist state propaganda began to take on the face of totalitarianism and world domination; the image of the 'evil empire' loomed. An extreme reaction came in the form of the anti-Communist hysteria of McCarthyism in America. The nuclear arms race that began also formed part of the distrust, and fear of nuclear war and 'the Bomb' sparked off campaigns for world peace that still continue to this day.

But the materialistic emphasis of mass consumerism also brought discontent from within America. Flaws began to show: inequalities between racial groups, between the 'haves' and 'have-nots' became evident. Civil rights activities simmered throughout the Fifties, one of a number of issues of power and equality that were soon to extend to other domains. At the same time, international inequalities started to surface as colonialism began to see its day. Triggered by crises such as the Bay of Pigs, Algeria and the Cuban Missile Crisis, it all exploded in the Sixties in waves of anger, protest and re-direction. The explosion was to resonate around the world and echo down through the decades, as shown in the graphic protests that follow.

3

3 Photographs from the West German 'Ban the Bomb' movement of the 1950s, which had strong support from the Social Democrats as well as renowned scientists, theologians and artists. The skeletons carry a banner saying 'Negotiations are better than sabre-rattling', and the dummy-bomb mounted on top of the bubble car reads 'The Bomb is suicide: Remember Hiroshima'. The vehicle was stopped several times by the police on its journey to Bonn, and was confiscated just before it could reach its destination.

4 The first Campaign for Nuclear Disarmament (CND) march from London to Aldermaston, Britain 1958.

4

3

Chapter one

2

National politics

Political parties, governments and leaders

1

The national politics of virtually any country comprises a mass of internal power struggles. The 'graphic voice' that emanates from those struggles has two forms: the official voice, and the unofficial voice. The official voice belongs to 'the establishment': governments, leaders and institutions that operate systems of control (political, economic or social), and define societal values and priorities. The unofficial voice belongs to those who question, criticize or even reject those systems and structures as well as the motives of the people behind them. The struggles may at times be waged over quite specific laws or taxes, such as Britain's poll tax, or they may be arguments over broader principles, such as the financing of AIDS research in America or the rise of neo-Nazi extremism in Germany. In the end, however, all of these struggles relate to power: either fighting for it, or against it.

This chapter does not aim to provide a comprehensive survey of different countries and their political graphics, but instead concentrates on a selection of significant graphic movements and projects. The examples shown illustrate the direct and confrontational roles that graphics can play in struggles of national import (as in the street posters of the Atelier Populaire in Paris or the resistance posters of

South Africa) as well as the equally important indirect roles such as consciousness-raising, generating aid or finance, or slowly eroding public support through graphic satire or abuse. In many cases this work reflects the social concerns and popular movements of particular countries, or recent historical changes that have taken place within them. The primary focus, however, is on particular graphic roles, techniques and traditions rather than historical sequences of events.

Both the official voice and the unofficial voice are represented graphically, for both are integral parts of the political landscape; even when the unofficial voice is stifled, its very absence is significant. Moreover both voices rely on propaganda techniques, even if the level of production and distribution differs greatly. The official voice usually has command of substantial funds and institutionalized methods of production and distribution: governments for example often produce heavily-financed media campaigns distributed through established channels. The unofficial voice may have motives that are equally propagandistic, but is often forced to resort to less extravagant (and potentially less effective) methods such as distributing home-made pamphlets by hand, or sticking up illegal posters at night.

PAY NO POLL TAX
All Britain Anti Poll Tax Federation

the**Demo**

Sat **31**st **Mar**ch
Meet at Kennington Park at 12 noon
March to Trafalgar Square LONDON

Contact Numbers:
London/National - 01 533 5551	East Midlands - 0246 231 631
Southern - 0773 231 005	Yorkshire - 0532 023 622
Eastern - 2268 506018	Merseyside - 051 226 4527
South West - 0272 622131	Manec/Lancs - 061 256 1974
Wales - 0792 485861	Northern - 091 262 6614
West Midlands - 4065 393620	Scotland West - 041 204 3502
	Scotland East - 031 557 4673

DON'T PAY, DON'T COLLECT

5

The 'unofficial' voice
of protest and social
comment.
1 Anti-fascist postcard
by Egon Kramer, West
Germany 1980.
2 Reworked billboard
(the original speech
bubble was blank)
protesting against the
poll tax, by 'visual
interventionists'
Saatchi & Someone,
Britain 1990.
3 & 4 Jenny Holzer's
series of 'Truisms':
t-shirts worn by John
Ahearn and Lady Pink,
New York City 1983.
5 Handbill announcing
the anti-poll tax
demonstration in
Trafalgar Square in
March 1990. A rally
of around 40,000
people, it turned into
one of Britain's worst
examples of civil
upheaval in recent
years.

4

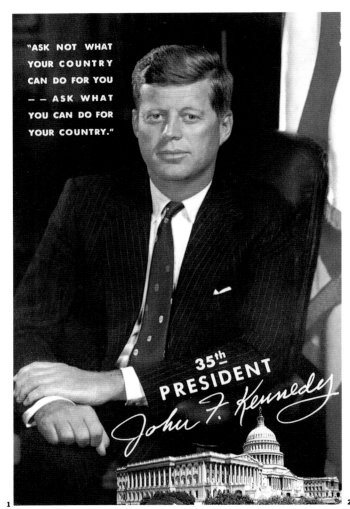

"ASK NOT WHAT YOUR COUNTRY CAN DO FOR YOU — — ASK WHAT YOU CAN DO FOR YOUR COUNTRY."

35th PRESIDENT John F. Kennedy

1,000 STAMPS
ONLY $2.95
JOHN F. KENNEDY
Worth Over $30 at Standard Catalog Prices!

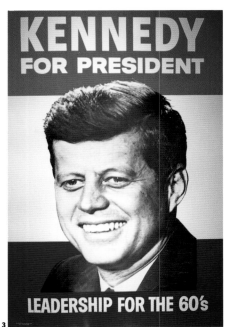

KENNEDY FOR PRESIDENT

LEADERSHIP FOR THE 60's

But the unofficial voice does have certain advantages. The fight to give 'power to the people', or to protest and be heard, draws upon the resourcefulness and ingenuity of individuals, the solidarity value of collective teamwork, and the emotional strength of commitment or resistance. Thus individual acts, as well as the work of small organized groups, can have substantial impact in the struggle against a much greater force. When American artist Robbie Conal sites his agitprop posters at very particular street junctions and at exactly the right height for captive viewing from a car (in Los Angeles, a city where no one walks), he is feeding more care and attention into his guerrilla tactics than most official bodies would lend to an average media campaign, because he knows that he must get maximum effect from economy of means. He is committed to getting his message across. He may not match the 'reach' of a televised campaign, but his effectiveness per square inch of image is probably just as high, if not higher.

The wealthier Western countries dominate the chapter in terms of the amount of imagery shown, for here the social and political roles of graphics are most complex, being heavily enmeshed in the workings of governments, economies and society as a whole. Both propaganda and protest techniques have been able to develop to an unparalleled level of sophistication, largely through an abundance of materials, new technology, and an audience accustomed to responding to newspapers, TV news, cartoons and other forms of open visual debate.

Party politics: propaganda and public image

Party politics present one of the most blatant uses of propaganda graphics and manipulative media techniques, particularly during election campaigns. The USA and Britain are used here as examples of highly developed but differing approaches to electioneering and visual debate. Both elected governments rely heavily on media publicity to win votes and explain party policies.

America has traditionally focussed on the electoral candidate as a personality: the projection of a 'public image' and use of supporting paraphernalia plays a large part in campaigning. Television has also played a crucial role in the development of this public image. Eisenhower may have been the first to employ an advertising agency or make TV commercial 'spots' to win an election, but Kennedy was the first truly to exploit the TV medium. His famous televised debate with Nixon was believed to have secured his narrow victory in the 1960 election, and from thereon he became the first presidential TV personality. Much of his popularity was based on the American public's ability (through TV) to get to know him – or rather his 'image' – personally, and to form judgements based on appearances.

Nixon however has been credited as having first engaged the controlled use of the TV medium (in the 1968 election), by tinkering, distorting and manipulating to the point where the 'image' was totally separate from the man. His strategy centred on the principle that the 'image' is what the voter psychologically 'buys' like any commodity. It heralded a new era in politics, where politicians and advertising went hand in hand and the 'image' that would win votes was no longer a matter of personality but a distortion created by media experts.

The campaigns conducted in America since then have taken this focus on public image and used it to wage an all-out media war. 'Sleaze tactics' are now commonly used to taint the opponent's image; issues are often lost in ambiguous manufactured TV messages; and candidates and their campaigns are moulded according to 'cultural strategies' and image-formulas, in other words, getting the production and the stage props right.

Britain, on the other hand, tends to wage electoral battles over parties and their policies, although Margaret Thatcher built up an international image in her own right throughout the 1980s. Televised interviews and party political broadcasts are a heavy part of the electronic media overload in the run-up to a national election, and great pains are taken to preserve the democratic notion that all is conducted with a sense of balance, lending equal media time to the airing of opposing views.

Great attention is also given to poster campaigns, which take the arguments directly to the man in the street. The famous Saatchi & Saatchi dole queue billboard of the 1979 election campaign (page 49) is considered to have been a contributing factor to the Conservative party's victory. Over ten years later, in the 1991 election campaign that threatened to dislodge Conservative Prime Minister John Major from office, the two main parties (Conservative and Labour) waged a battle of the billboards which reached comic proportions. No sooner was one poster unveiled by one party than a counter-poster would be rolled on by the other. So it continued at an impressive pace, sometimes drawing new retorts almost overnight in true argumentative style.

But no matter how frenetic or misguided the tactics may seem at times, an essential feature of both countries and their party politics (whether in campaigning mode or not) is the freedom to criticize and to present an opposing view. Propaganda plays an important role in this competitive scenario. It is part of the official voice that aims to win votes and to set policies; but it is also part of the unofficial voice that protests against the established order or encourages dissent. Both of these voices are allowed to vie for public attention, and both are allowed to manipulate the crowd.

Centralized government: propaganda and censorship

In societies with centralized power, propaganda and manipulation are exercised by one official voice. A prime example existed in the socialist graphics of the former Soviet Union and the Iron Curtain countries of Europe, where for many years propaganda strategies (such as media censorship) imposed authoritarian doctrines with complete intolerance of opposing views.

The Communist philosophy was reinforced through decades of Soviet image-building: the constant presence of Lenin in statues and portraits; the symbolic red of socialism on banners, flags and other elements of display; party slogans on buildings and posters; the

1 Postcard memorial of John Fitzgerald Kennedy, USA 1992.
2 Pack of matches, USA 1960s.
3 Presidential campaign poster for J.F. Kennedy, 1960.
4 Political sparring, British-style: Labour and Conservative billboards from the general election of 1992.

1 Postage stamps from Romania, 1990, commemorating the Popular Revolution of December 1989.
2 'Comrades, ADIEU', poster by István Orosz, Hungary 1989, commenting on the occupying Soviet army leaving Hungary.

3 Poster by Péter Pócs of Hungary, a memorial to the victims slaughtered during the Romanian Revolution of 1989; printed at the artist's own expense, 1989.

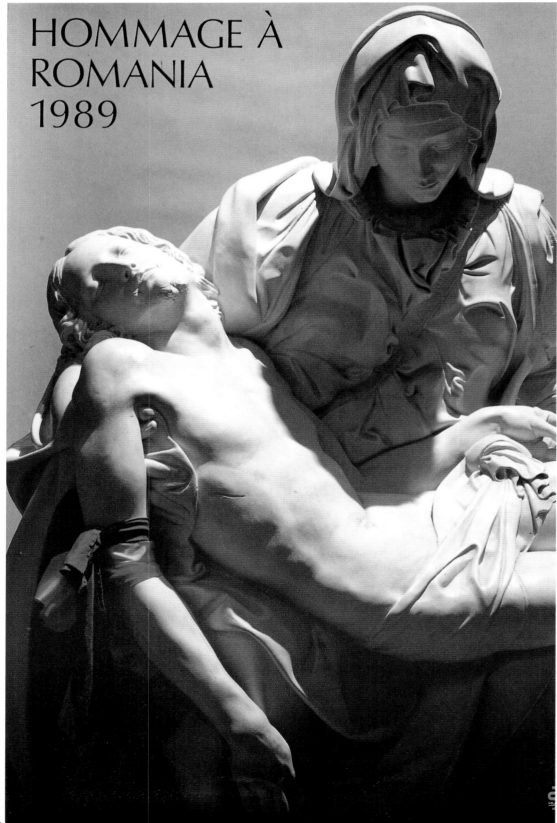

HOMMAGE À ROMANIA 1989

ubiquitous hammer and sickle emblem; and the officially promoted heroic peasant/worker imagery. The philosophy also found form in decades of poster art and other graphics that spoke with one ideological voice, and in the accepted style of Soviet Socialist Realism (originally introduced in the 1930s by Stalin). It is not surprising that the lifting of restrictions through glasnost and perestroika brought an immediate surge of poster work (one of the most popular art forms). Many of the posters were critical of society and its leaders; it was the release of decades of pent-up anger and criticism.

A centralized ideological voice also drove the propaganda graphics of Mao Tse-tung's Cultural Revolution in China (1966-76). With the aim of building a unified workforce, imagery was produced (in a hyper-Socialist Realist style) that projected the revolutionary spirit of collectivism and co-operative labour, led by the national hero figure of Mao and guided by his Little Red Book. Stereotyped representations of the masses, and heroic individuals demonstrating socialist ideals, became part of the graphic formula which taught people what to think and how to conduct themselves, while also eliminating individualism and other 'counter-revolutionary' elements.

Throughout the 1960s and 1970s, the graphic activities of both socialist revolutions suffered greatly from restricted artistic expression, the isolationist policies of their regimes and the dulling effect of producing repetitive idealized imagery that was divorced from the drama and reality of daily life or real people. Although both visual cultures contained interesting aspects – such as the monumental quality and stylized poses of the Soviet heroic-worker imagery, or the dynamic energy of the Cultural Revolution's depiction of the masses –

any fascination is mitigated by the hollowness of the message, and a recollection of the repressive aspect of the regimes the graphics represented. The imagery is a far cry from the colour, vitality and emotion of the poster graphics belonging to the 1960s socialist revolution in Cuba, which also spoke for a central ideology. But in Cuba, the spirit of internationalism was central to the revolution's aims, and artistic expression was not only encouraged but enlisted as a communicative tool for the revolution.

The Pro-Democracy protests

The liberation posters on pages 64-67 provide lasting memories of the Pro-Democracy movement of the late 1980s which swept Central and Eastern Europe. The strikes in 1980-81 that created Poland's independent trade union, Solidarity, provided an early rumbling of things to come. (The Solidarity logo was the first persistent symbol of the growing desire for democratic reform in Europe.) As the decade moved on, Gorbachev's policies of glasnost and perestroika placed the USSR on the road to economic reform and a free market economy – and inevitably led to the decline and break-up of the Soviet bloc. By the end of the decade, Eastern Europe was subjected to a wave of popular revolutions and uprisings – some quiet, some bloody. In highly simplified terms, the wave peaked in 1989 and encompassed Hungary, Poland, East Germany (accompanied by the opening of the Berlin Wall), Bulgaria, Czechoslovakia and Romania. It was followed in 1990 by the gradual break-up of Yugoslavia, and the controversial reunification of Germany. The year 1991 saw the collapse of the Soviet Union, and the independence of the Baltic States (Latvia, Estonia, Lithuania).

4 Painted banners from the Central Academy of Drama in Beijing, created for the Tiananmen Square protest of May 1989. 5 The Goddess of Democracy statue built by protestors in Tianamen Square, May 1989.

In graphic terms, the mood of openness and change (and eventually revolution) from the mid-1980s onwards allowed heavily censored cultures to emerge from behind the Iron Curtain. They exercised their new freedom in a wide range of extraordinary graphic statements: the historical resentment and social critique of the Russian perestroika posters; symbolic references to the removal of Communism, such as emblems cut or torn out of flags; clearly-expressed fears of the effects of Westernization and the dangers of embracing its 'hamburger culture'; as well as the proud but virulent imagery present on stamps and other documents from Romania's violent revolution.

Makeshift posters, signs, banners and other graphic ephemera also played a direct role in many of the uprisings, flooding the streets and plastering vehicles, walls and windows with the call to join in the struggle. The aftermath witnessed the gradual discrediting and dismantling of the Soviet State's visual identity. The hammer and sickle, red flags, party slogans and portraits of Lenin were seen to crumble with Gorbachev's reputation. The Communist Party was banned and Lenin's statues were torn down; by 1992 the USSR itself ceased to exist. Irreverence set in, and it wasn't long before the hammer and sickle adorned everything from bracelets to bustiers.

1

2

Out of the range of graphic statements released by the fall of the Iron Curtain, the most eloquent (and least damaged artistically) belonged to those countries – Latvia, Hungary, Poland, Czechoslovakia – whose poster traditions, although censored, had still managed to grow and maintain a life-line with the international art scene through poster competitions such as the Brno Biennale in Czechoslovakia and other forms of cultural exchange. Their poster artists had become skilled in bypassing censorship by the use of visual metaphor and symbolism, or had avoided it altogether by printing small editions at their own expense for entry into competition. This was in contrast to countries such as Romania, where resources and creativity had been sapped by a brutal regime.

In the period leading up to the revolutions in Europe, a Pro-Democracy event was staged on the other side of the world: the month of demonstrations held in May 1989 in Beijing's Tiananmen Square, where students, workers and intellectuals protested for the right to a voice in the government, only for many of them to be killed on 4 June by

troops from the hardline Communist regime. It was an event that interfaced old-style graphic methods with globe-shrinking new technology. The daily demonstrations employed makeshift banners and placards; students from the Central Academy of Art produced varied types of handbills and posters, often by means of simple woodcuts printed by hand, which were then pasted to walls and windows; and the Central Academy of Drama produced large banners painted with emotive figures of people pleading for help.

This was not the usual two-way dialogue between protestors and leaders, however: the Tiananmen demonstration was addressed to the world. There was live television coverage, and (at first) a festive sense of street theatre, with students addressing the crowds with loudspeakers and banners waving in the background. Fax and telex machines shot messages out to the rest of the world. And the world responded with high-tech solidarity, as shown by the Fax for Freedom project described in Chapter Two. The TV coverage of the demonstration produced immediate media icons: the Goddess of Democracy statue, the row of tanks stopped in their tracks by one lone protestor, and later, the horror of the injured and dying sprawled across the square.

In the Tiananmen Square demonstration new technology and TV were used to connect the demonstrators with the rest of the world and to invite viewers across the globe to be active and participate in the protest. Later, with the Gulf War, new technology and TV were used to do the exact opposite: to cloud activities, to encourage passive acceptance and to distance the viewer from real events and any association with death and destruction.

Graphics and war

Wars and conflicts have been more or less continuous over the past three decades, and Chapter Two deals with the general topic of war and militarism from a global perspective. This chapter, however, views wars as power struggles waged by particular governments, or by rival factions within a country. Such wars may extend beyond the boundaries of the country, or be fought from a distance, but the decision to wage war (and sustain it) rests with the government at home. The conflict becomes part of the internal workings of that country, and can generate intense protest from within.

America's anti-Vietnam War poster movement is represented here, along with other ephemera and projects that fuelled the American public's anti-war feeling and eventually forced the withdrawal of US troops. Protest posters of the 1991 Gulf War, however, were few and far between; indeed the ephemera of the time demanded support for the troops, so as not to repeat some of the mistakes of Vietnam (when American soldiers had difficulties re-integrating back into society). The Gulf War protests produced in other participating countries such as Britain involved general calls for peace, or centred on the horror of hi-tech, sanitized warfare and gloating media coverage.

Britain's military presence in Northern Ireland has generated little in the way of protest posters or exhibitable graphics, but a great deal of

3 The final salute, at Andersonstown, Belfast, on Thursday, for Bobby Sands, IRA Volunteer, H-Block hunger-striker and Westminster MP

יום העצמאות תשמ"ה

5

1 Postcard by the
Campaign Against
Plastic Bullets (design:
Stephen Dorley-Brown),
Britain 1980s.
2 Badge, Britain 1980s.
3 Front and back page
of *An Phoblacht* (May
1981), a Republican
newspaper published
in Belfast. This issue
appeared at the time
of the hunger strikes
in the early 1980s.
4 'Independence Day',
poster entwining the
Israeli and Palestinian
flags, calling for
reconciliation in the
Arab-Israeli conflict.
Designer unknown,
Israel 1988.

5 Poster for an
exhibition of masks,
by Israeli designer
David Tartakover, Israel
1989. The words that
appear are from a Purim
children's song: 'There
is no joy and happiness
like me – the mask, ha
ha!'. Pictured are a
masked Palestinian
sending a missile, an
Israeli soldier wearing
a protective mask,
another Palestinian
masking his face with
a picture of Yasser
Arafat and, at the
bottom, a baby girl
who was shot in the
eye by a rubber bullet,
masked with bandages.

4

'The Falklands Cards': from a series of postcards produced during the crisis in the Falklands by radical postcard press South Atlantic Souvenirs (Rick Walker and Steve Hardstaff), Britain 1982.

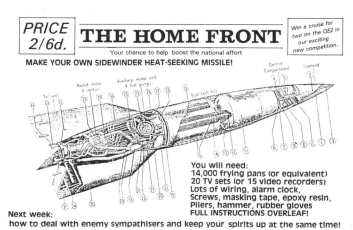

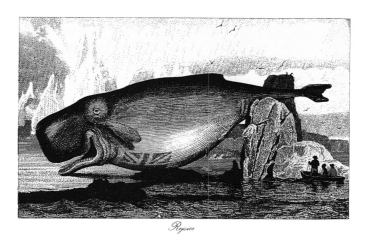

grassroots comment and criticism in the form of TV documentaries, films and ephemera such as pamphlets and postcards protesting against the use of plastic bullets by British armed forces in Northern Ireland. Certain artists, designers and cartoonists rallied against the war in the Falklands, producing some of Britain's most intense anti-war statements. These included postcards by the radical press South Atlantic Souvenirs, and illustrator Raymond Briggs' children's book *The Tin-Pot Foreign General and the Old Iron Woman* (obvious caricatures of Argentina's General Galtieri and Britain's Margaret Thatcher).

The Palestinian-Israeli conflict has generated many powerful political posters over the past three decades, reflecting the hard-fought struggle for Israeli independence as well as the intensity of Palestinian resistance. Appeals for understanding, reconciliation and peace have emerged from artists on both sides, particularly since the 1980s, resulting in eloquent universal graphic comments on pain and suffering.

Africa: anti-apartheid and reconstruction

It would be impossible to represent graphically all the conflicts and disasters that have beset the African continent over the past 30 years. The wave of African nationalism that brought de-colonization and independence for many new states in the 1960s also brought bloodshed and prolonged periods of instability. Wars between rival factions, apartheid policies, famine and other disasters have ensured that the plight of Africa and its people has never been away from our headlines for very long. There have been many artistic statements of support; many projects dealing with alternative technology and indigenous design issues; many aid appeals involving graphic art. Rather than encompass the broad spectrum, this chapter concentrates on two areas of concern where graphic design has played a very specific role in the social and political developments taking place.

The first area of concern is apartheid. Despite the rapid changes incurred elsewhere by African nationalism in the 1960s, the Republic of South Africa resisted and further entrenched itself in the separatist system of apartheid: the policy of white minority power over the black majority, involving racial segregation, economic exploitation, and the denial of basic rights to blacks, as well as Indians and people of mixed race. The years that followed represent a catalogue of despair and sacrifice: the attempted relocation of blacks onto Bantu homelands; the Sharpeville Massacre (1960); the banning of the African National Congress (1960-90) and imprisonment of its leader Nelson Mandela (1963-90); Steve Biko and the Black Consciousness movement (late 1960s and 1970s); and many other important events and protests, reinforced by economic sanctions and solidarity from the international community at large.

The turmoil culminated in a decade of intense mass resistance in the 1980s, and an extraordinary number of resistance posters and other graphics produced by screenprinting workshops and activists within South Africa. These acted as important tools for motivation, consciousness-raising and solidarity in the popular democratic struggle.

The second concern of this chapter is reconstruction after the damage of war. An example of the use of graphic design as a force for social development and change is shown in the work of the Maviyane Project in Zimbabwe. With the end of the war for independence in 1980, Zimbabwe (formerly Rhodesia) embarked on the building of a new socialist state. The Maviyane Project joined this movement wholeheartedly and their work mirrors many of the concerns and crises of the time, at both national and local level. These include the re-integration of guerrilla fighters from the war back into society; the need to raise literacy levels; worries over the disappearance of indigenous culture; and how to combat the ever-present spectre of apartheid. The project also represents an important attempt to find a graphic voice relevant to the black community, one which would challenge the dominating white voice of Western culture and thus provide the ideological revolution with a visual revolution.

The subjects of apartheid and solidarity appear often in the Maviyane Project's work. Apartheid's effects were far reaching. The apartheid regime's attempts to retain a dominant position by de-stabilizing its neighbours (the 'Frontline States', including Zimbabwe) took the form of South African-backed wars and terrorism, as well as the crippling social effects that they bring. Consequently solidarity amongst the Frontline States has been important both as a survival tactic and in order to foster the sense of 'shared destiny' cultivated by many of the African countries struggling to establish their own identity.

Africa has been the battleground on which many global problems and issues have been waged: the rebellion against exploitative multinational interests, the rise of nationalism and independence movements, human rights abuses, displaced and refugee populations, the battle against natural elements. The continent's national struggles therefore embody international significance, and have given rise to some of our most important solidarity efforts, such as the international anti-apartheid movement and the Live Aid appeal for famine relief, both of which appear in the next chapter.

Social change and home politics

Internal politics and protest relating to economic and social issues – such as civil unrest, workers' strikes, anti-racist campaigns and tax protests – provide this chapter with a variety of poster workshops, radical presses and other progressive publishing activities. Many have achieved international fame; all continue in the tradition of using graphics as a tool for revolution and social change.

The Cuban political posters of the 1960s were by far the most influential movement, and inspired grassroots poster workshops and art activists around the world. They were conceived as ideological tools for both the Cuban socialist revolution and the international (Third World) socialist revolution. Produced by a number of agencies, government departments and publishing houses within Cuba, they were distributed worldwide by an international propaganda agency. Unlike the cultural efforts of the USSR and China at that time, Cuba's posters were not

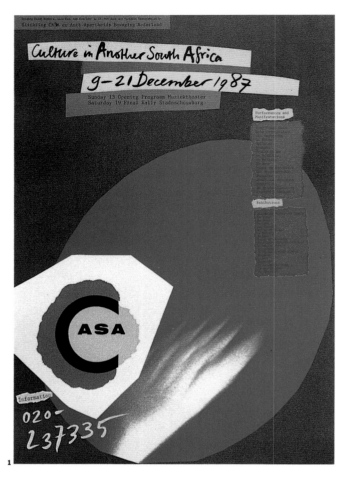

banal products of central party ideology but carriers of political education founded in the creativity of the people. In purely graphic terms, they provided a model of visual power and directness.

Other influential revolutionary tools included the street posters of the Atelier Populaire of May '68 in Paris which were similarly powerful in their directness and even more economical in their means and messages; they often consisted of nothing more than one image and a slogan, both carefully chosen and produced as a simple stencil, then screenprinted. The resistance posters, banners and t-shirts of South Africa that represented the popular struggle against the apartheid regime in the 1980s also carried the immediacy of relatively crude imagery and low-tech screenprinting. So did the Nicaraguan revolutionary posters produced during the 1980s by the Sandinista government and other agencies and dedicated to building a new society and fighting poverty, disease and illiteracy while also organizing people to political action and defence against the US-backed Contras. Australia has since the early 1970s harboured a fine tradition of graphic workshops that have not only serviced the labour movement and social concerns, such as education and health, but have also given a graphic voice to the plight of that country's Aboriginal people.

Revolution can take even more unusual or ephemeral forms. Guerrilla graphics, such as the night-time postering of Robbie Conal or the Guerrilla Girls in the USA, kept a protest undercurrent alive in America during the Reagan/Bush years. Meanwhile radical presses and community workshops in 1980s Britain worked persistently to challenge authority, promoting the peace movement and feminism through posters, postcards and other statements of graphic solidarity.

Powerful social comment can be found in low-budget community productions as well as high-tech repro.
1 Poster for 'Culture in Another South Africa', making use of sophisticated colour printing. It advertises a conference held in Amsterdam in December 1987 which featured over two hundred South African artists in exile. Designed by Wild Plakken (Frank Beekers, Lies Ros, Rob Schröder), Holland.
2 A simple but highly effective film poster by Alfredo Rostgaard for an anti-American documentary on the Vietnam War. Published by ICAIC, the film bureau of the Cuban government, 1967.

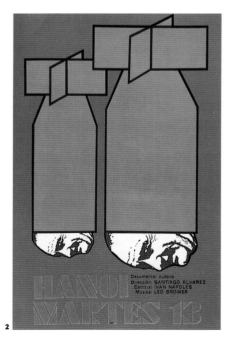

3 Low-tech screen-printing is used to powerful effect in this poster by Jayne Amble for an anti-racism campaign. Produced for the South Australian United Trades and Labour Council, Australia 1987.

The revolutionary activities described rely to a great extent on a powerful, direct statement produced by economy of means, often accompanied by low-cost, low-tech production methods such as screenprinting, photocopying or cheap offset litho. But powerful social comment is not exclusive to low-budget production. Germany, Holland and Japan all produce political comment and social critique that can be intellectual, surreal or drily witty, while also taking advantage of the best photographic and print production processes in the world.

Germany's Klaus Staeck has made sharp political comment in slickly-produced photomontages since the 1960s. Drawing references from advertising, his high-gloss imagery is often mated with contradictory text, which jars to make an acerbic comment about a rich, overfed, industrialized society and its excesses. The high-quality finish adds to the ironic wit of many of his statements. High-quality reproduction and attention to detail are also an integral part of Japanese visual language. Shigeo Fukuda's visual jokes and asides, for example, are short, sharp and meticulous. Japan is also responsible for glossy annual design exhibitions on ecology and peace, which have produced extremely beautiful social comment over the years (see the Hiroshima Appeals in Chapter Two). Finally, Holland's design group Wild Plakken can expect skilled printing to match the surrealistic effects used in some of their anti-apartheid statements – also helped greatly by the fact that the government has over the years supported and financed the anti-apartheid movement.

Developments in mass media and technology since the 1960s have meant that problems or movements occurring at national level now have the ability to grow into global movements. The Pro-Democracy movement in Poland, the peace movement in Britain, the anti-apartheid struggle of South Africa and the anti-fascist movement in Germany all started as national struggles, which then gathered solidarity to form international networks or found that similar organizations already existed in other countries. Graphic symbols, logos and other visual forms have aided the progression to internationalism in that they have the powerful facility to overcome language barriers, engage the emotions, and rally people to their cause. With graphics playing an instrumental role, we are gradually leaving the era of internal struggles and isolated protests, and are entering a new era of international movements and large-scale activism.

Personalities and paraphernalia

1

At the very heart of the American concept of democracy lies the principle of free elections. It is no surprise then that America stages its elections – at all levels – with a sense of celebration, flag-waving and showtime.

The identity of political parties and the direction of their election campaigns have traditionally centred around the candidate as a personality: the person in whom the electorate is placing their trust. Consequently, candidates' faces tend to appear on everything from posters to buttons.

Out of this emphasis on the candidate grew the modern concept of 'selling an image'. John Fitzgerald Kennedy was the first to exploit the TV medium to this end, and his televised debate with Nixon was believed to have secured his narrow victory in the 1960 election. Thereafter his charisma and youthful appearance won him great public support and provided an early example of television's ability to sway public opinion.

Because of the practice of 'backing' an individual, paraphernalia plays a large part in campaigning; buttons, badges and bumperstickers all allow the general public to take sides and feel involved. The personal touch also colours the conduct of the campaign trail: smear tactics are common, as are personal attacks and insults.

Whilst many artists, actors and writers lend their influence in support of election candidates, it is even more common for artists – both well-known and unknown – to generate protest against politicians and their policies.

2

5

MILHOUS I

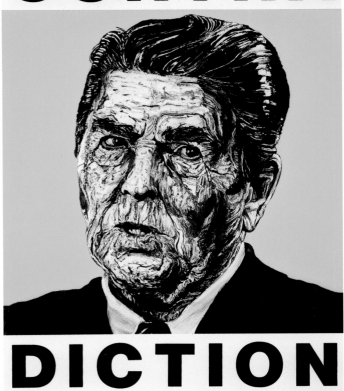

CONTRA

DICTION

3

IT CAN'T
HAPPEN

HERE

1 Assorted campaign
badges from
Presidential election
year, 1992.
2 Presidential campaign
poster for Lyndon
Baines Johnson, 1964.
3 Two posters by
guerrilla artist Robbie
Conal, commenting on
the more questionable
issues relating to
Presidents Ronald
Reagan and George
Bush, 1987-8.
4 Back-page ad from a
January 1968 issue of
the left-wing American
magazine *The New
Republic*.
5 'Milhous I', portrait of
Richard Milhous Nixon
by Edward Sorel for *The
Washington Post Book
World*, USA 1973.

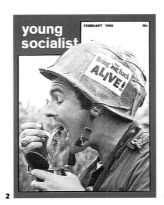

Protesting against the war in Vietnam

From the day that President Lyndon Baines Johnson ordered American troops into Vietnam in 1965, until their final withdrawal in 1973, the protests and demonstrations from within America were bitter and relentless.

Internal dissent and anti-war activities took myriad forms: there were citywide referendums, campus demonstrations, marches, sit-ins, strikes and draft card burnings. As involvement escalated, so did the anger and the protests. Campus unrest hit a peak in 1970, when four students were shot and killed by the National Guard in an anti-war demonstration at Kent State University.

American artists and designers poured out a prolific mass of anti-war posters, cartoons and other graphics, exemplified by the work of Seymour Chwast, Tomi Ungerer, Jules Feiffer and the Art Workers' Coalition – a large militant group of artists which, in addition to other activities, published the 'Q. And babies?' poster on page 44, an extraordinary piece of protest graphics.

Vietnam was the first broadcast media-covered war, and the influence of press and media was all-important. With constant live TV coverage and the emotional war photography of Tim Page, Sean Flynn, Don McCullin, Philip Jones Griffiths and others filling daily newspapers, magazines and books, there was no escaping the reality of the devastation. It fuelled public opposition to the war and made cries for withdrawal ever stronger: a pressure considered to have been instrumental in the eventual withdrawal of American troops.

ISN'T IT TIME YOU DID SOMETHING?

We think so.

We think it is time to speak out against the endless slaughter and suffering in Vietnam . . . time to redeem our United Nations pledge to seek the settlement of international disputes by peaceful means . . . time to admit that a military solution may lead to a nuclear war.

We must not commit the crime of silence. Freedom to differ with our government's policy is not a privilege to be withdrawn at the whim of the President; it is a right that is inherent and irrevocable in a democracy. We believe that it is the right, indeed the **patriotic duty**, of all Americans to question our presence in Vietnam . . . to ask whether the war is worth 15,000 American and untold thousands of Asian lives . . . whether it is worth $50 million per day . . . whether it is truly worth the risk of World War III.

Four out of ten people in the City of San Francisco recently voted for an immediate cease fire. We believe that the people of the City of Madison, whatever their differences as to the means of bringing peace to Vietnam, ought to have the opportunity to make their voices heard in the same manner. If our demands are clear and urgent, the government **must** listen . . . it **can** stop the bombing . . . it **can** negotiate an end to the agony in Vietnam.

We urge you to support us in placing the following referendum on the ballot of the city election to be held on April 2, 1968:

IT IS THE POLICY OF THE PEOPLE OF THE CITY OF MADISON THAT THERE BE AN IMMEDIATE CEASE FIRE AND THE WITHDRAWAL OF UNITED STATES TROOPS FROM VIETNAM, SO THAT THE VIETNAMESE PEOPLE CAN DETERMINE THEIR OWN DESTINY.

We need your signature on the petition to be presented to the Madison Common Council. We need your assistance in circulating the petition in every ward of the city. Above all, we need your generous financial support to implement an effective advertising and educational campaign.

JOIN WITH US! RETURN THE FOLLOWING COUPON TODAY!

MADISON CITIZENS FOR A VOTE ON VIETNAM

SPONSORS:
THOMAS ADAMS
DOUGLAS ANDERSON
PROF. MICHAEL N. BLEICHER
MONSIGNOR ANDREW BREINES
FATHER JOSEPH BROWN
DR. GEORGE CALDEN
DAVID CHENEY
HENRY CLARENBACH
DONALD EATON
FRANK EMSPAK
PROF. EDGAR FEIGE
PROF. TED FINMAN
MR. AND MRS. LAWRENCE FUELLEMAN
JAMES L. GREENWALD
FATHER JOSEPH HAMMER
MR. AND MRS. PAUL H. HASS
MRS. MARIANNE HOBBINS
DR. WILLIAM B. HOBBINS
REV. PAUL Z. HOORNSTRA
FATHER FREDERICK KREUZIGER
RICHARD KROOTH
REV. JAMES LA RUE
ROBERT LEVINE

MADISON CITIZENS FOR A VOTE ON VIETNAM
610 Langdon Street, Madison, Wisconsin 53703
Phone: 231-2852

☐ I wish to sign the petition.
☐ I wish to help circulate the petition.
☐ I wish to contribute $..........

Name ....
Address ....
City .... State .... Zip .....

SPONSORS:
ROBERT M. McCORMICK
REV. LOWELL MESSERSCHMIDT
JACK VON METTENHEIM
FATHER RICHARD OESTREICH
DR. GEORGE E. ORSECH
DR. AND MRS. H. K. PARKS
R. R. PAUNICK, JR.
MRS. LESTER RADKE
CLIFFORD ROBERTS
MR. AND MRS. GILBERT S. ROSENBERG
ADAM SCHESCH
RABBI GERALD SCHUSTER
DR. ADDIE SCHWITTAY
MR. AND MRS. IRA SHOR
WILLIAM SKAAR
PROF. AND MRS. WILLIAM STONE
RABBI MANFRED SWARSENSKY
MRS. MARY THOMPSON
GEORGE VUKELICH
LAURENCE A. WEINSTEIN
DR. AND MRS. PETER WEISS
RABBI RICHARD W. WINOGRAD
DR. ZAIN WOODRING
PROF. MAURICE ZEITLIN

1 Poster by renowned artist and illustrator Tomi Ungerer from a series of anti-war posters which he published privately, 1967.
2 Cover of *Young Socialist* magazine, USA 1968.
3 Sticker for a mass demonstration to be held in Washington DC, produced by the Student Mobilization Committee to End the War in Vietnam, 1968.
4 Poster showing young American burning his draft card, by the Dirty Linen Corp., New York City, late 1960s.
5 Handbill from Madison, Wisconsin calling for a city-wide petition and referendum to end the Vietnam War, 1968. Referendums were one of many forms of internal dissent over the war.

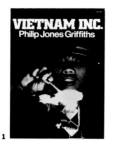

1

2

3

End Bad Breath.

1 Cover and inside spreads from the book *Vietnam Inc.* by photographer Philip Jones Griffiths, and the cover of *The New Soldier* by John Kerry and Vietnam Veterans Against the War, 1971.
2 'Q. And Babies? A. And Babies'. Offset litho poster by the Art Workers' Coalition (photo: R.L. Haeberle), New York, 1970.
3 Christmas card from Vietnam: a sarcastic note from an embittered generation (produced and posted by US servicemen while in Vietnam), Christmas 1970.
4 'End bad breath', anti-Vietnam War poster created in 1967 by Seymour Chwast, co-founder of Push Pin Studios. An undesirable war was depicted as Uncle Sam's bad breath; the title refers to sales-talk used to advertise toothpaste and mouthwash.

Taking sides again: America in upheaval

1

Discontent and anger shifted beneath the surface of a decade of conservatism with Reagan and Bush in the 1980s, producing isolated pockets of protest and agitation. As the decade progressed, the tensions increased and in some cases erupted. By the 1990s many of the protests had sharpened their bite, some had become full-blown movements, and all were employing visual formats as never before.

Jenny Holzer's 'Truisms' (1978-87) and other poetic messages appeared on everything from massive electronic signs in Times Square to t-shirts and phone booth labels. Enigmatic, sharp-edged, amusing or disillusioned, they became icons of modern culture. In addition, Barbara Kruger's use of text and image posed questions about consumerism, sexuality and societal values. Her haunting poster 'Your body is a battleground' was a call to arms in 1989 for the March on Washington for abortion and a woman's right to choose (page 141).

Robbie Conal produced a steady stream of caustic poster-portraits of 'bad guys' (politicians and public figures) that were wheatpasted on city walls across America. In addition AIDS activism, a movement born out of the gay community's anger at government inaction in the AIDS crisis, grew to be a formidable force – particularly through the demonstrations of ACT UP (AIDS Coalition to Unleash Power) and its effective use of propaganda graphics, created by art activist group Gran Fury and others.

2

STONEWALL '69

AIDS CRISIS '89

3

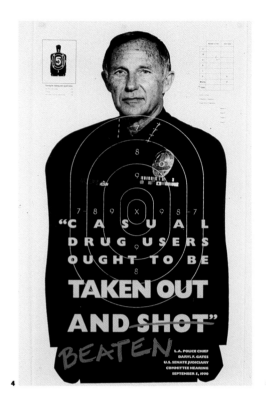

4

5

1 Badge and
bumpersticker
produced during the
Gulf War, USA 1991.
2 Sign message from
the 'Survival' series
by Jenny Holzer,
New York City, 1983.
3 'Riot' sticker by
the AIDS activist art
collective Gran Fury,
produced on the
twentieth anniversary
of the Stonewall Riots
(the beginning of the
Gay Liberation
movement), 1989.
4 Poster portrait of Los
Angeles police chief
Daryl Gates, by Robbie
Conal, 1992. The
altered text refers to
the Rodney King affair,
when four LA police
officers were tried for
the beating of black
motorist Rodney King.
5 Poster by Barbara
Kruger commenting
on some of the
inadequacies of the
Reagan/Bush years,
USA 1990.
6 Criticism of President
Bush's show of action
in the Gulf War and
inaction in the AIDS
crisis, designed by Gang
for ACT UP, 1992.

6

1

British politics: satire and restraint

The 'satire boom' that struck Britain in the
early 1960s was indicative of the social
upheaval taking place at the time –
highlighted by peace protests, the Pill, the
Profumo Affair, the Beatles, and other signs
of change. It brought a new wave of malicious
humour and entertainment, as exemplified
by the London review 'Beyond the Fringe',
the fortnightly magazine *Private Eye* and the
television programme 'That Was The Week
That Was' (or TW3). Many felt that it was not a
new movement, but simply a return to the
grand old satire tradition of Rowlandson and
others. Whatever the case, it revelled in abuse
and controversy aimed at public figures, the
government, class distinction, royalty and
religion, and set new standards of
outspokenness, subversion and public
humiliation that have been exploited by artists
and the media ever since.

2

Nevertheless, Britain's national election
campaigns tend to fight a 'clean' fight over
parties and their policies, taking great pride in
giving both sides equal time to make their
argument in televised debates or interviews.
Billboard campaigns, for example, are
considered to be a 'proper' form of argument
that takes place at the level of the man in the
street. Opposing parties often manipulate
each other's slogans and can act at great
speed in order to counter an attack. Although
messages and methods may be hard-hitting,
the opponents are still reasonably behaved.

However, outside this formal structure of democratic and restrained election sniping lies chaos. Throughout a normal year, the British public is accustomed to receiving its daily dose of politics, government and the economy, with heavy interlacings of irreverence, abuse and scandal. All British politicians can expect to be mercilessly mimicked and lampooned – and the agents of assault take many forms. Political cartoonists such as Steve Bell thrive in the national newspapers; satirical journals such as *Private Eye* (with its outrageous front covers) survive despite continual legal battles and attempts to restrain them; advertising agencies produce increasingly daring imagery; and the wickedly funny latex puppets of the weekly programme 'Spitting Image' ensure that the boundaries of good taste are stretched to the limit on television screens across the country.

3

4

1 Particularly known for the brazen jokes on its front cover, the satirical magazine *Private Eye* has for decades pushed both public and legal tolerances to the limit.
2 Prime minister John Major, by political cartoonist Steve Bell, 1991; published in the *Guardian* newspaper. 'Opportunity 2000' was an industry-led equal opportunities initiative; Major was criticized for having no women in his cabinet when it was introduced, and is shown mimicking a Jane Fonda workout.
3 The campaign billboard that helped contribute to the Conservative party's election victory in 1979 (during a period of high unemployment), by ad agency Saatchi and Saatchi.
4 Margaret Thatcher, Neil Kinnock and David Owen. Created by Yellowhammer ad agency during the 1987 election year, aiming to increase sales of *Today* newspaper. It received record complaints, and did not remain on view for very long.

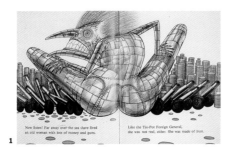

1

1 Spread from *The Tin-Pot Foreign General and the Old Iron Woman*, written and illustrated by Raymond Briggs. A children's storybook on the follies of war, it appeared in the wake of the Falklands crisis, Britain 1984.

2 'Maggie Regina', photomontage by Peter Kennard inspired by Margaret Thatcher's call for a return to Victorian values (such as hard work, duty and self-reliance) and making use of a well-known portrait of Queen Victoria. Produced as the front cover of the *New Statesman*

magazine in 1983, and later as a poster and postcard.

3 The British political satire tradition comes to life in *Spitting Image*, the television show where politicians, royalty and other public figures appear as caricature puppets – and malicious humour rules. The puppets, created by Peter Fluck and Roger Law, originated as 3D models photographed for use as illustrations in magazines. Once given motion, they achieved fame as one of Britain's most popular TV series in the late 1980s.

2

2

3

Home issues and youth politics

1

In the recession atmosphere of the 1970s, Britain's own particular method of fusing grassroots politics and the creative arts emerged in 1976 with Rock Against Racism, a group protesting against racism in the pop music industry. Originally consisting of people from the visual arts (graphic design, advertising, fashion and photography) they staged concerts, dances, demonstrations and other activities. The Anti-Nazi League was formed not long after, and both groups targeted their efforts on quelling the rising activities of the neo-fascist National Front party. Although tiny in comparison, Rock Against Racism paved the way for later global concerts such as Live Aid and the Nelson Mandela 70th Birthday Concert.

The 1980s brought attempts to breathe new life into the Labour Party by extending its appeal to the young, particularly via the efforts of young designers associated with the new breed of 'style magazines'. The decade also saw the strengthening of popular movements and the notion of 'personal politics' through the global charity concept of Live Aid, the Green activism of Greenpeace and Lynx (the anti-fur trade campaigners), and the continuing themes of anti-racism and anti-apartheid. By the 1990s, youth politics and consciousness-raising were communicated through music and visual culture, via rock stars, films, fashion, style magazines and other vehicles.

4

5   6 Cottons Gardens, London, E2.

6

Good at Sports   likes music   Needs surveillance

7

1 Logo for Red Wedge, a group of young people allied to the Labour Party. Designed in the early 1980s by Neville Brody. 2 Promotional literature, part of the visual identity designed by Neville Brody for *New Socialist*, 1986.

3 Cover for *New Socialist*, the Labour Party's monthly magazine, January 1987, designed by Phil Bicker. 4 Poster for Boy George's 'No Clause 28' single; designed by Jamie Reid and Malcolm Garrett, 1988.

The poster was part of a campaign against Clause 28, a new parliamentary bill outlawing the 'promotion' of homosexuality. 5 Sticker produced during the Queen's Silver Jubilee celebrations, 1977.

6 Poster for a fundraising concert on behalf of the Anti-Nazi League by Mervyn Kurlansky of Pentagram, Britain 1979. 7 'UK School Report', billboard and postcard by artist Tam Joseph, Britain 1983-4.

The Atelier Populaire

Paris became a focal point for the revolutionary Sixties in May 1968 when workers and students joined forces to stage a general strike. Factories, offices and schools were occupied, and civil unrest shook the city in the form of demonstrations and riots in a massive protest against the Gaullist government and an education system that upheld old traditions and values.

The Ecole des Beaux Arts went on strike, and students occupied the studios and print workshops. Under the title Atelier Populaire, they worked 24 hours a day producing a mass of posters and wall newspapers that were pasted up in the streets. By all accounts, it was a very organized operation. Atelier members met each day in a general assembly for the discussion and choice of poster designs and slogans, while also debating current political developments. The posters were produced in several of the workshops by silkscreen, lithography or stencilling and distributed all over Paris by student and worker representatives.

The ultimate aim was the rejection of bourgeois culture and the development of a popular culture at the service of the people. In this sense the Atelier became a guiding light. The workshop and its posters, with their crude vitality, have inspired students, poster groups and print workshops around the world, and their example of direct action remains an influence on the students and professionals of art and design today.

1 'The beginning of a long struggle': the recurring factory motif which appeared on the cover of a book produced by the Atelier Populaire, designed for use as a learning tool and to encourage other postermaking activities, 1969.
2, 3 & 4 Poster images from the Atelier Populaire workshop of May 1968.

1 & 2 Logo and poster; part of a visual identity designed by Grapus for the Secours Populaire Français, an organization for humanitarian aid (close to the French Communist party), 1981.
3 Poster by Grapus publicizing an exhibition of their work at the Musée de l'Affiche in Paris, 1982.

Children of the revolution: Grapus

No book on political graphic design in recent years would be complete without mention of Grapus. An offspring of the May '68 student revolt, Grapus design collective was founded in 1970 by Pierre Bernard, Gerard Paris-Clavel and Francois Miehe. They were joined in 1974-5 by Jean-Paul Bachollet and Alex Jordan; with Miehe's departure in 1978, the main core was set.

All members of the French Communist Party (PCF), they concentrated their early efforts on the new society visions of the Left, producing cultural and political posters for experimental theatre groups, progressive town councils, the PCF itself, the CGT (Communist trade union), educational causes and social institutions. At the same time, they rejected the commercial advertising sphere, with its principles of power and control and its constraints on creative freedom.

For 20 years they provided inspiration to graphic design students all over the world, with their idealistic principles (of bringing culture to politics, and politics to culture), and their highly distinctive form of image-making: an accessible and unpredictable mixture of child-like scrawls, bright colours, sensual forms and high-spirited visual pranks.

Throughout their history, Grapus remained Communists and idealists and continued to operate collectively: all work left the studio signed 'Grapus' even when their studio numbers had grown to around 20, operating in three separate collectives. They finally disbanded in January 1991, splitting into three independent design groups.

The Polish poster influence in France

France also acted as a haven for graphic artists who emigrated from behind the Iron Curtain during the 1960s, and who consequently thrived in the less restrictive climate of the West. Among these was Roman Cieślewicz, a representative of the second generation of Polish poster artists (heavily influenced by the father of Polish poster design, Henryk Tomaszewski). Cieślewicz left Poland to live in Paris in 1963, and has worked there ever since. He is particularly known for surreal photomontages which are intellectual, intriguing, and often broadly social or political in character.

Another famous emigrant from Poland was Jan Lenica, who also settled in Paris in 1963. Initially a poster artist who worked with the great Tomaszewski, he was soon drawn into experimental film-making and in the 1950s became one of the pioneers of animated film. His subjects often dealt with the struggles and fears of the individual in modern society such as loss of identity, and mistrust of technology and power politics, illustrated here by a graphic sequence from 1960.

The work of both Cieślewicz and Lenica underlines the tremendous influence of the Polish poster school and, in particular, the teaching of Henryk Tomaszewski at the Warsaw Academy of Fine Arts. Furthermore, two members of Grapus (Bernard and Paris-Clavel) had also travelled to Poland to study with Tomaszweski in the early 1960s.

AVEC L'ENFANT

LE COMITE   MONTREUILLOIS   DE L'ANNEE   DE L'ENFANT

4

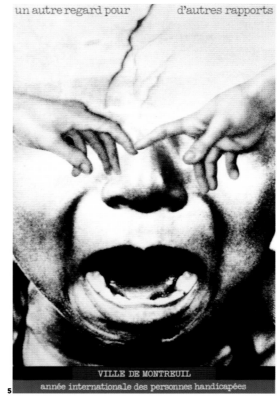

un autre regard pour   d'autres rapports

VILLE DE MONTREUIL
année internationale des personnes handicapées

5

**4 Poster for the International Year of the Child by Roman Cieślewicz, France 1979.
5 Poster for the International Year of the Disabled by Roman Cieślewicz, France 1981.
6 Graphic sequence by Jan Lenica showing a rise in status and position in a bureaucracy bringing loss of identity and humanity, Poland 1960.**

2

Germany: postcards, politics and popular movements

Germany's Klaus Staeck has been a major name in political graphics since the 1960s. His biting photomontages, produced in both postcard and poster form, have been known to spark off controversy and provoke anger among German conservatives. Images are matched with contrasting text or witty captions, usually with jarring results, and the high-quality production (often full-colour) enhances the comment. They owe much to the gloss and authority of advertising, but their power lies in subverting the viewer's sense of security.

Germany's Green politics and the peace movement have been well serviced by sympathetic artists and designers. But it is the web of issues surrounding reunification (the drain on the economy, the rise of neo-Nazi extremism and attacks on immigrant communities) that have recently provoked a ground swell of graphics and other activities generated by the popular movement against fascism and racism. This has included national media campaigns, anti-racist charity albums and videos, youth magazines and newsletters, and a large number of poster campaigns, demonstration announcements, and other ephemera produced by independent anti-fascist groups, individual activists and football supporters' clubs.

1

Konturen eines Amtsarsches
(Prototyp)
Gewidmet Herrn/Frau/Frl.

3

Ich bin der geistige Führer
in diesem unserem
krisengeschüttelten Land

4

5

1 Opening a breach
in the graffiti-covered
Berlin Wall at the
Brandenburg Gate,
December 1989.
2 Dry transfer sheet
carrying the symbols of
socialism and the old
German Democratic
Republic, and now a
relic after the fall of the
Iron Curtain in 1989.
3 'Outline of a
Bureaucrat's Arse
(prototype), Dedicated
to Mr/Mrs/Miss...',
postcard by Klaus
Staeck, West Germany
1974.
4 'I am the intellectual
leader of this our
troubled land', postcard
by Klaus Staeck, West
Germany 1982. The
pear is used here as
a symbol for 'head';
apparently the text was
supposed to mimic the
speech style of
Chancellor Kohl.
5 'Law and Order',
postcard by Klaus
Staeck, West Germany
1970.

1

2

5

3

4

1 Bolt of cloth showing
a fantasy vision of
'Happy Germany' and
European union: a far
cry from reality, 1992.
2 'Each day brings
everyone the
opportunity to refuse',
an anti-war poster
by Daniela Haufe and
Detlef Fiedler which
used bitmapped
typefaces and cursor
effects as a reference
to the technology of
the Gulf War in 1991.
3 'Death Rules OK in
Germany', poster for a
demonstration against
fascism and racism held
in Berlin, 1990.
4 & 5 'I am a foreigner',
a nationwide anti-racist
campaign initiated by
Herbert Gronemeyer
which brought together
radio and graphic
design in the form of
posters, ads and t-shirts
by ad agency Jagusch
and Partner, Hamburg
1992.

3

Radical design in Holland

1

Holland's liberal society has allowed substantial freedom for political movements to express themselves. For example, the government has over the years subsidized the anti-apartheid movement, which also receives heavy support from the public due to the past Dutch connection with South Africa. In addition, a long tradition of social and political design has centred around the Gerrit Rietveld Academy in Amsterdam because of its early connections with radical groups and movements such as De Stijl, Constructivism and the Bauhaus.

Jan van Toorn (professor of graphic design at the Gerrit Rietveld Academy, 1968-85) has been a constant radical voice in the Dutch design community. For three decades he has explored the theme of media manipulation and its social and political implications, as well as the ways in which graphic designers can challenge the packaging and transmission (through the media) of 'official culture'.

During the 1960s he was involved in movements pioneering a socially-relevant role for art, and in the 1970s designed calendars for the printing firm Mart Spruijt which were icons of their time. His collages of political events, politicians and ordinary people posed questions about media presentation – questions of fantasy versus real people, photographic manipulation as 'truth' and so on – while also making overt political statements. He continues to pursue issues surrounding perception and the media through his complex collages.

2

The original members of the Wild Plakken design collective – Frank Beekers, Rob Schröder and Lies Ros – met as students at the Gerrit Rietveld Academy's graphic design department. They worked together from 1977 until 1988, when Beekers departed. Other members have come and gone since then, but Schröder and Ros still remain. The name 'Wild Plakken' (roughly translated as 'wild pasting') can refer to making layouts in an unconventional manner, as well as to the illegal pasting of political posters on city walls.

Wild Plakken have worked mainly for cultural and political causes, designing a wide range of graphic materials. Their projects for the AABN (the Dutch anti-apartheid movement) are particularly powerful, demonstrating the group's commitment to a shared ideal of helping to change society through their work.

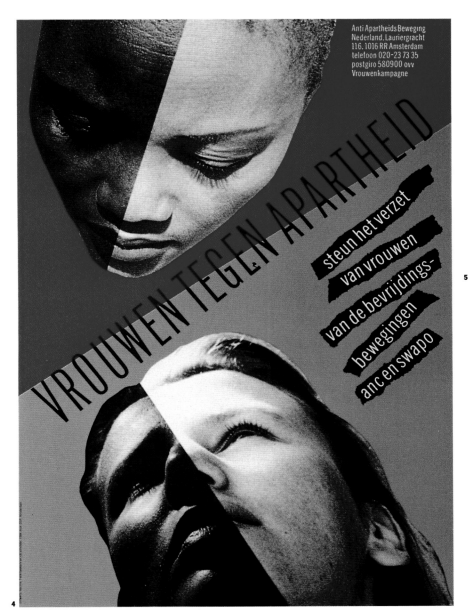

Anti Apartheids Beweging Nederland. Lauriergracht 116, 1016 RR Amsterdam telefoon 020-23 73 35 postgiro 580900 ovv Vrouwenkampagne

VROUWEN TEGEN APARTHEID

steun het verzet van vrouwen van de bevrijdings- bewegingen anc en swapo

5

1 '75 years of the ANC', poster celebrating the 75th anniversary of the African National Congress, designed by Wild Plakken for the Dutch anti-apartheid movement (AABN), 1987.
2 Jan van Toorn's series of commemorative stamps honouring past Dutch politicians: P.J. Troelstra, P.J. Oud and A.F. de Savornin Lohman. Their political orientation is suggested by colour and by their positioning against the depicted chair of the Speaker of the House in the Dutch parliament. (Troelstra, for example, was a socialist and is depicted on the left of the chair.)
3 'The trade union', postage stamp encouraging workers' participation. Designed by Wild Plakken, 1988-9.
4 'Women Against Apartheid. Support the struggle of the women of the liberation movements ANC and Swapo.' Poster by Wild Plakken for the AABN, Holland 1984.
5 Page from a calendar for the printing firm Mart Spruijt, 1974-5, by designer Jan van Toorn, showing Henry Kissinger and a bevy of beauty queens (all dubious showcase 'diplomats') as a comment on the Middle East situation.

4

1

POLSKA '80

The Pro-Democracy movement in Europe

The logo for Solidarity, Poland's independent trade union, appeared in the heat of the strikes staged under the leadership of Lech Walesa in the Gdansk shipyard in 1980. Designed by Jerzy Janiszewski, it quickly became the emblem of the national workers' movement. The logo was soon published worldwide, hailed as the symbol for unity, collective strength and the spirited resistance of the Polish people. A persistent and highly identifiable image, it helped to focus and sustain international sympathy throughout the decade for a struggle which finally achieved its goal of free elections in 1989.

It also signalled the beginning of unrest in Central and Eastern Europe. By 1989 a wave of popular revolutions and uprisings was sweeping across Europe, encompassing Hungary, Poland, East Germany, Bulgaria, Czechoslovakia, Romania and later Yugoslovia and the Baltic States (Latvia, Estonia, Lithuania). Makeshift street graphics in the form of posters, flags, handbills and handheld signs accompanied many of the demonstrations and uprisings. They carried symbols to rally around, names scrawled in anger, calls to action and protest, or messages telling people where to meet.

In addition, artists created posters during this period – for revolutionary groups, new political parties, international competitions or simply as personal statements – that provided insight into the many-layered bitterness that extended far beyond the TV news reports received by the West. The new climate of

2

change, and the freedom to criticize, brought a variety of new poster messages. Disillusionment with the Communist Party and its officials was expressed in their portrayal as broken objects, red animals (muzzled or chased out of town), or other sinister metaphors. The ghost of Stalin's image persisted, with all Soviet leaders viewed as a manifestation of Stalin. Reminders of past struggles and sacrifices were prevalent, particularly in the light of Soviet attempts to rewrite the history of occupied countries, but also to show the current struggles as part of a continuum. (The posters surrounding Czechoslovakia's Velvet Revolution in 1989, for example, make constant reference to the

Soviet invasion of Prague in 1968.) There were also images tinged with uncertainty over the future, showing fear of Westernization, or fear of the return of repression: a resounding remark on the fragile stability of many of the 'new dawns'.

The uprisings of Central and Eastern Europe did not occur in isolation, and neither did their visual manifestations. Poster artists involved in creating oppositional graphics in their home country travelled to add their visual support to revolutions in other countries and to help document the events as they occurred. The rage against the Communist regimes was common to all, and proved to be a powerful force of solidarity.

3

5

1 'Solidarity – Poland '80', logo and poster by Jerzy Janiszewski, Poland 1980.
2 Poster from the Solidarity headquarters in Cracow showing a variation on the Solidarity logo, 1989.
3 'We've already "voted" for them' by Jonas Varnas, Lithuania 1989. Independence poster commenting on Lithuania's loss of vote when it became a Soviet republic in 1940, with a collage of Soviet leaders (Stalin, Molotov, Khrushchev and Brezhnev).

4 'We know! We dare! We do!', poster triptych created by Péter Pócs in 1990 for the Kecskemet SZDSZ (Alliance of Free Democrats) to promote the election of the three pictured candidates to the Hungarian Parliament. The candidates strike a pose that is intentionally opposite to the classical three monkeys (hear nothing, see nothing, speak nothing). Instead they mime 'I hear, I see, I speak' to accompany the text of the title. In the foreground are symbols as they apply

to each candidate: anti-Communism (a muzzled red dog), the withdrawal of Russian troops, and the right way forward to a new future.
5 'May Day – SZDSZ, 1989', poster designed by Krzysztof Ducki for the SZDSZ, Hungary 1989. The poster represents the compulsory Communist May Day celebrations as a fork with broken teeth.

4

Images of solidarity and support.
1 Badge showing the symbol for the Civic Forum (OF: Obcanské Fórum), the movement for democracy in Czechoslovakia in 1989. Symbol designed by Pavel Stastny, Czechoslovakia.
2 'Civic Forum – Havel', poster by Rostislav Vanék, Czechoslovakia 1989.

3 'Civic Forum – Prague 1989', poster by S. Slavický and M. Cihlář, Czechoslovakia.
4 'Students 69-89', poster designed by Dusan Zdímal (Czechoslovakia) in 1989, in memory of students injured by armed police during the demonstrations of 1968 as well as the Velvet Revolution in 1989 in Czechoslovakia.

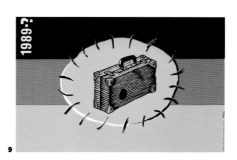

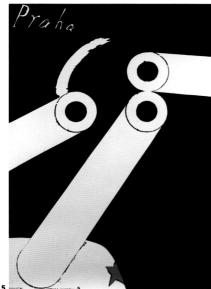

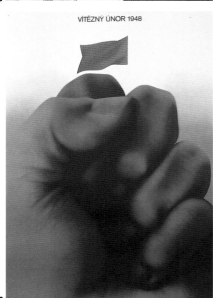

5 'Prague '68', poster designed in 1989 by Krzysztof Ducki of Hungary (present in Prague when the Velvet Revolution occurred) which recalls the Warsaw Pact tanks of the 1968 invasion of Czechoslovakia.
6 'Victorious February 1948', poster designed in 1980 by Radomír Postl (Czechoslovakia), commemorating the date the Soviet Union established itself as an occupying force. The poster is a model of ambiguity; the powerful fist could be read as popular support for the red flag – or an overwhelming desire to overthrow it.
7 'Hero City', poster by Feliks Büttner, East Germany 1990, commemorating the Leipzig demonstrations of 1989 which were instrumental in the downfall of the East German State.
8 'Eastburger' by Thomas Gübig, East Germany 1989; a depiction of the fear of being eaten up by the capitalist West, as well as associated fears of inheriting its culture.
9 '1989-?', poster designed by Péter Pócs of Hungary in 1989 which represents the mass emigration of people from East Germany in 1989; the Communist emblem on the GDR flag has been cut out and replaced with a symbol for travel.

The graphics of Romania

Romania's regime, and its consequent revolution, was one of the most brutal. The despot Nicolae Ceausescu kept an iron grip on the population through fear, hunger and the victimization of ethnic minorities. Having isolated the country from Moscow's rule, Ceausescu drained its resources for his own end, leaving nothing for the people and depriving them of all but the most basic necessities.

The graphics generated by that country depicted two contrasting faces: the full-colour 'folksy' image for export (accompanied by the extravagant personality cult of the dictator), and the internal reality of a drab and miserable daily existence where survival was the most important task. Resistance or criticism was not tolerated, but the brave sometimes managed to scribble a few words of hate on a wall.

When the uprising finally took place there was much bloodshed and Ceausescu was executed. The revolutionary demonstrations displayed the Romanian flag with the old regime's emblem cut out of it: a suitably harsh and emotive image that became the symbol of the Popular Revolution, and appeared in graphic form for a long time after.

5

4

1 Front cover of magazine showing the face of Romania for export, 1975.
2 Inside cover of a Romanian travellers' guide; Ceausescu's portrait appeared at the beginning of all books.
3 Postage stamp from 1990 commemorating the 1989 Popular Revolution; the franking stamp shows the flag with a hole in the centre, where the old regime's emblem was cut out.
4 Anonymous poster-drawing of the dictator Nicolae Ceausescu, with added graffiti from an angry public, 1989.
5 Wall graffiti in Bucharest: 'Hitler Stalin Ceausescu', 'Liberty and Bread', 'Down with the Cobbler'.
(Ceausescu was a cobbler before his rise to power.) Photographs by Sue Herron.

1, 2 & 3 Lapel button,
badge and coin,
USSR 1980s.
4 'The Victory of
October!', greetings
card, USSR 1986.
5 Desk calendar,
USSR 1987.
6 'More light, let the
party know...(Lenin)',
poster by Sachkov,
USSR 1988.

Soviet state graphics and the posters of perestroika

The Western view of the Russian 'evil empire', particularly during the 1960s, was heavily influenced by the visual display of the Soviet propaganda machine. Due to border restrictions and media censorship, the West could only capture a rare glimpse beyond the Iron Curtain – of military parades with red flags flying, of slogans, statues and portraits of Comrade Lenin adorning every building and boulevard, of official imagery of heroic peasants and workers, and the powerful USSR hammer and sickle emblem. These ingredients combined to create a picture of repression: a population locked in service to the state, where individuality and basic freedoms were denied.

There was in fact a great poster tradition to be upheld, stretching back to the powerful posters of the Bolshevik revolution. But avant-garde artistry had long since been suppressed by the Soviet Realism of Stalin. Without freedom of expression, the Russian poster had remained an ideological tool in the service of the state machine, carrying the cheerful stereotypes and bland slogans of 'official art'. Plakat, the Communist Party's official poster press, was the main producer of this official art and also held massive biennial poster competitions on approved subjects such as international peace.

When the policies of glasnost (openness) and perestroika (restructuring) were introduced in the mid-1980s, the Russian poster was one of the first art forms to embrace the new philosophies and act as a

mouthpiece for a society struggling to come to terms with new freedoms. Within a few years, the Russian 'posters of perestroika' were exhibited and published in book form in the West. They reflected the political changes taking place inside the USSR, as well as expressing the views of their creators; social criticism, and a call to build personal opinions and a sense of self, were prevalent.

In addition, many of the artists chose to create their posters as original works of art – not only because of the lack of photo-mechanical and other production facilities, but also due to an inherent suspicion of mass-produced or published posters (still associated with the official art of the past). Such limitations, or the confusion of some of the poster messages, only added to the potency of an art form struggling to find a new footing amid massive societal changes. A new era had begun for the Russian poster as an instrument of the people once again.

7

9 ЗАБВЕНИЕ ПРОШЛОГО ГРОЗИТ ЕГО ПОВТОРЕНИЕМ!

8

10

7 Poster designed by A. Kazhburskii, suggesting that Stalin's ghost still stalks Russia, 1989-90.
8 'Soviet Literature', poster by Kvadrat design firm in Moscow, 1989-90, a comment on the USSR's censorship and banning of books.
9 'To forget the past risks repeating it', poster by Alexander Faldin, Russia 1987, showing Brezhnev's dress uniform (Brezhnev awarded himself many medals of heroism in the 1970s).
10 'Don't make a mountain out of a molehill. We need glasnost and not gossip and rumours.' From the Russian saying 'Don't make an elephant out of a fly' – a man is shown buzzing and gossiping into an ear; poster by Zhmurenkov, USSR 1988.

Gorbachev: the fallen idol

1

The rise and fall of Mikhail Gorbachev occurred roughly within a six-year period. Elevated to Party Chairman in 1985, he set the USSR on the road to a free market economy – a move which began the fast but inevitable decline of the Soviet empire. His economic reforms took their toll, and incurred the wrath of the Russian people. By 1991 he had lost his position of leadership; the Communist Party was banned; and by 1992 the USSR itself had ceased to exist.

But at the height of glasnost and perestroika, Gorbachev was hailed as the man who brought the USSR out of the dark ages. He became an international celebrity and a media star, which led to the inevitable merchandising of his image. 'Gorbi-mania' had struck, as had a realization that on the slow road to change, the East would acquire some distinctly Western features such as fast food, and the desire to 'make a quick buck'. By the time Lenin's statues were falling to the ground, the symbols of state socialism had begun to appear on everything from fashions to board games, and its relics were being sold to the highest bidder.

2

3

5

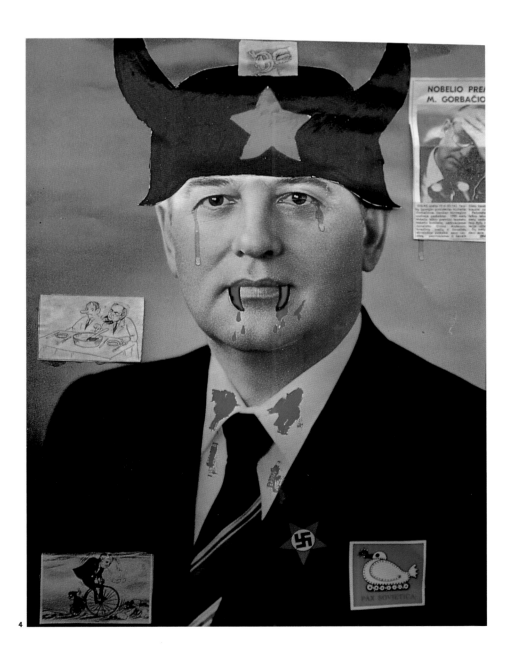

4

1 'I Love Gorby', t-shirt
by British fashion
designer Katharine
Hamnett, 1989.
2 An irreverent new use
for the hammer and
sickle: fashion models
posing in Red Square,
1992.
3 'McLenin's' poster,
part of an exhibition of
Soviet dissident art on
show in the Lenin
Museum in Red Square,
Moscow 1992.
4 A poster of Gorbachev
disfigured during the
August coup that
marked his downfall.
Moscow 1991;
photograph by Abbas,
Magnum.
5 Front cover of Central
Committee report (free
handbook available to
all), Moscow 1986.

BIKO AND SOLIDARITY

BLACK PEOPLE'S CONVENTION
TRIBUTE TO THE LATE
HONORARY PRESIDENT
BANTU STEPHEN BIKO
One Azania: One Nation

2

1 Albertina Sisulu, one of three joint presidents of the United Democratic Front and one of 16 UDF leaders charged for treason in 1985. South African women have been a powerful force in the mass struggle against apartheid.
2 Poster tribute to Black Consciousness leader Steve Biko who died in detention, 1977.

3 Poster portrait of Nelson Mandela while he was still in prison, painted from the descriptions of his visitors (publishing the photograph of a prisoner was illegal). Offset litho; produced by the Congress of South African Trade Unions (COSATU), Johannesburg 1989.

Apartheid: the graphics of resistance

1

The tide of African nationalism that swept through the 1960s created many new independent states. It continued to bring change and turmoil throughout the 1970s as the new states struggled to stabilize themselves and assert their own identity. Within this scenario the foundations of black resistance against the South African system of apartheid were laid: through Steve Biko and the Black Consciousness movement, the imprisoned Nelson Mandela, and many examples of protest and sacrifice that generated worldwide support and sympathy.

The 1980s therefore became the decade of mass organization, and graphics played a direct role in the course of events. Resistance posters (as well as t-shirts, banners, badges and other ready-made graphics) became a vital part of the popular struggle. They publicized meetings, promoted support for organizations and consciousness groups, memorialized events or crises and, most importantly, visualized the outrage and determination of the people. Resistance posters were produced throughout the 1980s, by silkscreen workshops, collectives and activists – often in secret and despite the threat of detention, beatings, or even death. They provided the visual bonding and solidarity that carried the democratic popular movement to its peak with the Defiance Campaign of 1989, and achieved the beginning of the dismantling of apartheid with the unbanning of the ANC and the release of Nelson Mandela in 1990.

RELEASE MANDELA

& all political prisoners

3

ASIYI eKHAYELITSHA

WE DEMAND HOUSES, SECURITY AND COMFORT

5

APARTHEID IS DEAD ITS INEQUALITIES REMAIN

6

10 FIGHTING YEARS 1976-1986

JUNE 16

SOUTH AFRICAN YOUTH DAY

PEOPLES' EDUCATION FOR PEOPLES' POWER!

4

**4 Poster
commemorating the
tenth anniversary of
Soweto Day (16 June)
when students made
a stand against Bantu
education and the
apartheid system.
Offset litho; produced
for the UDF, Transvaal
1986.
5 'We are not going to
Khayelitsha' (slogan of
resistance used when
the state forced people
in Cape Town's black
areas to leave their
homes), silkscreened
poster, Cape Town 1986.
6 A demonstration in
1991 on the steps of
Johannesburg city hall
by the members of the
Black Sash, a women's
organization devoted to
the protection of human
rights and parliamentary**

**democracy since it was
founded in 1955. The
organization's name
dates from early
years, when members
draped black sashes
over their right
shoulders to mourn
the 'killing' (violation)
of the constitution
by Nationalists.
Photograph by
Gill de Vlieg.
7 Friends write the
names of prisoners
and detainees on a
solidarity banner
dedicated to women in
the struggle against
apartheid, at the last
meeting of
the DPSC (Detainees'
Parents Support
Committee) before it
was banned in February
1988. Photograph by
Eric Miller.**

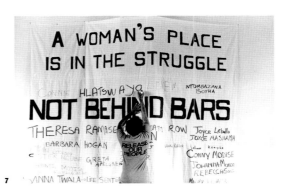

A WOMAN'S PLACE IS IN THE STRUGGLE

NOT BEHIND BARS

7

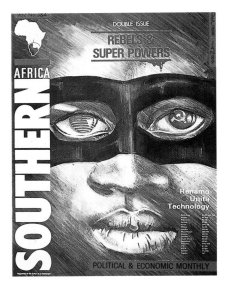

The graphics of reconstruction: the Maviyane Project in Zimbabwe

As in many African states, the move towards independence brought war to Zimbabwe (formerly Rhodesia) followed by a period of reconstruction. An example of the use of graphic design as a tool for social development is shown here in the work of the Maviyane Project in Harare.

At the end of the guerrilla war for independence in 1980, Zimbabwe embarked on the building of a new socialist state. The Maviyane Project, founded by graphic designer Chaz Maviyane-Davies in Harare, involved itself in many aspects of this reconstruction process. Consisting of a small team of designers and a photographer, they challenged the existing Western visual culture (produced by white-dominated advertising agencies) which they felt patronized the black community not only in the handling of images of black people, but in the attitudes and strategies employed to sell them products.

The Maviyane Project consequently aimed to create a new graphic language that would not only serve the communication needs of a new modernized society, but which would also be relevant to the black community,

respecting the strong indigenous visual culture present mainly in their traditional arts and crafts. The Project also addressed a wide range of issues accompanying social development, designing wallcharts that encouraged the preservation of indigenous culture and its artefacts, printed matter on contraception and health issues, and literacy materials and aids used to teach the history of the people's struggle.

Their cover designs for *Moto*, a current affairs magazine banned during the colonial period, depicted many of the social concerns of the time at both national and local level. These included the widening divisions between rich and poor, the existence of capital punishment (carried over from the previous white regime), election results, and the ever-present struggle against apartheid. Solidarity with the struggles of other African countries was a continuing theme in their work, stemming from a philosophy of determination and 'shared destinies', and was particularly important to the Frontline States (including Zimbabwe) battling against apartheid and South African aggression.

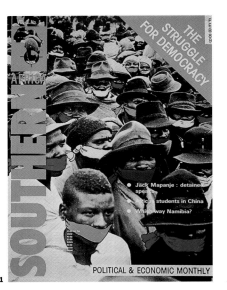

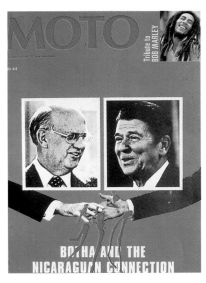

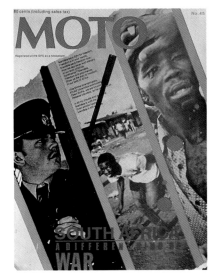

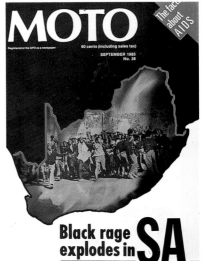

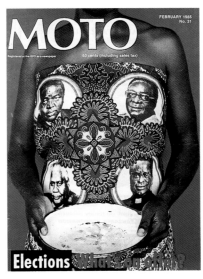

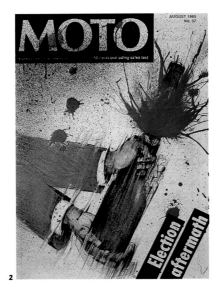

1 Covers of *Southern Africa*, a monthly political magazine aimed at an academic audience; design by Chaz Maviyane-Davies, illustrations by Fiona Paterson, Zimbabwe 1987-9.
2 *Moto* magazine covers, created in 1985-6 by the Maviyane project based in Harare, Zimbabwe (Chaz Maviyane-Davies, Ruhi Hamid and Navin Nagar; with photographer Alex Joe and others). 'Moto' means 'fire' in Shona, one of two major Zimbabwean languages, and was a monthly magazine covering political issues affecting the country at a fundamental level.

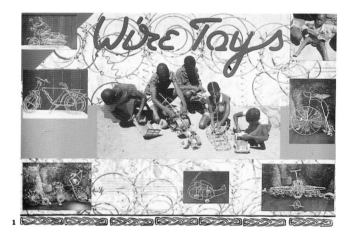

The Maviyane project addressed a wide range of social development issues after Zimbabwean independence in 1980.

1 & 2 A series of educational broadsheets aimed at reviving (and preserving) Zimbabwe's indigenous art and craft culture, such as the making of wire toys and beadwork; designed by Ruhi Hamid, 1985.

3 Poster protesting against misinformation by the press (and an analogy for a new country struggling to keep its footing); design by Chaz Maviyane-Davies, photograph by Alex Joe, Zimbabwe 1984. The poster carries a quotation from Pablo Neruda: 'How is the blind man supposed to live when the bees are constantly bothering him?'. As a result of his critical comment the designer was black listed by the media for five years.

4 Front cover from *Another Battle Begun*, a book on the co-operative movement in Zimbabwe; designed by Ruhi Hamid, photography by Bruce Paton, 1985.

5 A series of posters designed by Ruhi Hamid (showing photographs from *Another Battle Begun*) that were used to teach reading skills and the history of the co-operative movement. Each poster concentrates on a reconstruction issue. Shown here are No. 6, Education; No. 7, Industry and Work; No. 10, Agriculture.

6 Pages from a 1988 Solidarity Calendar in support of displaced Mozambiquens; designed by Chaz Maviyane-Davies with various photographers.

4

5

6

Palestine and Israel

The creation of the state of Israel in 1948 has been followed by four decades of Arab-Israeli border disputes (at times escalating into full-blown war) and terrorist tactics by Palestinians. The on-going turmoil, fed by various instances of international intervention and aid, has made the Middle East a focal point of international tension since the 1960s.

There have been many and varied graphic statements related to the conflict over the years. During the 1960s and 1970s, posters commemorating the struggle for Israeli independence were optimistic and uplifting; the Palestine liberation movement's appeals for revolution and resistance were much rougher in their execution.

Since then anti-war statements and calls for reconciliation have emanated from the artistic communities on both sides, showing widespread distress and fatigue after so many decades of fighting, and the use of graphic symbolism has produced eloquent pleas for a future of peaceful co-existence. But it is the humanitarian messages that directly confront pain and suffering that strike hardest, as illustrated by the posters of Tel Aviv designer David Tartakover (see also page 35).

1

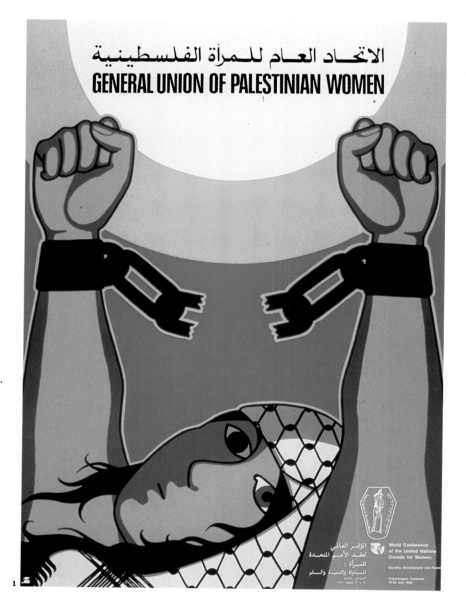

1 Poster for the General Union of Palestinian Women, by Palestinian artist Jihad Mansour. Designed for the World Conference of the United Nations Decade for Women, 1980.
2 'Shalom' (Peace), poster by Dan Reisinger, Israel 1965.
3 'Independence Day', poster designed in 1974 by Dan Reisinger for Israel's 26th anniversary.
4 & 5 Anti-war posters by Israeli designer David Tartakover make a humanitarian plea. Left: 'Mother', showing an Israeli soldier walking past a Palestinian woman – a comment on the duality of soldiers and mothers as sons and mothers, regardless of nationality, allegiance or cause. Photograph by Jim Hollander/ Reuters, Israel 1988. Right: 'Happy New Year', showing a cola bottle as a molotov cocktail. Photograph by Oded Klein, Israel 1987.

China's Cultural Revolution and the Pro-Democracy movement

The image of Mao Tse-tung was the central unifying feature of one of the world's most extensive national campaigns: the propaganda of China's Cultural Revolution (1966-76). The Revolution aimed to turn a vast, unstable population into a unified workforce, and at the same time establish a national culture.

In keeping with the spirit of collectivism, all artistic activity was created, produced and assessed by groups; individualism was discouraged, i.e. eliminated. Style and content were rigidly set, and Socialist Realism, borrowed from the USSR, was pushed to a further extreme of hyper-realism and utopian vision. Heroic stereotypes dominated, with endless representations of enthusiastic masses and the arm-in-arm comraderie of workers, peasants and soldiers. Heroic individuals dedicated to socialist ideals and glorified for deeds of merit were depicted as inspirational role-models, as of course was the all-knowing hero-figure of Mao with his Little Red Book.

The overall rigidity produced extremely banal imagery. The most impressive aspect was the manner in which revolutionary zeal was transferred through this vast media campaign. Demonstrations and banners filled Tiananmen Square in Beijing. Stereotyped imagery appeared everywhere: on outdoor billboards and posters; in books, magazines, newspapers, flyers; on lapel buttons and other ephemera; on household objects and

domestic products. Revolutionary image-saturation was total, and completely devoted to educating the masses on how to think and behave, and to the destruction of all 'counter-revolutionary' bourgeois elements.

In May 1989, over a decade after the Cultural Revolution ended, Beijing's Tiananmen Square was the site of demonstrations for the Pro-Democracy movement, where students, workers and intellectuals demanded a greater hand in the government and the end of corruption. It was a highly visual demonstration that reached out to the world through broadcast media and technology, and the world sat stunned at the massacre that followed – a grim reminder that in spite of popular protest, some regimes remain impervious to change.

4

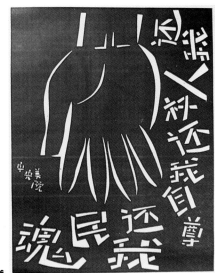

6

5

7

1 Badges paying homage to Chairman Mao, and declaring the people's gratitude.
2 'Unite and Win a Greater Victory', an image of Mao from the Cultural Revolution period in China, 1971.
3 'The People Are With You', Pro-Democracy poster, May 1989, Central Academy of Fine Art, Beijing.
4 Large demonstration banners painted by students of the Central Academy of Fine Art, Beijing, for use in the Tiananmen Square protest of May 1989.
5 Painting the demonstration banners. Photo: Fei Da-wei.
6 'Give Me Back Human Rights', Pro-Democracy poster May 1989, Central Academy of Fine Art, Beijing.
7 '1989 June 4', an image of China's national emblem defaced, created in protest against the massacre in Tiananmen Square. (The large red star represents the Communist Party, and the four small stars denote the people.)

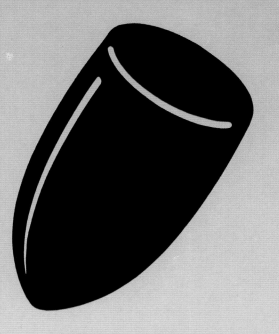

VICTORY 1945

Japan: the spirit of revolution and internationalism

In the 1960s Japan joined the world in anti-Vietnam War protests and campus unrest. Strikes and riots took place in the universities as a new generation rebelled against the conservative elders and their institutions. This spirit of revolt was represented in a post-war generation of designers – including art director Eiko Ishioka, poster artist Tadanori Yokoo and fashion designer Issey Miyake – who travelled the world for new influences. They broke taboos, and rejected clichéd images of Japanese culture, or existing attempts to merge Western Bauhaus or Swiss design philosophy with a traditional Japanese approach, and in so doing created a new image for contemporary Japan.

Tadanori Yokoo became one of the leading print and poster designers during the 1960s and 1970s; his surrealistic posters were as recognizable as the psychedelia of the USA. Shigeo Fukuda, whose posters also became world renowned in the 1960s, transcended the mould by creating his own unconventional form of design using visual puns, illusions and sculptural 3-D tricks.

An important event that furthered the use of graphic design to address global issues occurred in the early 1980s, when the Japan Graphic Designers Association launched its poster series 'Hiroshima Appeals' (see pages 98-99). It was accompanied by an annual exhibition of posters on peace which has continued ever since, expanding its message in the 1990s to include another crucial survival issue: the environment.

I'm here.

2

1 'Victory 1945', poster by Shigeo Fukuda, whose work makes powerful use of visual puns and illusions, Japan 1975.
2 Poster by Shigeo Fukuda for the 1992 Peace and Environment Poster Exhibition entitled 'I'm Here', held by the Japan Graphic Designers Association (JAGDA).

1

1 'We are still strong', poster by Chips Mackinolty, 1987. 'We are still strong', a modern-day rallying cry of Aboriginal people, appears on this poster in the Rembarrnga language of Central Arnhem Land, emphasizing the struggle for the continuation of Aboriginal tribal culture.

2 'Citizenship', poster by Aboriginal artist and writer Sally Morgan, 1987 – one of many unofficial art projects created for the Australian Bicentennial. (It was not until the referendum of 1967 that Aboriginals were conferred full citizenship rights.)

Australia's graphic arts workshops

Australia was also caught up in the wave of change in the 1960s that brought a broad questioning of establishment values, anti-Vietnam War activities, new liberation movements, and awareness and activism on the part of oppressed minorities.

One of the products of the new age was the start in the early 1970s of a modern tradition of posterwork and community art produced by graphic arts workshops using low-tech, low-cost screenprinting. They were dedicated to creating a socially-committed community art and expressing the politics of the Left, in addition to focussing on Australia's cultural diversity and the needs of the Aboriginal community.

The most influential workshop in the 1970s was the Earthworks Poster Collective established by Colin Little in 1972 and based at the University of Sydney Art Workshop, better known as the Tin Sheds. Initially under the heavy influence of psychedelic graphics, the workshop gradually became more politicized as the decade moved on. When it disbanded in 1979 its members spread throughout Australia to help form the next generation of workshops in the 1980s. The new generation included Redletter Community Workshop and Another Planet Posters (now combined to form Red Planet), Redback Graphix and many others. This new breed called upon elements of modern urban culture

such as the graphic style of Punk and modern music, advertising, mass media and technology as well as the symbolism and signs of Aboriginal culture.

The Australian Bicentennial of 1988 placed a sharp focus on Australia's contemporary cultural divisions, eliciting a grassroots movement that called for historical reassessment (as opposed to national celebration) in the light of the mistreatment of Aboriginal people. Many of the issues were eloquently expressed in unofficial art projects, exhibitions and poster-making. The call for an end to the oppression of the Aboriginal people continues to be a major theme for the graphic workshops and their oppositional art.

2

In 1944 Aborigines were allowed to become "Australian Citizens." Aboriginal people called their citizenship papers "Dog Tags." We had to be licensed to be called Australian.

3

3 'History', poster by Pam Debenham, 1987, a fabric-like collage of past and present.

4 'Kanaky Free and Independent', poster by Dianne Wells of Red Planet arts workshop in support of the indigenous people of New Caledonia, 1988.

5 'KCC Women's Auxiliary', poster by Redback Graphix (designer and printer: Alison Alder) for KCC Women's Auxiliary, Wollongong 1984.

6 & 7 A collaborative project between an Aboriginal and non-Aboriginal artist: 'We have survived' and 'Now let's crack the system', two posters by Alice Hinton-Bateup (Aboriginal Program artist) and Marla Guppy (artist in residence) at Garage Graphix community arts group, 1987. The group is based in Western Sydney, where Aboriginal interests have long been neglected, and where survival means fighting back with information and education as well as being armed with new technology.

Posters of the Cuban Revolution

Propaganda posters played a central role in the Cuban Revolution and its attempts to build a new society following Fidel Castro's takeover in 1959. As revolutionary tools, these posters were charged with the mission of communicating socialist ideology to the Cuban population. But unlike the cultural revolutions of the USSR and China, there was no attempt to stifle artistic expression and individual style in favour of repetition and dull stereotypes; art was seen as an aid to the Revolution.

The subjects were familiar: worker solidarity, cultural identity (especially in celebration of a world-renowned film industry), social development (education, literacy, health care), agricultural self-sufficiency and the emulation of heroes, most notably the charismatic guerrilla fighter Che Guevara. But the graphic influences reflected developments in film, fine art and graphic art in Europe and beyond. Hence the Cuban posters eloquently communicated the revolutionary spirit and colourful passion of their society, and did so with a boldness and economy that has been admired by generations since.

As internationalism was central to the Cuban Revolution's philosophy, posters were also used to promote the international (Third World) revolution. The propaganda agency OSPAAAL (The Organization of Solidarity with Asia, Africa and Latin America) distributed posters worldwide, providing a communication network of information and solidarity.

1 Cuban posters became symbols of revolution around the world; this Cuban poster was reprinted by the Chicago Women's Graphics Collective, USA, in 1972-3.
2 'El Salvador, Against Imperialist Intervention!', poster by the international propaganda agency OSPAAAL, Cuba c.1981.
3 'Day of the Heroic Guerrilla October 8', poster published by OSPAAAL, Cuba.
4 'Literacy, converting the darkness into light', poster produced by the Nicaraguan Ministry of Education in 1980, as part of the Sandinista government's national literacy campaign.
5 'Second Continental Congress for Study and Plenary Assembly, Against the Arms Race and Imperialist Domination in Central America and the Caribbean'. Poster produced by the Christian Conference for Peace in Latin America and the Caribbean, and the Christian Movement for Peace, Independence and Progress for the People; Nicaragua 1982.
6 'No intervention in Central America; victorious Nicaragua will neither sell out, nor surrender'. Poster produced by CEPA, the Agrarian Education and Promotion Centre which created peasant organizations to engage in political action, Nicaragua c.1985.

Nicaragua's Sandinista posters

Posters were also employed for political education and consciousness-raising by the Sandinista Revolution in Nicaragua. After the overthrow of the Somoza dictatorship of 1979, over fifty per cent of the population could neither read nor write. As in Cuba, posters were integral to the Sandinista government's struggle for literacy, health care and agrarian reform, and were used to strengthen cultural identity and commemorate heroes from the Revolution.

They also encouraged people to mobilize and defend themselves against the US-backed Contras aiming to destabilize the country. In addition, they often carried a broader call for solidarity with other Central American countries and for resistance to American intervention in Central America, as experienced in El Salvador in 1982, or the West Indian island of Grenada in 1985.

Chapter two

Global issues
Struggles for power, struggles for peace

The past three decades have been characterized by divisions and contrasts: the accompaniments to a shifting world map. We have witnessed the rise and fall of the Iron Curtain, symbol of the Cold War and of the ideological divisions between Eastern socialism and Western capitalism. Its chief manifestation, the Berlin Wall, has come and gone; East and West Germany have been reunited. The Soviet Union itself has moved from superpower to disintegration, and the collapse of the Communist empire has left in its wake a flood of weak economies, unstable governments and ethnic rivalry. As a result, the political and geographical map of Eastern Europe is now in a state of flux.

There has also been the overriding division of developed and underdeveloped. In the 1950s and 1960s the 'world order' consisted of two main superpowers and their associated blocs of countries, struggling against each other, while de-colonization took place in Africa, Southeast Asia and elsewhere. Many of the new states paid dearly for their independence with further internal conflicts, ethnic tensions or even war; few have managed to fulfill their hope of sharing the world's power and wealth. Now in the 1990s a new world order is envisaged, but it is an unstable and constantly changing one.

The underlying theme of power thus continues, and this chapter looks at the graphics generated by power struggles that have acquired an international perspective. It is therefore not concerned with specific wars, but rather with the general issues of war vs. peace, big vs. small, strong vs. weak, rich vs. poor, white vs. black, developed West vs. Third World. The chapter reflects the continuing instabilities and injustices presented by old scourges (such as multinational exploitation and racist policies) and new ones such as the global epidemic of AIDS.

This chapter also focusses on the ability of graphic art and design to communicate worldwide, transcending political and cultural boundaries through emotive and evocative imagery, and the faith that creative artists themselves often have in the ability of their art to make a difference in the way that people think.

The peace movement
After four decades of the nuclear arms race and strained relations between East and West, a new era of peacemaking and openness began in the 1980s with the Soviet policies of glasnost and perestroika, and the disarmament treaties struck between Reagan and

P E A C E

3

Schöne Aussichten

4

Gorbachev. But the subsequent euphoria didn't last long. Since then the Gulf War and the civil war in former Yugoslavia have served to remind us that after decades of a flourishing world arms trade, it is impossible effectively to gauge where military power lies, or what will be done with it. Peace can be broken at any time, from any direction.

The wish for world peace is consequently as fragile and pertinent as ever, and it remains an enduring theme for artists and designers everywhere. One of the most inspiring graphic design demonstrations for peace was the Hiroshima Appeals poster series, created from 1983 to 1990 and organized by the Japan Graphic Designers Association (JAGDA). Each year on behalf of the citizens of Hiroshima an appeal was made to the world – to remember the lesson of Hiroshima and to work for the survival of mankind – through the creation of an annual peace poster designed by a prominent Japanese graphic designer. The poster was distributed worldwide and exhibited in and around Hiroshima on the anniversary of the bombing of 6 August 1945. The series was launched in 1983 with Yusaku Kamekura's eloquent depiction of burning butterflies (page 98). Other JAGDA members added their own statements, printed at their own expense – marking the birth of an annual voluntary peace poster exhibition. (The annual exhibition still exists but has now been expanded to encompass a broader view of survival, including peace and the environment.)

There were other equally important offshoots. As a form of response and goodwill and to commemorate the fortieth anniversary of the Hiroshima bombing, a corresponding peace project was undertaken in 1985 in America by renowned designer and educator Charles Helmken, who died in 1989. (Helmken was also founder and head of the Shoshin Society, a group devoted to the exchange of design ideas between the US, Japan and Korea.) Seeing the potential for a worldwide campaign, Helmken organized the creation of a selection of original peace posters by America's best graphic designers, in co-operation with JAGDA. Under the collection title of 'Images for Survival', simultaneous exhibitions were staged in Hiroshima, Washington and New York. Helmken's project was not only a memorial to peace and a tribute to Japanese culture, it was also dedicated to the idea that graphic design can have an impact and 'make a difference'. (Driven by his belief in the efficacy of design, Helmken created a second project on AIDS posters under the title 'Images for Survival II' in 1989. (Both projects were published in book form by the Shoshin Society.)

Another significant visual contribution to the peace effort can be found in the graphics surrounding Britain's Campaign for Nuclear Disarmament (CND), founded in 1958 in protest against the nuclear bomb testing of that decade. The CND symbol – the circular peace sign, also adopted by the hippie movement in the 1960s – quickly became an international sign for peace. CND demonstrations in themselves achieved an international profile during the 1960s, and rose again in double strength in the early 1980s to protest against the housing of American Cruise missiles in Britain. This second wave was equipped with a highly visible profile provided by the skilful photomontages of

The international peace movement of the 1980s conveyed a powerful message in new and unusual ways.
1 'Impending Image', poster and postcard by Christer Themptander, Sweden 1984.
2 'Still Life', anti-war poster by David Tartakover, Israel 1989.
3 'Wave of Peace', poster created by McRay Magleby to mark the 40th anniversary of the bombing of Hiroshima. (The poster formed part of Charles Helmken's Images for Survival project.)
4 'Beautiful Prospects', postcard by Klaus Staeck recalling Ronald Reagan's Star Wars defence project earlier in the decade, West Germany 1987.

Peter Kennard, whose work was so prolific and popular at the time that he was labelled Britain's 'unofficial war artist' by the media.

Although global nuclear war and militarism are not in themselves a laughing matter, as products of human folly they offer a grand subject here for satirical comment. These include Christer Themptander's tendency to collage missiles in all the wrong (or rather, right) places, and Ronald Reagan playing Rhett Butler to Margaret Thatcher's Scarlett O'Hara while the world explodes in the background (pages 100-101). Humour provides a well-known release for anger and frustration, and has the invaluable asset of communicating across cultures. But it fulfills yet another role here, offering a lively variation on what are inevitably well-worn graphic clichés.

Peace posters and other anti-war graphics are constantly in danger of becoming redundant and ineffective through the use of tired symbols such as peace signs, missiles, gas masks, tearful children or wilting flowers. The variety of imagery included here demonstrates that in the 1980s and 1990s there has been a strong desire to avoid the old clichés – or at least to revitalize them. To this end, missiles are shown being shot down with sling-shots, painted into the English countryside or presented with heavy phallic associations – and then chopped in half. Women and children do not stare out at the viewer with tearful eyes. They are shown dancing in rings around peace camps, or making sarcastic remarks about financing military might with bakesales. The stiff, chubby, symbolic 'peace dove' so often depicted in the 1950s and 1960s makes only one brief, fluttering appearance on page 99 – and doesn't survive the trip. It is blasted by some unseen weapon or force, casting doubt over a future of peace in a dramatic gesture that warns society to come to its senses.

In today's modern graphic environment – where war and violence are often romanticized – the urgent call for peace provides artists and designers with one of their greatest challenges. Moreover the call is dependent on a constant turnover of fresh ways of approaching the subject, as an important means of counteracting the equally constant militaristic programming of the dominant cultural milieu.

Solidarity movements

Due to advances in modern communication media, our contact with the rest of the world has increased dramatically since the 1960s: it is possible to read and hear about hostages, political prisoners, injustices and discrimination around the world, or to see revolutions, civil wars, famine and drought. In the age of on-the-spot news coverage, solidarity projects have become an important means of connecting with – or supporting – the struggles of other peoples and countries.

Solidarity projects utilizing graphics have two major roles to play. They may offer general support for an issue, as in the posters supporting African nationalism and independence in the 1960s and 1970s. Or they may perform a more instrumental role, focussing attention on particular injustices such as the apartheid system in South Africa, disappearances and torture in South American countries, or hostages in the Middle East, and spurring people to take action that will apply pressure to the government or group at fault. Solidarity graphics are a particularly important tool for any situation where protest or resistance within the country itself is not tolerated.

In the global 'one world' spirit of the 1980s and 1990s graphic artists and designers have become increasingly involved in consciousness-raising projects and competitions, working in the belief

AMNESTY INTERNATIONAL

1 'Never Again',
photomontage poster
by Peter Kennard, one
of many anti-nuclear
posters he created
for the Greater London
Council, 1983.
2 Poster by Pam
Debenham on the theme
of no nuclear testing
in the Pacific Islands;
Australia 1984. It was
inspired by a 1950s
Hawaiian shirt depicting
a bomb blast, produced
to commemorate the
first Bikini Atoll tests.
In Debenham's shirt,
Pacific resorts are
replaced by the names
of nuclear test sites.
3 'Chile', poster
protesting against
political killings,
by Redback Graphix
(design: Michael
Callaghan; printers:
Alison Alder, Osmond
Kantilla) for Amnesty
International,
Australia 1987.
4 Human rights poster
for Amnesty
International by
Lanny Sommese,
USA 1980s.

that such efforts educate and lead to greater understanding, and in the long run can make a difference to the way the world behaves. Such projects also give designers the chance to take direct action as opposed to being passive observers of world events. Amnesty International, one of the best known organizations campaigning for human rights, has been a favourite design collaborator and inspiration of countless exhibitions, competitions, posters and other graphic works of solidarity.

Three projects are shown which present different approaches to the subject of human rights. The first project is from Paul Piech (Taurus Press), who has produced an impressive amount of graphic work on human rights issues through the medium of the lino-cut. His imagery and comments are extremely tough and raw-edged. Examples are shown here from the 'Abolish Torture' exhibition which Piech produced in collaboration with Colombian-born photographer Gustavo Espinosa in 1987. The exhibition strikes hard at the human conscience by combining expressionistic lino-cut imagery, fragments of photographed reality, and snippets of disturbing text. All elements work together to construct symbolic visions of the unseen and the unknown.

The second project is an exhibition for the 1989 Bicentenary of the French Revolution (produced by Artis 89), when the French poster group Grapus invited 66 internationally-known designers to produce posters on the 'Rights of Man' theme. The project is particularly significant in that it sparked off a new wave of international 'designer-exhibitions', usually involving large groups of designers producing work in order to give exposure to a cause. (Such exhibitions don't necessarily always show designers at their artistic best, but they do underline a socially committed role for design.) Unlike the 'Abolish Torture' project, the Artis 89 exhibition dealt with human rights in the broadest sense, and some of its best contributions cut through the vague universality of the subject to make one distinct and simple statement, as in Grapus' scribbled version of 'rich shits on poor'. Others make obscure or abstract comment, or present intriguing symbolic compositions as in Jan van Toorn's complex comment on the political shift to the right.

The third project shown here is an international designer-exhibition organized by Gallery Wabnitz in Holland in 1991. It celebrates 30 years of Amnesty International, and features a definite search for a new visual approach to the subject of human rights offences. A number of the compositions completely side-step the normal visual clichés, demanding participation and hard thought on the part of the viewer. Images and definitions derived from modern lifestyle are used to create soul-searching statements that are extremely effective. For example Edward McDonald's poster uses the modern obsession with logos (as marks of personal identity) to question the viewer's stance or personal sense of justice. Design group Hard Werken's contribution is more obscure: a photograph of an island paradise suggests the wishful thoughts of a prisoner. Along with other examples shown on pages 111-113, both explore new directions in poster communication as well as helping Amnesty International's humanitarian cause.

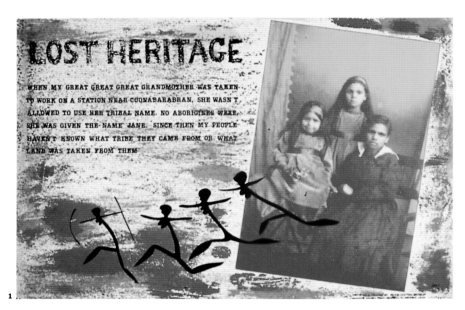

1

2

There has been a slow and steady stream of international solidarity movements related to the imperialism of the superpowers, racism, oppressed communities, or the injustices of particular regimes. This has included, for example, protest against US intervention in Central American countries (particularly strong in the early 1980s), and outcry against the repressive regimes of South America and 'disappearances' in Argentina, Brazil, Chile, Guatemala and elsewhere.

Anti-racism has been a powerful and continuing theme, with many variations. The international anti-apartheid movement has produced some of the strongest imagery to emanate from individual designers and groups. It has not only directed protest against the atrocities committed under the apartheid system in South Africa, but has also acted as a focus for the broader racial issues which are endemic to many countries. With the rise of neo-Nazi extremism in Germany in the early 1990s (and the threat of fascist groups active in other countries as well), there has been a recent popular ground swell of anti-racist activity in Europe – particularly generated by the young. Old campaigns have been resurrected (Britain's Anti-Nazi League has been revived, for example), and new campaigns and demonstrations have produced a wealth of anti-fascist and anti-racist material. Germany, once again, is clearly in the lead here.

In 1992, land-snatching and the plight of indigenous peoples were brought into sharp focus in protests concerning the 500th anniversary celebrations of Columbus's discovery of the New World. As had been the case with the Australian Bicentennial of 1988, the celebration of a history that represents one culture crushing another produced a surge of grassroots activism, often expressed in graphic form. The Columbus celebrations, for example, receive harsh attack from Doug Minkler's sinister posters in the style of children's games, an appropriate vehicle for questioning what children are taught to believe, shown here and on page 121. (The unofficial art produced for the Australian Bicentennial is discussed on page 86.)

Global connections and the Third World

Corporate relations with the Third World have provided another controversial theme for artists and designers, sparked off especially by the climate of social responsibility in the 1970s. This chapter includes the pioneering work of Hans Haacke, known particularly for his persistent explorations into the relationship between corporate power, art institutions, the media and the public. Haacke has made harsh comment on the 'unseen' activities of multinational corporations that have attempted to present an acceptable public face through funding of the arts. But his 'attacks' have always been executed in the style and language of corporate advertising and graphics (accompanied by the ever-present corporate logo). As art pieces and installations they turn media propaganda and rhetoric back on itself, presenting an unsettling view of the corporation and its interface with the public, as well as casting a shadow on the ethics of the creators of corporate image: the advertisers, PR men and graphic designers.

DRAW COLUMBUS
Liar   Slaver   Murderer   Thief

3

4

5

1 'Lost Heritage', screenprinted poster by Alice Hinton-Bateup, Aboriginal Program artist at Garage Graphix community arts group in Western Sydney, Australia 1983.
2 'I do not celebrate 200 years of war against the Aboriginal peoples and the land', screenprinted poster by Jan Fieldsend, Australia 1987. The poster depicts the ancient Aboriginal symbol of the Rainbow Serpent, the creator of the Earth and a representation of the Earth's life and power.
3 'Draw Columbus', poster in the style of a children's game by Doug Minkler, USA 1991.
4 'Never Again', artwork by Jamie Reid for a CD and album cover in support of the Anti-Nazi League, Britain 1992.
5 Front cover of the *Antifaschistisches Infoblatt*, an anti-fascist magazine from Berlin, Germany 1992.

1

2

Corporate 'nasties' and Western wealth are often best attacked in their own visual language. The photomontages of Sweden's Christer Themptander and Germany's Klaus Staeck (page 124) rely on the technique of making awkward juxtapositions of media imagery to achieve a greater symbolic message, and also demonstrate the extent to which corporate logos are now symbolically 'loaded'. Certain types of visual assault have had their casualties, however. The British charity War on Want employed an advertising agency to communicate its humanitarian messages, most of which were insulting to Western businesses with Third World interests. The result: the ad agency received a great deal of hype and applause from the media, while the charity found its existence under threat due to complaints and pressure by the companies concerned.

In a visual essay that he constructed for Britain's *i-D* magazine, stylist and designer Judy Blame has taken the theme of imbalances of power and wealth into a totally different expressive dimension, using style and fashion to present complex social and political contradictions. Like Staeck and Themptander he makes awkward juxtapositions, placing fashion models and imagery with text that contrasts the price of designer-label items with their equivalent in terms of humanitarian aid. But the fashion photographs are in themselves loaded images, posing pertinent questions relating to global power games and the West's entanglements with the Third World.

ACT UP (AIDS Coalition to Unleash Power), the AIDS activist group, has taken hold of the visual power-language of corporate design and advertising to fight government inaction on AIDS issues. A distinctive visual strategy lies at the centre of their political movement. They use propaganda graphics for group identification on demonstrations, for reinforcement and education on issues, and for 'keeping the pressure on', making sure that AIDS remains in the public vision as a live issue. They also exploit the possibilities of merchandising, using t-shirts, badges and other items to strengthen group identity while at the same time encouraging a personal political stance. Their symbol (Silence = Death) has come to be a sign for AIDS activism itself, and represents the ultimate modern-day challenge.

ACT UP's adoption of visual power-language however is a matter of professionalism and strategy. They know what they are up against; they know exactly who or what the enemy is: governments, bureaucracy, conservatism. Theirs is a struggle to get power back into the hands of the ordinary people: to change 'official' attitudes and policies. So they need to operate at the same level of sophistication, in terms of visual propaganda, as government departments, drug companies, insurance companies and financial institutions. Added to that, ACT UP is very much a global movement, committed to fighting the worldwide epidemic of AIDS. In the same way that multinationals employ global visual strategies through logos and corporate identities, so ACT UP relies on the strength of its graphics to keep their identity and profile intact, despite being translated into different languages or being subjected to the 'creative licence' exercised by different city chapters.

ACT UP also represents an important development in the trend towards 'personal politics', and the use of art and design for that political expression. Disillusionment with governments and political parties unable to deal with global crises has helped to generate grassroots involvement and activism, often through the popular vehicle of the creative arts and particularly through youth formats. The Live Aid rock concert of 1985 was a watershed: it proved what the creative arts could do to generate concern and caring for international causes (in this case, famine relief for Africa). In reality, Live Aid could only bring momentary relief – not solve the actual problem – but it did serve to magically shrink the world in an all-day 'global concert' which took place simultaneously in Philadelphia and London and was broadcast by the largest satellite link-up ever. It allowed people in many different countries to show solidarity over a common cause, and inspired a new young generation to action and involvement.

Live Aid also opened up politics and global issues to a wide range of art and design media and technology, again often exploited by the younger generation. Artists and designers have cast a creative but critical eye on the information and computer technologies, as shown in Keith Piper's anti-racist computer-based video installation *Surveillances* (page 130), while at the same time attempting to harness the new technology for direct action.

'You have the technology to change history' was the rallying cry printed in *The Face* magazine in Britain, as it encouraged its readers to take part in the Fax for Freedom, a protest-by-fax in support of the Tiananmen Square protestors. The protest was organized by *Actuel* magazine in France and involved 16 magazines around the world. The magazines all carried a cut-out manifesto and a multitude of fax numbers belonging to offices and institutions within China, so that readers could bombard them with the Fax for Freedom. *Actuel* also organized the production of a pirate edition of China's *People's Daily* newspaper. Written by students who had escaped to the West, it carried information about the democratic movement and was spread, secretively, in and around Beijing by French and German reporters.

The role of youth formats in the shift towards a new era of 'personal politics' has therefore been significant. Charity or 'awareness' rock concerts are now fairly common. Fashion items are used for a wide variety of causes, with t-shirts still operating as one of the best methods for parading personal politics (and one that is timeless in its appeal). Rap records and videos promote black awareness; football 'fanzines' attack fascism. Youth-orientated style magazines devote entire issues to activism and anti-racism, while ecology and Green issues have invaded beauty products, clothing, children's books and Saturday morning TV cartoons. All of these (and more) have become the expressive vehicles for the politics of a new generation. They have cut through the divisions and barriers existing in conventional attitudes and power structures, and have offered people (both young and old) the opportunity to be active and involved. In short they have all, in their way, brought power – and politics – back to the people.

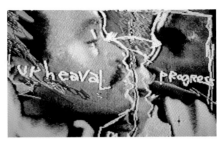

3

1 Cover and spreads from two of the 16 magazines carrying the Fax for Freedom manifesto in support of the Pro-Democracy movement in China: *The Face* **(Britain) and** *Actuel* **(France), November/December 1989.**

2 Pirated edition of China's *People's Daily* **written by students who had escaped to the West.**

3 'Step into the Arena', stills from Keith Piper's computer/video installation which explores gender and racial stereotyping

through the symbolic framework of a boxing ring, Britain 1991. Its four monitors represent the corners of a ring.

4 Poster announcing a demonstration (the hand sign symbolizes keeping death away) by the Dutch chapter of ACT UP, 1992.

PEOPLE WITH AIDS DO IT EVERYWHERE
demonstreer mee tegen discriminatie, tegen inreis- en immigratiebeperkingen
19 juli '92, 14.00 uur, Westerkerk

4

art direction, design: ryuichi kimekura
illustration: akira yokoyama
printing: toppan printing co.,ltd.
sponsor: hiroshima international cultural foundation, inc., jagda (japan graphic designers association)

2

The Hiroshima Appeals poster series

The Hiroshima Appeals poster series was one of the graphic design world's most emotional calls for peace. From 1983 to 1990 an annual appeal was made to the world – on behalf of the people of Hiroshima – to work against the threat of nuclear war, and for the cause of peace. Each year a poster was created by one of Japan's top designers, then distributed worldwide and exhibited in and around Hiroshima on the anniversary of the bombing of 6 August 1945. The series was organized by the Japan Graphic Designers Association (JAGDA), who then complemented it with an annual peace poster exhibition – a voluntary affair made possible by the enthusiasm of JAGDA's members, which still continues to this day. Other inspired offshoots included the 'Images for Survival' (I and II) poster exhibitions initiated by Charles Helmken in America, described on page 91.

Three of the Hiroshima Appeals peace posters are shown here. Yusaku Kamekura's 1983 poster launched the series with its tragic rendition of burning butterflies. Shigeo Fukuda, designer of the 1985 poster and known for his amusing visual puns and illusions, created an unusual and witty statement about keeping the world intact. In 1987 Kazumasa Nagai depicted a frozen moment of horror, as beauty and peace (symbolized by the wings of a white bird) were destroyed by some unseen force or weapon.

3

World peace: humour and satire

1

Humour and satire have provided the peace movement with a much-needed release for tension and anger over the years. This was particularly true during the early 1980s when the housing of American missiles in Europe was becoming an increasingly topical issue, and the close political relationship between Ronald Reagan and Margaret Thatcher was making peaceniks on both sides of the Atlantic extremely nervous, at the same time as providing an inspiring subject for cartoonists and satirists.

The 'Gone with the Wind' poster shown here was a distinctive graphic icon in Britain at that time, appearing in various radical haunts and highly indicative of the mood of popular protest. Other examples are much broader in scope. The Swedish photomontagist Christer Themptander, for example, has produced a large body of anti-militaristic collage work over two decades, all of it beautifully executed, and highly expert in capturing the lunacy of military matters.

2

1 Photomontage by
Egon Kramer, showing
West German
Chancellor Helmut Kohl
playing to the tune of
American supremacy in
the arms race, 1985.
2 'Gone with the Wind',
poster and postcard
by Bob Light and John
Houston, Britain
c.1984.

3 'Attention!', poster
and postcard by
Christer Themptander,
Sweden 1981.
4 'The Seducer' by
Christer Themptander,
Sweden 1984.

3

4

1

MOUVEMENT DE LA JEUNESSE COMMUNISTE DE FRANCE

"No Mr reagan"

Neutr ns

RELAIS de la PAIX
28 septembre / 25 Octobre 1981

2

1989
AN DEUX DU
DESARMEMENT

Pas de nouveaux missiles
Dimanche 23 avril
zone de Paix
Albion

4

NO
A TUTTI
I MISSILI

PARTECIPA
AL REFERENDUM
AUTOGESTITO

SCEGLI LA PACE

P.C.I.

3

6

The 1980s and the international peace movement

5

In the early 1980s the move towards NATO rearmament and the deployment of short and medium-range nuclear missiles in Europe (the US Cruise and Pershing, and Soviet SS20) brought the international peace movement roaring back to life. For many people, the missiles brought with them a fearful vision of Europe as a potential arena for a 'limited' nuclear war.

Britain's Campaign for Nuclear Disarmament (CND), which had achieved an international profile in the 1960s, rose again with a powerful and prolific visual campaign supplied by the political artist Peter Kennard; his immensely popular photomontages were seen on billboards, in the press, at demonstrations and on posters in the street. At the same time, the Women's Peace Camp at Greenham Common (established in 1981) made the international headlines, supplying a model for political activism and other peace camps. While protests and demonstrations swept across Europe, the USSR and Iron Curtain countries produced equally emotive statements through competitions such as those staged by the Communist Party poster press (Plakat), for international peace was one of the Party's 'approved' subjects during those pre-glasnost years.

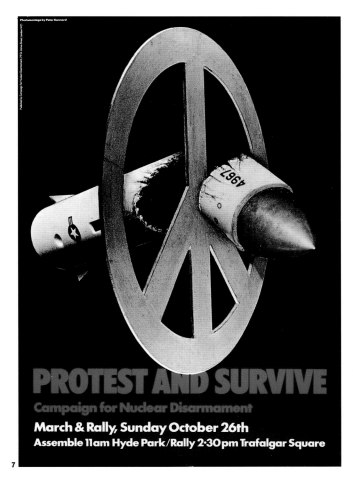

PROTEST AND SURVIVE
Campaign for Nuclear Disarmament
March & Rally, Sunday October 26th
Assemble 11am Hyde Park/Rally 2·30pm Trafalgar Square

7

1 Peace badges, USSR 1986. Both simply read 'No' (missiles).
2 Peace poster for the French Communist youth movement by Grapus design collective, France 1981.
3 'Choose peace', poster designed by Stefano Rovai of Graphiti studio in Florence, for the Italian Communist Party, Italy 1983.
4 'Year Two of Disarmament', poster for the Mouvement pour la Paix, Paris. Designed by Andrea Rauch of Graphiti studio, Italy 1989.
5 Nuclear disarmament symbol designed by Gerald Holtom in 1956, and adopted by Britain's Campaign for Nuclear Disarmament (CND) in 1958.
6 Photomontage poster by Peter Kennard which combines cruise missiles with John Constable's painting *The Haywain*. The poster was widely reproduced by the Greater London Council and also by the Labour Party; Britain 1980-83.
7 Badge and poster showing Peter Kennard's 'Protest and Survive' visual campaign, the result of a brief to revitalize the British CND symbol (and public image) for use on the first big march of the new 'revived' CND in 1979.

2

3

Peace protests: women and children

1

Women played a strong role in the protests of
the 1980s. The Women's Peace Camp at
Greenham Common led the way, in a protest
that saw women camped outside the gates of
a US missile base in Britain from 1981 to the
early 1990s. The camp came to symbolize the
strength of women united in a cause and their
ability to subvert male military power.

The Greenham experience involved a good
deal of theatre and visual symbolism. Many
direct actions were staged (such as 'Embrace
the Base', when in 1982 over 30,000 women
travelled to Greenham to link hands around
the base); banner-making enjoyed renewed
popularity; photo-journalists visited from far
and near. It inspired books, songs, print
portfolios and even a fashion collection by
Katharine Hamnett. The perimeter fence
remained a potent symbol: it was damaged or
pulled down during large demonstrations, but
was more often decorated with paint and
paper doves, pictures, dolls, photographs and
other momentos of humanity, womanhood
and childhood.

Greenham and its fighting spirit set the
tone for much of the imagery of that decade.
Women appeared often in the media and
were depicted as a source of strength,
unafraid to stand up for their rights, demand
a future of peace, or even to confront the
military machine.

4

5

6

7

1 One of a series of 16 'Post-Atomic' cards promoting an exhibition of 'postable art' on disarmament. Designed and printed by the exhibition organizers, the Fallout Committee (Michele Braid, Julia Church, Bob Clutterbuck and others); Australia 1984.
2 'Children ask the world of us', poster for Women's Action for Nuclear Disarmament (WAND) designed by Lance Hidy, with text by Margaret Wilcox, USA 1984.
3 Peace poster by Margus Haavamägi, Estonia 1986.
4 'No Neutron Weapons', poster (designer unknown), USSR c.1980.
5 Poster produced by the Women's International League for Peace and Freedom, USA 1980s.
6 Banner made in 1983 by Thalia and Jan Campbell and Jan Higgs, celebrating the 'Women for Life on Earth' Action for Peace at Greenham Common (27 August 1981 to 12 December 1983), Britain.
7 Cover and inside spread from *The Greenham Factor*, a newsheet and solidarity tool produced to document and raise funds for the Women's Peace Camp at Greenham Common, Britain 1983-4.

Graphics for human rights: Abolish Torture

Graphic artist Paul Peter Piech is internationally known for his expressionistic lino-cuts. His Taurus Press (founded in 1959) has generated a prolific output of radical comment over the years, born out of his passionate concern for the cause of human rights. Piech, his press and his collaborations represent the extraordinary potential and power of an individual voice.

Shown on this spread are selected pieces from 'Abolish Torture', an exhibition of works created for Amnesty International by Piech and Colombian-born photographer Gustavo Espinosa. It communicates the fears and horrors of its subject through the use of symbolic imagery and fragmented text. The juxtaposition of two very different graphic techniques – photography and lino-cut – is also extremely effective. The starkly symbolic photo-images emphasize the fear that lies behind unknown actions or reality; the primitive quality of the lino-cut text lends a dramatic edge to the thoughts and words. Both forces combine to create a disturbing and haunting call to action.

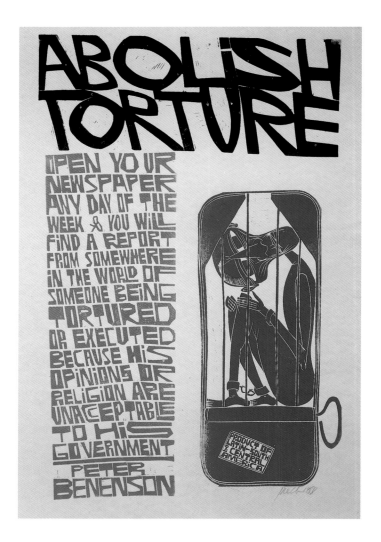

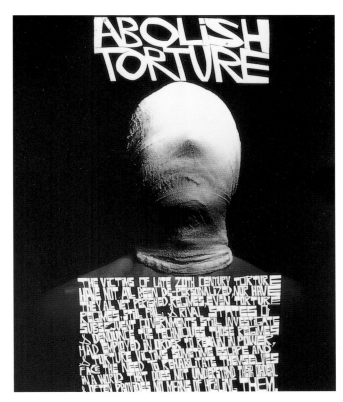

Selected prints from 'Abolish Torture', a touring exhibition of collaborative works created for Amnesty International by graphic artist Paul Peter Piech and Colombian-born photographer Gustavo Espinosa, 1987.

Posters for the Bicentenary of the French Revolution, 1989

1

The issue of human rights was the subject of an exhibition organized by French poster group Grapus for the 1989 Bicentenary of the French Revolution. Sixty-six well-known designers from around the world were invited to produce a poster on the theme of the Declaration of the Rights of Man and of the Citizen. The collection was then exhibited and published in the book *For Human Rights* (produced by Artis 89).

The collection featured broad interpretations of the subject, and a wide range of graphic approaches. Some posters distilled the all-embracing theme into one simple statement, as shown in Masuteru Aoba's 'we shall overcome' or Grapus' 'rich shits on poor'. Others dwelled on complexity: Jan van Toorn's rendition of 'the struggle continues' depicts confusion, contradictions, media-babble and other forces moving to the political right.

The exhibition also had its controversies, including a poster by Australian designer Julia Church which criticized the French nuclear presence in the South Pacific. The poster was an attempt by Church to question the exclusivity of the French government's interpretation of the 'Rights of the Citizen', and also represented the strained relations between France and nations of the Pacific Rim. It was one of a number of posters in the exhibition which caused certain French government officials concern, and provoked (failed) attempts at censorship.

The exhibition also sparked off a new genre of 'designer-exhibitions', where well-known designers were asked to create an original piece of work in order to aid a cause. In addition to creating some interesting collections of work, these exhibitions also helped to encourage the modern notion of design and style as politics.

2

3

4

Posters from the human rights exhibition organized by Grapus for the Bicentenary of the French Revolution, 1989.
1 Grapus, France.
2 Masuteru Aoba, Japan.
3 Jan van Toorn, Holland.
4 Julia Church, Australia.
5 Poster by Grapus, announcing the exhibition.

1

Poster exhibition: 30 years of Amnesty International

In 1991 the Poster Gallery Wabnitz in Arnhem, Holland, initiated a 'designer-exhibition' to celebrate 30 years of human rights campaigning by Amnesty International, with 50 well-known designers from around the world taking part. In addition to promoting a worthwhile cause, the collection featured new approaches to the subject of human rights.

The old clichés of prison bars and chains are forsaken for intriguing statements that demand thought on the part of the viewer, or that play with aspects of modern lifestyle. The notion of freedom appears in curious symbolic forms: a saw by Melle Hammer; a hellish vision of keys by Neville Brody; or a prisoner's wishful thinking, conjured up as an island paradise by design group Hard Werken.

Edward McDonald's resounding composition 'your choice is your identity' uses the modern obsession with logos and self-identity to pose questions of conscience; Rik Comello's conversational 'fuck justice' compresses an extraordinary amount of passion into a relatively small number of words; while the brash 'I am nasty' by Linda van Deursen and Armand Mevis highlights the hidden evils of the business world by using a camouflage of pinstripes. The visual language employed in all of the posters mentioned is rooted in the style and technology of today's society, with references to press photography, advertising, the quest for status, and other trappings of current lifestyles. Therein lies their strength and endurance: they use modern language to condemn modern evils.

to those *lusting* for power:

FUCK JUSTICE

(And she'll give birth to **Abuse & Despair** two sons who will kill **Integrity, Beauty & Truth,** your favourite brother and 2 most beloved sisters. **Believe me,** **THEY WILL!**)

thirty years amnesty international

2

30 JAAR AMNESTY INTERNATIONAL

3

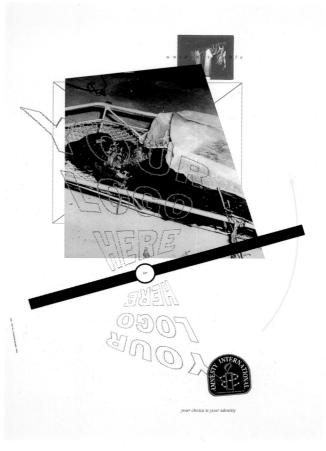

4

5

Posters from the exhibition '50 poster designs/30 years Amnesty International', organized by Poster Gallery Wabnitz of Holland in 1991.
1 Holger Matthies, Germany.
2 Rik Comello, Holland.
3 Hard Werken, Holland.
4 Gunter Rambow, Germany.
5 Edward McDonald, USA.

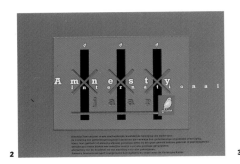

2

3

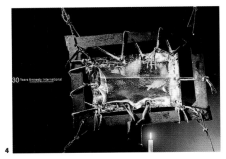

4

1

A further selection of
posters from the 1991
Amnesty International
exhibition.
1 Linda van Deursen
and Armand Mevis,
Holland.
2 Lex Reitsma, Holland.
3 Plus x (Melle
Hammer), Holland.
4 Hans Bockting,
Holland.
5 Neville Brody, Britain.

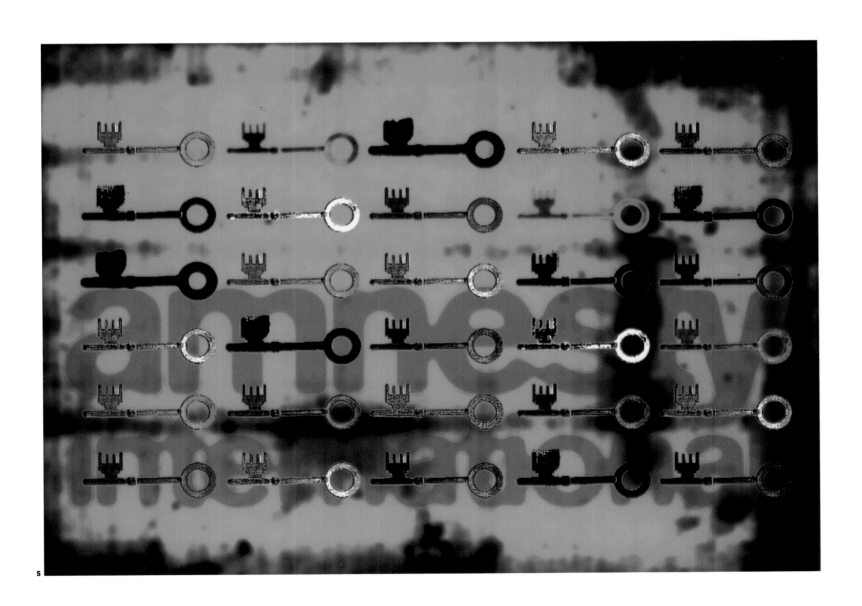

5

Uitgave: Anti-Apartheidsbeweging Nederland, tel 020-267525 ism.Komitee Zuidelijk Afrika, tel 020-270801. Ontwerp: Wild Plakken, Druk: SSP

Z AFRIKAANSE VROUWENDAG

**1 Poster celebrating 'South African Women's Day' on 8 August 1988 by Wild Plakken (Frank Beekers, Lies Ros, Rob Schröder), for the Dutch anti-apartheid movement.
2 'Apartheid', self-sponsored poster by Wild Plakken, Holland 1986.
3 & 4 Cover and inside spread from the handbook *How to Commit Suicide in South Africa*, with text by Holly Metz and illustrations by Sue Coe, USA 1983.**

1

3

Fighting apartheid: solidarity graphics

2

The anti-apartheid movement has inspired graphic work from designers in many countries. Activity was strongest during the 1980s when the popular resistance movement within South Africa itself was at its height (see National Politics, pages 74-5). International solidarity included such actions as campaigning for Nelson Mandela's release from prison, support for economic sanctions, and 'divestment', the withdrawal of public funds from companies investing in South Africa, in order to challenge apartheid. The projects shown here are highlights from a long and continuing stream of graphic support.

The handbook *How to Commit Suicide in South Africa* was an expression of outrage. Published by Raw Books and Graphics (New York 1983), it was created by artist Sue Coe and journalist Holly Metz after reading about people who died or 'committed suicide' in detention in South Africa – especially Black Consciousness leader Steve Biko (d. 1977). The book contained researched information concerning racism in South Africa – historical timelines, statistics on foreign investment and so on – and was illustrated by Sue Coe's expressionistic imagery. It was an important consciousness-raising document in both

Britain and America, and was used as an organizing tool on American campuses when divestment became a big issue.

Also shown here are posters from Wild Plakken design group in Amsterdam, who have made many anti-apartheid statements in photo-collage form, and imagery surrounding the Nelson Mandela 70th Birthday rock concert in London in 1988. These include Keith Haring's energetic cartoon-figures, and 'Hope and Optimism', an extremely popular lino-cut from one of Southern Africa's leading artists John Muafangejo, who had died the preceding year.

4

©K.HARING 88

1 Badges from the
British anti-apartheid
movement, 1980s.
2 Nelson Mandela 70th
Birthday Concert,
Wembley Stadium,
London 1988. The
concert was performed
before a backdrop of
work by artists Keith
Haring, Jenny Holzer,
John Muafangejo and
others.
3 'Hope and Optimism',
lino-cut by John
Muafangejo, Namibia
1984.
4 'Untitled', poster by
Keith Haring, USA 1988.

4

Solidarity with oppressed peoples of the world

The oppression of indigenous peoples in many countries around the world has been an on-going subject for graphic protest and focus for the past three decades. There have been many solidarity movements and individual protests along the way, some of them continuing in strength to this day. A selection is shown on the following pages, ranging from the national liberation struggles in Africa in the 1960s and 1970s, to the continuing struggles of the Aboriginal nation of Australia.

The 1990s however have brought further developments: new views and definitions of history, and new multicultural perspectives, reflecting the roles of women and ethnic minorities. Myths and legends surrounding historical 'heroes' have been subjected to scrutiny, and a fair amount of debunking. Attempts to celebrate the 'discovery' of new lands or new nations, which inevitably involved one culture 'civilizing' or conquering another, have continued to generate protest – as shown earlier in the Australian Bicentennial of 1988 (pages 85-6) and in the recent celebrations of the 500th Anniversary of Columbus's discovery of the New World, represented on page 95 by Doug Minkler's cynical historical lesson on Columbus.

1 Poster in solidarity
with the national
liberation struggles in
Africa, by The Poster
Collective, Britain
1970s.
2 Poster in support
of Guinea-Bissau
independence, by
Chicago Women's
Graphics Collective,
USA 1973.
3 Poster promoting
the book 'A for Africa'
written by Ife Ore; the
poster was also a
popular African
solidarity image.
Created by The Poster
Collective, Britain mid-
1970s.
4 'Nicaragua', poster
by Redback Graphix
(designers and printers:
Michael Callaghan,
Gregor Cullen) for the
Committee in Solidarity
with Central America
and the Caribbean
(CISCAC), Wollongong,
Australia 1984.
5 'Nicaragua must
survive', poster by Julia
Church (with Another
Planet Posters) for the
Trade Union Committee
on Central America
based in Melbourne,
Australia 1986.

1 'We'll never forget Wounded Knee', postcard and poster by Christer Themptander in solidarity with the cause of the Native Americans (and widely distributed in the USA), 1971. The title refers to the massacre of Sioux Indians by US troops at Wounded Knee in 1890.
2 'Night of Sorrow, 1492', a screenprinted poster by Pamela Branas of Red Planet arts workshop, Australia, contrasting the struggle of the indigenous peoples of the Americas and the historical view of the conquistadores. Produced in 1992 (the 500th Anniversary of the Conquest of the New World).
3 'Columbusters', poster in the style of a children's game by Doug Minkler, and an acerbic comment on the Columbus celebrations, USA 1992.
4 Screenprinted poster by Marie McMahon (Australia) designed in 1981 in solidarity with the people of the Tiwi Islands and in support of national Land Rights legislation.

1

2

COLUMBUSTERS

RULES: Spin Columbus, move to designated color.

Give back all native land.

Lose all slaves.

Receive molten gold throat treatment to relieve treasure lust.

Busted for incompetence. Go back to Spain.

Cholera infected blankets meant for native people kills all your soldiers.

Alcohol meant to stupefy native peoples intoxicates crew, your ship sinks.

Forced on white reservation for own good.

GOAL: Try to get from 1492 to 1992 keeping the mythical vision of brave Columbus the discoverer locked in your mind. The winner receives an American flag, and a Support the Troops bumper sticker.

4

3

1

1 The writers of the
Band Aid song: Midge
Ure and Bob Geldof
wearing a Feed the
World t-shirt (with
daughter Fifi), 1984.
2 & 3 The Band Aid
single (and cover
sleeve) recorded in
November 1984. The
Feed the World logo
was conceived by Bob
Geldof; sleeve artwork
was created by artist
Peter Blake.
4 Cover of Fashion Aid
programme; logo design
by Ostrich Graphics,
programme produced
by Concessions,
Britain 1985.
5 Cartoon by Pat
Oliphant commenting
on the charity-at-home
effort 'Hands Across
America', USA 1986.

2

3

Band Aid and Live Aid: famine relief

Two events of the mid-1980s changed the Western world's concept of charity, particularly in relation to the Third World, and at the same time inspired a young generation to action and involvement. They were the recording and release of the Band Aid pop single in November 1984, and the Live Aid rock concert held in July 1985. Both events were conceived and engineered by Irish musician Bob Geldof.

Sales of the Band Aid single 'Do They Know It's Christmas?', involving over 40 different pop singers and with record sleeve artwork by pop artist Peter Blake, produced over £10 million for Ethiopian famine relief in the winter of 1984. It was followed in the summer of 1985 by a sister event: the internationally-broadcast Live Aid rock extravaganza, an all-day 'global concert' which took place simultaneously in Philadelphia and London and was broadcast to 152 countries by the most ambitious satellite link-up that had ever been attempted.

Whereas Band Aid caught the imagination of the British public, Live Aid appealed to the hearts of the world. There were complaints at the time that it only supplied temporary relief and that it failed to solve Ethiopia's real problems, but there was no denying the effect the event had on its global audience. It provided people in numerous countries with the opportunity to unite on an issue of goodwill, and showed the astonishing rallying power of rock music and the possibilities of mass communication media.

Live Aid also produced a legacy of charity events, both in Europe and America. These included Fashion Aid, Cartoon Aid, and Artists' Aid, all of them trying to recapture that precious feeling of goodwill, some more successfully than others. America, for example, used the wave of goodwill as an opportunity to scrutinize its own poverty and homelessness, and staged 'Hands Across America', a Hollywood-style symbolic joining of hands across the country (with Ronald Reagan included). The event was heavily publicized, but relatively ineffective.

1 'Adapted to the Market', photomontage by Christer Themptander of Sweden, a portrait of consumerism and corporate aims.
2 'To commemorate the swearing in of the new world government', postcard by Klaus Staeck, West Germany 1981. Logos of the major oil companies are used to represent the global power of the multinationals.

The balance of wealth and power

The West's relations with the Third World, and the imbalances of power and wealth contained therein, have been long-standing themes in the art and design world. Attempts have been made to promote aid, or support indigenous projects: the climate of social responsibility in design in the 1970s, for example, created interest (and action) relating to alternative technology and Third World design needs. But there has also been a very large amount of on-going art and design activity devoted to attacking the instruments and causes of the imbalances.

Artist Hans Haacke's pioneering work purported to expose the 'concealed activities' of multinationals, particularly those using funding of the arts to create a presentable public face. Significantly, he conducted his attacks in the style of corporate advertising and graphics, thereby turning the rhetoric and propaganda back on itself. Christer Themptander, Klaus Staeck and others have also manipulated a wide range of symbols such as corporate logos, boardroom tables and fat men in business suits, to pose questions about commercial power and control. Other innovative approaches to the subject include Judy Blame's use of fashion and style to make cost equations between designer lifestyles and humanitarian aid, while also exploring themes of financial power, racial prejudice and industrial exploitation: all aspects of the global power games scenario.

1

marknadsanpassad

2

Zur Erinnerung an die Vereidigung der neuen Weltregierung

3

A selection of Hans Haacke's projects concerning Mobil.
3 'The Good Will Umbrella', 1976. A series of six panels displaying a speech delivered to a conference of advertising agencies in New York, outlining the company's new strategy to ensure that company concerns are seen in a good light.
4 'Mobil: On the Right Track', silkscreen print and photo-collage, 1980. Showing four liberal senators, all of whom were defeated when Reagan was elected, it alludes to Mobil's financial support of Republican candidates.
5 'Creating Consent', oil drum with television antenna, 1981. A comment on oil companies' financial support of TV networks.
6 'MetroMobiltan', fibreglass construction, three banners and photo-mural, 1985.

6

4

5

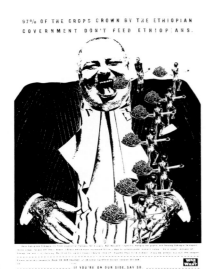

NORD-SÜD KONFERENZ

1

2

97% OF THE CROPS GROWN BY THE ETHIOPIAN
GOVERNMENT DON'T FEED ETHIOPIANS.

NO WONDER THE SOUTH AFRICAN GOVERNMENT FEEL
THEIR ECONOMY WOULD COLLAPSE WITHOUT APARTHEID.

IF YOU'RE ON OUR SIDE, SAY SO.

IF YOU'RE ON OUR SIDE, SAY SO.

3

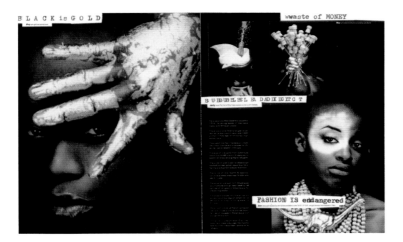

4

1 'North/South
Conference', postcard
by Klaus Staeck, West
Germany, 1979.
2 Klaus Staeck photo-
image put to use by a
human rights/protest
group making sarcastic
criticism of the World
Bank, Germany 1980s.
3 Two ads from a
controversial series
shown in the British
national press, created
by agency Boase
Massimi Pollitt for
charity War on Want,
Britain 1986-7.
4 Political fashion/style
essay commenting on
world power games and
imbalances of wealth,
by fashion stylist Judy
Blame for *i-D* magazine,
Britain 1991.

2 3

ACT UP and the graphics of AIDS activism

1

The powerful presence of AIDS activism since the late 1980s owes much to the efforts of ACT UP (AIDS Coalition to Unleash Power). ACT UP describes itself as 'a diverse, non-partisan group of individuals united in anger and committed to direct action to end the AIDS crisis'. Founded in New York City in 1987 as a result of US government inaction to the AIDS crisis throughout the 1980s, the coalition's anger encompasses a wide range of issues including government funding for research, the drug approval process, access to treatment and care, inaccuracies in reporting the AIDS crisis and the lack of safe sex education.

Within five years ACT UP had become a large network of independent city chapters with an international reach. With approximately 180 chapters spread through two dozen countries, it is now a global grassroots movement determined to combat a global epidemic, and committed to making an impact on national governments and the way they approach AIDS issues.

The genre of AIDS activist graphics was created by ACT UP, as visual propaganda and design strategies have been central to their operation as an organized movement. ACT UP's strong graphic identity has helped the network to 'connect' nationally and globally, while graphics have played a major role in demonstrations in the form of slogans and signs that highlight issues and target government officials. ACT UP's emblem 'Silence = Death' operates with an authority

4

normally assigned to corporate graphics. The pink triangle is a symbol of historical oppression: it originally marked gay men in Nazi concentration camps, but was positioned with the pink triangle pointing down. The triangle's inversion by ACT UP is a sign of resistance against new forces of oppression and annihilation.

Another graphic strength lies in the organization's use of the visual techniques and hard-hitting language of advertising, sometimes to the point of actually manipulating existing advertising images. They consequently force the propaganda of commercial culture to strike back at itself, targeting government departments, public health care authorities, drug companies and other institutions. Such turnaround tactics have been perfected by art activist groups such as Gran Fury (who started out as ACT UP's visual propaganda team) and have come to characterize the new and uncompromising genre of AIDS activist graphics.

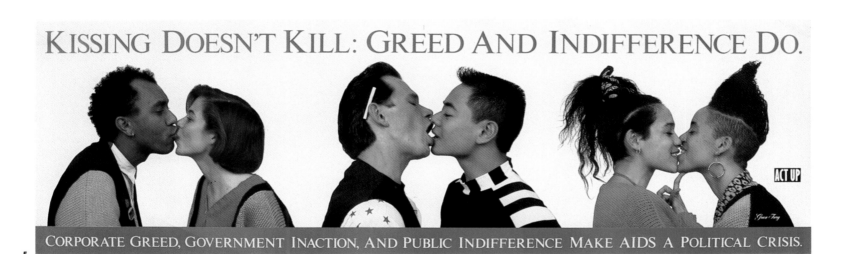

KISSING DOESN'T KILL: GREED AND INDIFFERENCE DO.

CORPORATE GREED, GOVERNMENT INACTION, AND PUBLIC INDIFFERENCE MAKE AIDS A POLITICAL CRISIS.

5

6

1 'Silence = Death' emblem and poster, the visual identity of ACT UP (the AIDS Coalition to Unleash Power). The original emblem was designed by the members of the Silence = Death Project in 1986, who then gave it to ACT UP on the organization's formation.
2 Poster from an international AIDS conference in Amsterdam, 1992.
3 Poster for ACT UP by Keith Haring, USA 1989.
4 ACT UP badges.
5 'Kissing Doesn't Kill', bus ad which ran in San Francisco and New York. By the AIDS activist art collective Gran Fury, USA 1989.
6 ACT UP t-shirts, with emblem variations by different chapters.

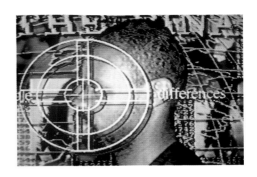

Combating racism and fascism in the New Europe

Worries related to the rise of racism and fascism have disrupted the once harmonious vision of the 'New Europe'. In Germany the overwhelming costs of reunification have given fuel to neo-Nazi extremists directing their anger at a heavy influx of refugee populations from Eastern Europe. Caught in the grip of global recession, the rest of Europe has also been experiencing a renewed strengthening of hard-right political groupings.

There has been a strong popular reaction against these developments, employing extremely varied graphic formats as highlighted by the examples shown here. In Germany, anti-fascist groups have offered continued resistance, producing a mass of information and printed material to announce meetings, accompany demonstrations and keep a strong voice of resistance alive. Artists have grappled with anti-racist themes: British artist Keith Piper's computerized photomontage/video piece *Surveillances* warns against the possible use of computer technologies and multi-media for the control and surveillance of aliens and non-Europeans, or any 'undesirables', within the structures and institutions of the New Europe.

Youth style magazines such as Britain's *The Face* and *i-D* have produced special editions on anti-racism and activism, pooling the artistic resources of an international collection of rock stars, artists, stylists, photographers and fashion designers. An English-speaking fax magazine called *Germany Alert*, published in Amsterdam and

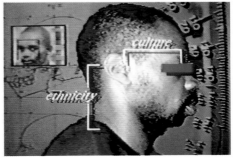

New York, was set up by a young German-born rapper to fax reports on the mounting racism and anti-Semitism in Germany to news media and other readers throughout the world. Football supporters' clubs in countries across Europe, meanwhile, have combined anti-fascist politics with a love for football. They produce 'fanzines', banners and stickers with the aim of combating racial abuse and a neo-Nazi presence at football games.

4

5

1, 2 & 4 Anti-fascist/anti-racist material produced by football supporters' clubs and groups in Europe, including the *Marching Altogether* fanzine for young people produced by Leeds Fans United Against Racism and Fascism (Britain), and stickers and banners produced by Millerntor Roar!, the St Pauli football supporters' club (Hamburg, Germany), 1991-2.
3 *Surveillances: Tagging the Other*, stills from Keith Piper's computer animation/video installation on the theme of control systems and Euro-racism, Britain 1992.
5 *Germany Alert*, an English-language anti-racist fax magazine, 1992.

Posters from a network of anti-racist and anti-fascist groups and organizations located throughout Germany. Some were produced, and the others collected, by Wolfgang Kreile, Germany 1992.

Chapter three

2 Students To Organize Peace Politically

STOPP

1 STRIKE because they murder students STRIKE against the war STRIKE to stop oppression STRIKE because the system lies STRIKE because they want you to be murderers STRIKE to give the people power STRIKE to make your country more human STRIKE before your life is over STRIKE

3 AMERIKA IS DEVOURING ITS CHILDREN

Shocks to the system
Alternative, anti-establishment and liberation movements

Many of our current popular movements have their roots in the groundbreaking activities of the anti-establishment and liberation movements of the 1960s and 1970s. Within a relatively short period of time (ten to fifteen years), youth challenged the old social order and its traditions and values; Feminism challenged the structures that determined women's expectations in life; the Civil Rights movement took the lid off racial tensions and set the streets ablaze; and gays and lesbians asserted their pride in a spirited call for their rights. The result was a changed world, both socially and culturally.

Extraordinary changes were in fact taking place internationally during this period: the Cultural Revolution in China, the independence movements of Africa and so on. But the graphic innovations that embodied this spirit of change to a great extent grew out of the social upheaval and youth revolutions of America. They spread to Britain, the rest of Europe, and beyond – and the graphic design industry has been under their influence ever since. However, the consciousness-raising and search for identity did not stop there. The youth movements and upheavals continue to this day, and views and protests are expressed in ever more inventive ways. This chapter is divided into two graphic 'eras':

the first comprises graphics produced by the upheavals and revolutions of the 1960s and early 1970s; the second includes both the graphic legacy of those revolutions and the new movements of the late 1970s, 1980s and 1990s.

The power struggles encompassed in this chapter relate to the fight for equality and recognition, which is essentially a fight against authority in the form of 'the establishment' or 'the system'. Some aspects of these struggles may be intensely personal, incorporating a search for individual identity, or for new aspirations and new values. But they are also about questioning the balance of power, and claiming it back for ordinary people. 'Power to the people' thus becomes an underlying theme throughout, regardless of the decade.

Whereas the chapters on National Politics and Global Issues invite a broader perspective – and sometimes grander formats for protest or concern – the revolutions of this chapter tend to be staged at street level. The struggles of the 1960s started the changes that would eventually grow into the 'personal politics' of the 1990s, and addressed themselves to essentially personal issues: sexuality, race, lifestyles, clothing and appearance, enjoyment and pleasure.

The Spirit of Che
lives in the new Evergreen!

Demand Evergreen *evergreen* at your newsdealer.

Signs of change and
student revolt in
America.
1 'Strike', poster by
the Student Strike
workshop at
Massachusetts College
of Art, 1970.
2 'Stopp', poster for
Students to Organize
Peace Politically, by
the Student Strike
Workshop at
Massachusetts College
of Art (artists: David
Majeau, Felice Regan),
1970.
3 'Amerika is Devouring
its Children' (inspired
by Francisco Goya's
Saturn), silkscreened
image on computer
printout paper
protesting against
the US invasion of
Cambodia. Artist
unknown, published
by the College of
Environment Design,
University of California
at Berkeley, 1970.
4 Advertisement for
the *Evergreen Review*
magazine, showing
the charismatic Che
Guevara, a hero-symbol
of revolution to many
American students;
illustrated by Paul
Davis, USA 1968.

4

1

2

Peace, love and revolution: a new visual language

The first signs of a youth revolution appeared on the West Coast of America in the mid-1960s. The younger generation 'dropped out', youth culture went 'underground' and developed a distinctive visual language by which young people could fight 'the system', or at least disassociate themselves from it. They created an identity of their own, for an important part of the rebellion against the establishment was rejection of its tastes and rigid codes for dress and appearance.

Thus the era of peace and love began in California and spread. Music was the great carrier; it transmitted the messages and generated the graphics that spoke for the new alternative culture. Music and drugs inspired psychedelic patterns, logos and colours that were painted onto everything from buildings to bodies. Long hair, jeans and a t-shirt became standard features, as distinct signs of lack of respect for the establishment suit-and-tie. A heady mix of decorative art movements and Far Eastern mysticism spread onto walls and textiles, and the work of artists such as Aubrey Beardsley and Alphonse Mucha became extremely popular, either reproduced in their existing form as popular prints and posters, or distorted to fulfill new decorative purposes.

Most importantly, the popular arts flourished. Posters, underground comics, cartoons in all forms, underground newspapers: all became part of the colourful visual display. Much of the typography was based on the decorated wood-type of old playbills or hand-drawn lettering, and many amateurs happily tried their hand at 'balloon lettering' and decorative borders.

The great masters of this period showed the art of the underground in its highest form: Victor Moscoso's psychedelic rock posters, for instance, or the work of Robert Crumb, Rick Griffin and others involved in underground comics. But the trend towards 'popular art' and personal image-making was equally important; it carried through all the succeeding revolutionary movements (Black Liberation, Women's Liberation, Gay Liberation) providing them with a common bond. Rough collages, crude drawings, cartoon comics and decorated lettering poured out of professionals and amateurs alike. Some of the products were bursting with liberated joy, others were bitter with anger, but all were powerful and full of vitality because of their bold lines, solid shapes and flat colours, often a product of having to print cheaply or by hand. The entire revolutionary period was documented and 'cartooned' through popular media, from the underground press to Women's Lib poster collectives and newsletters. The crude energy and immediacy of this popular art were in strong contrast to the photo-mechanical finesse to be found in corporate design and the Swiss and Germanic design influences of the same period.

The visual language of the revolution therefore popularized the struggles – and even personalized them. The graphic symbols of liberation became personalized icons; these included the female biological sign (for Feminism), black panthers (for Black Power) and raised fists (for everybody, and for all causes). They were all highly reproducible; they had no design blueprint, and thus appeared in varying renditions. These symbols were popular forms; they belonged to the masses, and were drawn and scribbled everywhere.

The new visual language also celebrated the new heroes and heroines: Che Guevara, Martin Luther King, Angela Davis and others. It was used to redress the imbalances in history; feminist presses researched 'herstory' and brought unsung heroines into view, as shown by the Helaine Victoria postcard press on this page.

The era of peace and love in itself was short-lived, quickly developing cracks from the strain of the many social tensions of the time. Thus an undercurrent of anger and violence also ran through the visual language of all the succeeding movements. The protest movement against the Vietnam War generated a wide range of angry posters, produced by professional studios as well as grassroots workshops. Violence surfaced most blatantly in the images surrounding campus unrest, and particularly racial tension. The Black Liberation and Black Power movements produced images that were full of suppressed tension and energy, ready to lash out at the first opportunity (hence the image of the panther, ready to spring). But very little graphic symbolism was in fact attached to the movement; its imagery dealt mainly with very real and powerful events: the protests in the street, the marches and the demonstrations. The posters of the time carried portraits of the movement's new leaders, and quotations from its main speakers were formed into inspirational slogans.

A more steady, slow and simmering anger was displayed in the clenched fists of Women's Liberation, a movement which used a great deal of graphic symbolism. Literary, artistic and historical references (for instance the legendary woman warrior) were often employed to create powerful images of struggle and fighting. There was also a heavy outpouring of images relating to freedom and release that used a variety of metaphors, such as the breaking of chains or the blossoming of flowers.

The visual language of the revolution was also out to shock: it challenged taboos on sex and nudity. Underground music and its graphics made heavy use of sexual references and nudity, as part of the sexual revolution and the attempt to break free from the repressive attitudes of the Establishment. Bodies were beautiful, sex was beautiful, and the imagery of the underground 'peace and love' era was full of both. Furthermore, the sexual exploitation of women in underground comics, magazines and other publishing vehicles became a contributing element to the anger that fuelled the Women's Liberation movement. Women went on to claim back their nudity, producing their own revolutionary publications such as Britain's *Spare Rib* magazine or America's *Our Bodies Ourselves*, the classic text of the women's health movement published in 1971 by the Boston Women's Health Book Collective. These publications employed body imagery for feminist learning purposes, such as encouraging women to regain control of their bodies and their health. All in all, bodies were very much a part of the revolution and its visual language throughout the 1960s and 1970s.

3

4

5

Rumblings against the Establishment, protest against the Vietnam War, and a host of liberation movements united a new generation.
1 'I Want Out', poster sponsored by the Committee to Help Unsell the War, a group comprising over 30 advertising agencies, USA 1971.
2 'Easy Rider' psychedelic image (a symbol of anti-Establishment attitude and dropping-out), poster by Theobald, USA early 1970s.
3 Postcards celebrating women's achievements from Helaine Victoria Press, established by Jocelyn Cohen in 1973 and still operating in the 1990s, USA.
4 'Women Working', poster sign by the Chicago Women's Graphics Collective, USA 1970-71.
5 Gay Liberation badge, Britain 1973-4.

The morality that guided the publishing of the sexual revolution was also brought into question many times along the way. Two obscenity battles are mentioned on pages 158-9: the fall of *Eros* magazine and the *Oz* trial in Britain. Both were well-known disputes and highly significant in graphic terms. But many similar disputes took place throughout that period – particularly with the underground comics – and it is important to remember that most of the imagery in this chapter caused consternation of one sort or another.

The legacy of the revolution was a far-reaching one, in visual terms. The revolution and its different liberation movements challenged sexual taboos, the use of gender and racial stereotypes – and broke through the all-white media construct, in recognition of the visual demands of a multi-ethnic society. There were new modes of expression and new media forms: underground comics, for example, reflected the spirit of the times and the interests of the drop-out community, while bringing some of America's existing social traumas and contradictions into sharp focus. They also created a new brand of cartoon art that had an international influence (the comics were pirated all over the world) and which gradually softened into subversive mainstream forms, as seen in the cartoon work of B. Kliban, or the film animation of Terry Gilliam and 'Monty Python's Flying Circus'.

The popularization of art, the search for new working structures and the concept of 'community art', generated by the liberation movements throughout the Sixties, brought about the creation of progressive publishing groups and poster collectives, some of which still exist today. However in the revolutions of the following two decades, the sentiments and ideas of the underground came crashing into the overground. The

nervous energy of urban culture and its newer manifestations was readily absorbed and harnessed by the commercial mainstream.

Urban culture: street style and attitude

The next era of 'revolution', in terms of graphics and the media, arose from the activities and counter-cultures of the city streets. Various forces were brewing throughout the 1970s which would bring tremendous change to mainstream design attitudes and tastes, and provide them with a much-needed recharge of energy.

The Punk movement in Britain began the new phase of change. It was similar to the Sixties revolt in America in a number of ways: young people revolted against the Establishment; music carried the message; drugs and sex were the main accompaniments, as well as social critique and shock. But there the similarities end, for as a movement Punk did not have its roots in the desire for ideological and political change; it did not have internationally agreed targets of protest; and in the end, it was not a social revolution with an international reach but more of a local dispute. Nevertheless, in terms of the visual arts, Punk's influence was phenomenal. It grew to be a highly creative cultural movement that encompassed art, music, graphics, fashion and photography, and spread to countries around the world. The designers and products involved in and around it broke existing conventions and continue to wield an influence on graphic design today.

Although not specifically a political movement in itself, Punk was affected by the art-politics of Situationism, a European avant-garde art movement which promoted participation in the creative aspects of city culture (with particular interest in subverting the established order)

1

2

3

4

5

THE ADVANTAGES OF BEING A WOMAN ARTIST:

Working without the pressure of success.
Not having to be in shows with men.
Having an escape from the art world in your 4 free-lance jobs.
Knowing your career might pick up after you're eighty.
Being reassured that whatever kind of art you make
     it will be labeled feminine.
Not being stuck in a tenured teaching position.
Seeing your ideas live on in the work of others.
Having the opportunity to choose between career and motherhood.
Not having to choke on those big cigars or paint in Italian suits.
Having more time to work after your mate dumps you
     for someone younger.
Being included in revised versions of art history.
Not having to undergo the embarrassment of being called a genius.
Getting your picture in the art magazines wearing a gorilla suit.

Guerrilla Girls CONSCIENCE OF THE ART WORLD

In the 1980s, the emphasis was on street art and urban creativity.
1 'Ice', by Chicago graffiti artist Mario Gonzalez Jr, USA 1991.
2 Invitation to an underground hip hop party, graffiti art by Rafa, USA 1992.
3 'Charm' (10ft x 25ft) by Mario Gonzalez Jr, USA 1989.
4 'Causes of Revolution', series of 12 posters by Jennie Kiessling pasted up in a Chicago Street, USA 1989. The series reads: 'People start an uprising when they are hungry and have nothing left to lose. As long as governments don't function so that people live in dignity there will be revolution.'
5 Poster and postcard by the feminist art activist group Guerrilla Girls, USA c.1990.

while drawing upon the graphic vocabulary of comics, advertising and other modern materials. In Punk terms, this subversion meant playing in bands, not going to work in boring jobs, and publishing street papers or 'fanzines'. The philosophy was transferred to Punk by Malcolm McLaren (manager of the Sex Pistols) and Jamie Reid; both had been involved with the Situationists and were later central figures in the Punk movement in Britain. Jamie Reid in particular, as art director of the Sex Pistols group and creator of all their graphic requirements, created the anarchic visual language associated with Punk. This was characterized by the use of 'ransom' lettering, labelling and other recycled elements; bright brash colours (indicative of supermarket packaging); crude photo-reproduction; aggressive cut-out or torn shapes; and perhaps most importantly, a chaotic and spontaneous layout.

The effect of this anarchic vision on the graphics world at that time was explosive. Graphic design shed its tired image as an élitist corporate tool, and once again became a populist means of personal expression. Punk's do-it-yourself graphics, 'fanzines' and music publicity opened up a new realm of possibilities for self-publishing and street magazines. Not surprisingly this emphasis on urban creativity led

to the 1980s preoccupation with lifestyles, street style and youth-related formats: most notably, British style magazines such as *The Face* and *i-D*. The 1980s were owned and operated by the youth generation: young people had financial power; young designers were at the top of the profession; young people were promoting environmental issues; and young people were redefining 'politics' in their own terms.

It was within this scenario that Band Aid and Live Aid were staged in the mid-1980s, and it's not surprising that their vehicles were youth formats: a record single and a global rock concert. The combination of youth politics and rock/pop music countered 'the establishment' by overriding the inaction of bureaucrats and politicians, and generated unprecedented amounts of famine relief for Africa. In the charitable 'one world' atmosphere that followed, social and political issues found their way onto a much broader range of public formats. Charity and humanitarian aid, animal rights, ecology matters, anti-drug campaigns and other issues were thrown at a receptive public by means of billboards and advertising campaigns, street fashions, street posters and magazines – creating a mood of social awareness that would carry through to the 1990s.

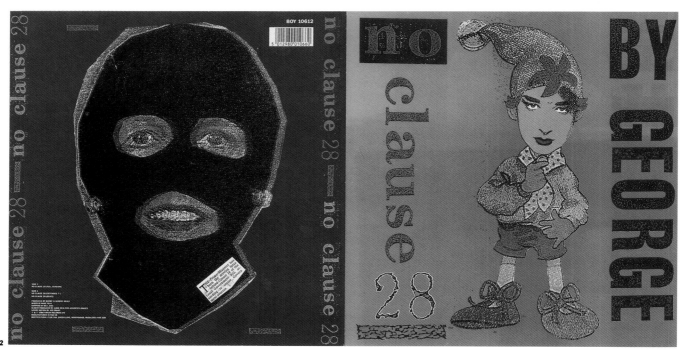

Another form of urban expression that evolved throughout the 1970s was graffiti art. Although graffiti in New York City harked back to street gangs marking out territory in the 1960s, it found a more expressive role in the graffiti writing of the early 1970s when teenagers began to 'tag' subway trains and buildings with their name (usually a pseudonym) and street numbers. This led to tags (stylized signatures) being treated as elaborate logos, and the development of spray painting on a larger scale; by the mid-1970s whole subway cars were being covered. With the development of 'wildstyle' lettering, 3-D effects and added cartoon characters, graffiti scrawls grew into highly sophisticated spray can art – a genre with its own codes, vocabulary, aesthetics, traditions and folk heroes. As a result of the hip hop explosion of the early 1980s, the graffiti/spray can art movement spread beyond New York and also began to impinge on the art gallery scene. In the 1990s a legitimate graffiti-based street art has evolved; what used to be illegal on subway cars as vandalism is now commissioned in some cities as 'street murals' for commercial walls.

It has also found an important role in US inner-city community life. Graffiti art and street murals are used to carry social messages and warnings in a language that is meaningful to the young inhabitants of the local community; hence graffiti art is seen as a creative alternative to gang involvement. Community programmes also exist which aim to introduce graffiti artists into conventional art or graphic design education. While the trend towards acceptance of graffiti art as a valid art form for galleries has been slow, its substantial influence on the field of graphic design has been readily acknowledged over many years.

Another cultural force came into sharp focus in the late 1970s: rap, the black American popular music that grew out of the hip hop subculture based in New York's Harlem and the Bronx. Rap hit the charts in 1979 and spread internationally, accompanied by other forms of urban expression such as break-dancing, disc jockeying, and graffiti art – all forms that achieved high levels of creativity from very limited resources. A mixture of poetry, music, style, fashion and attitude, rap was a cultural force that became a consciousness-raising vehicle and a political tool for the black community.

As the 1980s moved on, black identity and culture were explored (and celebrated) through an ever-growing variety of visual arts and graphic applications. These included the films of Spike Lee and their associated products; rap records, magazines, videos and accompanying graphics; pirate radio stations; and hip hop fashion. These vehicles also encouraged renewed interest in Black Nationalism, the heroes of the Sixties and Afrocentrism, an exploration of the historical contribution of African cultures and civilizations to the development of the world.

Other popular movements which fought for liberation in the 1960s found expression throughout the 1980s in both commercial and street graphics. Feminism carried on to achieve great commercial success in the 1980s through publishing houses such as Virago and the Women's Press in London. (The Women's Press was particularly known for its strong visual identity.) Equal graphic strength was shown at street level, through the poster campaigns produced by the Guerrilla Girls attacking discrimination in the New York art gallery world, the banners and photographs of the peace protests of Greenham Common, and other inspired projects.

Feminism rallied to meet one of its greatest conflicts in the American Pro-Life and Pro-Choice disputes of the late 1980s and early 1990s. In a battle that still rages, each side has employed highly contrasting graphic strategies. The Pro-Life movement has operated large, highly-organized visual propaganda campaigns that spread the movement's doctrine through a variety of 'selling' techniques – ranging from a 'clinical' approach incorporating statistics and medical research, to the hard-sell tactics of slapping slogans on everything from bracelets to balloons. The Pro-Choice movement, on the other hand, has been less of a propaganda machine; their strategy has been to argue through isolated projects of personal conviction. It has generated works ranging from the bold strength of Barbara Kruger's 'Your body is a battleground' to Ilona Granet's humourous 'State Womb': an image which mocks government possession or control of a woman's womb (page 173).

The lesbian and gay communities also moved from ground-breaking liberation to assertive pride in the 1980s. Having had to fight for so long for recognition of their sexuality, the 1980s became the decade when visual imagery in support of gay and lesbian lifestyles really began to flower. It was also the decade that brought us the AIDS crisis. Acutely aware of the vulnerability of its members, the gay community took the lead in AIDS activism, constantly pushing it from the marginalized sidelines into the very centre of political debate.

The surge in the popular arts during the 1960s, and the rise of urban creativity and its graphic forms in the late 1970s and 1980s, were extremely important developmental stages in the growing use of graphics for personal expression and the visual communication of 'attitude' by people in the street. Now anti-establishment attitudes and popular movements are widely expressed through visual culture. Graphics have merged with style, fashion, music, film and other creative arts to produce a vibrant show of the power of the people. After three decades of consciousness-raising and awareness activities, the 1990s has become the era of 'personal politics', and design and style are viewed as ways of expressing identity and awareness.

3

4

Debates about sexuality continue into the 1980s and 1990s.
1 T-shirt produced by the Golden Gate chapter of the AIDS activist group ACT UP, USA 1992.
2 'No Clause 28' record sleeve for pop singer Boy George, designed by Jamie Reid and Joe Ewart, 1988 – one of many protests against Clause 28, the British bill forbidding the 'promotion' of homosexuality.
3 Pro-Life bumperstickers, USA 1992 (Presidential election year).
4 Poster for the 1989 Pro-Choice March on Washington, by Barbara Kruger. The image was also used to promote women's rights issues in other countries: shown here are a subway poster from Berlin and a street poster from Warsaw (both 1991).

1

The underground: peace and love

In the early 1960s a new young generation
rebelled against the values and goals of 'the
establishment'. Youth culture went
'underground', devising its own vision of an
alternative society and finding cultural
expression through music, sex and drugs.
California became the epicentre of this youth
revolution, and the birthplace of many of the
new art and media forms.

The visual styles that emerged
encapsulated the energy and free-wheeling
spirit of the time. The most dominant visual
style was 'psychedelia', which dazzled the
eyes by twisting lurid day-glo colours into
complex patterns reminiscent of drug
experiences. Comics, cartoons and 'pop art',
the paintings and icons of Far Eastern
mysticism, decorative embellishments from
art nouveau and art deco, and the fat, chunky
alphabets of old circus and theatre playbills all
came into play. This decorative mixture
exploded onto clothes, textiles, posters,
badges and other products.

The psychedelic posters that advertised
rock events rate among the best work of this
period (particularly 1965-8), and their bright
colours and decorated lettering were soon
drawn into the mainstream. The best known
exponents of the genre included Victor
Moscoso (who studied with Josef Albers at
Yale and was responsible for the most vibrant

2

colour contrasts), Wes Wilson, Stanley Mouse, Alton Kelly and Rick Griffin, most of whom were also involved in another important vehicle of the time: underground comics.

A distinct revolt against the American way of life, underground comics flaunted sexuality, drugs, fantasies and street culture all in one package. The late 1960s to mid-1970s was their golden period and there were countless titles. (Robert Crumb's *Zap Comix*, begun in 1967, was probably the most famous series.) Stories and characters revolved around a hippie-style existence of sex and dope; and outrageousness was the main facet of their appeal. Robert Crumb, the most popular of the cartoonists, was responsible for the adventures of such bizarre characters as 'Mr Natural', and his images popularized the well-worn phrase 'Keep On Truckin' which became the hallmark of the West Coast attitude.

4

3

1 One of many 'Keep on Truckin'…' motifs by Robert Crumb.
2 Illustrated cover by Rick Griffin for *Zap Comix No. 3*, 1968-9.
3 Robert Crumb's 'Street Corner Daze', inside spread from *Zap Comix No. 3*, 1968-9.
4 Psychedelic rock poster *(Family Dog No. 81)* by Victor Moscoso, 1967. Family Dog was a producer of rock concerts and dances.

2

The underground press

1

Alternative culture developed its own communication lines, and accessories for daily living. The emerging underground movement needed a medium for expressing itself, and exchanging ideas within (or beyond) the community. Helped greatly by the advent of cheap offset litho printing, the underground press scene soon flourished and included such titles as the *Berkeley Barb*, *LA Free Press*, *San Francisco Oracle* and many other newspapers and magazines produced throughout America.

The underground press movement quickly developed into an international communications network. The prolific American papers made their way overseas, taking protest imagery, cartoons and cries for liberation with them. Europe supplied its own counter culture and magazines (such as *Provo* in Holland or *Ink*, *International Times* and *Oz* in Britain) which carried news of the Paris riots, the *Oz* trial and other events. Ideas spread rapidly; people travelled from country to country, and dropped into news offices or helped out in poster collectives as they were passing through. International connections were an important aspect of alternative culture throughout the 1960s and 1970s, and one of the outstanding characteristics of that period was that the smallest poster group – or the most obscure newspaper – could have an international reach.

3

1 Hippie hand-sign for 'peace', sew-on embroidered patch, *c.*1970.
2 Fake money from the 'Dick Gregory for President' campaign (reputed to operate change machines), 1968.
3 Cigarette rolling papers, more likely to be used for rolling a marijuana joint, 1970.

4 Street poster from the campaign promoting Dick Gregory as the underground's candidate for President in the 1968 election.
5 Front page of the underground newspaper *Berkeley Barb*, 1968.
6 Front page of the underground newspaper *Los Angeles Free Press*, with an illustration by Ron Cobb, 1968.

5

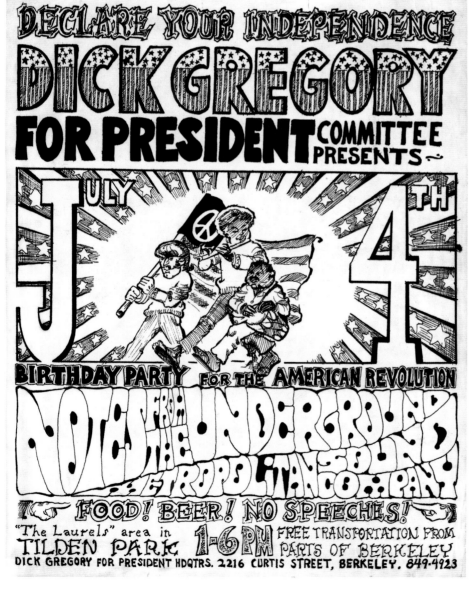

4

6

Icons from the era of peace and love

1

The era of peace and love was characterized
by a creative energy that gave rise to many
innovations; three icons of that visual
revolution are discussed here.

Push Pin Studios brought the best of West
Coast psychedelia into East Coast
mainstream graphic design. Founded in 1954
by Milton Glaser, Seymour Chwast and Edward
Sorel, their use of florid, decorative illustration
and a colourful mixture of influences (both
past and present) created a bright, punchy
and identifiable new genre of graphic design
that became highly popular during the 1960s.
Among their most influential graphic works
were Glaser's *Dylan* and *Mahalia Jackson* and
Chwast's anti-Vietnam posters.

How to Keep Your Volkswagen Alive was
a car repair manual for maintaining the
Volkswagen Beetle (the adopted car of
the hippie community), and a landmark in
information design. Written by the late John
Muir, it pioneered a friendly approach to
technology, as well as communicating
technical matters in layperson's terms. It
assumed no prior expertise, and no special
tools were required; these were replaced by
homespun methods using commonplace
equipment. The humourous, easy-to-follow
diagrams matched the laid-back,
conversational tone of the text, which
advocated communicating with the car,
respecting its karma, and carrying out all work
with a sense of Love. First published in 1969,
How to Keep Your Volkswagen Alive has
achieved cult status over the years.

2

John Lennon and Yoko Ono were the first real international rock couple, and dared to push their 'Power to the People' politics into the public view (often in a graphic format). Both were successful artists in their own right, but as a couple they broke barriers that rattled the conservative establishment to the core – particularly in America. They broke the nudity barrier, with their full-frontal nudity on the 'Two Virgins' album cover; they broke the racial barrier, as a mixed-race couple; they broke the age barrier, for when they met in 1966 Lennon was 26 and Ono was 33; and they broke the politics barrier, as rock artists showing a heavy political platform and an anti-Vietnam stance. Their anti-Vietnam protests were world famous, such as the 'love-in' staged in Amsterdam in 1969 when they had themselves photographed in bed as a protest for peace.

3 Cover and inside spreads from *How to Keep Your Volkswagen Alive* by John Muir, with illustrations by Peter Aschwanden; first published in 1969, the 1989 edition is shown here.

4 Many of the original drawings were retained but updated and refined: this illustration from the 1971 version hints at the original's rough charm.

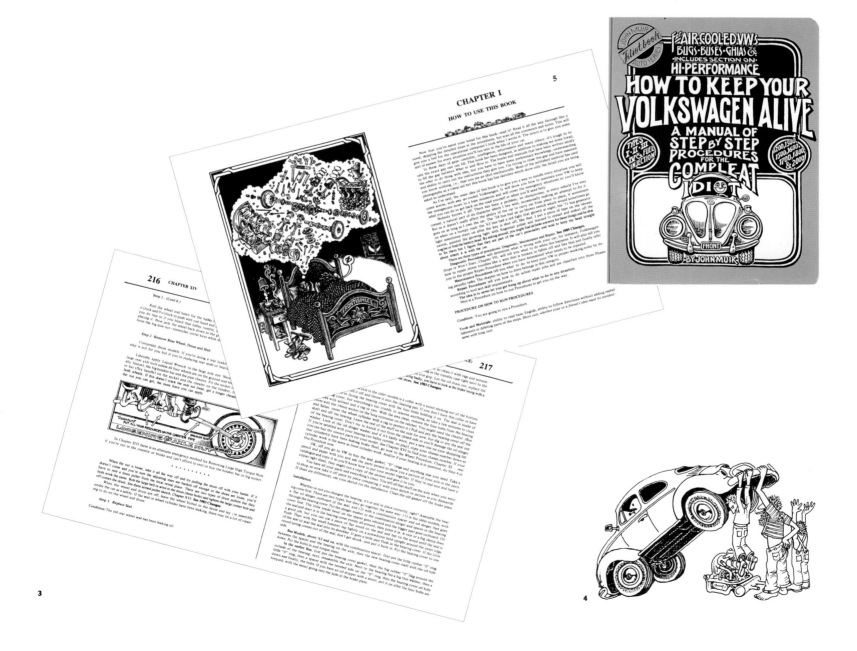

1 'Black Power, White
Power', poster comment
on US race relations by
Tomi Ungerer, 1967.
2 & 3 Images travelled
across the ocean: cover
and inside spread from
British underground
magazine *International
Times* (No. 133). The
cover shows a well-
known photograph of
a US student
demonstration at
Columbia University
in 1968.
4 'Two More in
Mississippi', from a
silkscreened poster
by the Student Strike
Workshop at
Massachusetts College
of Art showing solidarity
with the Black Power
movement, USA 1970.

1

Society in upheaval: images of tension

As the 1960s rolled on, the psychedelic mood of 'flower power' and the era of peace and love gave way to emerging social tensions.

J. F. Kennedy was assassinated in 1963. Civil rights marches grew increasingly strong; in 1965 tensions erupted with racial riots in the Watts area of Los Angeles. President Johnson took American troops into the Vietnam War in 1965 and anti-war protests and demonstrations increased in number and force. Student unrest and campus riots hit their peak during 1969-70 with the American invasion of Cambodia; violence, bloodshed and cries of police brutality grew to be common occurrences. In 1970 there was intense public outcry when four students were killed by National Guardsmen at a demonstration at Kent State University.

Social comment poured from a variety of sources: professional artists, designers and studios rallied; and countless art collectives and student workshops flourished during this period. One of the most famous was the Student Strike Workshop at Massachusetts College of Art founded in 1970 during a one-month anti-Vietnam strike staged by staff and students (the workshop still operates today as the Graphic Workshop in Boston). Many of these groups protested against the war or created public murals, protest projects, or art/publishing facilities for Women's Liberation, Black Liberation, Gay Rights and a broad span of other equality issues – and their imagery was gradually transported to Europe via the underground network.

3

Civil Rights, Black Liberation, Black Power

1 Photograph by Matt Herron, taken on the Selma-to-Montgomery march for voting rights, Alabama 1965. Many marchers put zinc oxide on their faces to prevent sunburn during the 54-mile march in the hot sun; this one wrote a message of conviction on his forehead.
2 Dr Martin Luther King memorial poster, produced by the Southern Christian Leadership Conference, USA 1968.
3 The mark of the Black Panther Party for Self-Defense, founded in 1966 in the wake of the Watts riots in LA.
4 'Free Bobby' (Bobby Seale, co-founder of the Black Panther Party), poster by the Student Strike Workshop at Massachusetts College of Art (artist: James DiSilvestro), USA 1970.
5 Poster carrying the liberation slogan 'Black is Beautiful', USA c.1968.
6 'I am a Black Woman', poster in support of the imprisoned Black Panther activist Angela Davis, designed and produced by Richard McCrary, USA 1971.

1

In the mid-1950s the Civil Rights movement gained a leader in the Reverend Martin Luther King, and began the long, slow struggle for equality. There were to be many traumas and conflicts over the next two decades. Riots occurred over the enrolment of the first black student, James Meredith, at the University of Mississippi in 1962. Weeks of city rioting and protest in 1963 climaxed in a peaceful demonstration in Washington DC, where Martin Luther King delivered his 'I have a dream' speech, presenting his inspired vision of dignity and equality for black Americans.

King himself led the march in 1965 from Selma to Montgomery, Alabama, to call for voting rights; and the summer brought the race riots in the Watts district of Los Angeles in which 34 people were killed. In that same year the revolutionary leader Malcolm X was shot and killed in New York, and in 1968 Martin Luther King was assassinated in Memphis, Tennessee. The movement reached boiling point, and there it remained into the 1970s. With the added thrust of Black Consciousness emanating from Africa, the Black Liberation movement was born.

The graphics associated with these developments mourned the leaders that the movement lost along the way, but brought solidarity and exposure to activists and groups such as the Black Panthers (a Black Power group formed by Bobby Seale and Huey Newton in 1966), and reinforced the assertiveness of Black Pride while popularizing slogans such as 'Black is Beautiful'.

4

5

6

Women's Liberation: sweet freedom and celebration

The call for women's equality and rights surged through the decade with all the other protests – and in the mid- to late 1960s, a mass movement was born. Women's Liberation called upon all women as a group to challenge the existing politics of male/female power relations.

Over the decade of the 1970s, the movement brought about many changes in the way women were viewed by society, and themselves. The revolution came through consciousness-raising groups, protests and many other vehicles. 'Women's issues' included women regaining control over their bodies and health; making choices over pregnancy and childbirth; gaining equal opportunities and equal pay at work; and combating violence against women. The movement was also characterized by international networking. Women's groups and feminist presses existed all over the world, and rallied around International Women's Day on 8 March.

Through feminist publishing a new focus was placed on women's creative work and writing, and attempts were made to start addressing the imbalance in reporting and assessing women's achievements throughout history. The movement benefited from a strong graphic symbol and from the protest graphics of poster collectives, college presses and women's groups; the most important of the time included the Chicago Women's Graphics Collective in America and the See Red Poster Collective in Britain.

In America Sheila de Bretteville pioneered a relationship between design and Feminism. She initiated the Women's Design Program at the California Institute of the Arts in Los Angeles in 1971, the first course of its kind. In 1973 she co-founded and directed the Woman's Building, a public centre for women's culture in Los Angeles, and within it the Women's Graphic Center which offered teaching and print facilities to women and women's groups. Both the Building and the Graphic Center became internationally known, and still exist today.

1 'Sisterhood is Blooming', poster by the Chicago Women's Graphics Collective, USA *c*.1970.
2 Poster for the conference 'Women in Design: the next decade' by Sheila Levrant de Bretteville, USA 1975.
3 Front cover of the graphic design magazine *Print*, USA 1970.
4 & 5 Posters from 'See Red' women's poster collective, Britain *c*.1974. Shown are 'Bite the Hand That Feeds You' (i.e. the bureaucracy) and 'My Wife Doesn't Work'.
6, 7 & 8 Images from early days in the movement showing variations on the Women's Liberation symbol.

The demand for women's liberation produced imagery that often underlined the violence of the struggle, or employed symbolism to powerful effect.
1 Badge, mid 1970s.
2 Front cover of Germaine Greer's influential book *The Female Eunuch*, published in Great Britain in 1970.
3 'Great Mother Sphinx', highly controversial poster by artist and writer Monica Sjöö, Britain 1969.
4 'In Celebration of Amazons', poster using the popular image of the female warrior, by the Chicago Women's Graphics Collective, USA 1974.

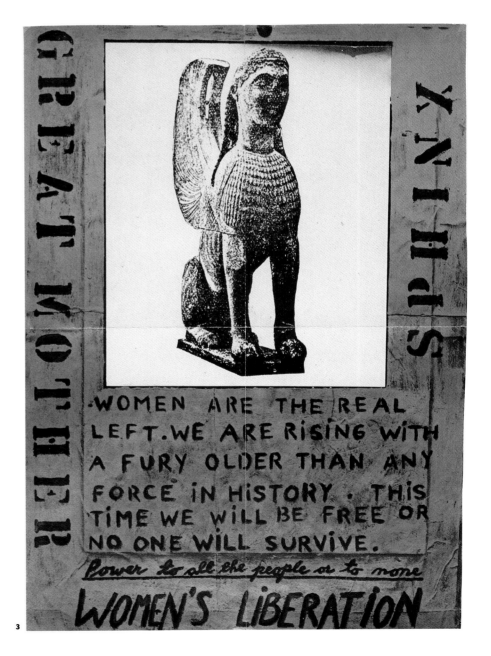

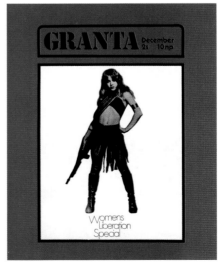

5 'Women Against Rape Unite!'. Poster announcing meetings of the Women Against Rape collective, France 1970s.
6 Poster, artist unknown, 1970s.
7 Front and back cover of a special issue of the Cambridge University students' literary magazine *Granta*, humorously depicting the feminist transformation from dolly-bird to revolutionary, Britain *c.*1971.

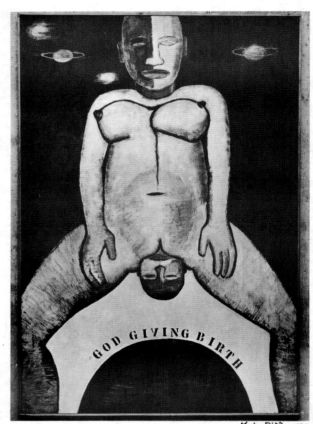

Britain: challenging taboos of sex and class

The Sixties mood of change in Europe brought the breakdown of the old social order, expressed in full force in the renowned Paris street riots of May 1968 (page 54). Britain however had been experiencing a slow erosion since the start of the decade, or even before.

The introduction of the Pill, the lifting of the publication ban on D.H. Lawrence's *Lady Chatterley's Lover*, the satire boom and the Profumo affair were just a few of the disturbances in the early 1960s that caused cracks to appear in the structures of the 'old guard'. By the middle of the decade 'Swinging London' was underway: a period of youth, energy and affluence marked by new forms of

3

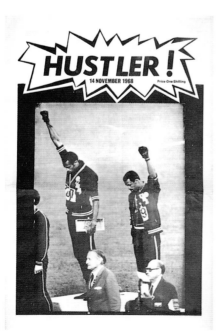

1

2

expression. The Beatles, Carnaby Street and innovations in fashion, film and photography brought worldwide attention, and within a few years 'the underground' was in operation. The psychedelic art forms of the American West Coast arrived and left their mark, and relaxed attitudes towards sex and morality permeated the imagery of this period.

America's tensions and revolutions also spread to Britain, transferred through both mainstream media and the underground press. By the early 1970s, Women's Liberation and other movements had caught on. But the buzz of optimism and hope, and the visions of a freer society crashed to the ground as the world moved into economic recession. Britain's radical spirit placed its strength behind the new libertarian movements and the urgent issues of home politics, and produced a whole generation of radical poster collectives, printshops and community art groups.

1 Front cover of British newspaper *Hustler*, showing the medal awards ceremony at the 1968 Olympics in Mexico, when two American athletes gave the Black Power salute.
2 Front cover of *Oz*, Britain's most famous underground magazine.
3 Poster reproduction of Monica Sjöö's painting *God Giving Birth*, Britain, 1968. The image came under threat for 'obscenity and blasphemy' and became an important feminist icon.
4 Front and back cover of *Bloody Women*, a publication by Scarlet Women (a women's liberation group in or around Cambridge University), Britain c.1971.

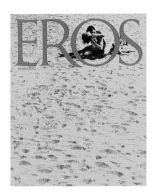

The obscenity battles of Eros and Oz

The sexual revolution that occurred in the 1960s and 1970s had its casualties. Many cries of obscenity erupted against the new art and media forms; two battles are mentioned here for their particular relevance to the graphics world.

Eros magazine, an expensively produced hardcover quarterly journal, was launched in the USA in 1962. Edited and published by Ralph Ginzburg, it was intended to be an intelligent publication on sex, love and romance, available by post on subscription. Illustration sources ranged from Salvador Dali to Albrecht Dürer; literature from *Mother Goose* to the Bible. It also benefited from the brilliance of the renowned graphic designer and lettering artist Herb Lubalin, whose expertise ensured that the magazine received many art direction awards at the time and has been hailed as one of the classics of Sixties publication design ever since. (Ginzburg and Lubalin also collaborated on *Fact* and *Avant Garde* magazines.)

More a lavish art journal than a 'dirty magazine', *Eros* had only produced four issues when Ginzburg was indicted for using the mail to distribute obscene materials. An appeal to the Supreme Court brought a conviction in 1966 and after five more years of appealing, Ginzburg was finally convicted of 'commercial exploitation', 'titillation' and 'pandering'. In 1972, after a ten-year fight, Ginzburg finally went to jail and served 18 months. The sexual revolution had lost a major battle, as well as an extraordinary publication.

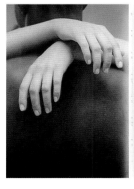

1

The rise and fall of *Oz* was a very different matter. Launched in 1967, *Oz* was Britain's most renowned underground magazine. It was rude and offensive (to the Establishment) and used sex as a revolutionary tool: to shock. Its content was a mixture of radical discussion of ecology and the new liberation movements, and underground interests such as drugs, music and mysticism. But its greatest asset was its anarchic appearance, the product of designers such as Martin Sharp and Jon Goodchild and their experimentation with the newly-developed offset litho printing process. The result was 'mind-blowing': whole pages of psychedelic splendour, with coloured text laid onto lurid backgrounds (at times completely unreadable).

The magazine reached its peak when in 1971 the 'School Kids' issue (produced by a guest editorial team of adolescents) was seized by police. The three *Oz* editors – Richard Neville, Jim Anderson and Felix Dennis – were charged with 'conspiracy to corrupt public morals'. There followed a six-week obscenity trial – the longest in British legal history – which turned into a battle between the Establishment and the 'permissive society'. There was public outcry and protest, and press and TV coverage from around the world. The three editors were cleared of conspiracy but *Oz* was condemned as obscene. The editors were sentenced, but were later acquitted upon appeal. The final issue was produced in 1973, and the magazine has remained an enduring symbol of social revolution.

1 Covers and spreads from *Eros* magazine, summer, autumn and winter 1962, including a portfolio of Bert Stern's studio photographs of Marilyn Monroe taken shortly before her death, and 'Black & White in Color', a photographic essay by Ralph M. Hattersley Jr.
2 Page from *Oz* relating to the results of the magazine's obscenity trial in 1971.
3 The 'School Kids' issue of *Oz* magazine that provoked the obscenity trial.
4 Inside spread from *Oz*, showing the magazine's renowned psychedelic printing effects.
5 Cover of *Oz* by Martin Sharp, Britain 1967.

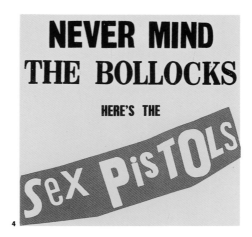

4

Punk graphics and street style

1

The British Punk movement of the mid-1970s was a distinct move away from the affluence and slick professionalism of the 1960s, and back to the energy of the streets. It borrowed its sense of subversion and politics from the French art/politics movement known as Situationism – particularly the notions of subverting the status quo by having fun, and developing the creative aspects of city culture. In Punk terms, this meant playing in or listening to aggressive bands in small, sweaty clubs (bands such as the Sex Pistols, the Buzzcocks, the Clash and Siouxsie and the Banshees); putting together small papers or magazines ('fanzines') and selling them in the streets; and having a good time while creating

a subversive counter-culture in the midst of a severe British economic depression.

With unemployment, gloom and disillusionment in the air, anarchy was seen to be creative. Style and fashion became an important means of self-expression (the more exhibitionistic, the better), and was led by fashion innovator and creator of bondage-wear Vivienne Westwood. Punk was maintained by the 'enterprise' and energy of 'kids' and the rejection of all that was boring and paternalistic. It was a highly visual movement that challenged the popular image of fashion and culture, and its subversive attitudes had a dramatic effect on art, music, graphics, fashion and photography.

Jamie Reid designed all of the graphic requirements (such as posters, album sleeves and t-shirts) for the first and most notorious Punk group, the Sex Pistols. In the process, he gave Punk its identifiable and aggressive graphic vocabulary: mixed typefaces and cut-out letters (ransom lettering), bright soapbox colours, crude photo-reproduction, cut-out or torn shapes, and spontaneous layout. This anarchic and irreverent design sense had an enormous impact on the restrained attitudes of mainstream design. It introduced a looser, freer vision; less restrictive ways of working; and new interest in self-publishing and street magazines. The graphic design world is still operating under its revolutionary influence.

2

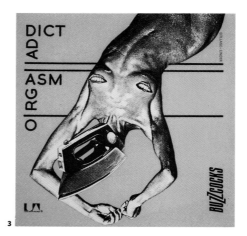

3

5

1 Page from Terry Jones' *Not Another Punk Book*, 1978, showing Vivienne Westwood wearing her 'Destroy' t-shirt. Westwood's designs for Seditionaries, the Punk clothes shop she ran with Malcolm McLaren, created a new style direction that saw clothing as a kind of subversion.

2 Stickers combining design and politics by Jamie Reid, created for his subversive community magazine *Suburban Press* based in Croydon, Britain 1973.

3 'Orgasm Addict', record single cover for the Buzzcocks. Design by Malcolm Garrett using a montage by Linder, Britain 1977.

4 Front cover of the 'Never Mind the Bollocks' album, designed by Jamie Reid and banned from many record shops following public complaints, Britain 1977.

5 Artwork for the record sleeve of the Sex Pistols' single 'God Save the Queen', designed by Jamie Reid, Britain 1977.

1

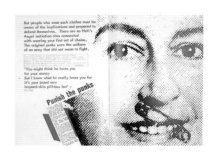

2

From Punk fanzines to style magazines

Punk had many modes of expression. One of the most important was the production of fanzines – products of the creative energy and 'enterprise' so crucial to the Punk movement. The flood of Punk fanzines, appearing in their hundreds from 1976 onwards, opened up a whole new genre of street publications and self-publishing projects. Anyone with a photocopy machine and a few bits of sticky tape could 'publish'. Fanzines were produced on many subjects – from 'gigs' to pubs – and were produced in cities and towns throughout Britain, as well as the rest of the world. (British Punk was by no means restricted to London; there was very heavy Punk activity in other cities such as Manchester.)

The emphasis on urban creativity and do-it-yourself publishing led to the 1980s preoccupation with street style. Terry Jones transferred Punk street style and anarchic graphics into the commercial avant-garde with his landmark publication *Not Another Punk Book* (London 1978). He soon followed it in 1980 with the launch of his magazine *i-D*, a catalogue of street style which hyped ordinary clothes and people in the street as fashion, and also employed 'instant design' methods and arbitrary, cluttered post-Punk layout. *The Face* magazine was also launched in 1980 and achieved fame through the radical art direction of Neville Brody. Both *i-D* and *The Face* became the most influential style magazines of the youth-orientated 1980s; and later in the 1990s expanded into art and design activism and youth politics.

3

1 Punk fanzines and street publishing, including Mark Pawson's 'Aggressive School of Cultural Workers' sticker, Pete Polanyk's *Ded Yampy* ('really crazy'), a fanzine on Coventry pub culture, and others from the late 1970s and early 1980s.
2 Punk as street fashion: cover and spreads from Terry Jones' *Not Another Punk Book*, 1978.
3 Covers of influential style magazines *i-D*, art directed by Terry Jones, and *The Face*, art directed (1981-6) by Neville Brody.

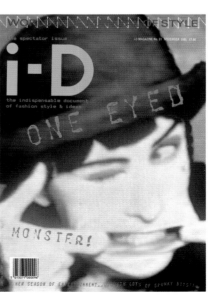

The culture of Black Awareness

1

The most powerful expression of urban culture to surface in the 1980s was rap music, a product of the hip hop subculture based in New York City. Rap and associated 'street arts' such as break-dancing, disc jockeying and graffiti art all formed part of the hip hop cultural explosion of the early 1980s that spread through countries from America to Japan. As the decade progressed, rap became a far-reaching vehicle for Black Awareness, and rap groups, such as the militant Public Enemy, voiced the turmoil and temperature of young African-Americans while also influencing the young black community around the world.

The music generated graphics in the form of distinctive record labels, typography and logos, and hip hop fashion became a highly commercialized uniform of baseball caps, jackets, hooded tops, track suits and particularly trainers, often endorsed by black rap or sports stars. As the 1980s moved on, Spike Lee's films focussed on black identity, revitalized the political heroes of the Sixties and encouraged a growing resurgence of Black Consciousness. They also became the source of intensive merchandising; the Spike Lee film *Malcolm X* (1992) generated a mini-industry of memorabilia, from baseball hats to pendants and watches. In addition, posters accompanying Spike Lee films became highly valued graphic icons.

Also part of the energetic and highly visual cultural scene were rap videos – many of them carrying moral or anti-drug messages –

2

and rap magazines such as *The Source*, *Black Beat* and *Right On*, all from the USA. Pirate radio stations that focussed on black music added to the crucial mix. Afrocentrism (which challenged the Eurocentric version of history) also became a popular educational and inspirational force. All have become part of a growing movement of renewed black pride in the 1990s, which has been aided by innovative projects in film, photography and graphics that find new ways to celebrate black culture and promote awareness in the black community worldwide.

4

5

6

3

7

1 Poster publicizing the opening of the Spike Lee film *Malcolm X* (USA 1992).
2 Poster, Britain 1992. This photograph of Malcolm X, accompanied by the quote 'by any means necessary', has become an enduring image of black radicalism. Similar posters are produced by community printshops and other organizations in the USA and internationally.
3 Film poster for Spike Lee's *Do the Right Thing* (USA 1989).
4 Poster for the Spike Lee film *Jungle Fever* (USA 1991).
5 Spike Lee t-shirt message inspired by the words of Malcolm X.
6 The logo for Spike Lee's film company, Forty Acres and a Mule (named after the promise given to slaves in America on their emancipation).
7 *Malcolm X* merchandise, USA 1992.

3

1 Cover and inside
spreads from the first
issue of *Origin* magazine
(December-January
1992), aiming to pro-
mote an awakening of
black culture in the
1990s; designed by
E-sensual Design (Arhon
Thomas and Gary Riley),
Britain.
2 & 3 Posters from
the ad campaign to
launch the newly
legalized dancefloor
station Kiss FM
(formerly a popular
pirate station, with
emphasis on soul, rave
and rap music), by Tom
Carty and Walter
Campbell of AMV BBDO
ad agency, London
1990. Although not
intended as a black
awareness statement
as such, the campaign
was ground-breaking
in visual terms in its
acknowledgement of
a young multicultural
audience.

2

On the streets: fighting talk

1

Throughout the 1980s, Feminism was pronounced a dying movement by the British media. Yet the anger and the protests continued. The battle against sexism, and particularly against the use of sexist imagery in advertising, was waged through very public formats. Graffiti was sprayed onto London walls and billboards; stickers shouting 'This Degrades Women' were applied to sexist book covers, ads or posters; and feminist groups such as Spare Rib magazine encouraged actions and marches. Jill Posener's photographs of graffitied billboards were widely reproduced, and became symbolic of women's grassroots resistance against the public images that dominated their lives.

A more recent battle of the streets (and one that is still in force) has been waged by the American feminist art activist group known as Guerrilla Girls. They have been exposing sexual and racial discrimination in the New York art world since 1985. Carrying on the tradition of the spontaneous street poster (often posted illegally at night), they attack the business practices of the New York galleries and museums through the use of salient facts, statistics and the 'naming of names' – usually conveyed with sharp ironic humour. The audiences they most often address are the artists and the public that support these establishments. One of their most popular posters, 'Do women have to be naked to get into the Met. Museum?' was originally refused space as a billboard and so instead became a bus ad.

2 **GUERRILLA GIRLS**
CONSCIENCE OF THE ART WORLD

BUS COMPANIES ARE MORE ENLIGHTENED THAN NYC ART GALLERIES.

% of women in the following jobs*	
Bus Drivers	**49.2%**
Sales Persons	**48**
Managers	**43**
Mail Carriers	**17.2**
Artists represented by 33 major NYC art galleries	**16**
Truck Drivers	**8.9**
Welders	**4.8**

*Sources: U.S. Bureau of Labor Statistics, Art in America Annual

Please send $ and comments to:
Box 1056 Cooper Sta. NY, NY 10276   **GUERRILLA GIRLS** CONSCIENCE OF THE ART WORLD

WHEN RACISM & SEXISM ARE NO LONGER FASHIONABLE, WHAT WILL YOUR ART COLLECTION BE WORTH?

The art market won't bestow mega-buck prices on the work of a few white males forever. For the 17.7 million you just spent on a single Jasper Johns painting, you could have bought at least one work by all of these women and artists of color:

Bernice Abbott · Anni Albers · Sofonisba Anguissola · Diane Arbus · Vanessa Bell · Isabel Bishop · Rosa Bonheur · Elizabeth Bougereau · Margaret Bourke-White · Romaine Brooks · Julia Margaret Cameron · Emily Carr · Rosalba Carriera · Mary Cassatt · Constance Marie Charpentier · Imogen Cunningham · Sonia Delaunay · Elaine de Kooning · Lavinia Fontana · Meta Warrick Fuller · Artemisia Gentileschi · Marguerite Gérard · Natalia Goncharova · Kate Greenaway · Barbara Hepworth · Eva Hesse · Hannah Hoch · Anna Huntingdon · May Howard Jackson · Frida Kahlo · Angelica Kauffmann · Hilma af Klint · Kathe Kollwitz · Lee Krasner · Dorothea Lange · Marie Laurencin · Edmonia Lewis · Judith Leyster · Barbara Longhi · Dora Maar · Lee Miller · Lisette Model · Paula Modersohn-Becker · Tina Modotti · Berthe Morisot · Grandma Moses · Gabriele Münter · Alice Neel · Louise Nevelson · Georgia O'Keeffe · Meret Oppenheim · Sarah Peale · Liubova Popova · Olga Rosanova · Nellie Mae Rowe · Rachel Ruysch · Kay Sage · Augusta Savage · Varvara Stepanova · Florine Stettheimer · Sophie Taeuber-Arp · Alma Thomas · Marietta Robusti Tintoretto · Suzanne Valadon · Remedios Varo · Elizabeth Vigée Le Brun · Laura Wheeling Waring

Information courtesy of Christie's, Sotheby's, Mayer's International Auction Records and Leonard's Price Index of Auctions

Please send $ and comments to:
Box 237, 496 LaGuardia Pl., NY 10012   **GUERRILLA GIRLS** CONSCIENCE OF THE ART WORLD

YOU'RE SEEING LESS THAN HALF THE PICTURE
WITHOUT THE VISION OF WOMEN ARTISTS AND ARTISTS OF COLOR.

Please send $ and comments to:
Box 237, 496 LaGuardia Pl., NY 10012   **GUERRILLA GIRLS** CONSCIENCE OF THE ART WORLD

DID SHE RISK HER LIFE FOR GOVERNMENTS THAT ENSLAVE WOMEN?

A PUBLIC SERVICE MESSAGE FROM **GUERRILLA GIRLS**

Closely-guarded anonymity is an important part of the Guerrilla Girls' operation. It keeps the focus on issues rather than personalities or status, safeguards members against retribution and also adds to the group's mystique and notoriety. No one knows their identity; they always appear in gorilla masks or full gorilla suits. But they are rumoured to include some of the USA's top female artists, as well as curators and critics from within the art establishment itself.

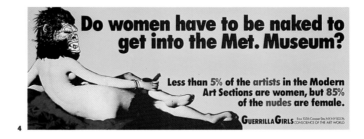

1 Badge created by Carole Spedding to help finance the feminist magazine *Spare Rib*, during the year of the royal wedding of Charles and Diana, Britain 1981.
2 Sticker and street posters from the Guerrilla Girls, attacking discrimination in the New York art establishment and other issues, USA *c*.1990.
3 Guerrilla graffiti as photographed and documented by Jill Posener, Britain 1979.
4 One of the most popular Guerrilla Girl posters. It was originally refused billboard space and so became a bus ad and street poster, USA late 1980s.

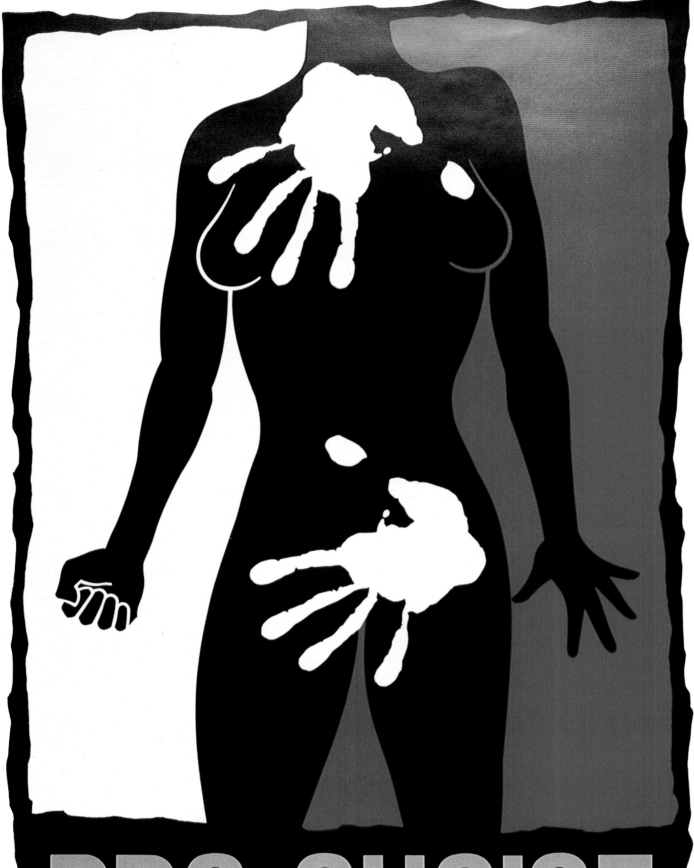

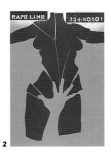

On the streets: fighting talk

Further examples of 'fighting talk' from the late 1980s included protests against violence towards women. The Rape Line poster shown here by Lanny Sommese provided a direct aid to victims of violence and rape, symbolizing the trauma and distress of rape through the image of a fractured body. The use of a body in a more angry and defiant posture appeared in a poster and t-shirt image by Rob Cheung, which juxtaposed a number of violations of freedom and hinted at the connections between them.

Barbara Kruger's billboard 'Get Out' captures the caged-in terror of domestic violence, with a cropped image that creates a sharp sense of urgency. The dramatic cropping of photographs, an expressive technique used in much of Kruger's work, stems from her background in editorial design.

The street signs shown here are from the 'Emily Post series' created from 1985-8 by New York artist Ilona Granet as an expression of her irritation with the cat-calls, whistles and suggestive comments that can bombard women pedestrians in certain areas of New York City. (Emily Post was one of America's best-known authorities on good manners and proper behaviour.) Posted for a period of six months on selected streets in lower Manhattan, they were bilingual (English/Spanish) for the benefit of their New York City audience and also displayed the wit and humour that has been a hallmark of Ilona Granet's work.

1 Pro-Choice poster using hand-prints to symbolize violation by laws and systems as well as by individuals, by Rob Cheung, USA 1989.
2 Poster for a rape help-line by Lanny Sommese, USA *c.*1988.
3 Billboard in San Francisco aiming to fight violence against women, by Barbara Kruger, USA 1992.

4 Street signs (approx. 2ft x 2ft) from the 'Emily Post series' by New York artist Ilona Granet, aiming to curb sexist street behaviour and bring back 'good manners'. Shown here are: 'Curb Your Animal Instinct', 1986; 'Are You Man or Mule', 1986; 'Are You Man or Martian', 1986; 'Are You Men or Mice', 1988.

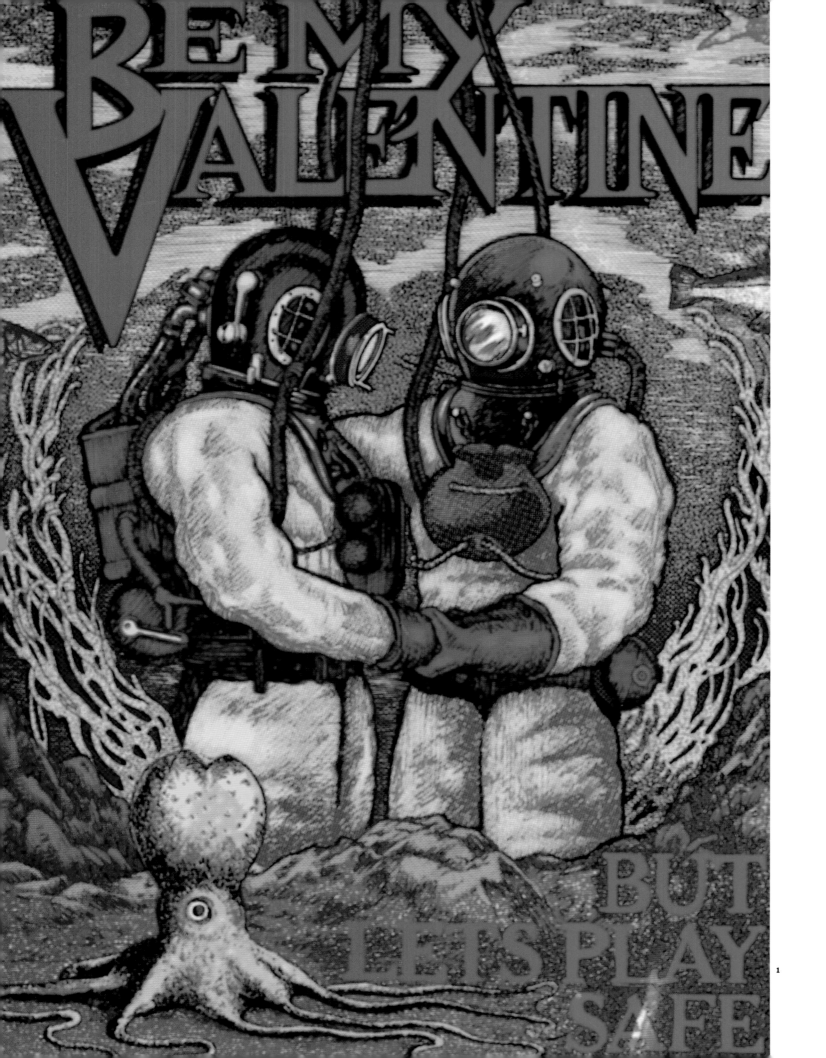

Sexual politics with a sense of humour

Humour can be used to make a sharp, satirical attack, or offer a means of 'letting off steam', particularly during long, drawn-out battles. If used carelessly, it can trivialize issues of importance. Much of the time however it can offer a welcome release, and the chance to momentarily laugh at life's problems and cares.

A new species emerged in the late 1970s and early 1980s: the feminist cartoonist, represented here by Viv Quillin's popular anti-sexist comment. Feminist publishing overall was approaching a period of great popularity and strength at this time, and flaunted a strong sense of humour while overcoming prevailing conservative attitudes. Fine examples of feminist wit included book covers for the feminist fairy tales published by the

renowned Attic Press in Ireland (shown here), and the logo for the Women's Press in London: a domestic iron, often accompanied by the line 'steaming ahead'.

The Gay Pride movement also had its moments of humour. The 'Defend the Meat Cleaver Seven' badge that is shown here protested against the arrest of a group of seven Gay Pride marchers (c.1982) in a campaign led by Julian Hows, known often to appear on marches in extravagant costumes. On this particular occasion Hows had worn a hat decorated with old gramophone records, and co-marcher Frank Egan had sewn a meat cleaver into his hat, to symbolize the oppression or 'butchering' of men in drag. At one particularly heated moment in the march, Egan was ordered by police to remove the

meat cleaver from his hat. On doing so (and obediently placing it in his bag), he was arrested for carrying an offensive weapon. There were further arrests, and a consequent rush to the marchers' defence – but all were released soon after. It is a humorous story now, but a sad remark on attitudes back then.

The issue of safe sex receives humorous treatment here, as does the highly emotive subject of abortion. The Pro-Choice and Pro-Life disputes of the late 1980s (and the question of the US government's stance on abortion) were the subject of Ilona Granet's 'State Womb' billboard, featuring a White House in the Womb and the symbolic American Eagle clutching two frightened sperm in its claws. It is a hilarious but biting comment on an extremely volatile issue.

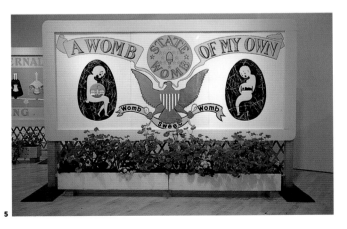

1 Safe sex Valentine postcard by South Atlantic Souvenirs (drawing by Steve Hardstaff), Britain 1986.
2 'Defend the Meat Cleaver Seven' badge, c.1982.
3 Front and back cover for a book of fairy tales for feminists published by Attic Press in Dublin, cover design by Wendy Shea, 1986.

4 Cartoon by Viv Quillin, from the book *Women Draw* (Women's Press, London 1984).
5 'State Womb' billboard, a Pro-Choice comment by artist Ilona Granet, USA 1989.
6 The graphic identity for the Women's Press in London (art director: Suzanne Perkins) symbolized the strength of feminist publishing in the 1980s.

LESBIANS IGNITE

1

The graphics of Lesbian and Gay Pride

2

The Stonewall Riots – a show of resistance to police raids on gay bars in New York City in 1969 – marked the beginning of the Gay Liberation Front, a movement aiming to combat society's oppressive attitudes towards homosexuals. The long fight for equality and legal reform has over the years encompassed issues such as the age of consent, the right to express sexuality publicly, equal opportunities and rights at work, parenting, and attacks on gay people.

Campaigning, marching and direct action have played an important part in a liberation movement that has had to continually defend its ground and demand its rights. Consequently, the movement's most memorable images tend to be street and demo-graphics (placards, posters and stickers as part of demonstrations or marches), as well as personal identity statements such as t-shirts and badges, and projects that support particular protests or campaigns.

The AIDS crisis has been a severe blow for the gay community, and the most difficult battle to date: a fight for recognition of the problem, safe sex education, and a host of other issues surrounding the illness. Although AIDS has provided yet another opportunity for societal prejudice and misunderstanding, it has also turned the gay community into a unified force. For it is the anger of the gay community that gave rise to AIDS activism, one of the most powerful popular movements of recent decades and a point over which all communities have locked arms.

3

4

GAY RIGHTS AT WORK!

1 'Lesbians Ignite' badge, 1980.
2 Gay Liberation badges. (The Gay Liberation Front badge dates from 1972.)
3 T-shirts from organizations forming the vanguard of the AIDS activism/gay rights movement of the 1990s, USA and Britain 1992.
4 Images used on posters and t-shirts created by the AIDS activist art collective Gran Fury, USA 1988-90.
5 Trade union members on the march: photograph and badge from a Gay Solidarity demonstration week held in Douglas, Isle of Man. Issues covered included homosexual law reform and rights at work; 1983.

5

Would you be more careful if it was you that got pregnant?

Anyone married or single can get advice on contraception from the Family Planning Association. Margaret Pyke House, 27-35 Mortimer Street, London W1 N 8BQ, Tel. 01-636 9135.

2

Mr. Camel's
LUMPS
CARTOON BAITED CIGARETTES
© RJ Renolds Youth Marketing Division (Cancer for Kids Project)

For posters or more information on DOC activities in your area call or write Doctors Ought to Care P.O. Box 7690, San Francisco, CA 94120-7690 (415) 882-3326

1

Chapter four

The caring society

Health, education and welfare

For God's sake give us a pound.

Post to Dept. 24, Salvation Army, 101 Queen Victoria Street, LONDON, E.C.4.

3

There ought to be a law against it.

There is.
Clunk-Click. The law of survival.

4

At the start of the decade, the 1990s was heralded as a new era of social responsibility: the 'caring, sharing decade'. Despite this tone of benevolent calm, the 1990s have been rocked by the continual surfacing of social crises, some of which have been highly explosive. The effects of the global threat of AIDS (its impact, for example, on the populations and economies of Africa) have become a haunting spectre, and promise a difficult future for those nations affected. In the West, growing urban poverty, strained health care systems, unemployment and homelessness are all problems that have been worsened by global recession and failing economies. The structures set up for ensuring the care and well-being of society have come under more strain than ever before. Consequently social issues – or the 'values' which in the 1990s define social well-being – have become a battleground. They rest high on the political agendas of governments; are argued and debated through the media; and have brought renewed interest in the concepts of social responsibility in design and community art.

This chapter is concerned with the graphics generated by the organizations that deal with social well-being – from large government departments to small charities – and encompasses projects or campaigns that put across messages broadly relating to health and welfare. It also includes graphics created by individuals or groups who challenge those messages, or the way that they are communicated. These challengers may create their own messages or forms, or even subvert or 'rework' existing imagery. As a consequence both the official voice of 'the establishment', and the unofficial voice that may criticize or question it, are present here.

The power and influence of advertising and the media are important points of focus throughout this chapter. Whereas in the past advertising and media channels mainly existed to extend the power of the commercial world, they are now also employed by organizations for public service or 'awareness' messages, or by protestors and artists for activist purposes – to subvert the status quo. A fine example of the latter is 'Death' cigarettes, a brand which challenges the lies and hypocrisy of cigarette advertising by projecting a totally 'honest' and upfront message. It represents a new progressive form of anti-smoking message, and the manufacturers donate a percentage of their profits to cancer research and related charities as part of their 'Pay as you Burn' policy (reminding their smoking customers that they are highly likely to need the benefits of such organizations one day). The 'Death' message is an obvious distortion of advertising tactics, used to drive home a harrowing message. Doug Minkler's poster, shown opposite, makes a different and equally effective comment on the power of advertising and image-building. It warns of the dangers for children taken in by cartoon cigarette ads and other stylish devices, and depicts a fantasy-horror of what may lie behind the 'cool' image.

The power struggles of this chapter therefore relate to the fight for (or against) the control of advertising/media channels. The power of commercial advertising to programme lifestyles and mould social attitudes is slowly being eroded – for its communication channels are now being used simultaneously to question those attitudes or to promote alternative views (sometimes by the hijacking of existing ads). The channels are no longer one-way power lines, they now contain mixed messages and mixed motives.

Changing attitudes and targeting audiences

Social attitudes have changed dramatically over the past three decades – and with them, the way that we visually or graphically handle health issues, social problems and 'public service' information. It began as a long, slow process of challenging taboos. The social revolutions of the 1960s and 1970s brought visions of a freer and more open society, and a bold new era of 'changing attitudes'. A product of this climate was a new breed of information and advertising campaigns. While America led the way in creative commercial advertising in the 1960s, Britain pioneered a daring new form of public service information. The best of the innovative campaigns included Cramer Saatchi's poster of a pregnant man, promoting contraception on behalf of the Health Education Council, and the shocking David Holmes/Terence Donovan poster of a distressed pregnant child, produced for the Salvation Army. This 'age of daring' reached its peak in Britain in the early 1970s with the Clunk-Click seatbelt campaign, the first time sensationalism and shock tactics were used for the public good in a national campaign.

Other groups exploited the new climate of liberation. Women faced new liberated attitudes to sex, and took control of their bodies and health care. Feminist groups and public health organizations produced a flood of graphic informational material on contraception, reproduction, sexually-related diseases and rape, which was handed out in liberal-minded community clinics and women's health centres. In the mid-1970s, too, the disabled began to fight for their rights, and soft-spoken charities adopted the new label of 'pressure group'. Publications for the disabled, promoting self-care and independence, began to receive heavy media coverage and support. There was new interest in providing wheelchair access to buildings, public transport and entertainment venues; ergonomics and social responsibility in design were hallmarks of this period. Significantly, the disabled at this time began finally to acquire visual representation in the media, and a place in public considerations. In visual terms, society was becoming more than a white, male, middle-class, able-bodied group.

5

1 An anti-smoking poster which parodies existing cartoon-style cigarette ads, USA 1992. The poster was created by Doug Minkler for Doctors Ought to Care, a national organization of doctors in the USA focussing on preventive medicine.
2, 3 & 4 Pioneering statements in shock: campaign to promote contraception by ad agency Cramer Saatchi for the Health Education Council, Britain 1970-71; poster promoting the work of the Salvation Army, by agency Kingsley Manton & Palmer (photo: Terence Donovan), Britain 1967; poster from the landmark Clunk-Click campaign to promote the use of seatbelts, conducted by the Central Office of Information for the Ministry of Transport, Britain 1971-3 (first test phase), then continued until 1980.
5 Publicity paraphernalia, including coffin-shaped packaging, for Death cigarettes, Britain 1991.

1

But despite these advances, certain areas remained curiously unchecked. Drugs were still considered to be a 'containable' problem in most countries in the 1960s and 1970s, and apart from isolated campaigns produced by government departments or charitable organizations, received little graphic attention. In America in particular, drugs were part of the underground youth culture, as well as a broader social scene that was looking for fun and experimentation. Marijuana was affordable and popular, and even cocaine was considered a 'party drug' until the late 1970s. It was not until the early 1980s that the first signs of a broader problem began to appear. Hard drugs became cheaper, addiction and the effects of long-term drug abuse began to surface, and drugs soon became heavily crime-related. The mid-1980s brought a new development in the form of crack (crack cocaine), not a social 'high', but an extremely addictive, often crime-related street drug. At that point drugs shifted onto the political agenda and America turned to face a national problem.

In 1986 the Partnership for a Drug-Free America set up as a coalition of volunteers from the communications industries and set about the problem of 'unselling' illegal drugs. Their efforts have created the largest public service media initiative in America's history. 'Anti-drug messages' are the heart of their mission, and with unprecedented participation by the media, they can claim that every American sees at least one anti-drug message per day. Participation is wide-ranging – from TV networks (the three major networks have contributed over 10,000 spots) to newspapers, theatres and home video companies – and messages are carefully targeted to specific audiences such as children or parents. According to the Partnership's research, their

crusade has produced results: their annual national tracking studies show significant attitude shifts away from drugs since 1987. Furthermore, drug abuse centres and clinics have now become commonplace. Federal and local government devote much of their time and money to prevention, and the entire problem has become part of the social fabric. In addition, definitions have been broadened: alcohol and drug dependency (hard or soft) are viewed as one and the same. Lobby groups such as MADD (Mothers Against Drunk Driving) now have substantial clout and are able to exert great pressure on legislators to tighten laws.

In other countries, where programmes relating to drug use lack the Partnership's financial resources and power, the most interesting efforts are still those which tend to target a specific audience and localize their message, as well as their media and visual language. Their approaches to the subject, however, can differ greatly. For example, the non-judgemental drug-related information provided by the Youth Awareness Programme (YAP) of the Newham Drugs Advice Project in London (pages 186-7) is targeted to the tastes, interests and street-life of young people, from the age of ten upwards, and speaks to them in a visual language they will relate to and understand. NDAP are close to their audience and its needs, taking their expertise into local schools, housing estates and youth clubs; they also target groups normally neglected by drug treatment agencies, especially the Asian and black British and African communities. The British mainstream drugs information strategy, on the other hand, is typified by the overly broad and condemnatory approach of the poster 'Skin Care by Heroin' on page 187, or the sensationalized needles and scars shown here.

"I ignore them."

"I don't want to look like this."

"I'd rather stick anchovies in my ears."

"Take a chill pill..."

"I respect my body, man."

5

"Grrrrr"

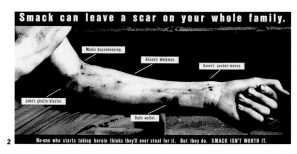
2 No-one who starts taking heroin thinks they'll ever steal for it. But they do. SMACK ISN'T WORTH IT.

3

The approaches used in communicating social messages range from shock tactics to friendly familiarity.
1 Anti-drugs poster by Alexandr Faldin and Alexandr Segal, USSR 1987.
2 'Smack', street poster from a campaign against drug abuse by

ad agency TBWA for the Central Office of Information (COI), Britain 1988.
3 'Kebab', poster from a campaign against drug abuse by Yellowhammer agency for the COI, Britain c.1988.
4 Poster warning about drug use and AIDS, USSR 1990.

5 Stills from computer-animated TV spot: an anti-drug message targeted at eight- to eleven-year-olds, by Richard Hsu (New York) for the Partnership for a Drug-Free America, 1991. The characters shown were asked 'When others ask you to do drugs, what do you say?'

Other examples of sharp targeting of audiences include the work of Bob Linney's charitable organization Health Images, which was founded in Britain in the mid-1980s. Health Images conducts poster and print workshops in underdeveloped countries, and teaches local health workers to create their own health materials and visual aids, thereby incorporating local customs, superstitions, symbolism and other issues which determine the way that images are read. In Australia, Redback Graphix provides a broad range of educational/information graphics, especially in consultation with Aboriginal communities and other specific groups. Their no-smoking and drinking message aimed at pregnant mothers (page 188) was designed to illustrate a story developed by health workers in conjunction with Aboriginal communities. They also devised a number of messages warning against the effects of Grog (alcohol), as shown here, in the form of picture stories or narrative strips for use in communities where people didn't necessarily speak, read or write English – and which were reminiscent of an Aboriginal style, and its use of symbolism.

As many of the examples in this chapter show, there was a growing awareness in the early 1980s of escalating social problems in the countries of the West, with many groups and individuals working to find radical solutions, despite the inaction of conservative governments. In the mid-1980s a number of forces converged, creating a new mood of public awareness and concern. The Live Aid rock concert of 1985 generated famine relief for Africa and saw people in 152 countries join forces in televised international solidarity. In the climate of social awareness that followed, advertising agencies were commissioned to produce media campaigns on social issues and ecology, and public formats normally reserved for commercial use were press-ganged into social use. Animal rights were popularized when the Lynx poster campaign (page 221) made wearing fur unfashionable; reports of a 'greenhouse effect' and the depletion of the ozone layer suddenly made ecology a publicly-acknowledged fight for survival; and the spectre of AIDS became not only a health crisis, but a communication crisis. How to change people's social and sexual behaviour after years of liberated permissiveness became the ultimate education and information design problem. The old 1970s trend towards social responsibility in design had returned, in an updated and highly urgent form.

AIDS education: the missing strategy

The spread of the HIV virus and the illness it can cause (known as AIDS) has created the public health crisis of the century. Now recognized as an epidemic seated in countries around the world, it presents challenges on many levels: medical and scientific (in the search for new and better drugs); economic (from the collapsing medical system of America, to the collapse of economies in Africa); cultural (for sex and morality are central issues and subject to tradition and religious influences); legal (in the attempt to ensure the rights of people with AIDS); and social (in terms of the effect of AIDS on relationships with lovers, family, and the community).

Despite the complexity and scale of the problem, there is a general lack worldwide of national strategies for AIDS education. The examples shown in this chapter are largely from poster campaigns, which play an important role in AIDS/safe sex education in that they offer support and promote discussion. But they do not compensate for the lack of a national strategy that incorporates a broad range of media, with clear and up-to-date information, specific targeting and evaluation tests for effectiveness. (What America does for anti-drug matters, for example, with the Partnership for a Drug-Free America, it does not do for AIDS and HIV.) Consequently, the best AIDS education is shouldered to a great extent by grassroots campaigners and organizations.

However poster campaigns do exist worldwide, and vary dramatically with regard to cultural traditions and audiences. They tend to be generated by two types of sources: government agencies and institutions; or community/voluntary groups and concerned individuals. The two sources operate very different approaches. Government agencies normally address a broad general audience; worried about offending the status quo, or aligning themselves to issues that may prove to be politically embarrassing during an election campaign, they tend to talk from a distance, using generalized and often bland imagery conjured up by large ad agencies. The community sector, on the other hand, is obviously more directly involved; it will target a specific audience or community and attempt to communicate with that audience on its own terms.

The community sector will also search for new audiences – very important in such a fast-changing milieu – and will attempt to respond to the needs of neglected communities, such as gay teenagers. The Swedish Federation for Gay and Lesbian Rights (RFSL) is a good example of an organization that uses careful targeting. Their safe sex posters are produced to be sited in very specific settings and to provoke reaction and discussion; their imagery therefore tends to be bold, humorous or shocking: and just right for the job. They also have a very specific aim, for although knowledge about the HIV virus in Sweden is widespread, the level of new infections particularly among young gay men is still high. A selection of their posters is shown below.

Thus in targeting specific audiences, the community sector tends to cover groups the government fails to address properly: lesbians and gay men, the young, the sexually active – in short, all those people most at risk. As one of our greatest information challenges to date, AIDS and safe sex education demands imagination and modern design strategies that will change attitudes and behaviour and at the same time combat the effects of misinformation, sensationalism and prejudice – the trademarks of much government strategy until now.

4

1 'Beat the Grog' (alcohol), poster by Redback Graphix for the Central Australian Aboriginal Media Association, Alice Springs, Australia 1986.
2 'Are you in good health?', anti-smoking poster by Margus Haavamägi, Estonia 1988.
3 A series of posters produced by the Swedish Federation for Gay and Lesbian Rights (RFSL) targeted for use in specific settings: (left) for sex clubs and other places where men meet for occasional sex; (centre) for use in nurses' offices and surgeries in schools and similar contexts; (right) mainly for schools. All of the images were used in gay bars and restaurants around the country, as part of a large campaign, Sweden 1992.
4 Stickers from RFSL, Sweden 1992.

TAKE·CARE · BE·SAFE

Take care be safe

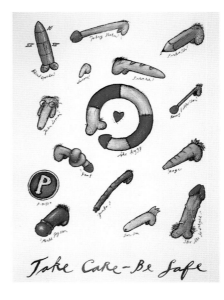

Take Care–Be Safe

Billboards have become an important public format for protest and social issues.
1 Billboard project by British artist Philippa Beale to raise public awareness of child abuse, for the benefit of various children's societies; site: London, 1987.
2 & 3 Billboards from the Randolph Street Gallery project in Chicago 1990 entitled 'Your Message Here', which aimed to provide a means of communication and an awareness of issues within inner-city communities: 'Treat a brother like your brother, with respect' designed by Julian Akins of Artists of Color United/School of the Art Institute of Chicago; 'It's the best solution' (peace and an end to street violence) by Sam Gomez, with Kharl Walker of GATE (Graphic Arts Through Education), a programme designed to help introduce and guide young street graffitists into the art gallery and education world.

The billboard: from commercial ad to public forum

Since the early 1980s billboards have become an increasingly popular format for agitation and social comment, and a powerful demonstration of the subversion of advertising power by non-commercial groups or an angry public. Billboards are one of advertising's most imposing vehicles, whether sited in city streets or in the countryside for long-distance viewing by a captive audience of highway motorists. Since they command such a direct and overbearing place in people's sights and thoughts, it is not surprising that guerrilla artists and groups have formed over the years to interfere with this process – to reclaim an imposition on public space, stop the cluttering of the environment, attack adverts or concepts they find offensive, or strike back at the faceless commercial authority and materialism that billboards represent. As the voice of commercial 'programming', billboards are an authoritative and exploitative device, a one-way form of communication. Defacing and graffiti magically transform this into a two-way conversation: the voice of authority is overtaken by the voice of resistance, and commercial power is subverted to people power.

This form of subversion has a strong tradition. In the late 1970s, while graffiti art was reaching its prime in New York City, political 'guerrilla graffiti' was being developed in other countries by groups or individuals expressing the social movements of the time. Spray-can comments or defacings normally came from 'street writers', often feminists, peace protestors, anti-racists and other activists reacting to the offensive content of existing ads, or expressing personal resistance to current politics. (As this form of defacing was usually a criminal offence, they were often operating at great risk.) Photographer Jill Posener carefully documented the range of these activities in Britain, and also the existence of groups such as BUGA UP (Billboard Utilizing Graffitists Against Unhealthy Promotions) in Australia, founded in 1979 and dedicated to assaulting corporate advertising. BUGA UP exercised a particular loathing for the tobacco industry, but in fact retaliated against all advertising and its growing imposition on everyday life.

The 1980s brought a move towards self-publishing and urban expression. Art activists such as Jenny Holzer and Barbara Kruger began to put across social messages through a wide variety of environmental formats: electronic signs, billboards, stickers or invented street signs. At the same time (and in the charitable atmosphere following Live Aid) London advertising agencies were producing charity campaigns on social and environmental issues which were displayed on billboards, the most famous being the Lynx '40 dumb animals' poster.

By the late 1980s and early 1990s, both artists and ad agencies were communicating social issues and protest comment by billboard, providing occasional disruption to the usual commercial patter. More extreme disruptions for commercial advertisers also arrived, in the form of new-generation guerrilla-graffitists who no longer worked in the mode of 'defacing' but of 'refacing'. A number of examples of this art of 'visual intervention' were carried out by the company Saatchi and Someone: in reality, an individual named David Collins, operating with a few helpers.

Saatchi and Someone aimed to hijack the images and production values of high-profile advertising imagery; and the quality of their 'seamless' alterations often subjected viewers to a 'double-take' effect. They reworked 15 billboards in the Leeds and Bradford area between the summers of 1990 and 1991. Needless to say, most of the interventions were done at night; they usually lasted for one or two weeks before being pasted over with a different poster.

Commercial advertisers have also tried to promote social concerns through public formats with varying results. In 1991 global fashion companies Benetton and Esprit took on 'global problems' and began to produce socially-conscious campaigns aimed at young people on issues such as racism, violence, literacy and AIDS. Esprit's press and TV campaign, inviting young people to write in and express their suggestions for a better world, created a flood of earnest and sometimes witty responses; while Benetton's use of highly controversial photographs on billboards and in the press evoked intense public debate, outcry and protest (page 205). A more interesting use of commercial billboard advertising stemmed from the unusual concept of 'recycled advertising' created by London ad agency Chiat/Day to promote Ecover environmentally-conscious household products. In April 1991, an advertising campaign was devised which involved 52 artists, each collaging a billboard image by tearing up redundant advertising posters. Prizes were awarded and the new billboards appeared all over London – an extraordinary way of creating ads without waste, while promoting green products and a green philosophy (pages 232-3).

Yet another function assigned to billboards in the 1990s has been that of public forum, whereby commercial advertising sites are acquired (sometimes donated) for public art projects that address issues relevant to inner-city communities. The billboard project 'Your Message Here', for example, was co-ordinated by the Randolph Street Gallery in Chicago in co-operation with the artists' collective Group Material. It produced and printed 40 designs from community-based organizations and individuals, and posted them for three months (changing their location each month), thus providing an opportunity for people and groups to address each other, or the public. Thus the billboards were used to carry hand-written messages from the homeless; promote peace in the streets, protest against unjust treatment of immigrants; celebrate diverse ethnic backgrounds; or simply talk about having respect for the neighbourhood.

The growing use of billboards, posters and other public formats as a means of expression, represents an attempt to claim the communication power and presence of these formats for use by people in the street. Such a movement offers everyone the opportunity to have a voice, argue issues, and confront crises; and presents a challenge to commercial control systems and the dominant voice of traditional news media. Street graphics and other public formats look set to become an increasingly important alternative channel for involvement and education on political issues.

4 Reworked Benetton ad by Saatchi & Someone, 1990-91, site: Leeds, Britain.
5 The Saatchi & Someone logo.

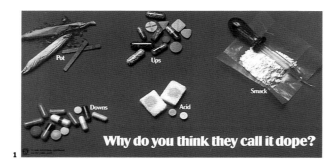

Why do you think they call it dope?

1

On the road to a drug-free America

Although occasional anti-drug statements
were produced in the US in the 1970s, it was
in the 1980s that America declared a national
problem and waged an all-out war against
drugs. The communications industries rallied
with the formation in 1985 of the Partnership
for a Drug-Free America, a voluntary coalition
of professionals from advertising, public
relations, entertainment and associated areas
all working together to expose the dangers of
illegal drugs. They create and disseminate
'anti-drug messages' with the help of massive
contributions of *pro bono* design work,
information and research services and
donated broadcast time and press space;
they now claim to be the largest public service
media campaign in history.

Each message is targeted to a specific
audience, and reviewed for accuracy,
appropriateness and effectiveness. Targeted
audiences receiving the heaviest attention
tend to be children (from aged eight upwards)
and teenagers; but messages are also
produced for parents, managers and
employees, healthcare professionals and
minority communities. The Partnership's
strategy also includes an increasing use of
non-traditional media to carry anti-drugs
messages, which may appear for example in
school packs and on children's toys, sports
equipment, direct mail materials, book covers
and video games.

7. Drugs can get you in big
trouble.

8. You could go to the principle's
office.

9. ...

10. Or go to jail.

2

14. Drugs are bad. I wouldn't
do drugs.

Introduce your nine year old to drugs.

Nine years old isn't too young for kids to learn about drugs. The question is, who will teach them? Show your kids this ad. Tell them about the dangers. Let them see what drugs and drug paraphernalia look like. Because if you don't, someone else will. **Partnership for a Drug-Free America**

3

This is the weed that Jack bought. Jack got it from Bobby. Bobby is Jack's best friend. Bobby bought it from his pal at school. Tony. Tony knew this neighborhood connection—Sid or someone. Sid made a deal with a guy downtown who scored it from some dude down south who knew two cops to get it over the border. Just for Jack.

POT HOOKS YOU UP WITH A WHOLE NEW CIRCLE OF FRIENDS.

PARTNERSHIP FOR A DRUG-FREE AMERICA

4

ENCOURAGE YOUR KID'S HABIT.

KIDS NEED SOMETHING BETTER TO DO THAN DRUGS. LIKE SPORTS. DANCE. OR MUSIC. BECAUSE GOOD THINGS CAN BE HABIT-FORMING, TOO. SO GET THEM INTO A GOOD HABIT. TODAY. OR THEY MAY GET INTO A VERY BAD ONE.

PARTNERSHIP FOR A DRUG-FREE AMERICA

5

"Use drugs? I'd rather stick anchovies in my ears"

Partnership for a Drug-free America

6

Can You Find The Drug Pusher In This Picture?

We all know what drug pushers look like. We've seen them often enough on television. But the frightening thing is, a kid is more likely to be pushed into drugs by some innocent-looking classmate.

Studies show that kids are eight times more likely to use drugs if their friends use drugs. As a parent, how do you beat odds like that?

First, realize that your preteen children *are* at risk. Then, find out everything you can about drug abuse. Next, talk to your kids. Let them know how you feel about drugs. Find out how they feel. Then, and this is very important, get to know your kids' friends – and their parents.

In other words, if you're in the picture, chances are a pusher won't be.

Partnership for a Drug-Free America

7

You have to scare the wits out of an addict.

Even if he sits in the next office.

Nothing you do in business will be much tougher than this.

You may have to confront your next-in-command, the one you hoped would someday fill your shoes.

And you'll have to say, "Get well or get out." There's no other way for you to break through an addict's defenses.

But you're not alone. Confidential help is only a phone call away when you contact your Special Health Services representative.

Saving the career of the person next door isn't easy. But who ever said being a friend was easy?

Partnership for a Drug-Free America

Texaco is a Member of the Partnership for a Drug-Free America

8

1 Drug abuse message by the Advertising Council of America, USA 1971.
Anti-drug messages from the Partnership for a Drug-Free America:
2 Sequence of stills from a television spot featuring 'Penny', a popular character from 'Pee Wee's Playhouse'. Target: six- to eight-year-old children.
3 Full-page newspaper ad. Target: parents.
4 An ad which makes a connection between drug use and a crime network. Target: teenagers.
5 Print ad included in all of the basketball packaging used by a sporting goods company. Target: young adults and parents.
6 One of six posters in an educational pack for teachers. Target: five-to nine-year-olds.
7 Print ad. Target: parents.
8 Print ad for Texaco. Target: managers and co-workers.

Approaches to drugs, alcohol and smoking

1

An assortment of graphic imagery relating to drugs, alcohol and smoking is shown on the following pages, representing a variety of audiences, approaches and countries.

The examples on this spread show strategies for communicating with the young through their own language and culture. For example, Studio Graphiti in Italy makes use of the popularity of comics and spray stencils among young Italians; the British fashion designer Katharine Hamnett politicizes a youthful fashion scene; and E-sensual Design produce attention-grabbing visual effects for YAP, the Youth Awareness Programme of Newham Drugs Advice Project in London. The collection also demonstrates an interesting variation in aim and tone, ranging from the scare tactics of campaigns such as 'Skin Care by Heroin' to the street-wise straight-talking of the YAP graphics, which offer advice and help.

A broader selection of audiences appears on pages 188-9. Some of the work is specifically targeted, as in the 'Pregnancy' poster aimed at Aboriginal communities in Australia, while other images – for example, the anti-smoking poster from Singapore – make a more general appeal.

2

1 'Stay Alive in 85',
t-shirt by fashion
designer Katharine
Hamnett for an anti-
heroin campaign,
Britain 1985.
2, 3 & 4 Created by
young people, for young
people: non-
judgemental drugs-
related information
from YAP, the Youth
Awareness Programme
of Newham Drugs
Advice Project in
London. Designed by
E-sensual Design (Arhon
Thomas and Gary Riley),
1992. Shown here are
information cards,
posters and a postcard.
5 'Skin Care by Heroin',
ad campaign by
Yellowhammer agency
for the Central Office of
Information, Britain
1989.
6 'Drugs are the dark
and frightening
unknown', road stencil
and poster image from
the 'Drugs Out'
campaign, illustration
by Angelo Stano, design
by Andrea Rauch of
Graphiti studio in
Florence, Italy 1992.

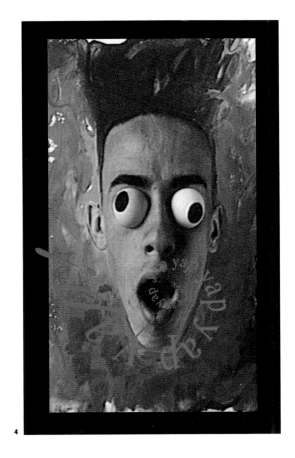

SKIN CARE BY HEROIN.

Take heroin and before long you'll start looking ill, losing weight and feeling like death.
So, if you're offered heroin, you know what to say. **HEROIN SCREWS YOU UP**

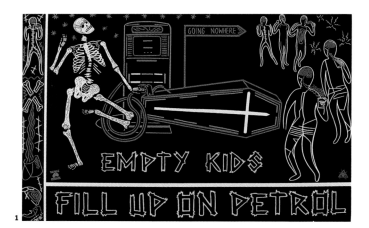

1

1 'Empty Kids', poster
by Redback Graphix
(design: Marie
McMahon; printer:
Peter Curtis) for the
National Campaign
Against Drug Abuse
in Canberra; Australia
1987.
2 'Pregnancy', poster
by Redback Graphix
(design: Marie
McMahon; printer:
Alison Alder) for the
National Campaign
Against Drug Abuse in
Canberra; Australia
1988.
3 Anti-smoking poster
by Miroslav Jiránek,
Czechoslovakia.
4 'Don't Drink!', poster
by Alexandr Gelfenboim,
Russia, 1990.
5 'Bad Habits Die Hard',
poster by Ketchum
Advertising (design
by Gordon Tan, Jim
Aitchison and Heintje
Moo) for the Ministry of
Health in Singapore,
1992.

2

PUFF PUFF
PUFF PUFF
COUGH PUFF
PUFF COUGH
COUGH PUFF
COUGH COUGH
COUGH COUGH
COUGH COUGH

3

4

 **BAD HABITS DIE HARD**

Ministry of Health

5

1

2

3

4

Safe sex and AIDS education

The term AIDS entered our vocabulary as early as 1980, but it took another five years for the apathy, misinformation and inaction of governments to reach a point where a grassroots reaction in America was forced into play – and yet another five years to bring acknowledgement of the global spread of the disease. Over ten years after the arrival of the problem, AIDS education is still in its infancy.

AIDS education materials are however produced worldwide and vary dramatically in approach and style. Poster campaigns continue to play an important role, produced either by government agencies or by community groups and concerned individuals.

A scan over the examples shown gives some indication of the complexity of the design issues involved. Target audiences can vary from country to country (in Africa, heterosexuals are most vulnerable; in Northern Europe, gay men) and cultural background, visual language and tastes will differ. Tolerance levels differ with regard to 'indecent' imagery, often resulting in the use of visual metaphors, while the atmosphere conveyed can range from ice-cold British sophistication to the sinister symbolism of Russia and Eastern Europe.

The campaigns for safe sex on pages 192-3 take an adventurous and modern tack. Rather than revert to moralizing, scare tactics or an attempt to impose restrictive behaviour, these images are seductive, lustful and full of fun: they are a tempting invitation to safe sex, aimed at a modern and sexually-active audience.

WET YOUR APPETITE FOR SAFER SEX.

Safer sex protects us all from HIV (the virus that can lead to AIDS), STDs and unwanted pregnancy.
Call the Terrence Higgins Trust Helpline on 01-242 1010, 3pm-10pm.

1, 2, 3 & 4 Safe sex posters (from a series of six) designed by Big-Active for the Terrence Higgins Trust, Britain 1992.
5 Poster from the Take Care Be Safe campaign by the Swedish Federation for Gay and Lesbian Rights (RFSL), design by Ola Johansson, photography by Robert Nettarp, Sweden 1992.
6 Poster promoting 'Red Hot + Blue', an AIDS benefit album of Cole Porter songs. Design by Helene Silverman, photography by Steven Meisel, USA 1991.
7 Magazine ad produced by the Health Education Authority, Britain 1993.

NO RISK
IN
A KISS.

TAKE CARE ★ BE SAFE

safe sex
USE A CONDOM EVERYTIME
¡CUIDATE, USA CONDONES!
is hot sex

HE'S INTO SAFER SEX, SO WHY NOT GIVE HIM A HAND?

A matter of life and death

Poster campaigns for AIDS education rightly focus on changing social attitudes or sexual behaviour. But there are also other roles for graphics to play, for example the dissemination of life-saving information through more everyday graphic forms, as shown here by The Kitchen calendar, an events listing for a New York arts venue.

Another communication role can be seen in the 'Images for Survival II' project created by designer and educator Charles Helmken. The project involved 31 graphic designers; all produced AIDS posters in 1989 for an exhibition intended to tour Korea (only just beginning to discover cases of the virus) as part of a campaign to increase public awareness of the problem. Helmken's own poster contribution appears here.

Memorials and interpretative pieces have been another type of activity over the years, to honour the memory of loved ones lost through AIDS. The most famous expression of the humanity behind the statistics has been the NAMES Project, America's national AIDS memorial, which takes the form of a huge quilt. Started in Sacramento in 1987, the quilt consists of thousands of panels: each panel measuring 3ft x 6ft, and each representing an AIDS victim. In 1988 the panels numbered 35,000 and were still rising. The project has continued as an artistic venture unparalleled in size and emotion, and an overwhelming expression of human loss and love.

Although not a piece of graphics in itself, the quilt has inspired further forms of graphic

1

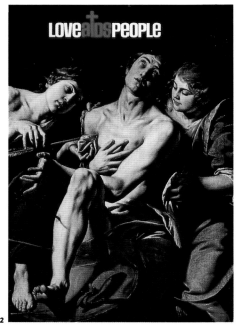

2

expression such as films, photographs, and posters – for instance Joseph P. Ansell's 'Eternal Summer' designed in 1989, which couples William Shakespeare's sonnet with a photograph of the quilt by David M. Green. (Green not long after died from AIDS; there are now two panels in his memory in the NAMES Project quilt). The poster, like the quilt, is a reminder that AIDS is robbing the world of interesting, creative people and, in Ansell's words, 'a promise to those who have already died and those who may yet die – they will not be forgotten'.

4

*B*ut thy eternal summer shall not fade,
Nor lose possession of that fair thou owest;
Nor shall *D*eath brag thou wander'st
in his shade,
*W*hen in eternal lines to time thou growest;
So long as men can breathe, or eyes can see,
So long lives this, and this gives life to thee.

Wm. Shakespeare
Sonnet XVIII

3

1 Street poster announcing events for The Kitchen (a performing arts centre in New York) while also publicizing a help line number for the AIDS Drug Assistance Program, which provides help for people needing drugs for the treatment of HIV. Design by Bureau (Marlene McCarty and Don Moffit), USA 1990.
2 Poster by Charles Helmken for the 'Images for Survival II' project on AIDS awareness, USA 1989.
3 'Eternal Summer', poster designed by Joseph P. Ansell using a photograph by David M. Green, for the 'Images for Survival II' project, USA 1989.
4 Photographs by Marc Geller of the NAMES Project quilt, USA 1987-8.

The politics of food, nutrition and health

Problems relating to food, nutrition, medicine and health care differ greatly from country to country; most however are entangled in a web of politics and economics. In the Third World in particular, food is a fiercely political issue and is inextricably linked with the imbalance of wealth between the underdeveloped countries and the industrialized West.

It is not surprising then that the posters in this section are a mixture of straightforward health instruction and bitter political comment. Projects shown include posters from a Food and Nutrition kit designed in 1982 for the Organization of Consumer Unions in Malaysia by Chaz Maviyane-Davies (head of the Maviyane Project in Zimbabwe,

page 77). They mix harsh statements about the industrialized world's economic exploitation of underdeveloped countries with comments about sanitation and nutrition. The visual language however is damning: energy crises are depicted as a starving child peering out of the shadows of the control panel of a car (symbol of the rich, petrol-guzzling West), and further messages of persuasion or protest are conveyed through obvious signs of Westernization such as pills or dollar bills.

Bob Linney's poster on the activities of transnational food companies makes equally harsh comment. His British-based charity, Health Images, conducts poster and graphic workshops in the poor countries of the world.

They teach community health workers to design and produce their own health materials and visual aids, thereby incorporating relevant symbolism, customs, colours, local art, and other issues affecting the reading of an image. For example, both the Hindu goddess Kali and the Hindu elephant god are used to carry health messages in the posters shown here, which were produced by local health workers in the slum of Dharavi in Bombay.

But political comment is never far away. A Health Images workshop was held in 1989 in association with the Asamblea de Barrios, a grassroots group in Mexico City that pressurizes the Mexican government on a wide range of issues. Their figurehead is

Superbarrio (a costumed ex-wrestler) who campaigns against homelessness, poor sanitation and air pollution, and features on one of the posters produced by local people attending the Health Images workshop, shown on page 199.

Other matters relating to health and well-being on pages 198-9 include irradiated food, anorexia and culture clash, as shown in the nutrition poster by Redback Graphix in Australia which focusses on those forced to exist between two different cultures, and urges children to 'Eat Good Food'.

3

4

5

6

1 & 2 Posters from a Food and Nutrition kit for the International Organization of Consumer Unions in Malaysia, designed by Chaz Maviyane-Davies of Zimbabwe, 1982. 3 & 4 The products of Health Images poster workshops: two posters produced in the large slum of Dharavi in Bombay by local health workers, 1988. Ganapati, the Hindu elephant god, is holding a syringe (for immunization), vitamin A solution, de-worming **solution and oral rehydration solution. The Hindu goddess Kali is holding a mango, milk, a carrot and some dark green leafy vegetables. These are all good sources of vitamin A, a deficiency of which causes xerophthalmia and eventually blindness in children. 5 Front cover of Health Images information leaflet. 6 Poster by Bob Linney on the socio-political causes of low health status, Britain 1980s.**

1

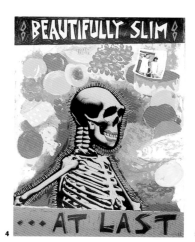

1 'Eat Good Food' by Redback Graphix (design: Leonie Lane; printer: Peter Curtis) aimed at children in bush communities, Australia 1987.

2 & 3 Two posters printed and designed by local participants of a Health Images workshop (see page 196) held in association with the grassroots pressure group Asamblea de Barrios, Mexico City 1989. Left: featuring the group's figurehead Superbarrio, an ex-wrestler who appears dressed up in a Superman suit at the Asamblea's demonstrations and meetings. The slogan says 'Deficient Health, Indifferent Government'.

Right: poster about the severe problem of air pollution in the city (*contaminación*). The words at the bottom say 'In Danger of Extinction'.

4 'Beautifully Slim, at Last' by Carol Porter of Red Planet arts workshop, a silkscreened poster on anorexia and women's self-perceptions, Australia 1992.

5 'Yuk', a poster comment on food irradiation by Sue Anderson of Red Planet arts workshop, Australia 1989.

The Road to Social Success

Education

Unemployment

Employment

Financial Insecurity

Financial Security

Reduced Consumer Power

Consumer Power

Poor Housing

Home Ownership

Greater Consumer Power

Urban Deprivation

Social Alienation

Superior Social Standing

3

Financial Disaster

Civil order and social welfare: from housing to homelessness

1

2

Poverty and homelessness have increased over the past three decades, and promise to be the plague of the 'caring 1990s'. Whereas the 1970s brought attempts to deal with the alienation and poverty of public housing plans and estates, the 1990s has brought homelessness and *The Big Issue* (a newspaper produced on behalf of the homeless), as well as concern over social services unable to cope.

Social critique and protest centering on unemployment, strained health systems and rising crime, is therefore increasing, as are attempts to provide the homeless with an identity in order that they are not simply forgotten. In America, community art projects are now seen as a way of combating gangland violence in cities and producing local pride in inner-city neighbourhoods, while handgun control still remains a hotly-debated issue.

1 'Benefits', poster alluding to life on housing estates, London 1970s.
2 *The Big Issue*, newspaper produced on behalf of the homeless, Britain 1992.
3 Young designer's comment on future prospects in the British recession (the symbols are derived from British road signs), Chris Shuff, Britain 1990.
4 'Welcome to America: the only industrialized country besides South Africa without national healthcare', billboard by Gran Fury, USA 1990.
5 Billboard from the public art project 'Your Message Here', showing a mass of signatures of homeless people. Created by Greg Boozel and Sara Fredrickson for the Union of the Homeless, USA 1990.
6 'Caring is hard work!', poster in support of the restoration of historic architecture, by Alexander Vasilchenko, USSR 1988.
7 Poster concerning the housing shortage and its harmful effects on family life in the USSR, by Levshunova, USSR 1980s.

WE'RE ALL ONE COLOR

STOP THE KILLING

3

4

2

5

Controversies surrounding the right to carry arms.
1 'We're All One Color', poster calling for a stop to Los Angeles gang violence and depicting a soul handshake by members of different LA gangs. Designed by Robbie Conal and Debbie Ross, USA 1989.
2 'My Boys Didn't Die for Me', billboard message against gang violence by graffiti artist Mario Gonzalez Jr, as part of the Randolph Street Gallery's public art project 'Your Message Here', which placed 40 billboards around Chicago neighbourhoods in 1990.
3 'One Child a Day', poster produced by the National Coalition to Ban Handguns, USA 1992. Photograph by James Wood. The text refers to the number of children reported to be killed annually with handguns in the USA.
4 Press ad calling for support to stop the sale of military assault weapons in California; created by the Public Media Center, USA 1990.
5 Issues of safety and self-defence are given glossy graphic treatment in *Women & Guns* magazine, USA 1992.

Global issues and global promotions

The year 1991 brought a new form of
advertising: global issues were used to
promote commercial products as part of
socially-responsible business philosophies.

San Francisco-based Esprit, one of the
world's largest manufacturers of women's
and children's clothes, decided to develop a
dialogue with its customers through television
and print advertising by asking the question
'What would you do?' (to change the world) –
and reeled from the weight of response it
received on a wide range of social issues,
from the rainforest to abortion. Their heavily
publicized aim was to give their customers a
chance to 'get involved' in issues, as part of
a socially-conscious corporate philosophy.

Benetton, also one of the world's largest
casual clothing companies, decided to 'make
people think' by displaying 'universal' and
socially-orientated photographs as part of
a global corporate image communicating to
audiences in a hundred different countries.
Although an international perspective had
marked their campaigns throughout the
1980s (leading to the adoption of their slogan
'United Colors of Benetton' in 1989), by the
1990s the ads had become increasingly
provocative. Clothes no longer featured;
instead there were controversial social images
aimed at promoting awareness of world issues
– and the Benetton name. Some audiences
were infuriated by the combination; others
were not. An image of a black woman
breastfeeding a white baby was banned in the
US; it won awards in five other countries.

1

A blood-spattered newborn baby went up on billboards in Britain – and promptly came back down, due to public outcry. A photograph of a deathbed scene involving AIDS sufferer David Kirby threw British magazine editors into moral dilemmas, and caused outrage by AIDS activists such as ACT UP, who immediately boycotted Benetton shops.

There is no denying that both Esprit and Benetton broke new ground in advertising;

Benetton in particular, for better or worse, opened up a debate on how images are used in the public domain, and for what purposes. But the underlying controversy remains: in the caring 1990s, social and political 'involvement' has become enmeshed with commercial sales strategy. It is an uncomfortable mating no matter how well it is handled, and one that will continue to elicit mixed reactions and protest from the public.

1 Press ads from the 'What would you do?' campaign by Esprit clothing company, USA 1991.
Benetton's provocative ad campaigns produced a mixed response from their international public:
2 Reworked billboard ad by Saatchi & Someone (original text: 'United Colors of Benetton'),
Britain 1990-91.
3, 4 & 5 Controversial Benetton ad showing a dying AIDS sufferer. *The Face* magazine carried the ad but insisted that any revenue gained should go to charity; *Elle* magazine refused and left a blank space and explanation to its readers; AIDS activists ACT UP boycotted Benetton shops and produced this poster for display on streets and in bus shelters.

There's only one pullover this photograph should be used to sell.

1 2 3

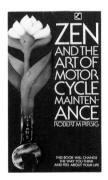

5 Foreword by Anita Roddick

Saving the earth

Ecology and the Green movement

The disruption of eco-systems and exhaustion of natural resources are not new issues, even for the design world; the rumblings and warnings have been fairly constant over the past few decades. The forerunners of today's Greens were not only present in the science corridors of universities and colleges, but also in the drop-out hippie culture of the 1960s, when living in a commune was the path to self-sufficiency and a better relationship with Mother Earth. This consciousness continued to develop into the 1970s cult for 'alternatives', spurred on by the world oil crisis of 1973 and subsequent shortage scares. People began not only to take a critical look at their own lifestyles and values but also to develop a sense of responsibility for their society and the planet. Ecology, alternative technology and survival began to be seen as the passwords to the future.

This chapter takes a brief look at those early days of the 'Earth movement', when the foundations for many present-day attitudes were laid. But it then jumps quickly to the 1980s, for that was the decade when 'Greening' really became a viable force: in politics, pressure groups, business and consumerism, education and daily habits. The effect of this change in attitude, in what ad agencies now refer to as

'the great Green boom' of the mid-1980s, was phenomenal – and it revolutionized the way in which artists and designers viewed and handled environmental subjects.

The power struggles examined in this chapter are between conflicting attitudes: consumption vs. conservation; industrial and economic expediency vs. planning for the future; government complacency vs. popular protest or individual determination. The conflicts do not divide neatly between the Establishment and the agitators; they encompass everyone and at all levels – personal, national and global. A graphic revolution of sorts has also taken place, in the sense that Green issues have now penetrated our everyday thoughts, tastes and visual language.

Beginnings of the Earth movement

Much of the imagery and philosophy from the early days emanated from America. The first Earth Day was held on 22 April 1970 to focus public attention on environmental concern, and consolidate a new and fast-growing movement. Robert Rauschenberg's poster for the event was a design classic; and the aggressively staring eagle became a

Over 20 years after its conception, Earth Day USA remains America's tribute to community action on environmental issues.

1 The revival in 1990 of Earth Day celebrations, which continue annually on 22 April.

2 Local Earth Day activities poster from a shop window in Morgantown, West Virginia, 1992.

3 An Earth Day 1990 poster by Seymour Chwast, USA.

4 Poster by Robert Rauschenberg for the first Earth Day held on 22 April 1970, USA.

5 Evidence of greening: from the early days (*Blueprint for Survival* led to the founding of the Ecology Party in Britain in 1973), to the height of the green publishing boom with *The Green Consumer Guide* of 1989.

DIE GRÜNEN

lle Gründe sprechen für Grün

1

symbolic guardian of the Earth movement – and a symbol for survival. US Earth Day was revived on its twentieth anniversary in 1990, with the more specific aim of building environmental commitment through personal action. Although global in scope – some 200 million people in 140 countries participated in 1990 – it remains America's annual tribute to the value of local, community effort on environmental issues.

The early movement also had its champions and theoreticians. These included consumer rights crusader Ralph Nader (see page 213); the Club of Rome, an international group of scientists and industrialists intent on persuading governments, industrial leaders and trade unions throughout the world to take heed of global environmental problems; the British Ecology Party, formed in 1973 (the first in Europe); and later the German Green party, Die Grünen – led by the dynamic Petra Kelly – which made an impact in West German politics in the national elections of 1983, and then entered the European Parliament in 1984.

Casting a heavy influence on design education in the 1970s were Buckminster Fuller with his geodesic domes and concept of 'Spaceship Earth', and Victor Papanek and his treatise on moral responsibility vs. industrial design, *Design for the Real World*. Together they introduced a

generation of students to the concept of 'economy of means' and the plight of the Third World. Valuable work was carried out by organizations such as UNICEF in the study of literacy and health problems, as well as the communication of health matters to non-literate groups through the use of pictures and drawings. This began a pioneering phase in the visual design of instructional information and educational aids.

Alternative living also had its bibles, for example Charles Reich's *The Greening of America* (1970), Stewart Brand's many versions of the *Whole Earth Catalog* (1968-85), E. F. Schumacher's *Small is Beautiful* (1973), and Robert Pirsig's *Zen and the Art of Motorcycle Maintenance* (1974) which achieved a massive cult following. They all influenced and fed the prevailing mood of 'social conscience', and the move towards socially-responsible design. Ergonomics was the buzz word of the day, and equally popular were the notions of recycling, alternative technology and economical use of materials and energy. The graphic design world also strove to be socially relevant, showing new interest in community art, photo-journalism, design for special needs, health education, literacy and readability. Attention was focussed on the audience or user, and the concept of 'user feedback'. Graphic design

The Green movement took a particularly strong hold in Germany where it received enthusiastic support from artists and designers.
1 Poster publicizing Die Grünen, the Green political party in West Germany, by Gunter Rambow, 1983. The bottom line reads: 'All of nature supports the Greens'.
2 Postcard by Egon Kramer, West Germany 1984.
3 'No Place for Trees', a poster comment on how trees have difficulty surviving in city environments, by Manfred Butzmann, East Germany 1990.
4 Postcard by Egon Kramer, West Germany 1988.
5 Poster promoting Green politics, by Manfred Butzmann, Germany 1990.

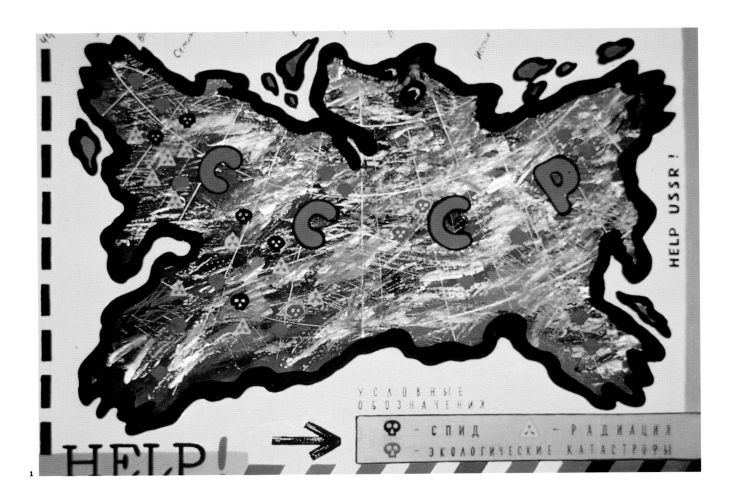

1

2

3

education responded to all these interests with a flowering of college courses specializing in information design, teaching a research-and-analysis approach to communication graphics and, for better or worse, widening the existing gap between graphic design and advertising.

But despite such educational trends, ecology and its concerns were still marginalized. They had no political weight, and were ignored by industry and the broader general public. The visual handling of environmental issues consequently suffered from not being taken very seriously, and at best offered a soft-centred approach, or a clichéd conservationist-hippie attitude. Although Rauschenberg's eagle had cast a rather sinister, watchful eye over the decade, the imagery from the 1970s was generally not hard-hitting enough to impose a dramatic shift in attitude. The vision of a gentler and more caring planet failed to make sufficient impact on dog-eat-dog industrial society.

The Green movement and new attitudes

With Thatcher elected in 1979, Reagan elected in 1980, NATO rearmament underway and other evidence of a shift in world politics to the Right, the alternative politics of the Left began to rise with a

vengeance. In alignment with the growing anti-nuclear lobby came the rise of the Green movement, and in 1984 Petra Kelly and Germany's Die Grünen made their significant move into the European Parliament, accompanied by a bright, punchy visual identity.

The period of change had begun. The pressure group Greenpeace acquired an international profile as nature's vigilantes through televised reports of their courageous 'direct actions'. Although Greenpeace never operated a global corporate identity, their name came to have tremendous impact and authority. The graphic campaigns associated with Greenpeace also took on this confrontational stance. Their famous offshoot Lynx, the anti-fur trade campaigners, teamed up with Yellowhammer ad agency in London to produce the '40 dumb animals' campaign in 1985 (page 221). The campaign was a landmark in modern graphic design history, and helped create a widespread stigma against wearing fur (nearly ruining the British fashion-fur industry).

The Live Aid rock concert that took place in July 1985 was another crucial force in the period of change. Through the medium of a globally-televised rock concert, it helped create a new mood of 'public awareness'. Although the concert was specifically for famine relief in

Africa, it heightened public sensibilities and consciousness of global problems. Within a few years life-threatening crises such as the greenhouse effect and global warming also loomed into view, along with disasters such as the world's worst ever nuclear accident at Chernobyl in 1986 and the Exxon Valdez oil spill in 1989. With growing reports of pollution and irreparable damage to forests and wildlife, ecology suddenly became a battle for the survival of humankind and the planet.

Accompanying this shift in attitude came a crucial change in visual strategy. Environmental campaigns stopped concentrating on the pleasanter aspects of conservation; they instead started focussing on the destruction and stupidity taking place. They began 'talking tough', and seeking help from ad agencies to get their message across. Pollution became a more urgent and popular topic, producing clever twists in approach, as in the litmus paper billboard shown on page 223. By this time (and with the Lynx campaign setting an example) advertising agencies had also realized that much kudos was to be gained in hard-hitting environmental campaigns. Consequently such campaigns were eagerly snatched up by the media industry.

Oil spill disasters around the world brought intense public outcry and an inspired form of despair and protest from creative artists, including the fantasized image 'Changing the Face of America (Genetically Speaking)' by Alaska Visual (page 223) and fashion stylist Judy Blame's controversial and harrowing sequence 'Dying Waters' (pages 224-5). Pollution, animal rights, endangered species and other environmental campaigns would never be the same.

In addition, educational efforts were targeted at the young (shown on page 229 in the form of Britain's Captain Eco, and America's Captain Planet and the Planeteers) and Green marketing and consumerism came into existence with the creation of 'Green companies' such as Anita Roddick's Body Shop. Consumers increasingly began to turn to 'natural' products, from food and clothing to beauty-without-cruelty cosmetics. As specifiers of paper and print, and as visual communicators (able to help mould the attitudes of consumers and clients alike), graphic designers themselves found an instrumental role to play in the 'selling' of the whole issue of recycling.

The 1990s have seen environmental issues find their way onto the agendas of mainstream political parties, and the 1992 Earth Summit in Rio marked an important attempt to see them enter the arena of international politics, even though the outcome may have disappointed many. But if the environmental politics of governments ultimately fail to go global, perhaps protest will. The 'Visualize the Future' event held in 1992 by Parco – the youth subsidiary of Seibu department store in Tokyo – was intended to raise ecological consciousness in Japan, but also points to a potential future format for graphic agitation. Parco's event took the form of an open art exhibition where artists, designers, illustrators and students from all over the world produced slogans, designs or pieces of art relating to their vision of the future. These were faxed directly to the exhibition, or sent on computer disk and printed out and displayed. In addition to encouraging new types of environmental statements, such an event also suggests a futuristic scenario – where revolutions might no longer take place in the streets, but instead take the form of global movements of protest and solidarity, carried by a network of messages, images and manifestos, shot round the world through fax signals and computer technology.

Ecology imagery takes on a greater urgency in the 1980s.
1 'Help!' (the legend reads: AIDS; Radioactivity; Ecological catastrophe), poster relating to the USSR's urgent problems, designer unknown, USSR 1989.
2 'Chernobyl 1986', poster by Dan Reisinger, Israel.
3 'It's better to live nuclear free', poster by Stefano Rovai of Graphiti studio, Italy 1987.
4 'The Proof of the Pudding...is in the Heating', postcard showing nuclear reprocessing plant as a Christmas pudding, by South Atlantic Souvenirs, Britain 1985-6. On the back it carries a humorous recipe for a (lethal) party cocktail entitled 'Meltdown'.
5 Poster picturing mankind as a greedy pig destroying the world, by Bokser, USSR 1989.

4

THE PROOF OF THE PUDDING····

5

1

Forerunners of the Green movement

3

2 ECOLOGY NOW!

The search for alternative lifestyles and technology, and the growing climate of 'social conscience', provided the foundation for the early days of the Earth movement in America. It was a movement heavy with philosophy, publications and personalities, all of which influenced design directions and attitudes for years to come.

Highlights from that period included the crusading lawyer Ralph Nader, who emerged in the early 1960s as the watchdog of consumer rights and protection. He was particularly known for taking Chevrolet to task over the production of the rear-engine Corvair, which he declared unsafe – a legal battle described in the 1965 publication *Unsafe at*

any Speed. Having made a historic confrontation with a major corporation, Nader was instrumental in strengthening the consumer movement in America and influencing issues of environmental and social import for a long time after.

Design education also declared its gurus and bibles. There was the architect and inventor Buckminster Fuller, best known for his geodesic domes, concept of 'Spaceship Earth', and dedication to the development of modern technology and science for the good of humankind. Designer and educator Victor Papanek authored *Design for the Real World* which examined moral responsibility in design, and promoted alternative, energy-saving

methods. In 1968 Stewart Brand started the 'access-to-tools' compendium known as the *Whole Earth Catalog*. Six versions were completed up to 1985, including *The Last Whole Earth Catalog* (1971) shown here: a directory of sources, places and people relating to alternative living and a monumental collection of research that aimed to make technology accessible to everyone.

Ecology posters also emanated from diverse sources, including the Graphic Workshop in Boston, a group founded in 1970 as the Student Strike Workshop at Massachusetts College of Art and renowned for their protest graphics on a number of issues in the early 1970s (see page 149).

4

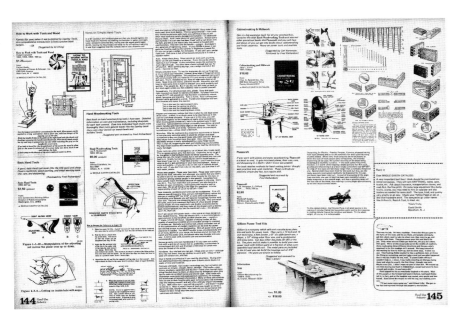

A nuclear catastrophe is too big a price for our electric bill.

Ralph Nader calls a national meeting of citizens to stop the development of nuclear power until it can be proven safe.

Critical Mass74

A national gathering of the citizens movement to stop nuclear power.
November 15-17   Statler Hilton Hotel   Washington, D.C.   Phone 202-546-4936

5

1 Victor Papanek's book *Design for the Real World*, with an introduction by R. Buckminster Fuller, first published in 1971.
2 'Ecology Now', poster (artist unknown), USA 1970.
3 Poster for a recycling group by The Graphic Workshop (formerly Student Strike Workshop) in Boston, *c.*1972.
4 One of many versions: *The Last Whole Earth Catalog*, an illustrated compendium of technology and research for alternative living, USA 1971.
5 'Critical Mass 74', poster designed by Arnold Saks announcing a national meeting in Washington DC for Ralph Nader's movement against nuclear power, USA 1974.

Early Green collaboration: art and business

The 'Save Our Planet' series of six anti-pollution posters by well-known creative artists was sponsored by Olivetti in 1971, representing an early example of collaboration between the art world and large corporations. Olivetti was known for its modern image and innovative graphics and publicity; its alignment with the new movement was in keeping with a progressive corporate vision.

Of the images in the series, three remain outstanding products of that period. Georgia O'Keeffe's 'Save Our Air' is a hypnotic comment on the beauty of pure, never-ending sky and the rhythm of life itself; it is probably the most widely reproduced poster of the series. With appropriate quirkiness and charm, architect Buckminster Fuller's 'Save Our Cities' captures the high-spirited enthusiasm of the man, his theories of 'Spaceship Earth', and his commitment to harnessing technology for the good of all. Roy Lichtenstein's 'Save Our Water' however is perhaps the most startling image, for his enlarged Ben Day dots hint at mechanization, technology and other potential evils that are hovering above the water line.

The 'Save Our Planet' series sponsored by Olivetti, 1971.
1 'Save Our Cities' by Buckminster Fuller.
2 'Save Our Air' by Georgia O'Keeffe.
3 'Save Our Water' by Roy Lichtenstein.

1

The rise of Green politics in Europe

2

The Ecology (or Earth) movement began to develop as an alternative political grouping in Europe in the 1970s. The British Ecology Party was formed in 1973; and soon after Petra Kelly set about founding a political party in Germany, where Green issues were beginning to have tremendous impact. The West German Die Grünen (Green Party) was thereby formed to stand as a nationwide party in the European parliamentary elections in 1979. They made a great show of strength in the national elections of 1983 (gaining 27 seats), and in 1984 entered the European parliament. By the mid-1980s the enthusiasm had spread, and most Western European countries had Green parties.

From their founding in 1979, Die Grünen employed the emblem of a bright, bold sunflower, and made use of the emotional appeal of graphics derived from children's illustrations, as well as handwritten slogans. Die Grünen also benefited from the allegiance of world-renowned artists and designers, including Joseph Beuys and Andy Warhol.

The East German Green Party was later able to draw upon the greater resources of the European Green network and produced a sophisticated photographic poster by Holger Matthies to contest the March 1990 East German free elections; the image, shown here, is still in use by Die Grünen today. Also represented is a poster by Manfred Butzmann for the left-wing ecology pressure group Grüne Liga, used to help promote green politics in the March 1990 elections.

3

WIR HABEN DIE ERDE VON UNSEREN KINDERN NUR GEBORGT.

GRÜNE PARTEI

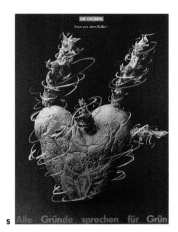

5 Alle Gründe sprechen für Grün

bei dieser Wahl:

Beuys: Der Unbesiegbare

die GRÜNEN

4

GRÜN! ROT!

6

UMWELTSCHUTZ

WIR KÄMPFEN UM JEDEN MILLIMETER

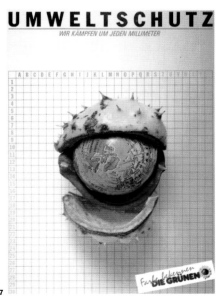

7

1 Sticker from the British Green Party, showing the sunflower emblem adapted from the West German symbol, mid-1980s.

2 Anti-nuclear power sticker, early 1980s.

3 'We have only borrowed the Earth', the first major poster produced by Die Grünen, West Germany 1979.

4 'By this election: the Green Party', poster issued by Die Grünen that reproduces a work entitled 'The Invincible' by the artist Joseph Beuys, West Germany 1979.

5 'Come out into the open', poster for Die Grünen by Gunter Rambow, West Germany 1983. The bottom line reads: 'All of nature supports the Greens'.

6 'Green! Red!', poster by Manfred Butzmann for Grüne Liga (Green League), an East German environmental pressure group, 1990.

7 'Protecting the Environment: we fight for every millimetre', poster and postcard issued by Die Grünen, designed by Holger Matthies 1990.

GREENPEACE

Greenpeace: international environmental action

The international environmental pressure group Greenpeace began their protest activities in 1971. Although they staged important campaigns against nuclear testing and other issues throughout the 1970s, it was in the early 1980s that they moved into the international spotlight. Their dramatic direct actions, when flashed across television screens in news reports, caught the public imagination. Greenpeace became the champions of the natural world, and by the mid-1980s had become a household name.

Since its founding, the organization has grown worldwide, with offices in over 20 countries. Non-violent direct action is employed to pressurize governments and industries, and the organization's list of accomplishments includes stopping the French testing of nuclear weapons in the Pacific, halting radioactive waste dumping in the Atlantic and bringing an end to legalized commercial whaling. They have also suffered along the way: in 1985 their sea-going vessel, the *Rainbow Warrior* (on a mission to evacuate victims of the French nuclear testing programme) was bombed by the French Secret Service as it lay moored in Auckland harbour, causing the death of the Greenpeace photographer on board.

The main administrative office, Greenpeace International, acts as an umbrella to national offices – but there is no international logo or corporate image, except for the authority of the name itself. (The logo shown here, for example, is well known in Europe, but not necessarily in America.) The UK national office has a history of producing hard-hitting, openly controversial print campaigns: they initially commissioned Yellowhammer in 1983 as their first full-service ad agency, an association which led to the '40 dumb animals' poster on page 221. From that point onwards, the use of advertising as a means of provocation was one of their hallmarks. By the late 1980s they were pushing media tolerances to the limit, and ad agencies and designers were clamouring to be associated with them.

FORD GIVES YOU MORE.

A <u>Ford</u> in Britain pumps out 100% more toxic fumes than a <u>Ford</u> back home in America.

6

GREENPEACE

MICHIGAN
F·U·GB
HAVE A NICE DAY!

A <u>Ford</u> in Britain pumps out 100% more toxic fumes than a <u>Ford</u> back home in America.

GREENPEACE

5

1 The Greenpeace logo used in Europe; one of a number of versions used around the world.
2 A pipe-blocking action at Portman, Spain (the pipe was dumping solid industrial waste into the Mediterranean), 1986.
3 In the Mediterranean near Gibraltar: a Greenpeace inflatable intercepts a British carrier loaded with nuclear spent fuel from an Italian reactor and bound for Sellafield reprocessing plant in Britain, 1986.
4 The *Rainbow Warrior* in the Gulf of St Lawrence, Canada, as part of a seal cull action, 1982.
5 & 6 Posters for a Greenpeace print campaign in Britain, highlighting the fact that, at the time, Ford motors did not fit catalytic converters on its British cars (as it did in America).

2

Lynx: the anti-fur campaign

YUCK!
YOUR
DISGUSTING
FUR COAT

LYNX

1

In 1985 Mark Glover formed a splinter group of the environmental organization Greenpeace that was solely devoted to fighting the fur trade. He teamed up with Lynne Kentish and Carol McKenna, and together they formed the main core of Lynx, the national organization campaigning against the fur trade.

Although small in size, the charity made a very big noise with their '40 dumb animals' campaign (originally commissioned by Greenpeace) which involved a billboard poster showing a fashion model dragging a bloody fur coat behind her. It was followed by a cinema ad which simulated a fashion show; models paraded down a catwalk and in the course of twirling round to show off their fur coats, sprayed their audience with blood. (Both were created by London ad agency Yellowhammer at minimal cost, through the *pro bono* work of sympathetic colleagues.) The campaign became one of the classic advertising award-winners of the 1980s and played a role in damaging the industry: fur shops were boycotted, fur sales plummeted and the British public's attitude towards fur-wearing changed significantly.

Other Lynx campaigns followed which were equally hard-hitting, and some much more gruesome, such as the cinema ad named 'Scavengers' which showed a customer pulling a fur coat off a shop mannekin, causing the maggot-infested guts of an animal to spill out onto the floor. Lynx campaigns were continually controversial, and their boldness earned them strong reaction

3

from the fur industry. It all eventually led to a torrent of litigation and Lynx was forced into liquidation.

The ground-breaking effects of their campaigns were substantial: Lynx pioneered a new form of aggressive charity and pushed public tolerances to the limit. Their message was driven home by extensive merchandising, with badges and t-shirts bearing hard-hitting slogans. Their symbiotic working relationship with Yellowhammer started a fast-growing trend that saw ad agencies teaming up with charities, and using charitable issues as a showcase for their creative talents (producing many admirable campaigns as a result). The public communication of social issues was thus changed forever, and the issues acquired a sense of urgency as never before.

It takes up to 40 dumb animals to make a fur coat.

But only one to wear it.

If you don't want millions of animals tortured and killed in leg-hold traps, don't buy a fur coat.

LYNX
Fighting the fur trade
Visit the Lynx Shop at 79 Long Acre, London WC2.
PO Box 509. Dunmow. Essex. Tel: 0371 2016.

1 & 2 Badge and t-shirt from Lynx merchandising, known for its hard-hitting messages.
3 Cinema ad by Yellowhammer, 1985.
4 History-making billboard and poster for Lynx anti-fur campaign by Yellowhammer (art direction by Jeremy Pemberton; photograph by David Bailey). It was originally commissioned by Greenpeace in 1985.
5 Poster for Lynx by John Silver and Kevin Thomas of TBWA ad agency, 1988.

ACID RAIN

It falls on everyone.

1 'Acid Rain', poster by Takayuki Itoh (art director) and Chikako Ogawa (designer), Japan 1989.
2 Billboard constructed of litmus paper which turned from blue to red in a rain shower, conceived and constructed by Roger Akerman and John Lewis of McCann-Erickson ad agency in London for environmental charity Friends of the Earth, Britain 1989-90. The sequence was filmed to make a cinema ad.
3 'Save San Francisco Bay', poster by Doug Akagi and Kimberly Powell of Akagi Design, USA 1992.
4 A sci-fi vision: postcard and t-shirt inspired by an oil spill off the Alaskan coast, designed by Vern Culp of Alaska Visual, USA 1989. Most stores in Alaska refused to carry the t-shirts for fear of offending the oil companies who were financing the clean-up.

A survival strategy for the 1990s

A new mood of public awareness began in the mid-1980s that was a product of many converging forces – among them the global charity efforts of Live Aid, the activities of pressure groups such as Greenpeace and Lynx, the growing threat of AIDS, and the 'great Green boom'. Added pressure came from disasters such as the nuclear accidents of Three Mile Island in 1979 and Chernobyl in 1986, the Exxon Valdez oil spill in 1989, and reports on the greenhouse effect. By the late 1980s, environmental issues had become an urgent matter of survival.

This shift in attitude dramatically changed the way that creative artists viewed and handled environmental issues. No longer considered 'soft subjects', environmental issues became part of the cutting edge. Old graphic clichés – drawings of cute, cuddly animals and exotic photographics of majestic wildlife – did not completely lose their attraction, but the range of environmental comments, and the visual methods used to convey them, expanded enormously. The following pages include a number of unusual and pioneering statements, such as a litmus paper billboard; a style and graphics essay by Judy Blame inspired by a major oil disaster; and the cartoon characters Captain Eco and Captain Planet, both aiming to educate new generations of environmentally-friendly children (and their parents).

Cover and inside spreads from *i-D* magazine, showing fashion stylist Judy Blame's controversial 'pollution style' essay, inspired by an Alaskan oil disaster (1989) and using human models to symbolize oil-slicked birds. Informative statements about pollution appear throughout the sequence, woven into the murky background; Britain 1990. By the end of the 1980s *i-D* had incorporated the growing trend towards youth politics, and in the 1990s was pioneering the concept of fashion and style as an expression of personal identity and political awareness.

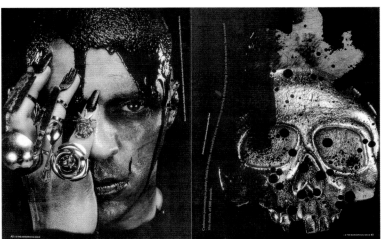

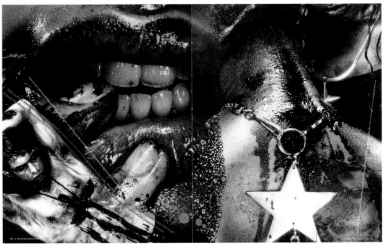

1 'Antarctica', a screenprinted poster on environmental issues related to Antarctica by Carol Porter of Red Planet arts workshop, Australia 1992.
2 Two posters from the Endangered Species series, started in 1975 and still continuing, by The Graphic Workshop in Boston, USA: 'Endangered Cuban Crocodile' (artist: Judy Kensley McKie, 1985) and 'The Kangaroo' (artist: Felice Regan, c.1989).
3 'Life and Death', an ecology awareness symbol designed by Svetlana Amoskina, Odessa 1989-90.
4 Ad campaign for the Whale and Dolphin Conservation Society by James Spence and Julie Crawford of Yellowhammer ad agency, Britain 1988.

1

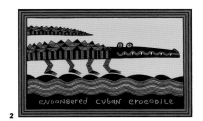

2

3

What the Japanese mean by preserving whales.

4

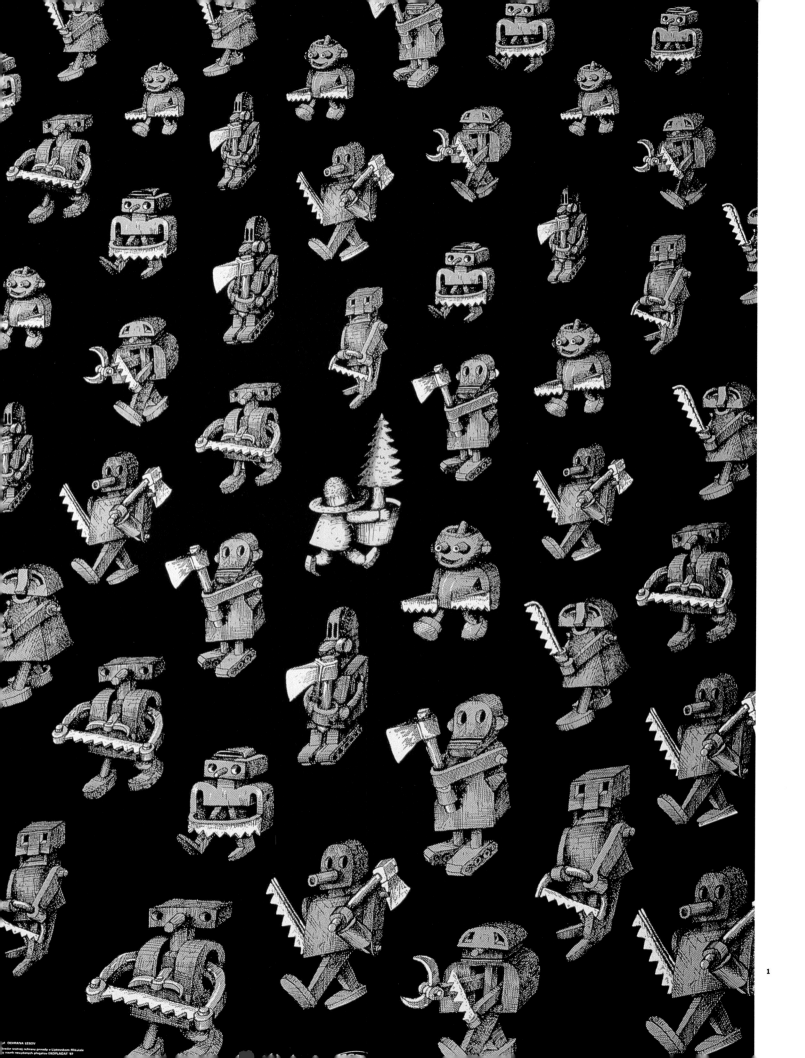

2

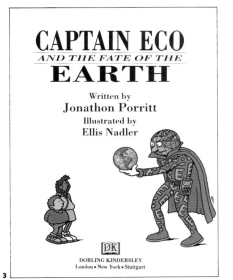

3

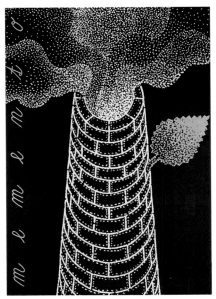

4

1 Poster for the protection of forests by Václav Houf, Czechoslovakia 1987.
2 Captain Planet from *Captain Planet and the Planeteers*, the world's first animated environmental action-adventure TV series which made its debut in 1990. It was syndicated in over 80 countries and became the number one children's show in the USA. Created by Turner Broadcasting System and DIC Enterprises.
3 Title-page and spread from the highly popular *Captain Eco and the Fate of the Earth*, written by Jonathon Porritt and illustrated by Ellis Nadler, Britain 1991.
4 'Memento', anti-pollution poster by Jozef Dóka, Czechoslovakia 1989.

The Green consumer movement

1

The 1980s saw the rise of the Green consumer movement, involving a growing demand for environmentally responsible consumer products, renewed interest in recycling, support for environmental campaigns and a new breed of Green companies with caring images or philosophies.

Most large corporations developed environmental policies to cope with consumer expectations for 'environmentally friendly' goods, and many new companies and products were formed. For example, beauty without cruelty (cosmetics not tested on animals) became a big issue, as part of the general move towards 'natural' products. In the graphics world, attempts were made to minimize unnecessary packaging, encourage recycling and refill systems and explore the possibilities of recycled paper. Graphic designers in particular occupied a position of influence on clients and consumers, and consequently were targeted by paper manufacturers, or took upon themselves the role of catalyst for change.

The 'greening' of the design world has yielded many innovative projects. Shown on pages 232-3 is ad agency Chiat Day's adventurous concept of 'recycled advertising' for Ecover, a Green detergent manufacturer. Faced with the problem of how to get across the environmental message without creating more pollution in doing so, they devised a massive 'street art project' and asked 52 artists to create collaged billboard posters,

2

made from cutting and tearing up redundant advertising posters; the billboards were then displayed all over London. It was followed by a TV campaign which used old black-and-white commercials from the 1950s, dubbed with new voices and colour packs, thereby delivering an environmental message while making fun of the absurdities of the genre of soap advertising.

Some companies have taken on the heavier mission of environmental education, as well as marketing environmentally responsible products. The most famous UK representative of this is the Body Shop, the international Green company founded in 1976 and managed by Anita Roddick. Now trading in 41 countries, their products for skin and hair are naturally based and no animal testing is allowed. The company operates strict recycling and refilling practices, runs community projects all over the world and interestingly has a policy of no advertising. In addition it has run over 20 issue-led campaigns over the years, from Stop the Burning (of Brazilian Rainforests) to Human Rights for Amnesty International.

5

1 Poster for the Body Shop's Reuse Refill Recycle campaign to reduce post-consumer waste, design by Richard Browning, 1990.
2 Poster for the Body Shop campaign to stop the burning of the Brazilian rainforest, design by John Crossland, 1989.
3 Informative comic book explaining the

Body Shop's 'Trade Not Aid' relationship with the people of the Brazilian rainforest, and suggesting possible ways of ensuring their survival.
4 Annual report for the Body Shop (and the first annual report in Britain to be produced on recycled paper) designed by Neville Brody, Ian Swift and Liz Gibbons, 1988.

5 Still from promotional video to launch Ark, an environmental charity which markets its own range of ecologically responsible consumer products as well as educating on Green issues. The video features comedienne Dawn French as a scolding Mother Earth; created by Reg Boorer and Kevin Godley, Britain 1988.

1

2

3

4

1 Stills from two TV ads from Green detergent manufacturer Ecover's 'recycled advertising' campaign. Created by the ad agency Chiat Day, Britain 1992.
2-8 Collaged billboard posters from Ecover's 'recycled advertising' street art project, organized by Chiat Day, London 1991. The collages were created by cutting and tearing up redundant advertising posters.
2 Nick Gonzalez
3 Kendrick/Bickel
4 The team at Ecover
5 Kathryn Jackson
6 Rachel Withers
7 Sarah Kelly
8 Robert Stevens

2

Environmental issues and international connections

1

The Earth Summit in Rio de Janeiro (Brazil, May 1992) disappointed many in terms of concrete action and the adoption of hard-core policies. But the significance of a meeting of world leaders to discuss environmental issues was beyond dispute. The problem of reconciling economic development with environmental preservation had finally entered the arena of international politics.

Internationalism and global solidarity on environmental issues has become a new and exciting theme for designers, and two examples shown here hint at the potential for global working methods and collaborations. The first is the poster 'The Earth is our Mother', created by Chaz Maviyane-Davies,

the only African representative to the World-wide Visual Celebration for the United Nations Conference in Rio which ran parallel to the Earth Summit. In addition to the poster's symbolic importance as a representative of Africa within that cluster of international artistic statements, it also embodies internationalism in its very creation. It was conceived in Zimbabwe; images were mixed on a graphic paintbox computer in England; they then went back to Zimbabwe for completion of design; and finally the poster travelled to Rio for printing and exhibition. The project brings to fruition the idea of the 'global design studio', a concept which looks set to become increasingly important in the future.

Also displayed at the Rio conference were posters created by Swiss designer Cornel Windlin for the 'Visualize the Future' exhibition/event staged by the Parco company in Japan later that year. In an attempt to raise ecological consciousness in Japan, Parco offered an open invitation to artists and designers around the world to send their environmental messages (in artwork or slogans) by fax or on computer disk for display in the exhibition. The event provided a prime opportunity for designers to explore the global potential for social and political comment through information and computer technologies, as well as allowing them to link into a network of concerned creative people.

3

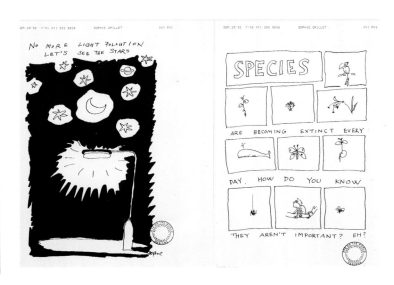

1 Logos and emblems
designed by Cornel
Windlin for the
'Visualize the Future'
exhibition held in Parco
department store,
Tokyo 1992.
2 & 3 Graphics faxed
to the exhibition.

(Top) Trevor Jackson;
(bottom left) Ian
Wright; (bottom centre)
Terry Jones; (bottom
right) Sophie Grillet,
Eye on the World
Designs.
4 Promotional posters
by Cornel Windlin.

5 Inside and outside
views of the exhibition.
6 'The Earth is our
Mother', poster by
Chaz Maviyane-Davies
of Zimbabwe, for
the United Nations
Conference in
Rio, 1992.

Selected bibliography and further reading

Atelier Populaire. *Mai 68: Posters from the Revolution, Paris, May 1968*, London 1969. Texts and posters by Atelier Populaire.

Barnicoat, John. *Posters: A Concise History*, London 1972.

Bertsch, Georg C. et al. *SED: Schones Einheits-Design – Stunning Eastern Design*, Cologne 1990.

Blinderman, Barry et al. *Keith Haring: Future Primeval*, New York 1990. Exhibition catalogue.

Brand, Stewart (ed.). *The Last Whole Earth Catalog*, New York and London 1971.

Briggs, Raymond. *The Tin-Pot Foreign General and the Old Iron Woman*, London 1984.

Coe, Sue and Metz, Holly. *How to Commit Suicide in South Africa*, New York 1983. Illustrations by Sue Coe, text by Holly Metz.

Conal, Robbie. *Art Attack: The Midnight Politics of a Guerrilla Artist*, New York 1992.

Cooper, Martha and Chalfant, Henry. *Subway Art*, London 1984.

Cries of Freedom: Women in Detention in South Africa, London 1988. Originally published as *A woman's place is in the struggle, not behind bars* by DPSC/Descom (Detainees' Parents Support Committee and the Detainees Support Committees), Johannesburg, February 1988. Within weeks of publication, the DPSC and the book itself were banned.

Dormer, Peter et al. *The Illustrated Dictionary of Twentieth Century Designers*, London 1991.

Dyrenforth, James and Kester, Mark. *Adolf in Blunderland: A Political Parody of Lewis Carroll's Famous Story*, London 1939. Illustrated by Norman Mansbridge.

Elkington, John and Hailes, Julia. *The Green Consumer Guide*, London 1988.

Elliott, David (ed.). *Alexander Rodchenko*, Oxford 1979. With essays by Alexander Lavrentiev (grandson of A. Rodchenko) et al.

English Caricature: 1620 to the Present, London 1984. Exhibition catalogue.

Estren, Mark James. *A History of Underground Comics*, Berkeley, California 1986 (revised edition 1989).

Evans, David and Gohl, Sylvia. *Photomontage: A Political Weapon*, London 1986.

Feaver, William. *Masters of Caricature: from Hogarth and Gillray to Scarfe and Levine*, London 1981.

Friedman, Mildred et al. *Graphic Design in America: A Visual Language History*, Minneapolis and New York 1989. Exhibition catalogue.

Garrigan, John et al. *Images of an Era: The American Poster 1945-75*, Washington DC 1975. Exhibition catalogue.

Griffiths, Philip Jones. *Vietnam Inc.*, New York 1971.

Graphic Communication through Isotype, Reading 1975 (revised edition 1981). Exhibition catalogue. Introduction by Michael Twyman.

Grapus. *Grapus 85: various different attempts*, Utrecht 1985.

Great Propaganda Posters: Paper Bullets, Axis and Allied Countries WWII, New York and London 1977.

Harper, Paula. *War, Revolution & Peace: Propaganda Posters from the Hoover Institution Archives 1914-1945*, Stanford 1969. Exhibition catalogue.

Harsch, Ernest et al. *Art from the Frontline: Contemporary Art from Southern Africa*, London 1990.

Heller, Steven (ed.). *Man Bites Man: Two Decades of Satiric Art*, London 1981. Drawings and cartoons by 22 comic and satiric artists, 1960 to 1980.

Hendrik Nicolaas Werkman 1882-1945: A selection of 'druksels', prints and general printed matter, Amsterdam 1977. Exhibition catalogue.

Henrion, FHK. *AGI Annals*, Zürich 1989.

Henrion, FHK. *Top Graphic Design*, Zürich 1983.

Holborn, Mark. *Beyond Japan: A Photo Theatre*, London 1991.

Holzer, Jenny. *Jenny Holzer: Signs*, London 1988 (revised edition).

Home, Stewart. *The Assault on Culture: Utopian Currents from Lettrisme to Class War*, Stirling 1991.

Hughes, Robert. *The Shock of the New: Art and the Century of Change*, London 1991 (revised edition).

Jacobs, Karrie and Heller, Steven. *Angry Graphics: Protest Posters of the Reagan/Bush Era*, Salt Lake City 1992.

Jungwirth, Nicholas and Kromschröder, Gerhard. *Die Pubertät der Republik: Die 50er Jahre der Deutschen*, Frankfurt 1978.

Kerry, John and Vietnam Veterans Against the War. *The New Soldier*, New York 1971.

Kruger, Barbara. *Love for Sale: The Words and Pictures of Barbara Kruger*, New York 1990. Text by Kate Linker.

Kunzle, David. *Posters of Protest: The Posters of Political Satire in the US, 1966-1970*, Santa Barbara 1971.

Litvinov, Victor. *The Posters of Glasnost and Perestroika*, London 1989. Introductory articles by Alexander Yegorov and Victor Litvinov.

Lucie-Smith, Edward. *Cultural Calendar of the 20th Century*, Oxford 1979.

Marnham, Patrick. *The Private Eye Story: The First 21 Years*, London 1982.

McDermott, Catherine. *Street Style: British Design in the 80s*, London 1987.

McGinniss, Joe. *The Selling of the President 1968*, London 1969.

McQuiston, Liz and Kitts, Barry. *Graphic Design Source Book*, London 1987.

Millon, Henry A. and Nochlin, Linda (eds.). *Art and Architecture in the Service of Politics*, Cambridge, Mass. 1978. Article: 'Votes for Women: A Graphic Episode in the Battle of the Sexes' by Paula Hays Harper, pp.150-161.

Minick, Scott and Ping, Jiao. *Chinese Graphic Design in the Twentieth Century*, New York 1990.

Muir, John. *How to Keep Your Volkswagen Alive: A Manual of Step by Step Procedures for the Compleat Idiot*, Santa Fe, New Mexico 1969 (revised edition 1989). Illustrations by Peter Aschwanden.

Nader, Ralph. *Unsafe at Any Speed: The Designed-in Dangers of the American Automobile*, New York 1965 (revised edition 1973).

Nicholls, C. S. (ed.). *Power: A Political History of the Twentieth Century*, New York 1990.

Owusu, Kwesi (ed.). *Storms of the Heart: An Anthology of Black Arts and Culture*, London 1988.

Papanek, Victor. *Design for the Real World: Making to Measure*, London 1972.

Philippe, Robert. *Political Graphics: Art as a Weapon*, Oxford 1982.

Pirsig, Robert M. *Zen and the Art of Motorcycle Maintenance*, London 1974.

Porritt, Jonathon and Nadler, Ellis. *Captain Eco and the Fate of the Earth*, London 1991.

Posener, Jill. *Louder Than Words*, London 1986.

Posener, Jill. *Spray It Loud*, London 1982.

Poster Book Collective of the South African History Archive. *Images of Defiance: South African Resistance Posters of the 1980s*, Johannesburg 1991.

Reid, Jamie. *Celtic Survivor: More Incomplete Works of Jamie Reid*, London 1989.

Reid, Jamie. *Up They Rise: The Incomplete Works of Jamie Reid*, London 1987. Text by Jamie Reid and Jon Savage.

Rose, Cynthia. *Design After Dark: The Story of Dancefloor Style*, London 1991.

Rowe, Marsha (ed.). *'Spare Rib' Reader: 100 Issues of Women's Liberation*, Harmondsworth 1982.

Rowland, Kurt. *A History of the Modern Movement: Art Architecture Design*, New York 1973.

Selz, Peter et al. *Photomontages of the Nazi Period: John Heartfield*, London 1977.

Shocks to the System: Social and political issues in recent British art from the Arts Council Collection, London 1991. Exhibition catalogue.

Sparke, Penny et al. *Design Source Book*, London 1986.

Stermer, Dugald. *The Art of Revolution: 96 Posters from Cuba*, London 1970. Introductory essay by Susan Sontag.

Sylvestrová, Marta and Bartelt, Dana. *Art as Activist: Revolutionary Posters from Central and Eastern Europe*, London 1992.

Toop, David. *The Rap Attack: African jive to New York hip hop*, London 1984.

Thompson, Philip and Davenport, Peter. *The Dictionary of Visual Language*, London 1980.

Waldenburg, Hermann. *The Berlin Wall Book*, London 1990.

Wallis, Brian (ed.). *Hans Haacke: Unfinished Business*, New York and Cambridge, Mass. 1986. Exhibition catalogue. Essays by Rosalyn Deutsche et al.

Weill, Alain. *The Poster: A Worldwide Survey and History*, London 1985.

Wenborn, Neil et al. *The 20th Century: A Chronicle in Pictures*, New York 1989.

Wombell, Paul (ed.). *PhotoVideo: Photography in the Age of the Computer*, London 1991.

Wye, Deborah. *Committed to Print: Social and Political Themes in Recent American Printed Art*, New York 1988. Exhibition catalogue.

Yanker, Gary. *Prop Art*, New York 1972.

Fetal life is ... an ... throughout our live... begin to prepare **...ce of the conditions set out below** ...etus can demonstrate a remarkably robust res... ...enge... ...itely sensitive phase of development. It is now well recognized that ... al Association. fetal environment can influence and even undermine our state of h...h well into adult... . This exciting new publication provides a valuable insight into fetal growth and development of all the main body systems, and examines the influence of the materno-fetal environment on adult-onset diseases. Additional chapters on the embryo, the placenta and parturition make this a fully self-contained introduction to life before birth. Written by world-renowned experts from leading centres of excellence, this account will be an invaluable introductory text for students of medicine, reproductive biology and human biology. It will also serve as an excellent introduction to fetal medicine for trainees in materno-fetal and reproductive medicine and obstetrics and gynaecology.

Fetal growth and development

Edited by

Richard Harding

Monash University, Victoria, Australia

and

Alan D. Bocking

University of Western Ontario, Canada

CAMBRIDGE
UNIVERSITY PRESS

PUBLISHED BY THE PRESS SYNDICATE OF THE UNIVERSITY OF CAMBRIDGE
The Pitt Building, Trumpington Street, Cambridge, United Kingdom

CAMBRIDGE UNIVERSITY PRESS
The Edinburgh Building, Cambridge CB2 2RU, UK
40 West 20th Street, New York, NY 10011–4211, USA
10 Stamford Road, Oakleigh, VIC 3166, Australia
Ruiz de Alarcón 13, 28014 Madrid, Spain
Dock House, The Waterfront, Cape Town 8001, South Africa

http://www.cambridge.org

First published 2001

Printed in the United Kingdom at the University Press, Cambridge

Typeface Minion 11/14pt   *System* QuarkXPress™   [SE]

A catalogue record for this book is available from the British Library

ISBN 0 521 64237 X hardback
ISBN 0 521 64543 3 paperback

Contents

Contributors

Alan D. Bocking
Department of Obstetrics and Gynaecology
and Physiology,
The University of Western Ontario,
London, Ontario N6A 4V2,
Canada

Robert A. Brace
Department of Reproductive Medicine,
University of California (San Diego),
San Diego, California 92093,
USA

A. Nigel Brooks
Astra Zeneca,
Cancer and Infection Bioscience,
Alderley Park, Macclesfield,
Cheshire SK10 4TG, UK

John R. G. Challis
Department of Physiology,
University of Toronto,
Toronto, Ontario M5S 1A8,
Canada

James C. Cross
Department of Biochemistry and
Molecular Biology,
University of Calgary,
Health Sciences Centre,
Calgary, Alberta T2N 4N1,
Canada

Abigail L. Fowden
Department of Physiology,
University of Cambridge,
Cambridge, UK

Mark Hanson
Centre for Fetal Origins of Adult Diseases,
Princess Ann Hospital,
Southampton SO16 5YA,
England, UK

Richard Harding
Department of Physiology,
Monash University,
Clayton, Victoria 3800,
Australia

Stuart B. Hooper
Department of Physiology,
Monash University,
Clayton, Victoria 3800,
Australia

Torvid Kiserud
Unit of Fetal Medicine,
Department of Obstetrics and Gynecology,
Bergen University Hospital,
POB 1, N-5021 Bergen,
Norway

Stephen J. Lye
Department of Obstetrics and Gynaecology
and Physiology,
University of Toronto,
Samuel Lunenfeld Research Institute,
Toronto, Ontario M5G 1X5,
Canada

Sandra Rees
Department of Anatomy and Cell Biology,
University of Melbourne,
Parkville, Victoria 3010,
Australia

Janet Rossant
Samuel Lunenfeld Research Institute,
Mount Sinai Hospital,
Toronto, Ontario M5G 1X5,
Canada

Danny W. Rurak
British Columbia Research Institute for
Children's and Women's Health,
Vancouver, British Columbia V5Z 4H4,
Canada

Jeffrey Trahair
Department of Anatomy and Histology,
University of Adelaide,
Adelaide, South Australia 5005,
Australia

David Walker
Department of Physiology,
Monash University,
Clayton, Victoria 3800,
Australia

Charles E. Wood
Department of Physiology,
University of Florida,
Gainesville, Florida 32610,
USA

Preface

The purpose of this book is to provide a concise account of the major factors involved in the regulation of fetal growth and development and to review the processes by which the fetus responds and adapts to a potentially stressful intrauterine environment. This topic is of considerable relevance to human health as numerous epidemiological studies indicate that impairments in early growth and development can have a significant bearing on an individual's later predisposition to serious adult-onset diseases such as hypertension, diabetes, emphysema and schizophrenia. Although the focus of this book is the growth and functional development of the human fetus, the majority of information relating to this topic has been obtained from animal experimentation. As a subject, the fetus is difficult to study as it is physically inaccessible to the researcher and the reductionist approach, employing isolated material, is often not rewarding. However, the use of chronically implanted sensing and sampling devices in animals and the increasing sophistication of ultrasound techniques used in studies of pregnant human subjects have provided an increasing amount of new information on physiological processes underlying fetal growth and the functional maturation of the fetus and placenta under normal and adverse intrauterine conditions.

A key concern in preparing this book was to ensure that current concepts relating to the growth and development of the fetus were explained succinctly yet clearly. We were also concerned that it should deal with important issues related to fetal development such as the formation of the embryo and the function of the placenta. From the start it was considered that the format most likely to benefit readers was a systems approach. In choosing body systems for inclusion in the book, we have been influenced by the degree to which they are important to the well-being of the fetus, the extent to which they enable the fetus to withstand adverse intrauterine conditions, and its ability to make the transition from intrauterine to extrauterine life. These include the cardiovascular, respiratory, endocrine, digestive, neural, muscular and reproductive systems. As the fetus grows and develops in an aqueous environment, it is important to understand the factors regulating fluid balance within the fetal-placental-maternal unit. In addition to the fetal genome, growth depends upon both adequate nutrition and metabolic activity of the fetus and placenta. A major clinical problem in perinatology which interrupts fetal growth and development, and which has far-reaching implications for later health, is preterm labour; hence a review of the control of parturition is included. Another important factor which has a potent influence on the developing fetus is the cluster of maternal adaptations that take place in response to pregnancy. If they occur as expected, these adaptations ensure that the fetus is adequately nourished and oxygenated, but if they are incomplete, fetal growth and later health will likely be compromised.

Our hope is that this book will be of interest to undergraduate and graduate students in the biomedical sciences, clinical trainees and healthcare professionals. This book is, therefore, dedicated to our past, present and future students. Finally we wish to express our thanks to our colleagues for their excellent contributions, and to our families for their forbearance during the book's gestation period.

Richard Harding
Alan D. Bocking

Development of the embryo

James C. Cross and Janet Rossant

Embryonic development is a remarkable process that requires carefully regulated cell proliferation, the formation of distinct cell lineages that adopt unique cell functions, and finally the concerted interaction between cell types to produce complex tissues. In eutherian mammals these events take place within the uterus of the mother after the conceptus implants. This feature demands that the conceptus orchestrates additional events, beyond its own development, related to controlling maternal physiological functions, growth of the uterus and provision of a supply of nutrients and oxygen through the formation of the placenta; these processes are amongst the earliest events to occur during embryogenesis. They are critical early steps during development and can be viewed as 'checkpoints' that must be achieved for the embryo to survive (Fig. 1.1).

This chapter will discuss the details of the cellular and molecular basis of early mammalian embryonic development. Information on these processes has largely been learned through research on rodents, the reason for which is that all developmental stages are readily accessible and therefore the detailed timing of developmental events is well known. In addition, whole embryos or tissue explants can be cultured to analyse the role of intercellular interactions and, finally, the critical functions of individual genes and molecular pathways can be probed using genetically engineered (transgenic and 'knockout') mice. Therefore, much of the following discussion will concern embryonic development in rodents unless otherwise stated.

Preimplantation development

After fertilization the zygote undergoes a series of symmetrical cell divisions creating a mass of cells called the morula. The first differentiation event during development occurs after compaction of the morula (approximately day 3.5 in the mouse) with formation of the blastocyst (Fig. 1.2). Cells that lie on the outside of the morula differentiate to become trophectoderm, leaving

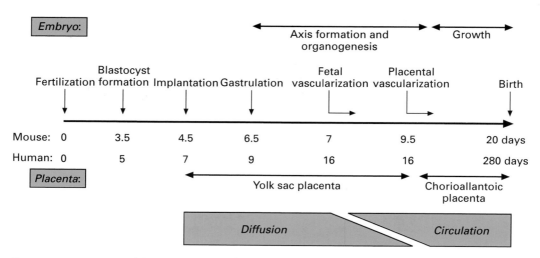

Fig. 1.1. Sequence of the major developmental events that occur during murine and human embryogenesis.

undifferentiated cells of the inner cell mass (ICM) surrounded by trophecto-derm. Blastocyst formation occurs in vivo after the embryo has passed from the oviduct into the uterus but there is no evidence that the maternal environment is required for blastocyst formation since embryos produced by in vitro fertil-ization can easily be cultured to the blastocyst stage.

During the morula to blastocyst transition, the Na^+/K^+-adenosine triphos-phatase (ATPase) becomes redistributed to the basolateral plasma membrane of the mural trophectoderm. By virtue of this relocalization this enzyme estab-lishes a Na^+ gradient that drives the accumulation of fluid in the blastocoel (cavitation). Trophoblast cells that overlie the ICM (polar trophectoderm) con-tinue to proliferate whereas cells away from the ICM that surround the blasto-coel (mural trophectoderm) stop dividing. This is the first example during development of how cell–cell interactions regulate development.

The mitogenic signal emitted from the ICM is probably a member of the fibroblast growth factor (FGF) family of growth factors (FGF4), since muta-tions in the *Fgf4* gene as well as the FGF receptor 2 gene (*Fgfr2*) in mice result in early defects in trophoblast development. In addition, FGF4 can maintain murine trophoblast cell proliferation in vitro. A major unanswered question of early development is how a cell's position in the morula stage embryo ulti-mately results in changes in gene expression that result in trophectoderm differentiation.

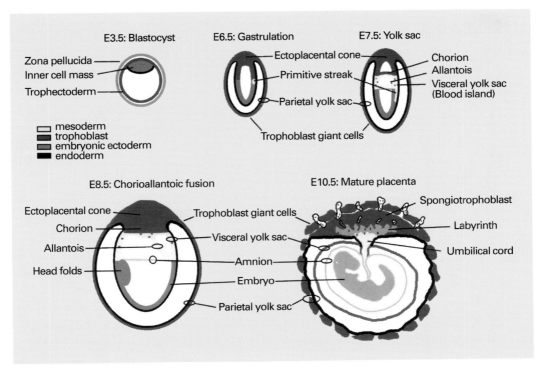

Fig. 1.2. Diagram of the major transitions in structure during murine embryonic and placental development (different stages are not drawn to scale). E, embryonic day.

Implantation

Preimplantation development to the blastocyst stage proceeds similarly in different mammalian species. However, considerable differences occur thereafter. In rodents and primates, implantation occurs soon after the blastocyst hatches from the zona pellucida. In contrast, blastocysts of domestic animals remain free within the uterus for several days (pigs, sheep, cattle) or weeks (horse) before implantation. The implantation process involves an initial attachment phase in which the trophoblast epithelium adheres to the uterine epithelium, and then is followed by considerable changes in the uterine stroma. For example, in rodents, within a few hours of attachment, several remarkable events occur, including transformation of the uterine stroma (the decidual response), recruitment of inflammatory and endothelial cells, transepithelial invasion of trophoblast cells into the endometrium, and apoptosis of the uterine epithelium. Whereas the preimplantation conceptus can develop without maternal cues, implantation involves an active interchange between the mother and blastocyst. The process demands exquisite synchrony in development of the uterus and blastocyst, a fact that may account for the high rate of embryo transfer failure in humans and animals.

Development of the uterus during the preimplantation period is primarily controlled by ovarian steroid hormones, oestrogen (periovulatory surge) and progesterone (luteal phase), which prime the uterus for implantation. In rodents, a secondary surge of oestrogen is the trigger that induces implantation and the secretion of growth factors from the endometrium, including members of the epidermal growth factor (EGF) family and leukaemia inhibitory factor (LIF). The primary target of these growth factors is unknown, but is unlikely to be the blastocyst as mouse embryos that lack either EGF or LIF receptors are still able to implant. LIF-deficient female mice, while viable, are infertile as implantation does not occur, regardless of the genotype of the blastocyst. LIF may therefore be required for inducing the decidual response.

At implantation, the previously nonadhesive apical surface of the trophectoderm becomes adhesive. The molecules that are critical for binding of trophoblast cells to the uterine epithelium are not well defined, although a number of candidate receptor systems have been implicated including selectin/carbohydrate and integrin/extracellular matrix (ECM) interactions. Integrins are critical for trophoblast–ECM interactions, at least in culture. The preimplantation mouse blastocyst expresses a number of integrins and ECM ligands but, so far, only integrins recognized by an antiserum against $\alpha V \beta 3$ integrin have been detected on the apical surface of the trophoblast cells. A novel cell–cell adhesion molecule called trophinin has also been implicated in blastocyst attachment. Trophinin is a homophilic adhesion receptor that is expressed on both the trophectoderm and uterine epithelium in mice around the peri-implantation period.

The decidual response that occurs in rodents and primates shares some features with the acute inflammatory response, including increased permeability of uterine blood vessels, influx of inflammatory cells to the implantation site and local production of several proinflammatory cytokines. In addition, angiogenesis in the uterus is induced rapidly, an event that is probably promoted by factors produced by trophoblast giant cells after implantation, including vascular endothelial growth factor (VEGF) and the placental-specific angiogenic factor proliferin.

Maternal recognition of pregnancy

The term 'maternal recognition of pregnancy' was originally used to describe how the ovarian cycle is extended during pregnancy such that the uterotrophic hormone progesterone continues to be produced by the ovary beyond the length of the normal nonpregnant oestrous cycle. How this process occurs varies between species, although in all cases the conceptus, and specifically placental cells, produce hormones that initiate the process. In humans and other primates, a luteotrophic hormone (human chorionic gonadotrophin, hCG) is secreted by trophoblast cells into the maternal circulation during the first few days after implantation. Rodents do not produce a chorionic gonadotrophin, but instead prolactin and prolactin-related hormones have luteotrophic effects. Copulation induces prolactin surges from the mother's pituitary gland that result in a 'pseudopregnant' state that lasts about 10 days, or about half the length of gestation (versus a 4 day nonpregnant or nonmated cycle). By mid-gestation the placenta secretes placental-specific, prolactin-related hormones (e.g. placental lactogen-I, -II) that further stimulate progesterone production from the ovaries until the end of gestation.

Placental formation and early nutrition of the embryo

The yolk sac placenta

The second cell type to differentiate at the blastocyst stage of development is the primitive endoderm, which develops as a monolayer of cells on the blastocoelic surface of the ICM (Fig. 1.2). This layer of cells, like the trophoblast, is concerned solely with formation of extraembryonic membranes and does not contribute to the later development of the fetus itself. It consists of parietal endoderm cells, which move away from the ICM to line the blastocoelic cavity, and the visceral endoderm cells, which cover the developing epiblast of the embryo itself. The parietal endoderm and the overlying trophoblast giant cells form the parietal yolk sac (Fig. 1.2), which is the first layer of interchange with the maternal environment. However, the parietal yolk sac is not vascularized and so only allows exchange of materials by diffusion. The visceral yolk sac develops after around 7.5 days of gestation and consists of an outer layer of visceral endoderm and an inner layer of mesoderm, derived from the embryo itself. In the mesoderm layer are the blood islands that mark the site of the first embryonic hematopoeisis and vasculogenesis. The establishment of the yolk sac circulation, linking the yolk sac and the embryo, at around 8 days of development, means that the yolk sac can act as a means of transferring nutrients and gases from the maternal environment to the embryo. In the rodent, the yolk sac comes to surround the entire embryo and is a major extraembryonic membrane of the conceptus. The yolk sac persists late into pregnancy, even after the establishment of the chorioallantoic placenta, but in other mammals, the importance of the yolk sac as an exchange organ varies considerably. In humans and ruminants the yolk sac does not surround the embryo, lasts only for a few weeks and is largely vestigial through much of gestation, although it is also the site of first embryonic hematopoeisis.

Although both trophoblast and primitive endoderm are specialized for roles as extraembryonic structures interacting with the maternal environment, it should not be concluded that they play no direct role in the development of the fetus itself. The establishment of the basic body plan requires intercellular signalling from multiple tissue sources, as will be discussed below. It has become increasingly clear that both trophoblast and visceral endoderm provide some of the critical signals that are required for patterning of the early postimplantation embryo.

The chorioallantoic placenta

The mature placental structure (chorioallantoic placenta) is formed largely from two cell lineages that have distinct embryological origins: trophoblast and mesoderm. The epithelial component of the placenta is derived from the trophoblast lineage. The ICM of the blastocyst gives rise to the three germ layers of the embryo proper as well as to the mesodermal cells that later make up the stromal and vascular components of the placenta. Trophoblast cell derivatives interacting with the underlying stroma develop into the vascular exchange unit of the placenta, a structure whose gross anatomy varies widely between species. For example, in humans the surface of the placenta elaborates into a villous tree which 'floats' in a large blood-filled space, whereas in rodents a labyrinth is formed consisting of a series of small maternal blood channels.

In humans, the blastocyst implants into the uterus 7–8 days after conception. Soon after implantation the trophectoderm layer gives rise to distinct differentiated cell types: a multinucleated syncytial layer (syncytiotrophoblast) that covers the conceptus, and an underlying villous cytotrophoblast layer which continues to proliferate. The chorionic villi are formed slightly later in development as stromal cells derived from extraembryonic mesoderm invade beneath the villous cytotrophoblast layer. Individual villi therefore have an overlying syncytiotrophoblast layer, underlying cytotrophoblasts and a stromal cell core. Villous cytotrophoblast cells are progenitor cells that differentiate and fuse to form new syncytiotrophoblast as the villi grow. The placental vessels form within the stromal compartment as a result of angiogenesis. In addition, the stromal cells also probably produce signals that control the differentiation of adjacent trophoblast cells. Most of the chorionic villi remain free of the uterine wall (floating villi) and function in nutrient and gas exchange. Other villi attach to the decidua (anchoring villi). At the tip of these anchoring villi, cytotrophoblast cells differentiate and migrate out of the villus, forming columns of cytotrophoblasts that contact endometrium, and eventually invade into the decidua and myometrium (extravillous cytotrophoblasts). They eventually enter maternal arterioles and arteries through both endovascular and perivascular migrations. At these sites they replace the smooth muscle walls of the arteries thereby producing low-resistance blood flow to the implantation site.

In rodents, there are several trophoblast cell subtypes and structures in the mature placenta: an outermost layer of trophoblast giant cells, an intermediate layer called the spongiotrophoblast and the innermost labyrinthine layer (Fig. 1.2). The labyrinthine layer functions like the chorionic villous tree in humans. It starts forming at day 9 of mouse gestation, following the attachment of the allantois (mesoderm) to the trophoblast-derived chorion. The bulk of the tissue consists of two layers of trophoblast syncytia that separate the maternal blood space from the fetal stroma/blood vessels. Trophoblast giant cells lie at the periphery of the placenta, analogous to the extravillous cytotrophoblast cells in humans, and differentiate from precursor cells in the spongiotrophoblast layer. Giant cells get their name from the fact that they are very large, polyploid cells that form as a result of endoreduplication. These cells remain mononuclear but continue to undergo episodes of DNA replication in the absence of intervening mitoses. By contrast, syncytiotrophoblast cells, which are also polyploid, are multinucleated cells.

Molecular control of mature placental development

Abnormalities in placental development can compromise the growth of the fetus (intrauterine growth restriction: IUGR) or, if severe, even result in fetal death. It is thought that this could occur by one of two developmental mechanisms. First, defective trophoblast invasion may result in reduced maternal blood flow to the implantation site. Second, restricted development of the chorioallantoic placenta (e.g. the chorionic villous tree in humans, the labyrinth in mice) would limit the ability of the placenta to take up and deliver nutrients and oxygen to the fetus. Considerable progress has been made in identifying molecular pathways critical to these developmental events.

Regulation of trophoblast invasion

The ability of cytotrophoblast cells to invade depends upon the appropriate expression of both surface cell adhesion molecules (e.g. integrins) as well as proteases that degrade the extracellular matrix (e.g. plasminogen activator and matrix metalloproteinases). Cytotrophoblast cells can differentiate into invasive cells in vitro, under relatively simple conditions, indicating that this progression is regulated autonomously. Several transcription factors have been implicated in the regulation of trophoblast growth and differentiation in mice. Hand1 and Mash2 are of particular interest because they regulate, positively and negatively respectively, the formation of trophoblast giant cells in mice, the cell type most analogous to the invasive extravillous cytotrophoblast cells in humans. Their roles in human placentation have not yet been elucidated.

In addition to their initial differentiation, the invasiveness of cytotrophoblast cells is influenced also by growth factors and cytokines produced either by cytotrophoblast cells themselves, having an autocrine action, or by fetal stromal and maternal decidual cells. Potentially anti-invasive factors that are expressed in the placental bed include transforming growth factor (TGF-β). Tissue oxygen levels may also have a significant effect on placental development. Early in the first trimester of human pregnancy, blood flow velocity in the intervillous space is normally low and direct measurements have shown that the oxygen levels in the placenta are much lower than in the endometrium until about 12–13 weeks. This suggests that the normal environment for early first trimester trophoblast development is low in oxygen. Culture of first trimester villous explants in 2.5% O_2, compared with 20% O_2, results in better maintenance of syncytiotrophoblast viability, and isolated cytotrophoblast cells continue to proliferate only in low oxygen levels.

Development of the chorioallantoic placenta

Even after the trophoblast cell lineage has been segregated at the blastocyst stage in early development, it continues to interact with the ICM and its derivatives throughout development. By midgestation in mice, the proliferating trophoblast cell population is in contact with mesodermal cells, an interaction critical for subsequent development. Mouse embryos that lack either the cell adhesion molecule α4 integrin, or its ligand VCAM-1, die at midgestation due to a failure in attachment of the allantois to the chorion (chorioallantoic fusion), demonstrating roles for these cell adhesion molecules in this interaction. Chorioallantoic fusion can occur in a fraction of VCAM-1 mutant embryos, but they still die at midgestation, showing defective formation of the labyrinthine layer. This implies that functions other than cell adhesion are mediated by VCAM-1/α4 integrin to direct trophoblast proliferation and morphogenesis of the labyrinthine layer. There are several candidate growth factors produced by mesodermal derivatives of the placenta that could regulate trophoblast growth and differentiation. EGF and several EGF-related factors are expressed during pregnancy and are thought to affect trophoblast development based on the phenotype of EGF-receptor (EGFR) mutant mice. On certain mouse genetic backgrounds, EGFR-deficient conceptuses show a loss in spongiotrophoblast cells by midgestation. Mutations in the genes encoding the growth factor SF/HGF and its receptor c-Met are associated with poorly developed spongiotrophoblast and labyrinthine layers. SF/HGF is produced by the allantois and probably maintains trophoblast growth. Wnt2 is another signalling molecule expressed by the allantois, and *Wnt2* mouse mutants show abnormal placental structure.

Mesodermal cells within the allantois undergo the process of vasculogenesis, in which blood vessels and blood cells form *de novo*. Although this occurs in a cell compartment that is separate from the yolk sac where fetal blood cell formation begins, it seems likely that similar molecular mechanisms control both. VEGF and its receptors Flt-1 and Flk-1 are critical for blood vessel formation throughout the conceptus, and are all expressed in the placenta of mice and humans, supporting the idea that they may play a role in fetoplacental blood vessel formation. Other factors appear to control the outgrowth, branching and survival of established blood vessels during embryonic development, as suggested by mutations in genes encoding angiopoietin-1 and its receptor Tie-2. While there may be conservation of mechanisms controlling blood vessel formation in the embryo and placenta, there is some evidence that development of the placental vasculature may depend on unique genes as well. Mutations in the *Arnt* and *Vhl* genes result in embryonic mortality due to placental defects. Interestingly, while blood vessel formation in the placenta is compromised in both of these mutants, it appears to be normal in the yolk sac and embryo itself.

Establishment of the embryonic body plan

The development of the embryonic body plan begins with the events of gastrulation (embryonic day 6.5 in mice), in which the definitive germ layers, ectoderm, mesoderm and endoderm are formed. The first morphological sign of asymmetry in the embryonic ectoderm (epiblast) occurs with the formation of the primitive streak at one point around the circumference of the apparently radially symmetrical embryo (Fig. 1.2). At the primitive streak, the embryonic ectoderm undergoes an epithelial to mesenchymal transition and the newly formed mesenchymal cells migrate away from the streak to form the mesoderm layer between the ectoderm and the visceral endoderm. The site of primitive streak formation marks the future posterior end of the embryo and so establishes not only new cell layers but also the primary body axis of the embryo.

The mechanism involved in establishing the site of primitive streak formation is not clear. There appears to be some influence of the maternal environment as the site of streak formation is always perpendicular to the long axis of the uterus. However, it can be in either orientation in this plane, suggesting that there may be stochastic events in the embryo leading to primitive streak formation which can be influenced by the uterine environment. This differs from the situation in other vertebrate embryos, such as amphibians, in which there is evidence for initial asymmetries in the egg, based on maternally inherited components, leading to later axis development. In mammals it has generally been thought that the events that pattern the postimplantation embryo are established zygotically around the time of implantation and are independent of events occurring during preimplantation development. This conclusion is based on the resistance of the preimplantation embryo to many kinds of cellular manipulations, including adding, subtracting or rearranging cells.

However, it has recently been shown that the site of second polar body formation in the fertilized egg marks the future boundary between the ICM and the trophectoderm. Since other studies have predicted that asymmetries in the blastocyst may relate to future streak formation, this raises the possibility that there may indeed be an early egg asymmetry that relates to future axis development. Future experiments will resolve this issue and indicate where to search for the molecules involved in initiating mammalian gastrulation.

As the mesoderm develops it acquires different fates depending on what region of the primitive streak produces it. The most anterior tip of the primitive streak gives rise to a specialized structure called the node, which produces the midline notochord (Fig. 1.3). The definitive endoderm also arises from the

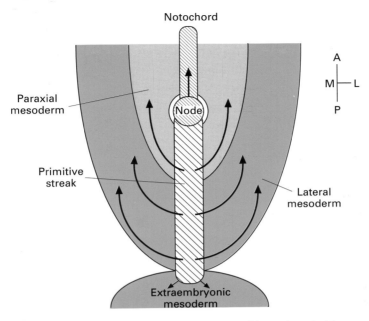

Notochord

A

M—L

P

Paraxial mesoderm

Node

Primitive streak

Lateral mesoderm

Extraembryonic mesoderm

Fig. 1.3.   Fate map of the mesoderm populations derived from the primitive streak.

anterior region of the streak. Slightly more posterior, the mesoderm produces the paraxial mesoderm of the somites. The lateral plate mesoderm, which produces structures such as the urogenital system, arises from a more posterior position. The most posterior part of the streak, closest to the boundary with the extraembryonic regions, gives rise to the cells of the extraembryonic mesoderm, which migrate out to form the yolk sac blood islands and, slightly later, the allantois. Studies in many different vertebrate species have implicated multiple growth factor signalling pathways in establishing and patterning the developing mesoderm of the streak. There is evidence for involvement of Wnts, FGFs and multiple members of the TGF-β/BMP (bone morphogenic protein) gene family. Mutational analysis in the mouse has supported the importance of these families.

For example, mutations in both FGF8 and the receptor, FGFR1, cause major disruptions in formation of the developing mesoderm. The TGF-β-related gene, *nodal*, is essential for an organized primitive streak, and mutations in putative receptors and downstream signalling molecules of the TGF pathway also lead to gastrulation defects. The complex interactions of these pathways during mesoderm development are still being defined.

Once the mesoderm layer is formed, the ectoderm at the anterior end of the embryo starts to develop into the neural plate. As the neural plate forms it rapidly acquires anterior–posterior (A–P) positional information that leads to the later patterning of the nervous system. This information is evident in the carefully regulated boundaries of expression of a number of important genes involved in A–P patterning, including *Hox* genes and other transcription factors involved in more anterior patterning of the brain. The induction and patterning of the nervous system is brought about by interactions between the overlying ectoderm and the underlying mesendoderm tissues. In particular, the node has been proposed to be a critical source of signals for inducing and patterning the body axis. This stems from experiments in frogs which showed that the dorsal lip of the blastopore, the frog equivalent of the node, could induce a whole new body axis when transplanted ectopically. Similar experiments in the mouse, while not so dramatic, also showed that the node could induce new axial structures. However, mutation of the transcription factor HNF3β in mice causes loss of the node and its derivatives, but still allows formation of the neural plate, and some degree of normal A-P patterning. This suggests that the node is not the only source of signals for early neural patterning. Recently attention has focused on a region of the anterior visceral endoderm (the AVE) as a potential separate source of signals particularly for patterning of the head region. In addition, some signalling molecules, such as FGFs and retinoic acid, which may be important for more posterior patterning, are produced from regions around the node and are not depleted in HNF3β mutants. Thus interactions between the AVE, the node and streak-derived tissues, are probably required for full patterning of the A-P axis of the embryo (Fig. 1.4).

Although the node may not be as critical for A-P patterning as once thought, it does play a critical role in embryonic patterning by virtue of giving rise to the notochord. The notochord is critical for dorsal–ventral patterning of the developing nervous system and the somites. Ablation of the notochord prevents production of the floor plate and ventral patterning of the neural tube, while addition of a second notochord induces ectopic floorplate (Fig. 1.5). The main signalling molecule responsible for these effects of the notochord is sonic hedgehog (Shh), a secreted molecule related to a critical embryonic signalling molecule in *Drosophila*. Shh plays many critical roles in mammalian development but its earliest role is in midline patterning. Mutations in the human *Shh* gene have been detected in some forms of familial holoprosencephaly, a syndrome in which there is fusion of midline structures as a result of failure of midline patterning.

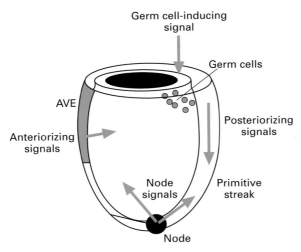

Fig. 1.4. Interacting signalling sources involved in early embryonic patterning. AVE, anterior visceral endoderm.

The node appears also to be critical for establishing the last major axis of the embryo, namely the left–right axis. Mammals show reproducible left–right asymmetry of a number of internal organs, including the heart, lungs, liver and gut. Several mutations in both mouse and man affect the directionality of asymmetry, leading to situs inversus. The first morphological sign of left–right asymmetry is the directionality of heart looping at around 9 days of development. However, asymmetric expression of a number of genes, including *nodal* and *lefty*, which encode TGF-β-related signalling molecules, and downstream transcription factors such as Pitx2, is seen in the lateral plate mesoderm earlier in development. It has been proposed that the initiating event for establishing left–right asymmetry must reside in some process with built-in chirality. Recent evidence that the node has motile cilia on its surface that beat in a polarized manner has suggested that directional flow of fluid around the node may be the trigger for all later events, perhaps by setting up a gradient of growth factors across the node and lateral plate. Mutations that affect the node or its cilia all produce situs defects.

After formation of the placenta, the heart is the first critical organ to develop in the fetus. The heart develops from two distinct cell lineages during early mammalian embryogenesis. Most of the heart develops from anterior mesodermal cells whose initial migrations and cell differentiation steps may be under the control of the overlying primitive endoderm. The layers of the heart wall

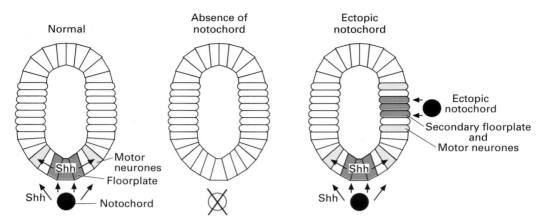

Fig. 1.5. Induction of the floorplate and ventral motor neurones in the neural tube by notochord-derived signals.

(endocardium, myocardium and epicardium) and the valves all develop from the mesodermal progenitors. Initially the cardiogenic region exists as twinned tubes that converge at the midline into a single linear heart tube that begins contracting as early as day 8 in murine and day 21 in human embryos. Besides mesoderm, neural crest cells also contribute to heart, specifically to the outflow tracts of the aorta and pulmonary arteries. After the linear heart tube stage, it undergoes a left-to-right looping event that establishes the positions of the four heart chambers and the outflow tracts, and in doing so establishes the natural asymmetry to the heart structure. Signalling molecules, such as Shh, Nodal and Lefty, which establish left–right asymmetry in the embryo, also have an effect on the direction of heart looping. However, these factors are not involved in the process of looping *per se*, as alterations in their expression affect only the direction of looping. As such, these factors are implicated in establishing left–right asymmetry along the body axis but other downstream factors, thus far unknown, must control the looping process. The cellular events that underlie the mechanics of heart looping morphogenesis are poorly understood although asymmetrical rates of cell division, changes in cell shape and/or cell migration have been suggested.

Another critical event during mesoderm development is the formation of the somites, which develop as segmental units of mesoderm, in a progressive rostral to caudal manner, on either side of the midline. Later in development the somites give rise to the individual vertebrae of the spinal column, the musculature and the dermis of the fetus. Only the spinal column retains clear evidence of its segmented origin, but it is clear that the initial segmentation of the somites is essential for later development of all somite derivatives. Several mutations that disrupt the orderly process of segmentation exist and all are lethal. Interestingly, a number of mutations that disrupt somite development are in genes of the Notch signalling pathway, implicating this pathway as critical for the correct allocation of cells into the segmental units. The later patterning of the somites into dorsal dermatome, intermediate myotome and ventral scleratome is largely controlled by the Shh pathway, the same pathway used for dorsal–ventral patterning of the developing nervous system.

Clearly much of the early patterning of the body plan of the mammal depends on complex intercellular signalling pathways, the identity of which are now beginning to be determined. There is one cell lineage, however, which in most animals seems to be set aside very early in development and depends on segregation of cellular determinants rather than later cell–cell interactions. That lineage is the germ cell lineage, which gives rise to the gametes, the eggs and sperm. In several invertebrate species, there is a special cytoplasmic region in the egg, called the germ plasm, which is segregated to a subset of cells in the early embryo. These cells are thereby committed to the germ cell fate. However, in mammals there has never been any convincing cytological evidence for germ plasm, and chimera studies show that single cells from the ICM can give rise to both germ cells and somatic cells, arguing against early segregation of the germ cell lineage. Indeed, cell lineage marking in the early postimplantation embryo has shown that the germ cell lineage is not set aside until around 7 days of development, as a small group of cells in the embryonic ectoderm close to the extraembryonic junction. Transplant studies have shown that more distal epiblast cells can also form germ cells when placed adjacent to the extraembryonic region, implicating local signalling in germ cell determination. Recently it has been proposed that BMP4 produced by the extraembryonic ectoderm is a necessary signal for germ line development (Fig. 1.4), another example of the importance of the extraembryonic lineages for the development of the embryo itself.

Common developmental defects of the embryo

Developmental abnormalities that arise during the embryonic period can manifest themselves much later during gestation or even during postnatal life, particularly if the defects are relatively minor. Cardiac defects are common in newborns, and estimated to be present in 1 of every 100 liveborn babies. These probably represent the less severe developmental defects, but can be traced back to defects in very early embryonic development. Anomalies of mesodermal and myocardial origin include looping defects, heterotaxy, and left and right side-specific myocardial hypoplasias. Cardiac neural crest defects affect outflow tract development.

Also, and importantly, many tissues and organs such as the brain, lung, gut and kidneys are not essential for intrauterine life. Therefore, for example, while neural tube defects are common among fetuses, they do not necessarily compromise fetal survival. By contrast, survival through the embryonic period is dependent on function of the placenta, the yolk sac and fetal liver (sites of hematopoeisis), and the cardiovascular system. The phenotypic spectrum of single gene mutations in mice generated by gene knockouts indicates that the vast majority of embryonic lethal phenotypes can be accounted for by defects in one of these systems. Formation of these structures therefore truly represents a series of 'checkpoints' for embryonic and early fetal development. Although the incidence of first trimester embryonic loss is very high in humans, spontaneous abortion material is often very poorly described from a developmental perspective. However, it is very likely that embryonic mortality in humans can be accounted for by molecular mechanisms similar to those defined in mice.

FURTHER READING

Cross, J.C., Werb, Z. and Fisher, S.J. (1994). Implantation and the placenta: key pieces of the development puzzle. *Science*, **266**, 1508–18.

Kaufman, M.H. (1992). *The Atlas of Mouse Development*. New York: Academic Press.

Beddington, R.S. and Robertson, E.J. (1999). Axis development and early asymmetry in mammals. *Cell*, **96**, 195–209.

Hogan, B., Beddington, R., Costantini, F. and Lacy, E. (1994). *Manipulating the Mouse Embryo. A Laboratory Manual*, 2nd edn. Cold Spring Harbor, NY: Cold Spring Harbor Laboratory Press.

Kingdom, J.C.P. and Kaufmann, P. (1997). Oxygen and placental villous development: origins of fetal hypoxia. *Placenta*, **18**, 613–21.

Rinkenberger, J.L., Cross, J.C. and Werb, Z. (1997). Molecular genetics of implantation in the mouse. *Dev. Genet.*, **21**, 6–20.

Development and function of the placenta

Danny W. Rurak

Amongst mammalian organs the placenta must be considered unique for a number of reasons, the most striking of which is perhaps its composition of cells from two genetically distinct organisms, the mother and fetus, and these cells live in apparent harmony for the whole of gestation. Other unique features of the placenta have been succinctly outlined by G.S. Dawes :

> The placenta combines in one organ many of the functional activities which are separate in the adult. It is a partial barrier to the transfer of cells from the mother to foetus or vice versa, and hence provides an immunological fence; it acts as the foetal lung; it assists in the preferential transfer of amino acids to the foetus but limits the transfer of large molecules; it provides the substrates for foetal metabolism and disposes of waste products; it is a site of hormone production; it grows rapidly in early gestation, adapts to the increasing metabolic requirements of the foetus, becomes separated at birth and is expelled harmlessly, despite its extreme vascularity. Not only is it marvellously designed for its biological functions, but the strange species variations in design have long attracted the interest of the biologist and the artist.

In this chapter, fundamental aspects of the development, structure and function of the placenta are reviewed. For more detailed information see the reading list at the end of the chapter.

Anatomy and development of the placenta

The placenta exhibits in different species a wide diversity of structure that includes macroscopic differences in shape and the pattern of distribution over the inner lining of the uterus, as well as variations in cellular organization (Fig. 2.1). Placentae can be classified into four major types that relate to the degree to which the placenta is localized into a single discrete organ. In diffuse placentae, as in the horse, pig, camel and whale, the placenta is distributed over most of the entire inner surface of the uterus. With cotyledonary placentae, as found in sheep, goats and other ruminants, there is restriction of the placental tissue

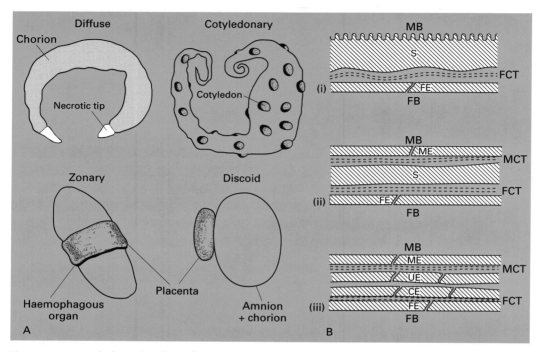

Fig. 2.1. Morphological and histological variations in placental structure. A. The four main types of placenta based on gross morphology (from M.B. Renfree, in: Reproduction in Mammals:2, Embryonic and Fetal Development, edited by C.R. Austin & R.V. Short, pp. 26–69, Cambridge University Press, 1982). B. Diagrammatic representation of the three main types of placenta classified histologically: (i) haemochorial, (ii) endotheliochorial, (iii) epitheliochorial. MB, maternal blood; FB, fetal blood; S, syncytiotrophoblast; MCT, maternal connective tissue; FCT, fetal connective tissue; ME, maternal endothelium; FE, fetal endothelium; UE, uterine epithelium; CE, chorionic epithelium. (Redrawn from C.P. Sibley & R.D.H. Boyd, in: *Fetal and Neonatal Physiology*, vol. I, ed. R.A. Polin and W.W. Fox, pp. 62–74. Philadelphia: Saunders, 1992.)

to specific areas of the endometrium, termed caruncles. Each placental element is termed a cotyledon, the number of which varies from about 4 to 100 in different species. In zonary placentae, found in dogs, cats and related species, there is further concentration of the placenta to an equatorial band; incomplete zonary placentae, in which the equatorial band is not complete, are found in bears and mink-like animals. The most localized placenta is the discoid type in which there is a single plate, as found in humans and other primates, in rodents, rabbits and guinea-pigs. A double-discoid placenta is found normally in some primate species and as an abnormality in humans.

Based upon cellular structure, there are three main types of placenta (Fig. 2.1B). These differ in the number of cell layers separating maternal and fetal blood, and this in turn is related to the extent to which the trophoblast layer of the conceptus invades and erodes maternal uterine tissue. In epitheliochorial placentae no uterine cell layers are destroyed. Thus there are six layers that separate maternal from fetal blood and the uterine epithelium is in contact with the trophoblast layer of the conceptus. Such placentae are found in ruminants, pigs and horses. The endotheliochorial placenta, found primarily in carnivores, lacks the uterine epithelium, which is destroyed during placentation; thus on both sides of the placenta the capillary endothelium is in contact with the trophoblast. The haemochorial placenta, as found in primates and rodents, exhibits the greatest extent of uterine tissue destruction, with the uterine epithelium, underlying basement membrane and maternal endothelium all being lost. Maternal blood in the placenta is thus in direct contact with the trophoblast. Intuitively one might think that the number of layers separating maternal and fetal blood would affect placental permeability, so that the haemochorial placenta would be most permeable and the epitheliochorial placenta least. However, it is now clear that for many substances, other factors are more important in determining the degree of placental transfer.

Given the great diversity in placental structure, it is not surprising that there is also diversity in the formation and development of the placenta. As it is not possible to cover this issue in depth for all placental types, placentation in two species will be outlined: the human and the sheep. The human placenta is discoid and haemochorial, while that in the sheep is cotyledonary and epitheliochorial. The human placenta is of critical importance to human reproduction, and it is now clear that abnormalities in its development can have adverse consequences on fetal development and may affect health in later life. The sheep placenta is important as it has provided much of our knowledge on the mechanisms of placental transfer and on the factors which affect maternal and fetal placental perfusion.

Placentation in the human

Implantation in the human occurs 6–7 days following conception at which time the developing embryo has reached the blastocyst stage, comprising an inner cell mass and the trophoblast cells (trophectoderm) forming the blastocyst wall

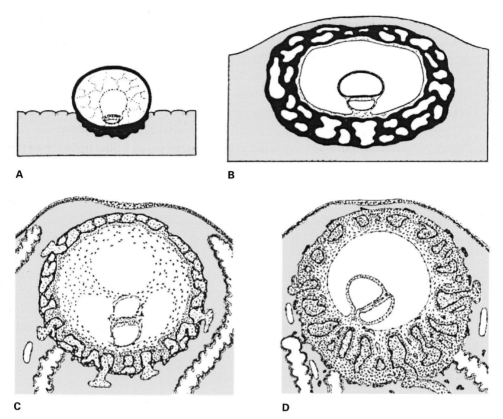

Fig. 2.2.   Diagrammatic representations of early placentation in the human. A. Implantation, B. Expansion of the syncytiotrophoblast (in black) and formation of the lacunar spaces, C. Development of primary chorionic villi, D. Formation of the cytotrophoblast shell. (Redrawn from J.D. Boyd and W.J. Hamilton, *The Human Placenta*. Cambridge: Heffer.)

(Fig. 2.2A). The process involves attachment of the blastocyst to the uterine wall followed by burrowing of the blastocyst into the uterine wall; by 7.5–8 days postconception the blastocyst is already completely or partially embedded in the uterine wall. This form of implantation, which involve the blastocyst invading and destroying maternal uterine tissues, is termed interstitial implantation. In contrast, the superficial type of implantation found in some other species (e.g. sheep) involves the uterine epithelium remaining intact, and the placenta thus forms at the inner surface of uterine wall. Implantation in the human also involves characteristic changes in the histology of the uterine endometrium (stroma), termed the decidual reaction. The changes include loss of the uterine epithelial cells and their replacement with epithelialized stromal cells, termed decidual cells. There is also local oedema in the stroma surrounding the blastocyst, due to increased vascular permeability. Inflammatory cells rapidly migrate to the implantation site and restructuring of the connective tissue matrix, blood vessels and uterine glands occurs.

At the time of the initial attachment of the blastocyst to the uterine epithelium, some of the trophoblast cells at the interface fuse to form a syncytium, the syncytiotrophoblast, and this layer appears to be involved in the initial invasion of the uterine tissues. Soon after implantation there is expansion of the synctyotrophoblast layer and by days 8–9 cavities, termed lacunar spaces, form within the layer (Fig. 2.2B). These will ultimately form the spaces into which the maternal blood supplying the placenta will flow. A few days later (about day 13) columns of cuboidal trophoblast cells (cytotrophoblasts) which underlie the syncytiotrophoblast, begin to grow outwards towards the outer margin of the conceptus (Fig. 2.2C). These are the primary villi and it is the multiple branching from these columns that forms the villous structure of the mature placenta. When the cytotrophoblast columns reach the outer boundary of the syncytial layer, cells at the tip expand laterally to join with cytotrophoblast cells from adjacent columns. This forms the cytotrophoblast shell, a complete layer of cytotrophoblast cells surrounding the conceptus, a process that is complete by about day 20 (Fig. 2.2D). At this point, the basic organization of the placenta is present. There is a chorionic plate of cytotrophoblasts from which the villi arise, a basal plate to which some villi (termed anchoring villi) attach and an intervillous space into which nonattached villus branches (termed floating villi) project and into which maternal blood will soon flow. Syncytiotrophoblast is now largely restricted to the outer layer of the villi, i.e. in direct contact with maternal blood in the intervillous space, and within the villi fetal vascular elements are developing.

There is another important fate for cytotrophoblast cells in the villous columns; they can migrate outward from the conceptus into the uterine tissue as extravillous cytotrophoblast (Fig. 2.3A). This process begins in the first month, with cytotrophoblast cells moving into the decidua, and in a later second wave of migration into the myometrium that ends by about 18 weeks of gestation. Some of these cells appear to undergo differentiation and fusion to form multinuclear giant cells in the decidua and myometrium.

Another important decidual location of extravillous cytotrophoblast is around and within the lumen of the spiral arteries, ultimately extending down the arteries as far as the inner third of the myometrium. These cells, termed endovascular cytotrophoblast, replace the endothelial cells lining the arteries, a

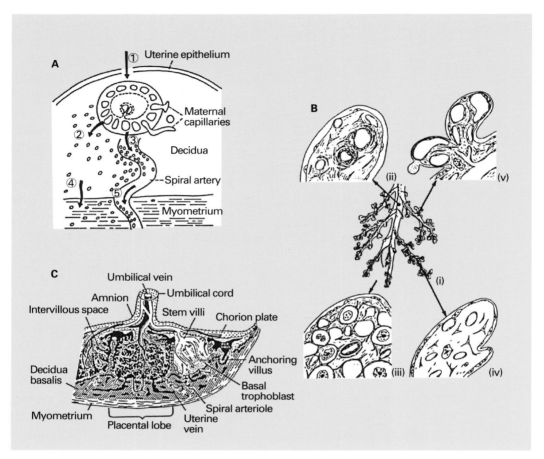

Fig. 2.3. Placentation in the human. A. Diagram illustrating successive steps in invasion in the human. 1. Implantation, 2. Extravillous cytotrophoblast in the decidua, 3. Invasion of the spiral arteries by endovascular cytotrophoblast, 4. Second wave of extravillous cytotrophoblast invasion that extends into the myometrium. (Redrawn from R. Pijnenborg, in: *Trophoblast Invasion and Endometrial Receptivity, Trophoblast Research*, vol. 4, ed. H.-W. Denker and J.D. Aplin, pp. 33–47. New York: Plenum Press, 1990). B. Chorionic villous structure in the human placenta. (i), simplified drawing of a peripheral part of a villous tree. The surrounding cross sections represent stem villus (ii), immature intermediate villus (iii), mature intermediate villus (iv) and terminal villus (v). (Redrawn from P. Kaufmann (1985), *Contrib. Gyncecol. Obstet.*, **13**, 5–17.) C. A section through a mature human placenta. (Redrawn from G.S. Dawes, *Fetal and Neonatal Physiology*. St Louis: Year Book Medical, 1968.)

process involved in the 'physiological changes' in the spiral arteries that occur in early pregnancy. These changes comprise, apart from loss of the endothelial cell layer, destruction of the elastic and muscular components of the vessel wall and their replacement with fibrous tissue. Through these processes, the muscular spiral arteries of the nonpregnant uterus are converted to wide-diameter, flaccid vessels that can accommodate the tremendous increase in maternal placental blood flow that occurs in late pregnancy. Interest in this phenomenon has been stimulated by the evidence that cytotrophoblast invasion of the spiral arteries does not appear to proceed to completion in pregnancies later complicated by preeclampsia, a disorder characterized by endothelial cell dysfunction in the mother, associated with reduced uterine perfusion, maternal hypertension and fetal growth restriction.

The basic organization of the human placenta is present by about day 20 of pregnancy. Development beyond this time largely comprises elaboration of this basic structure as well as growth of the placenta. Initially, when the conceptus remains entirely embedded within the uterine wall, it is completely surrounded by chorionic villi and decidua. With further growth the conceptus first projects into and then fills the lumen of the uterus, and the villi and decidua over the exposed portions degenerate, leaving the definitive, discoid placenta at the maternal–fetal interface.

Three main elements are involved in the elaboration of placental structure: growth and expansion of the cytotrophoblast shell/basal plate into the uterine stroma to tap the spiral arteries, continued branching of the fetal villi, and formation of partial septa arising from the basal plate and projecting into the intervillous space. The branching of the villi that occurs results in increases in both anchoring and floating villi. At term there are 50–60 fetal villi, each with a complex structure. Villous elements are denoted as stem villi, immature and mature intermediate villi and terminal villi, based upon histological appearance (Fig. 2.3B). It is the terminal villi that form the final branches of the villous tree and they comprise approximately 50% of its surface area. They are the most important elements in maternal–fetal exchange. At term, the placenta is 15–20 cm in diameter, 2–3 cm in thickness and weighs 500–600 g (Fig. 2.3C).

Maternal blood supply

Maternal blood is supplied to the uterus via the uterine and ovarian arteries, which anastomose and send 9–14 branches to the lateral margins of the uterus. These vessels divide to form the arcuate arteries, which pass circumferentially to the anterior and posterior uterine walls, there to meet with the arcuate vessels from the other side. From the arcuate system arise radial arteries which pass deeper into the myometrium. Each radial artery then divides to form several spiral arteries, which supply the intervillous space, and basal arteries, which supply the myometrium and decidua. Maternal blood enters the intervillous space in discrete spurts or jets and travels upwards towards the chorionic plate before dispersing laterally. Maternal blood leaves the intervillous space via veins that drain into the uterine veins. Uterine blood flow increases during pregnancy from ~200 to ~700 ml/min, about 12% of maternal cardiac output.

Fetal blood supply

Fetal blood is supplied to the placental villi via the paired umbilical arteries, which contact the chorionic surface of the placental disk, usually at the centre. The arteries then divide to send chorionic arteries over the surface of the placenta, and these in turn give off a branch to each stem villi. These pass down the stem villi into the immature and mature intermediate villi, giving off branches to supply the villous branches. In intermediate villi, the vessels are transformed into arterioles and venules, and in the terminal villi into capillaries with sinus-like dilations. These may serve to reduce blood flow velocity in the terminal villi and promote maternal–fetal exchange. Venous drainage from the villi flows into a single umbilical vein. Umbilical blood flow increases dramatically during pregnancy from ~40 to 450 ml/min, approximately 33% of fetal cardiac output.

Cellular mechanisms in implantation

The use of immunohistochemistry and cell culture has provided important information on the characteristics of trophoblast cells and on the mechanisms involved in implantation and trophoblast differentiation and invasion. Much attention has been focused on the cell surface receptors involved in cell–cell and cell–extracellular matrix (ECM) interactions. Two classes of receptors have received particular attention. One is the integrins, a diverse family of heterodimeric, glycoprotein cell surface receptors composed of α and β subunits; they are involved in both cell–cell and cell–ECM matrix interactions. The other class of receptors is the cadherins, made up of two subfamilies, type 1 and type 2 cadherins, both of which are involved in calcium-dependent, homophilic cell adhesion.

As trophoblast cells differentiate into the various subtypes (i.e. the cyto- and syncytiotrophoblasts in the anchoring and floating villi and the extravillous and endovascular cytotrophoblasts) there appear to be characteristic changes in the expression of the integrins and cadherins. The villous cytotrophoblast cells express E-cadherin, a type 1 cadherin involved in intercellular junctions and cell polarity in epithelial cells, and the α_6 and β_4 integrin subunits, which form receptors for the ECM component, laminin. In contrast, syncytiotrophoblast and extravillous cytotrophoblast cells express cadherin-11, a type 2 cadherin, rather than E-cadherin, and cadherin-11 is also expressed in decidualized endometrium. Moreover in extravillous cytotrophoblast, there is downregulation of the α_6 and β_4 integrin subunits and upregulation of first $\alpha_5\beta_1$ and then $\alpha_1\beta_1$ integrin, which are fibronectin and collagen/laminin receptors, respectively. Endovascular cytotrophoblasts, which invade the maternal spiral arteries, also appear to express cell adhesion molecules characteristic of endothelial cells, including cadherin 5, $\alpha V\beta_3$ integrin and several other receptors.

Another feature of the invasive extravillous and endovascular cytotrophoblast is expression of proteinases that degrade the ECM. The predominant enzymes are zinc-dependent matrix metalloproteinases (MMPs), particularly MMP-9 (92 kDa). Expression of these enzymes peaks in the first trimester and there is downregulation in the second trimester, at the time at which trophoblast invasiveness diminishes.

Implantation and trophoblast invasion in the human thus appear to involve a coordinated change in the expression of ECM receptors, cell adhesion molecules (CAM) and proteinases. These mechanisms control cellular differentiation, migration and aggregation. The use of specific antibodies to integrin subunits and tissue inhibitors of MMPs in cultured trophoblasts has suggested that these changes are of functional importance to trophoblast differentiation and invasiveness, rather than only being a consequence of the processes. Thus antibodies against $\alpha_5\beta_1$ integrin stimulates trophoblast invasion in vitro, whereas antibodies against $\alpha_1\beta_1$ and $\alpha V\beta_3$ integrins and tissue inhibitors of MMPs inhibit invasion.

What is not yet completely understood, however, is the way in which trophoblast differentiation and invasion are regulated. It has been long recognized that progesterone and oestradiol play a critical role in preparing the endometrium for implantation, through the initiation of decidualization of the endometrium. More recently, it has been reported that progesterone increases expression of cadherin-11 in cultured endometrial stromal cells, an effect that is enhanced by cotreatment with oestradiol. As noted above it is this CAM that is expressed in syncytiotrophoblast, extravillous cytotrophoblast and decidualized endometrium during trophoblast invasion. It is also clear that the uterine tissues must play some role in limiting the extent of trophoblast invasion, since invasiveness is enhanced in human ectopic pregnancy and when mice blastocysts are experimentally transplanted into extrauterine tissues.

A number of growth factors and cytokines may be involved in regulating placentation; these include transforming growth factor β-1 (TGF-β), insulin-like growth factor-II (IGF-II), epidermal growth factor (EGF), activin and interleukin-1. IGF-II, activin and EGF stimulate invasion of isolated cytotrophoblasts, as does the cytokine interleukin-1β and the effects of activin can be inhibited by its binding protein, follistatin. In contrast, TGF-β inhibits the invasiveness of first trimester cytotrophoblasts, at least in part by inducing production of tissue inhibitors of MMPs, and promotes fusion of the cells to form syncytiotrophoblast, effects mediated by its high-affinity receptor, endoglin. Thus it seems possible that these agents could regulate the early events of placentation by altering expression of CAMs and ECM components and by coordinating the interplay between the trophoblast and endometrial cells.

The local microenvironment in different regions of the endometrium may also be involved in the control of cytotrophoblast proliferation and differentiation. Thus, culture of cytotrophoblast cells under hypoxic conditions promotes proliferation, but not differentiation, whereas in normoxic cultures, the latter process is favoured. Moreover, there could be differences in endometrial and trophoblast tissue oxygen concentrations during the course of placentation, depending on the extent of vascularization and hence tissue perfusion. However, the precise regulatory framework has not yet been fully elucidated nor have the key regulatory mechanisms that determine the extent of trophoblast invasion, the precise architecture of a normal placenta or its ultimate size.

Placentation in the sheep

The sheep placenta is composed of numerous (about 60–70 in a singleton pregnancy) discrete placental elements, termed placentomes or cotyledons, which are distributed over the inner surface of the uterine wall (Fig. 2.1A). At term, each placentome is 2–4 cm in diameter, but weights of individual cotyledons vary widely, from about 0.5–16 g; the total weight of the placenta is ~350 g. The placentation sites are restricted to specialized aglandular areas of the endometrium, termed caruncles, which are apparent in the nonpregnant uterus. Caruncles do not regrow if surgically removed, and this has been exploited experimentally as a way to reduce the ultimate size of the placenta in a subsequent pregnancy, thereby producing the carunclectomy model of fetal growth restriction. The structure of the sheep placenta is commonly termed epithelio-chorial as there is no gross invasion of the trophoblast into the endometrium and hence no disruption of the uterine epithelium (Fig. 2.1B). However, the cuboidal uterine epithelium becomes modified to a system of syncytial plaques.

Blastocyst formation in the sheep occurs at 6–7 days postconception but implantation is delayed until about day 15. In the intervening period, the blastocyst grows from a sphere of ~1 mm in diameter to an elongated sac ~100 mm long by days 13–14, with the embryonic disc located in the centre of the long axis. By day 15, the blastocyst has filled the uterine lumen and come into contact with the uterine epithelium; in the regions of the caruncles, the trophoblast cells have become closely adherent to the caruncular epithelium. This then represents implantation of the superficial or indeciduate type, which is in marked contrast to the invasive, deciduate type of implantation that occurs in the human.

The first obvious signs of placentome formation occur at about day 28, when the trophoblast epithelium adjacent to the caruncles forms a series of ridge-like projections into the caruncular epithelium, which develops corresponding sulci or crypts into which the trophoblast extends to remain adherent. These trophoblast folds rapidly increase in height to ~0.25 mm and develop villous-like projections along the long axis of the ridge summits (Fig. 2.4A). While this process is occurring, the caruncular cellular epithelium is transformed into syncytial plaques each containing 20–25 nuclei and connected to adjacent plaques by tight junctions. Further maturation of the villi involves an increase in length and further branching to form secondary and tertiary branches. This process occurs up to about day 75 (midgestation). Subsequent maturation involves shrinkage of the mesenchyme that forms the tissue core of the villi, so that they are less bulky. Thus, the villi become delicate, frond-like structures embedded in crypts of maternal uterine tissue (Fig. 2.4B).

Blood supply

Maternal blood supply to the sheep placenta is similar to that in the human, the main difference being that within the sheep placenta maternal blood remains contained within blood vessels, rather than flowing into an intervillous space, as in the human (Fig. 2.4C). The fetal blood supply is via paired umbilical arteries, which divide to send branches to each placentome. There has been considerable controversy over the relative directions of blood flow in the maternal and fetal placental capillaries, which as discussed below, is a factor that affects the

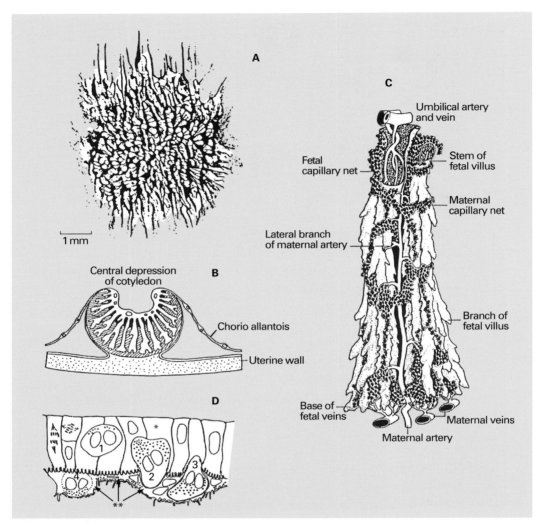

Fig. 2.4.   Placentation in the sheep. A. External surface of a cotyledon at 32 days gestation. At this stage, primary villi are forming from the parallel ridges that developed earlier. (Redrawn from W.A. Wimsatt (1950), *J. Anat.*, **87**, 391–457.) B. Section through a mature cotyledon illustrating the chorionic villi (in white) projecting into the maternal uterine crypts. (Redrawn from D. Steven, in: *Comparative Placentation*, pp. 25–57.) C. Diagram of a chorionic villus at 135 days gestation showing the relationship between maternal and fetal placental vessels. (Redrawn from M. Silver & D. Steven, in: *Comparative Placentation*, ed. D. Steven, pp. 161–88). D. Schematic representation of the migration of binucleate cells (stages 1–4) in the sheep placenta. * denotes trophectoderm, ** indicate the uterine epithelial syncytium. (Redrawn from F.B.P. Wooding (1982), *J. Reprod. Fertil.* (Suppl.), **31**, 31–9.)

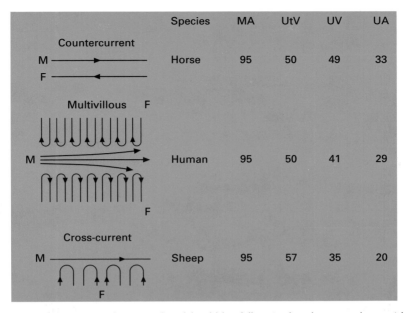

Species	MA	UtV	UV	UA
Horse	95	50	49	33
Human	95	50	41	29
Sheep	95	57	35	20

Fig. 2.5. Three orientations of maternal and fetal blood flow in the placenta, along with representative values of PO_2 (mmHg) in the mother and fetus for species that appear to have that particular orientation. MA, maternal arterial blood; UtV, uterine venous (intervillous space in the human) blood; UV, umbilical venous blood; UA, umbilical arterial blood. (Redrawn from G.S. Dawes, *Foetal and Neonatal Physiology*, Chicago, Year Book Medical Publishers, 1968; PO_2 data from D.W. Rurak, in: *Textbook of Fetal Physiology*, ed. G.D. Thorburn and R. Harding. Oxford: Oxford University Press, 1994.)

efficiency of placental transfer. The currently accepted view is that there is a cross-current arrangement, i.e. maternal and fetal blood flow at right angles to each other (Fig. 2.5).

A unique feature of the placenta of sheep and other ruminants is the presence of characteristic binucleate cells in the trophoblast (Fig. 2.4D). Apart from having two nuclei, these cells contain a large number of electron-dense granules. Throughout ovine pregnancy, these cells comprise 15–20% of the trophoblast population, and seem to have at least two functions. One is the synthesis of ovine placental lactogen, a polypeptide hormone released primarily into the maternal circulation, and progesterone, another major endocrine product of the sheep placenta. The second function is involvement in the transformation of the uterine epithelium into syncytial plaques. This occurs via migration of the binucleate cells from the trophoblast into the uterine epithelium where they fuse with the maternal cells to form the multinucleated plaques. At any given time, 15–20% of the binucleate cells are migrating into the uterine epithelium. While this process has been well described, the cellular and molecular mechanisms that underlie it and other aspects of implantation and placentation in the sheep are largely unknown.

We have then in the human and sheep two very different sorts of placenta in terms of structure, formation and development. Yet these two very different placentae are able to meet the metabolic requirements of the fetus, and in the case of these two species, the fetuses at term are of comparable size. However, the placentae of these and other mammalian species share a number of common features. One is the elaboration of the trophoblast layer that forms the fetal component of the placenta into highly branched villous structures, which continue to branch throughout pregnancy, thereby greatly increasing the surface area available for maternal–fetal exchange. A second feature is the close apposition of maternal and fetal blood in the placenta, which minimizes diffusion distances. Finally, there is the tremendous augmentation of maternal and fetal placental blood flow which, coupled to the increase in villous surface area, allows the placenta to meet the increasing metabolic demands of the growing fetus.

Placental functions

The placenta is a multifunctional organ and most or all of these functions appear to optimize the intrauterine environment for normal embryonic and fetal development, either directly via influences on the fetus or indirectly by modifying maternal physiological functions.

Protection of the fetus from the maternal immune system

As the interface between the fetus and the mother, the trophoblast layer serves an important role in protecting the fetus from the maternal immune system. It is important to recognize that the maternal immune system can and does recognize the fetal semiallograft as foreign tissue in certain clinical conditions and experimental paradigms. Thus in Rh disease in human pregnancy with an Rh+ fetus and an Rh− mother, fetal red cells that leak into the maternal vasculature can trigger maternal antibody production against the fetal cells. These antibodies can then cross the placenta, leading to red cell destruction and severe anaemia in the fetus. Similarly in animals, fetal tissue (not associated with trophoblast) transplanted into maternal tissues is subject to a typical transplantation reaction and rejected. Conversely, fetuses in ectopic pregnancies in humans and transplantation of animal blastocysts (which subsequently implant and form a trophoblast layer) to an extrauterine location in the mother are not subject to attack by the maternal immune system, illustrating the key protective role played by the trophoblast.

Two main mechanisms seem to be involved in this protection. The first is the production of various molecules with immunosuppressive properties. These include progesterone, oestrogens and several cytokines, and in the human, placental lactogen and several pregnancy-associated proteins. The second mechanism involves the major histocompatibility complex (MHC) molecules that are expressed on cell surfaces and which are used by immune cells to distinguish between self and nonself. They are thus intimately involved in transplantation rejection reactions.

Trophoblast cells do not express the classical polymorphic class I and II MHC molecules that are present on other cells, and this would limit the ability of the maternal immune system to recognize the trophoblast as foreign. However, invasive, extravillous trophoblast cells in the first and second trimester produce a nonclassical MHC molecule, HLA-G, which, in contrast to the classical MHC molecules, exhibits a very limited polymorphism. When expressed in other cells, HLA-G inhibits the cell lysis mediated by natural killer (NK) cells, and it is thought that, in the placenta, it could function to inhibit the activities of both maternal NK and T cells in the decidua, i.e. the cells that mediate transplantation rejection reactions. In several other mammalian species, there is the production of similar nonclassical MHC molecules.

The mechanisms involved in the altered expression of MHC molecules by trophoblast cells have not yet been delineated. Thus it appears that the trophoblast is capable of limiting the effectiveness of the maternal immune system in both recognizing and attacking the conceptus. Failure of these mechanisms has been implicated in early pregnancy failure in humans; however, the significance of this cause in relation to other factors remains to be established.

Placental transfer functions

Virtually all maternal–fetal transfer occurs via the placenta, and transfer via other potential routes (e.g. from uterine tissues to amniotic membranes or fluid) is of minimal importance. An exception to this in some species, such as rodents and the guinea-pig, is transfer of immunoglobulin molecules via the yolk sac (choriovitelline) placenta. This yolk sac placenta forms early in embryonic development following the development of an endodermal layer in the blastocyst wall and association of this choriovitelline layer with maternal uterine tissues. In most species, including the human, it regresses early in pregnancy or never completely forms and thus is of little functional importance. However, in the species mentioned above, the yolk sac placenta persists throughout gestation and serves the important function of conferring passive immunity to the fetus prior to birth via transfer of maternal immunoglobins.

The chorioallantoic placenta possesses the same transfer mechanisms found in other epithelial systems. These include passive diffusion, facilitated diffusion, active transfer and receptor-mediated endocytosis. Before discussing the mechanisms in more detail, it is important to note that the placenta is not much of a barrier and most substances present in the maternal or fetal circulations can cross the placenta. With the haemochorial placenta of the human, this even includes fetal red cells, which can be detected in maternal blood in many pregnancies. They presumably get there through leaks in the trophoblast layers of the placenta villi. In a minority of pregnancies, this fetal to maternal blood loss can be severe, resulting in haemorrhagic stress in the fetus.

Diffusion is the most common and quantitatively the most significant transfer mechanism in the placenta. It accounts for the transfer of oxygen, carbon dioxide, fatty acids, steroids, nucleosides, some electrolytes, fat-soluble vitamins, and most therapeutic agents. As in other epithelial systems, placental diffusion permeability varies inversely with molecular weight, degree of polarity and electric charge, and directly with solubility.

For lipophilic substances, transfer can occur via transcellular routes and the placental permeability to these compounds is high. They are termed flow limited (i.e. placental transfer is limited by maternal and fetal placental perfusion), and well-studied examples include oxygen, carbon dioxide and ethanol. With these compounds, there is complete or near complete equilibration between maternal and fetal blood in the placenta.

In contrast, the diffusion of hydrophilic molecules appears restricted to postulated water-filled transmembrane channels, and the placental permeability is lower. These latter compounds are termed diffusion limited (i.e. placental transfer is limited by diffusion, and not greatly affected by changes in maternal or fetal placental blood flows), and there is incomplete equilibration between maternal and fetal blood in the placental exchange area. Examples that have been well studied are urea and mannitol.

For diffusion-limited clearance, there are marked species differences in the degree of placental permeability. Species which possess haemochorial placentae (e.g. rabbit, guinea-pig, human) behave as if they had a placental pore radius of ~30 nm, i.e. they mimic capillary walls. Species with epitheliochorial placenta (e.g. sheep, goat) behave as if they had a placental pore radius of ~0.4 nm, i.e. they mimic the plasma membrane and thus are much less permeable to hydrophilic molecules than is the case in a haemochorial placenta.

Evidence has been obtained recently for a small number of much larger diameter pores (~400 nm) in parallel with the small pore system. These do not contribute to diffusion permeability, but have a physiologically significant filtration coefficient and low electrolyte reflection coefficients and may be important in regulating fetal fluid balance and arterial pressure. Similar pores may occur in other placental types. There are much less data available for endochorial placentae, but results obtained from dogs indicate permeability characteristics intermediate between those of the human and sheep.

For flow-limited clearance, the relative orientations of maternal and fetal blood flow in the placenta affect the efficiency of placental transfer (i.e. the concentration of a given substance in fetal blood leaving the placenta versus the concentration in maternal blood). In the species that have been studied there is evidence for several different arrangements of maternal and fetal vascular channels in the placental exchange areas, namely counter-current, concurrent and cross-current (Fig. 2.5). In the human placenta, there are no maternal vascular channels in the intervillous space. The maternal blood flows through small spaces between the villous branches in which fetal blood flows towards and then away from the villous tips. Such a maternal–fetal flow arrangement is termed multivillous. The counter-current flow arrangement, in which maternal and fetal blood flows in opposite directions, is the most efficient and there is good evidence that this arrangement occurs in the placentae of the horse, guinea-pig and rabbit. The multivillous arrangement is next in efficiency, an arrangement present in placentae of humans and some other primates. There has been considerable controversy over the vascular relationships in the sheep placenta, but the current consensus is that there is a cross-current arrangement, which is less efficient than the counter-current and multivillous arrangements (Fig. 2.5). These differing efficiencies are reflected in species-related differences in the normal values of oxygen partial pressure (PO_2) in umbilical venous blood, in comparison to the values in uterine venous blood. In the horse, PO_2 values are 49 and 50 mm Hg for the fetus and mother, respectively (i.e. nearly equal), while in the human they are 41 and 50 mmHg and in the sheep 35 and 57 mmHg. Thus the counter-current placenta of the horse is associated with the highest umbilical venous PO_2, whereas the cross-current placenta of the sheep has the lowest value. However in all three species, maternal arterial PO_2 is ~95 mmHg, so that fetal vascular PO_2 is much lower.

The relatively low umbilical venous PO_2 appears due to two factors. One is oxygen consumption by the placenta, which has a high metabolic rate probably due to its active transport and synthetic activities (see below). These and other metabolic activities require oxygen and this must come from maternal and/or fetal blood perfusing the placenta, which results in a lowering of fetal vascular PO_2. The other factor that appears to contribute to the low fetal PO_2 is inequalities in maternal and fetal placental blood flows in different regions of the placenta. Thus, if in one region of the placenta fetal blood flow is higher than the maternal flow, the available oxygen in the maternal blood will be depleted before the fetal blood is fully saturated. Conversely, if in another region fetal flow is lower than the rate of maternal perfusion, the fetal blood will be fully saturated before all the available oxygen in the maternal blood has been transferred. Both situations reduce the efficiency of maternal–fetal oxygen transfer and contribute to the low PO_2 in fetal blood.

Fetal oxygenation

The relatively low fetal PO_2 is not associated with correspondingly low values for fetal blood oxygen saturation and content. This is because of a higher haematocrit and haemoglobin concentration in fetal blood compared with maternal blood, which increases the oxygen carrying capacity of fetal blood. In addition, in most species, the oxygen affinity of fetal blood is higher than in the mother, so that over the physiological range of fetal vascular PO_2, fetal oxygen saturation is higher than it is in maternal blood at the same PO_2 (Fig. 2.6). However, the magnitude of the difference between the oxygen affinity of fetal and maternal blood varies considerably in the species that have been studied to date. It is greatest in the sheep, with the difference in the PO_2 values at which fetal and maternal blood is 50% saturated (P_{50} value) being 17 mmHg. In contrast in the human the P_{50} difference is only 4 mmHg and in the cat it is 0. It may be that this mechanism is most important in those species, such as sheep where fetal PO_2 is lowest. Regardless, both of these factors increase total oxygen content of fetal blood, so that the oxygen saturation and content of umbilical venous blood returning from the placenta is not much lower than the values in arterial blood in the adult. However, the only portion

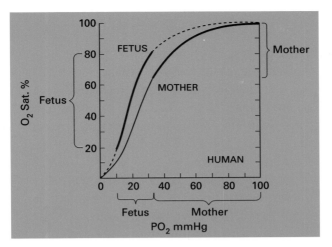

Fig. 2.6.   Oxygen dissociation curve for human maternal and fetal blood. The thick portions of each curve indicate the approximate physiological ranges for PO_2 (mmHg) and O_2 saturation. (Redrawn from M.E. Towell, Fetal Respiratory Physiology, in: *Perinatal Medicine*, ed. J.W. Goodwin and G.W. Chance. Toronto: Longman, 1976.)

of the fetus that is perfused with undiluted, oxygen-rich umbilical venous blood is a part of the fetal liver. Owing to the vascular shunts in the fetal circulation, the arterial blood that perfuses the rest of the fetus is a mixture of umbilical venous and deoxygenated systemic venous blood. As a result, fetal arterial PO_2 and oxygen saturation and content are much lower than can be tolerated in adult terrestrial mammals. This is compensated for by a high fetal cardiac output and systemic blood flows, which are much larger than the resting values in the adult, when normalized for weight. Consequently, the rate of oxygen delivery (i.e. blood flow times oxygen content) to most fetal tissues and organs is actually higher than during postnatal life. Moreover, in spite of the fetus being hypoxaemic relative to the adult, its basal rate of oxygen consumption (per kilogram of body weight) is about 1.7 times that in the adult. This applies in species in which the adult is large, such as the human and sheep. In smaller mammals, such as the guinea-pig, where the weight-normalized metabolic rate in the adult is much higher than in larger species, the rate of fetal oxygen consumption is lower. This is because, in contrast to the situation after birth, fetal oxygen consumption/unit weight appears the same in different species, irrespective of fetal size, and this is another feature that is different from the adult situation.

Gas transfer

For compounds such as oxygen whose placental transfer is flow limited, the major factor that affects the rate of transfer is changes in maternal and/or fetal placental blood flow. Both flows increase progressively during gestation, but there are also frequent changes in flow that are of short duration. One cause of such changes is the small amplitude (nonlabour) uterine contractions that occur throughout pregnancy and which result in transient decreases in uterine and umbilical blood flow. The decreased flow results in transient hypoxaemia in the fetus. Much larger decreases in uterine blood flow are associated with the large amplitude uterine contractions that occur during labour and these result in larger declines in fetal PO_2. However, these are tolerated by the fetus, at least during normal labour and with a healthy fetus. Fetal PO_2 is chronically reduced in pathophysiological situations such as preeclampsia, which as discussed earlier is associated with incomplete trophoblast invasion and reduced maternal placental blood flow.

Carbon dioxide production by fetal tissues occurs at about the same rate as oxygen is consumed, and to maintain fetal carbon dioxide and pH balance, the carbon dioxide must be transferred to the mother at the rate at which it is produced. Carbon dioxide exists in blood as dissolved gas and is also hydrated to carbonic acid via the enzyme carbonic anhydrase. The carbonic acid spontaneously breaks down to form bicarbonate ion and a proton. As carbonic acid levels are very low, dissolved carbon dioxide and especially bicarbonate are the dominant species; there is also carbon dioxide reversibly bound to haemoglobin. Fetal to maternal transfer of carbon dioxide appears to occur mainly in disolved form and, as with oxygen, the placental permeability for carbon dioxide is high. In contrast to the situation with oxygen, there are only small differences between maternal and fetal partial pressure of carbon dioxide (PCO_2) values in placental venous blood, probably because of the higher placental permeability for carbon dioxide. For example, in the human, the difference between the PCO_2 values in the intervillous space and in umbilical venous blood is only ~2 mmHg, compared with the 7 mmHg difference for PO_2. Because of the shunts in the fetal circulation, fetal arterial PCO_2 is much higher than in the mother (42 versus 28 mmHg in the human). However, because maternal PCO_2 in pregnancy is lower than in nonpregnant adults (see Chapter 11), fetal arterial PCO_2 is not much higher and pH not much lower than the normal adult values. As is the case with oxygen, fetal PCO_2 is altered by changes in uterine and/or umbilical blood flow, and it increases when flow decreases.

Glucose and lactate

These are examples of substances transferred across the placenta by facilitated diffusion, that is coupled to a membrane-bound carrier at rates far greater than could be achieved by simple diffusion. Placental glucose transport appears to be independent of fetal or maternal insulin and is also sodium independent. Transport is also stereospecific and can be inhibited competitively by glucose analogues. The specific glucose transporter in the placenta appears to be Glut 1, the same one found in red blood cells. As with other types of facilitated diffusion, the rate and direction of transplacental glucose transfer is dependent upon the maternal–fetal glucose concentration gradient. In the fetal lamb, a doubling of the arterial glucose concentration will result in net placental uptake of glucose from the fetus. As with oxygen, the placenta consumes glucose, and at a high rate. The placenta has a high metabolic rate which is much higher than overall fetal metabolic rate. In sheep in late gestation, placental glucose consumption is equal to about 67% of the rate of uteroplacental glucose uptake from the maternal circulation, although not all of the glucose consumed comes directly from this pool. About 60% of the glucose utilized by the uteroplacenta is converted to lactate and fructose. The lactate is released into both the maternal and fetal circulations, while fructose is delivered only to the fetus. Placental fructose production occurs only in certain species, such as the sheep and pig; it is absent in the human.

Amino acids

Amino acid concentrations in the fetus are higher than in the mother, although the magnitude of the difference differs with the various amino acids. Overall, fetal amino nitrogen concentration is twice the maternal value, and trophoblast concentrations of amino acids are higher still. This suggests the involvement of active transport mechanisms in placental uptake of amino acids from the maternal circulation, but not necessarily from placenta to fetus. Studies of isolated trophoblast membrane vesicles have demonstrated the presence (on the maternal facing membrane) of both sodium-dependent (e.g. system A) and sodium-independent (e.g. systems L and y^+) transporters, as well as transporters found in the blastocyst, but not in mature tissues. Some of these transporters may be under hormonal control (e.g. insulin). Fetal amino acid supply involves more than just placental transfer, as the placenta possesses a variety of enzymes that can metabolize amino acids. In sheep fetal glycine supply is derived from placental production, and amino acid cycles between the placenta and fetal liver have been identified for some amino acids (e.g. glycine–serine, glutamine–glutamate), with net excretion of glutamate into the maternal circulation. Active transport mechanisms also operate in the placental transfer of iron and calcium.

Lipid transport

Lipids are another class of nutrient molecules that are required in large amounts for fetal growth and maturation. However, knowledge of lipid transport and metabolism by the placenta is limited, in part because, in contrast to the situation with glucose and amino acids, there are wide species differences in the extent of placental lipid transport. These seem to correlate with the fat content of the fetus at term, which varies widely (e.g. 2%, 1%, 2%, 4% and 16% in the sheep, pig, mouse, cat and human respectively). Free fatty acids cross the haemochorial placenta relatively readily and there is a rise in transport capacity in late gestation, at a time when fetal fat deposition is increasing. However, in the epitheliochorial placenta, fatty acid transfer is much more limited, and in late gestation, white adipose tissue deposits actually decrease in the fetal lamb. Fatty acids are released from triglycerides in maternal blood by lipases located on the maternal-facing trophoblast membrane. The free acids can then be transferred directly to the fetus by carrier-mediated mechanisms, but there also appear to be chain-shortening reactions in trophoblast peroxisomes to result in the preferential transfer of medium chain (< 16 C) fatty acids to the fetus. This could be important for fetal lipid metabolism because of a limited ability to oxidize long chain fatty acids due to low carnitine levels. Low-density lipoprotein (LDL) cholesterol is taken up by the placenta by receptor-mediated endocytosis and then degraded by lysozymes to provide the free cholesterol needed for placental steroid synthesis. This cholesterol (as well as that from high-density lipoprotein (HDL) cholesterol) may also be transferred to the fetus, but the quantitative importance of this is uncertain, since the fetal liver has a high capacity for cholesterol synthesis. Given the importance of lipids in many aspects of fetal growth and maturation (e.g. membrane synthesis, myelination, steroid and ecosanoid production), further study of maternal–placental–fetal lipid relationships is clearly required.

Immunoglobulins

Endocytosis operates in the placenta for lipoproteins and in some species, including humans, is also important for the transfer of immunoglobulins from mother to fetus to provide passive immunity. The process occurs at the base of the microvilli lining the mucosal surface of the syncytiotrophoblast that is exposed to maternal blood. It is most important in late gestation in preparation for birth and exposure of the newborn to the pathogenic microorganisms present in the postnatal environment. In rodents, rabbits and guinea-pigs, immunoglobulin transfer occurs via the yolk sac placenta. In other species, such as ruminants, the offspring receive maternal immunoglobulins only after birth, in the first secretions (colostrum) produced by the mammary gland. The devastating consequences of the lack of these immunoglobulins on the newborn are most easily observed in such species. When colostrum is not provided, the newborn usually quickly succumbs to infective processes.

Placental synthetic and endocrine functions

The placenta makes a large variety of hormones and other substances in great quantity. These are released into the maternal and fetal circulations as well as being present in high concentrations in placental tissue. The list includes steroid, peptide and protein hormones, biologically active amines and a number of other proteins, which appear specific to the placenta or at least present there in much higher concentrations than in other tissues. Some of the latter compounds have immunosuppressive properties. Most of the substances appear to be synthesized by trophoblast elements, for example the syncytiotrophoblast in the human and binucleate cells in the sheep. The placenta also synthesizes steroid hormones, comprising progesterone, oestrogens and perhaps some of their metabolites, which are important for the initiation and maintenance of pregnancy.

Progesterone

Progesterone has been termed the 'hormone of pregnancy' and, as well as maintaining uterine receptivity to the conceptus, appears involved in the inhibition of uterine activity and in immune suppression. It is also involved in some of the maternal adaptations to pregnancy such as hyperventilation. Progesterone is synthesized from maternal cholesterol which, as noted above, is taken up by the trophoblast as LDL. Through a series of enzyme-catalysed steroidogenic reactions, the 27-carbon cholesterol is converted to the 21-carbon progesterone, with the key enzyme being cytochrome P_{450} side chain cleavage enzyme. Most of the progesterone formed by the placenta is released into the maternal circulation. At the onset of pregnancy, however, the important progesterone source is the corpus luteum. In some species (e.g. goat), the corpus luteum remains the important source for the entire pregnancy, and this requires that its lifespan be extended. In other species (e.g. humans, sheep), the placenta takes over in early pregnancy. This occurs at about 8 weeks gestation in the human, so that even here the lifespan of the corpus luteum must be extended. This difference between species in relation to the source of progesterone during pregnancy is accompanied by other differences including the shape of the curve relating maternal plasma progesterone concentration to time of gestation. In some species (e.g. humans), the concentration increases progressively and is highest at the end of pregnancy, whereas in others (e.g. rat, guinea-pig), the peak concentration occurs closer to midpregnancy, while in others (e.g. sheep, rhesus monkey), there is a rapid decline in maternal progesterone concentration shortly before the onset of parturition. The factors responsible for these patterns probably include placental mass, steroidogenic enzyme activities and the rate of steroid metabolism.

Oestrogens

As well as being involved in implantation, oestrogens appear to be important in eliciting many of the maternal physiological and metabolic changes during pregnancy (e.g. increased blood volume), and in some species (e.g. sheep, rat) are involved in the initiation of parturition. Oestrogens, which are 18-carbon steroids, are formed from 19-carbon androgenic precursors in reactions catalysed by the enzyme aromatase. These precursors are in turn formed from 21-carbon progestogenic steroids (progesterone and pregnenolone) via the activity of the enzyme, 17α-hydroxylase/17,20 lyase. Both this enzyme and aromatase are required for full steroidogenic potential, as they are able to synthesize oestrogens from progesterone. There are species differences in the extent to which the placenta possesses this full capacity. In the human, sheep and cow, for example, the placenta lacks or has very low levels of 17α-hydroxylase/17,20 lyase for all or most of pregnancy and thus cannot synthesise oestrogens from progesterone. However, in the sheep and cow there is increased expression of the enzyme in late gestation, associated with a dramatic rise in maternal circulating oestrogen levels. Through some unknown mechanism, the increased enzyme expression appears due to the associated rise in fetal plasma levels of cortisol, and both the maternal oestrogen and fetal cortisol rise serve as important triggers for the initiation of parturition.

In the human the placenta lacks 17α-hydroxylase throughout pregnancy and a completely different strategy is employed for oestrogen synthesis. The androgen precursors, dehydroepiandrosterone sulphate and 16α-dehydroepiandrosterone sulphate, are synthesized in the maternal and fetal adrenal glands and fetal liver, respectively. These are taken up by the placenta and converted to oestrogens via desulphurylation followed by aromatization. Maternal plasma oestrogen concentrations (primarily oestrone, oestradiol and oestriol) increase progressively and dramatically during human pregnancy. Because their production involves the 'fetal–placental unit', measurements of maternal plasma oestrogen concentrations or 24-hour urinary excretion of oestrogens have been employed as diagnostic tests of fetal well-being.

The rat provides a final example of the species variation in placental oestrogen synthesis; the rat placenta expresses 17α-hydroxylase, but lacks aromatase. Thus the placenta produces androgens during late gestation and releases them into the maternal circulation. They are taken up by the maternal ovaries and aromatized there, leading to a rise in maternal plasma oestrogen concentrations in the last few days of pregnancy.

Protein hormones

The primary and most well-studied protein hormones produced by the placenta are the chorionic gonadotrophins and the placental lactogens, which are produced by trophoblast cells in some but not all species. In relation to chorionic gonadotrophins, the best-studied species are the human and the horse.

In the human the molecule is human chorionic gonadotrophin (hCG), which is a double-chain glycoprotein, with the chain identical to that in luteinizing hormone (LH), follicle-stimulating hormone (FSH) and thyroid-stimulating hormone (TSH) and a distinct β chain. It first appears at the time of implantation and is synthesized by the blastocyst. It has an important function in maintaining the life of the corpus luteum until placental progesterone production takes over, which as noted above occurs at about 8 weeks of pregnancy. Peak maternal plasma concentrations of the hormone occur at about 10 weeks gestation, and thereafter the levels decline markedly, although it can still be detected at term. hCG has also been postulated to be involved in sexual differentiation of the male fetus and in the maintenance of the fetal zone of the adrenal gland. However, the evidence for these two roles of the hormone is not overwhelming. The mechanisms involved in the regulation of hCG synthesis are not known.

In the horse, the gonadotrophin is pregnant mare serum gonadotrophin (PMSG) or equine chorionic gonadotrophin (eCG). It is produced by unique populations of binucleate trophoblast cells which migrate into the endometrium and multiply to form surface cup-like structures ~2 cm in diameter. PMSG's general structure is similar to hCG and it also functions to maintain corpus luteal function in early pregnancy, in this case by eliciting the formation of secondary corpora lutea. The extension of the lifespan of the corpus luteum in early gestation is an important requirement for the maintenance of pregnancy in many species. However, not all these species produce a chorionic gonadotrophin. Examples include sheep and other ruminants. In these species, the pregnancy recognition and antiluteolytic molecule appears to be interferon tau, a unique subclass of 172 amino acid type I interferon that is not inducible by viruses. Rather it is synthesized constitutively by the blastocyst trophectoderm just prior to implantation and acts to prevent regression of the corpus luteum. A similar mechanism may operate in the pig and horse.

Placental lactogens have been detected in several species including the human, rodents and ruminants. Human placental lactogen (hPL) is the major placental protein produced by the placenta (at term HPL mRNA comprises 25% of total placental mRNA). It is composed of a single polypeptide chain with 96% homology to growth hormone. As with hCG, hPL is synthesized by syncytiotrophoblast (and mature cytotrophoblast) and released mainly into the maternal circulation, although much lower levels are present in the fetus. Maternal plasma hPL concentrations increase progressively during gestation and are highest at term. It is thought to have at least two major metabolic roles in the mother, increasing lipolysis and inhibiting glucose uptake (i.e. anti-insulin, glucose-sparing actions). These effects can maintain an adequate maternal supply of glucose to the fetus in late gestation. It has also been suggested to be involved in fetal growth regulation. However, in some women, specific gene deletions result in low or undetectable hPL levels in pregnancy, yet these pregnancies are uneventful, suggesting that hPL is not essential, at least in normal pregnancies. The regulation of hPL production is not clear. However, the increasing levels of hPL in maternal blood appear to correlate with syncytial trophoblast mass, so that the factors that regulate placental growth may also control hPL synthesis. Ovine placental lactogen is produced by binucleate cells. In contrast to the situation in the human, plasma levels of the hormone are higher in the fetus than in the ewe in the first half of pregnancy, but after about

50 days gestation, maternal plasma levels increase dramatically. As in the human, the maternal hormone concentration in late pregnancy is related to placental mass, for example it is higher in twin compared with singleton pregnancies. The regulation and functions of ovine placental lactogen have not yet been definitively elucidated.

FURTHER READING

Aplin, J.D. (1997). Adhesion molecules in implantation. *Rev. Reprod.*, **2**, 84–93.

Boyd, J.D. and Hamilton, W.J. (1970). *The Human Placenta.* Cambridge: Heffer.

Conley, A.J. and Mason, J.I. (1994). Endocrine functions of the placenta. In: *Textbook of Fetal Physiology*, ed. G.D. Thorburn and R. Harding, pp. 16–29. Oxford: Oxford University Press.

Cross, J.C., Werb, Z. and Fisher, S.J. (1994). Implantation and the placenta: key pieces of the development puzzle. *Science,* **266**, 1508–18.

Damsky, C.H., Mousi, A., Zhou, Y., Fisher, S.J. and Globus, R.K. (1997). The solid state environment orchestrates embryonic development and tissue remodelling. *Kidney Int.*, **51**, 1427–33.

Dawes, G.S. (1968). *Fetal and Neonatal Physiology.* Chicago: Year Book Medical.

Faber, J.J. and Thornburg, K.L. (1983). *Placental Physiology.* New York: Raven.

MacCalman, C.D., Getsios, S. and Chen, G.T.C. (1998). Type 2 cadherins in the human endometrium and placenta: their putative roles in human implantation and placentation. *Am. J. Reprod. Immunol.*, **39**, 96–107.

Roberts, R.M., Ealy, A.D., Alexenko, A.P, Han, C.S. and Ezashi, T. (1999). Trophoblast interferons. *Placenta*, **20**, 259–64.

Steven, D.H. (ed.) (1975). *Comparative Placentation, Essays in Structure and Function.* London: Academic Press.

Taylor, R.N. (1998). Immunobiology of human pregnancy [foreword]. *Curr. Prob. Obstet. Gynecol. Fertil.*, **21**, 5–23.

Wooding, F.B.P. (1992). Current topic: the synepitheliochorial placenta of ruminants: binucleate cell fusions and hormone production. *Placenta*, **13**, 101–3.

Growth and metabolism

Abigail L. Fowden

Intrauterine growth involves the coordinated increase in mass of a wide variety of different tissues and organs. Generally this growth is measured in terms of changes in weight or size in relation to gestational age, but it also involves alterations in body composition and the functional development of the different tissues. Normal fetal growth depends on an adequate supply of nutrients and on a strict temporal relationship between tissue accretion and differentiation. During early development, the pattern of intrauterine growth is largely determined by the fetal genome but, as size increases, growth may become constrained by environmental, or epigenetic, factors. If the constraints are severe, the fetus will become growth restricted with adverse consequences for its survival at birth and subsequent postnatal development.

Measurements of growth

Fetal growth is defined as the increase in mass that occurs between the end of organogenesis (the embryonic period) and birth. In the human fetus, growth was originally inferred from measurements of symphysial–fundal height or palpation of uterine size but fetal growth can now be assessed more directly using ultrasound. Ultrasound measurements can be made throughout most of pregnancy both serially in individual fetuses and cross-sectionally in large populations. By midgestation, the majority of fetal organs can be imaged by ultrasound and their development monitored for specific abnormalities. The ultrasound measurements most commonly used to assess fetal growth are body length, femur length, biparietal diameter, and head and abdomen circumference. Fetal body weight can be estimated from these measurements or measured directly at delivery. Normative growth curves constructed from ultrasound measurements are used clinically to identify abnormal intrauterine growth and predict the risks of obstetric and neonatal complications. However, the curves vary with ethnicity (genetics), altitude, socioeconomic status, parity and multiple pregnancy. It is therefore important in assessing fetal growth to use growth charts appropriate for the population and geographical location.

Normal growth of a fetus can be defined using standard statistical methods such as measurements of weight or dimensions that fall within two standard deviations of the mean. Clinically, the 10th percentile is commonly used to identify infants who are growth restricted. However, this cut-off fails to allow for the baby who is genetically small and has grown normally to its full potential or for the baby whose growth rate has deteriorated in utero but whose birthweight is within normal limits. Therefore, a range of morphometric measurements, in addition to weight and length at birth, have been used as an index of the growth rate in utero. These include ponderal index (weight/length^3), body mass index (weight/length^3), skin fold thickness and the ratios of midarm to head and abdominal to head circumferences. Using these parameters, different patterns of fetal growth can be identified. For instance, babies who are small for their gestational age at birth may be symmetrically small or show an asymmetrical, or disproportionate, pattern of development. Symmetrically small babies may be genetically small or have suffered an insult early in development which has resulted in a slow growth trajectory throughout most of gestation. In contrast, asymmetrically small babies are believed to result from a relatively late restriction in the growth rate.

In experimental animals, more invasive methods can be used to assess fetal growth although direct morphometric measurements of the fetus and its individual organs have been made at different gestational ages in a number of species including the sheep, pig, horse, guinea-pig and rodents (Fig. 3.1). In sheep, serial measurements of crown rump length (CRL), girth, limb lengths and biparietal diameter have been made in individual fetuses using indwelling growth measuring devices and ultrasound transducers (Fig. 3.2). Measurements of blood volume can also be made at weekly intervals in chronically catheterized fetuses to provide an indirect assessment of fetal body growth (Fig. 3.1). In addition, ultrasound has been used in fetal sheep and horses to measure the diameter of structures such as the aorta and eye orbit as indices of fetal size. At a cellular level, rates of proliferation can be measured directly in individual fetal tissues by using tritiated thymidine to label DNA during cell division.

Growth rate and body composition

The actual rate of fetal growth varies widely between species and ranges from 0.9% to 30% per day during late gestation (Table 3.1). However, the general

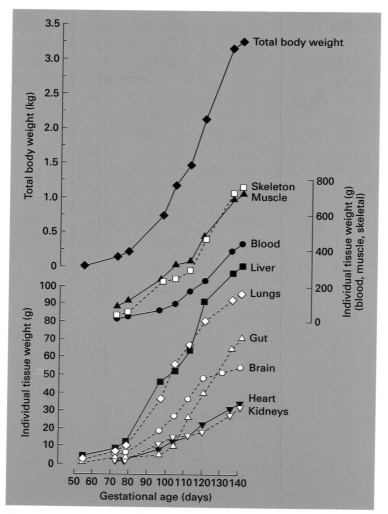

Fig. 3.1. The body weight and weight of individual tissues of the sheep fetus with respect to gestational age. (Data redrawn from J. Barcroft, *Researches in Prenatal Life*. Oxford: Blackwell, 1946.)

pattern of fetal growth is similar in many mammalian species. Weight curves are generally sigmoid in shape and growth slows towards term (Fig. 3.2). In the human fetus, there is a steady increase in weight at a rate of 15 g/kg per day from about 24 weeks to 37–39 weeks of gestation. The weight curve then flattens and the increment in weight falls to 6 g/kg per day in the last 2–3 weeks of gestation. When pregnancy is prolonged beyond 42 weeks, the average body weight of the

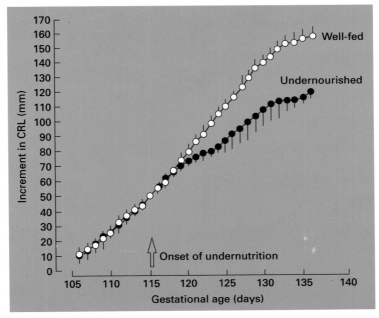

Fig. 3.2. The increment in crown rump length (CRL) measured using an indwelling device during the last 30–40 days of gestation in sheep fetuses from well-fed (open circles) and undernourished (filled circles) mothers. (Data redrawn from Mellor and Matheson (1979), *Q. J. Exp. Physiol.*, **64**, 119–31 and Fowden *et al.* (1996), *J. Endocrinol.*, **151**, 97–105.)

human fetus may actually fall. Similar reductions in growth velocity are observed for length, biparietal diameter and head circumference after 37 weeks of gestation.

In the sheep fetus, the daily increment in CRL is 5–6 mm/day before 120 days, 4–5 mm/day between 120 and 130 days and less than 3 mm/day thereafter (term 145–150 days). In the last 5–10 days before birth, the CRL increment declines to just 1–2 mm/day (Fig. 3.2). There is therefore a 70% reduction in fetal growth rate over the last 30–40 days of gestation with the most pronounced fall in the last week before delivery. The changes in growth rate just before term are accompanied by marked alterations in the structure and function of key fetal tissues such as the lungs, liver and gut, which are essential for neonatal survival. Similar changes in tissue maturation occur in the human and other species close to term. The prepartum decline in fetal growth rate observed in these species therefore appears to reflect a switch from tissue accretion to tissue differentiation in preparation for extrauterine life.

Table 3.1. The growth rate, birthweight and fat content of fetuses of different species during late gestation (≥85% gestation)

| Species | Birthweight (kg) | Growth rate (g/kg fetal wet wt/day) | | | % body fat at term |
		Total	Nonfat dry wt	Fat	
Rat	0.006	300.0	32.4	3.0	1.1
Guinea-pig	0.09	68.0	21.2	10.7	11.7
Pig	1.2	32.8	6.6	0.5	1.0
Sheep	3.0	36.0	6.5	0.8	2.0
Human	3.5	15.0	2.3	3.5	16.0
Horse	52.0	9.2	2.8	0.4	2.6

The changes in growth rate and tissue maturation that occur towards term are also accompanied by alterations in body composition, particularly of body fat. Body fat content increases during the last third of gestation and accounts for 1–16% of body weight at birth depending on the species (Table 3.1). The absolute rate of fat accretion therefore varies widely among species during late gestation (Table 3.1). Close to term, the human fetus is accumulating fat at 4–7 times the rate of the fetal sheep or pig even though its total growth rate is only half that of the domestic animals (Table 3.1). In contrast, body protein content at birth varies little between species and accounts for 12–14% of birthweight. The accretion rate of nonfat dry weight therefore closely parallels the total growth rate of the fetus in the different species (Table 3.1). During intrauterine growth restriction, fat deposition is disproportionately reduced in fetuses such as the human which normally have a high fat content. In species with little fat at birth, growth restriction is associated with a disproportionate reduction in fetal skeletal muscle accretion.

Factors affecting fetal growth

In the human, 40% of the variation in body weight at birth is due to genetic factors while the remaining variability is due to environmental factors. In developed countries, low birthweight or small for gestational age babies account for 5–6% of all deliveries and a significantly higher proportion of those requiring intensive neonatal care. In these countries, the major factors associated with

Table 3.2. Factors affecting fetal growth

Maternal factors
Maternal size: weight and/or weight for height
Uterine size
Nutritional state: calorific intake and dietary composition
Uterine blood flow
Anaemia
Tobacco smoking
Substance abuse: alcohol and narcotic drugs

Placental factors
Size
Microstructure: villi density, vascular density and architecture
Umbilical blood flow
Transporters and binding proteins
Nutrient utilization
Nutrient production
Hormone synthesis

Fetal factors
Genome: chromosome number, imprinted genes
Nutrient production
Hormones: feto-placental steroidogenic units and fetal endocrine glands
Growth factors: see Table 3.3.

reduced birthweight are small maternal size (height or weight for height), smoking in pregnancy, increased parity and preeclampsia, previous history of a low birthweight infant and low maternal glucose concentrations. For example, babies born to mothers who smoke are on average 200 g lighter than those born to nonsmokers. However, the incidence and causes of low birthweight vary both between populations and with time as dietary habits and substance abuse change. Studies in experimental animals have shown that fetal growth can be manipulated by varying maternal diet, placental and uterine size, uterine and umbilical blood flow, exercise, ambient temperature, atmospheric pressure and the availability of various hormones and growth factors in the fetal circulation. Thus, maternal, placental and fetal factors all influence the ability of the fetus to reach its genetic growth potential (Table 3.2).

Maternal factors

Cross-breeding experiments using horses demonstrated that maternal size had a greater influence on size at birth than paternal size. The maternal effect on foal size also persisted for 3 months after birth. The smaller foal from the small mother remained small and did not catch up in size to the reciprocal cross delivered from the large mare. More recent studies using embryo transfer techniques to eliminate genetic differences have confirmed that maternal size is a constraint on fetal growth in the horse and other species. Space in the uterus is therefore the ultimate limit to fetal and perhaps placental growth.

In experimental animals such the rat, rabbit and guinea-pig, ligation of one uterine artery impairs fetal growth in the ipsilateral but not the contralateral unligated horn. Similarly, in sheep, reducing uterine blood flow by blocking the maternal placental vasculature with microspheres retards fetal growth, particularly in late gestation. Reducing uterine blood flow in late gestation is associated with fetal hypoxaemia and hypoglycaemia and leads to an asymmetrical pattern of fetal growth with relative sparing of the brain at the expense of the fetal liver and gut. During human pregnancy, the maternal spiral arterioles supplying the placenta adapt structurally and functionally to produce a 700-fold reduction in vascular resistance to blood flow. These adaptations do not always occur in pregnancies complicated by intrauterine growth restriction (IUGR). The number of spiral arteries recruited to form the maternal vascular supply to the placenta is also reduced from 120 to 80 during human IUGR. Uterine blood flow and, hence, the supply of oxygen and nutrients to the placenta are therefore important factors in the control of fetal growth (Table 3.2).

Maternal undernutrition has been shown to reduce fetal growth in a number of species. The type of fetal growth restriction observed depends on the severity, duration and gestational age at onset of the nutritional insult. Even alterations in maternal nutrient intake around the time of conception can have effects on fetal development. In late gestation, maternal undernutrition tends to produce an asymmetrical pattern of IUGR similar to that seen in response to reducing uterine blood flow. In sheep, a 20–30% reduction in fetal glycaemia induced by maternal undernutrition in late gestation produces a similar percentage fall in the daily girth and CRL increment (Fig. 3.2). The temporal pattern of fetal growth is not significantly altered by this relatively moderate undernutrition (Fig. 3.2). The increment in CRL still decreased progressively towards term with the lowest increments in the last 5–10 days before delivery. The actual increment in CRL observed in the undernourished animals just before birth was similar to that found in well-fed controls which suggests that 1–2 mm/day may be the basal growth rate of the sheep fetus. Maternal under-nutrition in early gestation tends to produce a more symmetrical type of IUGR, which may be less severe than seen in response to late-onset undernutrition. However, although early maternal undernutrition appears to have relatively little effect on fetal organ size, it can alter the functioning of certain tissues and endocrine glands later in gestation and in postnatal life. The fetal effects of early maternal undernutrition in the ewe are also complicated by the enhanced pla-cental growth that occurs in these circumstances.

Much less is known about the effects of maternal nutrition on growth of the human fetus. Birthweight is positively associated with the maternal glucose levels but a caloric intake of less than 1500 calories per day is needed to produce clinical IUGR. In the Dutch famine of the 1940s reduced birthweight was only observed in babies exposed in utero to famine conditions late in gestation. Babies suffering famine in utero earlier in gestation and returned to normal conditions by mid to late gestation were not growth restricted. However, there may be generational effects of undernutrition early in pregnancy as females exposed to famine in utero early in gestation delivered smaller babies as adults even though their own birthweight was unaffected. Undernutrition early in pregnancy may therefore cause abnormalities in the development of the repro-ductive tract and oocytes of female fetuses that only become apparent when they themselves become pregnant. In rats, the effects of undernutrition during pregnancy are known to take several generations before they are reversed entirely. In human pregnancy, variations in dietary composition within the caloric norm have been linked to changes in the pattern of intrauterine growth. For example, a high carbohydrate intake in early pregnancy coupled with a rel-atively low protein consumption in late pregnancy is associated with delivery of infants with a lower ponderal index than seen when a more balanced diet is con-sumed throughout pregnancy. Relatively subtle changes in maternal diet may therefore influence fetal growth and development.

Placental factors

In all species studied so far, fetal weight is positively related to placental weight at term. Experimental reduction in placental size also reduces fetal growth in a number of species. In the ewe, removal of the placental implantation sites before pregnancy reduces placental mass and lowers body weight at term by as much as 70%. Similarly, destruction of the secondary placental disc in primates by ligation of the interplacental vessels leads to severe growth restriction of the fetus. The reduced weight and size of the foal of the smaller mare in the cross-breeding experiments also reflect, in part, a decrease in placental mass as the horse has a diffuse placenta which normally covers the entire surface of the uterus. Reductions in the functional mass of the placenta by umbilical artery ligation or partial embolization of the fetal placental vasculature with micro-spheres also results in IUGR. Fetal growth is therefore highly dependent on the functional and structural integrity of the placenta (Table 3.2).

In early pregnancy, placental growth exceeds fetal growth but in the second half of gestation placental weight increases at a much slower rate and does not parallel the steep rise in fetal weight. In ruminants such as the sheep and cow, placental weight decreases by 20% between mid and late gestation. In other species, including the human, placental weight gain slowly continues up to term. However, the slowing or cessation of placental growth in the second half of pregnancy is compensated for by major changes in the microstructure and transport characteristics of the placenta. In a number of species, total villous surface area of the placenta increases between mid and late gestation by division and elongation of the fetal villi. There is also proliferation and dilation of the fetal capillaries and a reduction in the diffusion distance between the fetal and maternal circulations with increasing gestational age. Moreover, resistance of the fetoplacental vasculature falls towards term, which results in a rise in fetal blood flow to the placenta. The capacity for transfer of certain ions and nutrients across the placenta also rises towards term on a unit weight or volume basis in both the human and ovine placenta. This reflects, in part, the increased surface area for exchange but also involves gestational increases in the density and gene expression of specific transporter proteins involved in the carrier-mediated transfer processes. During human IUGR, the concentration of particular transporter proteins in the placenta is reduced and placental remodelling appear to be less extensive during late gestation.

The placenta is a metabolically active organ and uses a significant proportion of the nutrients derived from the uterine circulation before they can reach the fetus. In the sheep, the proportion of oxygen and glucose used by the placenta declines with increasing gestational age but, even in late gestation, placental consumption accounts for 50% of the oxygen and glucose leaving the uterine circulation. The nutrients taken up by the placenta provide energy for the transport and biosynthetic activities of the placenta. They also provide precursors for the synthesis of hormones and other molecules that are released into both the umbilical and uterine circulations. Some of the substances synthesized by the placenta such as lactate and certain amino acids are used by the fetus for growth and oxidative metabolism. The hormones produced by the placenta may also have effects on fetal growth and development either directly or indirectly via changes in placental or maternal metabolism.

Fetal factors

Fetal growth is affected by internal constraints independently of the maternal and placental factors. Ablation of certain fetal organs such as the thyroid, pancreas and kidneys results in IUGR in sheep. Insulin deficiency in utero causes a proportionate type of growth restriction with little, if any, specific effects on the individual fetal tissues. Fetal thyroid hormone deficiency, on the other hand, reduces body weight to a greater extent than CRL and leads to specific developmental abnormalities in tissues such as the skin, bones, lungs and muscle. Similarly, congenital absence of the thyroid and pancreas in the human fetus leads to abnormalities in bone development and low birthweight. Hormones such as thyroxine and insulin therefore appear to have an important role in regulating tissue accretion and differentiation in the fetus and are required throughout late gestation for normal growth and development. In contrast, hormones known to regulate postnatal growth, such as growth hormone (GH), appear to have little effect on fetal growth although they are present at relatively high concentrations in the fetal circulation. The growth-promoting actions of insulin and thyroxine are believed to be due primarily to their anabolic effects on fetal metabolism (see below) but they may also involve fetal growth factors such as the insulin-like growth factors (IGFs). Circulating and tissue levels of the IGFs in the fetus are lowered by intrauterine deficiency of either hormone and are restored to normal values by replacement of the deficient hormone.

Glucocorticoids also play an important role in fetal development although their effects appear to be confined to the period of gestation just before term when fetal glucocorticoid levels normally rise. In sheep, the increase in fetal plasma cortisol towards term is responsible for the fall in growth rate just before birth (Fig. 3.2). It also initiates and controls the sequence of prepartum maturational events that occur in fetal tissues such as the liver, lungs and gut in preparation for extrauterine life. These processes are all abolished when the cortisol surge is prevented by fetal adrenalectomy. Cortisol therefore appears to be the agent switching the cell cycle from accretion to differentiation in the period immediately before birth. It may also contribute to the slowing of growth observed in growth-restricted human fetuses and during adverse intrauterine

Table 3.3. Growth factors identified in fetal tissues

Growth promoting
Insulin-like growth factors (IGF-I and IGF-II)
Epidermal growth factor (EGF)
Transforming growth factor-α (TGF-α)
Platelet-derived growth factor (PDGF)
Fibroblast growth factors (FGF)
Nerve growth factor (NGF)
Haematopoietic growth factors

Growth inhibitory
Transforming growth factor-β (TGF-β)
Inhibin/activin family
Müllerian inhibitory substance
Binding proteins

conditions in experimental animals as fetal cortisol levels are raised in these circumstances. Its effects on fetal growth and development are mediated directly via changes in gene transcription and indirectly through other hormones and growth factors.

A large number of growth factors have been identified in fetal tissues (Table 3.3). They are synthesized locally and act largely by paracrine and autocrine mechanisms on tissue development. Their main role is to regulate cell division but they affect many different aspects of cell growth including proliferation, induction, migration, aggregation, programmed cell death and regeneration. They have both growth-promoting and inhibitory actions and can be either competence or progression factors in the cell cycle. The growth factors that have been studied most extensively in relation to fetal, as opposed to embryonic, growth are the IGFs. Disruption of either the IGF-I or IGF-II gene leads to IUGR in mice. Birthweight is reduced by 40–60% and abnormalities occur in the development of the lungs and skeletal muscle which can prove fatal at birth. Similar changes in growth and development have been observed in fetal mice after disruption of the IGF type 1 receptor that mediates the action of the IGFs. In part, the changes in fetal body weight observed in these knockout experiments may have been due to the concomitant reductions in placental weight. But, in fetal sheep and rodents, infusion of IGF-I enhances fetal tissue growth independently of effects on placental weight, which suggests that IGF-I has direct effects on fetal growth.

Long-term consequences of the pattern of intrauterine growth

Recent epidemiological observations in humans have shown that the pattern of growth observed in utero may have lifelong consequences. IUGR is associated with an increased incidence of cardiovascular, metabolic and other diseases in later life. These associations are observed both in babies who were below the 10th percentile and in those who were within the normal birthweight range but were small relative to their placental size. Hence, restricted growth in utero rather than size *per se* appears to be the predisposing factor to adult-onset diseases. Babies of low birthweight or with a low body to placental weight ratio had higher systolic and diastolic blood pressures in adult life. They also had a greater risk of glucose intolerance, type 2 diabetes, syndrome X (hypertension, glucose intolerance and hyperlipidaemia), ischaemic heart disease, respiratory disease and abnormal reproductive function as adults. The association between low birthweight and adult disease occurs independently of other risk factors such as obesity and inactivity, and is observed in populations with different ethnic origins. More detailed analysis of the data has shown that certain types of IUGR are linked to specific adult diseases. For instance, it is the thin baby with a low ponderal index, not the symmetrically growth-restricted baby, that has the higher incidence of glucose intolerance and type 2 diabetes. Both types of baby are equally at risk of adult hypertension.

The association between low birthweight and adult disease has been linked to poor nutrition during pregnancy. Certainly, the babies growth restricted by undernutrition late in gestation during the Dutch famine of the 1940s have a higher than normal incidence of glucose intolerance and type 2 diabetes as adults. In experimental animals, abnormalities in adult glucose metabolism and cardiovascular function are observed after prenatal nutrient restriction. In rats, specific deprivation of protein during pregnancy leads to hypertension and glucose intolerance in the adult offspring. The lifespan of the offspring who were protein deprived in utero is also altered in a complex manner related to their sex and postnatal diet. The adaptations that the fetus makes to its pattern of growth to survive adverse nutritional conditions in utero may therefore program tissues for subsequent pathophysiology. Hence, the availability of nutrients in utero and their metabolic fate in the fetus have important implications for adult morbidity and mortality.

Fetal metabolism

Normal growth and development of the fetus requires a supply of carbon, nitrogen, ions and water. These substances are used for the accretion of new structural tissue, the deposition of fuel reserves such as glycogen and fat, and for the production of energy for the growing tissues. The total nutrient requirement of the fetus therefore depends on its growth rate, body composition and rate of oxidative metabolism. In turn, these factors vary with species and gestational age. Fetal oxygen consumption (per kilogram of body weight) decreases towards term but, in late gestation, varies little between species (Table 3.4). Fetal growth rate and fat content also change towards term and differ widely between species in late gestation (Table 3.1). There are, therefore, wide interspecies differences in the fetal requirements for nutrients during late gestation.

Measurements of metabolism

A number of methods have been used to quantify the rates of uptake and utilization of oxygen and the different metabolic fuels in the fetus. Most involve the Fick principle which can be expressed for any individual organ or the whole fetus by the following equation:

Rate of substrate uptake (or output) = blood flow × arteriovenous (AV) concentration difference in the substrate.

Precise measurements of fetal nutrient consumption can therefore be made provided that the umbilical blood flow and umbilical venous and arterial blood concentrations of the substrate can be obtained. Quantitative studies of fetal metabolism have been confined largely to domestic species in which the fetus can be catheterized and studied after recovery from anaesthesia (Table 3.4).

Umbilical and regional blood flow can be measured using either flow meters implanted around major vessels or microspheres which become trapped in the capillary beds in proportion to the fractional distribution of blood flow. Umbilical blood flow can also be measured indirectly using transplacental disappearance of inert freely diffusible substances (e.g. antipyrine, tritiated water, ethanol). Measurements of AV concentration differences across individual organs or the umbilical circulation depend on the percentage change in substrate concentration across the vascular bed. With current methods, only

Table 3.4. The mean rates (μmol/min per kilogram fetal bodyweight) of urea production and umbilical uptake of oxygen and various substrates in fetuses of different species in the fed state during late gestation ($\geqslant 85\%$ of gestation)

Species	Oxygen	Glucose	Lactate	Acetate	Urea[a]
Sheep	315	30	20	17	10
Cow	300	30	50	20	7
Pig	340	40	30	–	3
Horse	315	45	15	–	5
Human	350	45	10	–	4

Note:
[a] Calculated from placental urea clearance.

substrates with extraction coefficients greater than 1% can be quantified with any degree of accuracy.

Infusion of radioactively labelled substrates (e.g. 14 C-glucose) or their stable isotopes (e.g. 13 C-glucose) have been used to quantify the flux of substrate carbon between pools and into the various intracellular pathways of metabolism. By measuring the production of labelled carbon dioxide, the rate of oxidation of labelled carbon in a particular substrate can be measured directly. The main assumption of these tracer methods is that, at steady state, the labelled and unlabelled substrates, and their products, are treated identically by the transport mechanisms and biochemical pathways of the cells. The measurements can be refined to provide specific rates of substrate utilization by using the Fick principle to establish the amount of tracer lost across the placenta. The equation used to derive specific rates of nutrient utilization in the fetus is as follows:

Rate of fetal substrate utilization = [rate of tracer infusion into the fetus − rate of tracer loss from fetus to placenta] ÷ fetal arterial specific activity of the substrate.

Substrate utilization calculated in this way should equal or be greater than the umbilical uptake derived simultaneously by the Fick principle. If the tracer-derived value is greater, there must be endogenous production of the substrate by the extraplacental fetal tissues.

Nutrient supply

Nutrients are supplied to the fetal tissues by three different routes. First, they may be transported across the placenta from the maternal circulation. Second, they can be synthesized in the placenta and released into the fetal circulation. Finally, they may be produced endogenously by the fetal tissues themselves by mobilization of stored reserves or by *de novo* synthesis. The relative importance of these different sources of nutrients to the total requirement varies with the specific substrate and the maternal nutritional state. However, in normal conditions, the primary origin of most of the fetal substrates is the mother.

Placental transport

Nutrient transfer across the placenta can occur by simple diffusion across the cell membranes, paracellular diffusion between the cell membranes, active and facilitated transporter-mediated transfer and by endocytosis–exocytosis across the cell layers. The actual mechanism of transport used by a particular substance depends on its physicochemical properties. Small molecules such as respiratory gases and metabolic substrates generally cross the placenta by simple diffusion or by carrier-mediated processes if fat insoluble. Larger molecules such as insulin and immunoglobulins can be transported by paracellular diffusion or endocytosis–exocytosis depending on their water solubility. The rate of nutrient transfer is therefore determined by the fetomaternal concentration gradient across the placenta, the availability of specific transporters and binding proteins and by the metabolic activity, surface area, microstructure and blood flow of the placenta itself (see above).

Oxygen crosses the placenta by simple diffusion down a concentration gradient from maternal to fetal blood. Its transfer is flow limited but only falls when placental blood flow is reduced by 50% or more. The transplacental oxygen gradient varies amongst species and depends on a variety of factors including placental vascular architecture, placental oxygen consumption and the oxygen affinity of the fetal blood. The uteroplacental tissues use 50% of the oxygen delivered to them by the mother and have a rate of oxygen consumption four- to sixfold greater than the fetus and 10-fold higher than the adult rate of oxidative metabolism.

Glucose is taken up and transported across the placenta by facilitated diffusion. This process requires glucose transporters (GLUT) and a glucose concentration gradient from the maternal to the fetal circulation. This gradient varies with species and is less in the human than in ruminants although the actual fetal glucose level is higher in humans than in the sheep or cow. In normal circumstances, the main determinant of the transplacental glucose concentration gradient is the maternal glucose level but, during adverse conditions, fetal glucose levels can rise independently of the maternal concentration and can lower the gradient, leading to a reduction in placental to fetal glucose transfer.

In man and sheep, the rate of glucose transport across the placenta increases during the second half of gestation as the nutrient demands of the growing fetus rise. This increased capacity for glucose transfer may be due to a number of factors. First, structural remodelling of the placenta increases the surface area and reduces the diffusion distance for transfer. Second, there is an increase in the transplacental glucose concentration gradient with increasing gestational age as fetal glucose levels are lower at term than earlier in gestation. Third, there is a redistribution of uterine glucose uptake between the fetus and uteroplacental tissues with a proportionate increase in glucose delivery to the fetus. Finally, the density of the placental glucose transporters may increase towards term. Two glucose transporters, GLUT 1 and 3, have been identified in the placenta of most species but their abundance and cellular localization varies between animals. In human placenta, GLUT 1 is the major transporter. It is located on both the maternal and fetal facing membranes of the placenta and shows no apparent change in abundance with increasing gestational age. In ovine and rat placenta, GLUT 1 and 3 are both expressed at midgestation but GLUT 3 rises in abundance thereafter to become the predominant glucose transporter at term.

The majority of amino acids required by the fetus including all the essential ones are derived from the mother and are transferred across the placenta by active transport against a concentration gradient. Throughout the second half of gestation, fetal amino acid levels are higher than those in the mother but the precise ratio of fetal to maternal concentrations varies between species and with physiological state. Placental amino acid levels are higher than those in either the fetal or maternal circulations, which indicates that it is uterine and not the umbilical uptake that is the active process.

At least nine different amino acid transport systems have been identified in the human placenta. These systems are either sodium dependent or sodium independent and are selective for specific groups of amino acids. They may be polarized in their distribution or located on both the microvillous (maternal facing) and basal (fetal facing) membranes of the placenta. Their activity is regulated by a variety of factors including calcium concentration, pH and the level of certain hormones and growth factors such as the IGFs. During human IUGR, activity of the neutral amino acid transport system is reduced per milligram of placental protein. This is consistent with the reduced levels and narrower umbilical venous–arterial concentration difference of these amino acids found in growth-restricted human fetuses. Placental amino acid uptake is also lowered by substances such as nicotine and alcohol, which are known to impair fetal growth in the human.

In the human and sheep, measurements of umbilical venous–arterial concentration differences in individual amino acids show a net uptake of neutral and basic amino acids but not of acidic ones despite their accumulation in fetal protein. In fact, there are significant effluxes of amino acids such as glutamate from the fetus to the placenta. The placenta is therefore not only transporting amino acids but also metabolizing them throughout the second half of gestation (see below). Even essential amino acids are not simply transported across the placenta but may be modified en route. During adverse intrauterine conditions such as undernutrition, the efflux of certain amino acids from the fetus to the placenta may rise although there is little change in the net uptake of amino acid into the umbilical circulation.

The amount and rate of lipid transport across the placenta varies widely between species. In rabbits, rats, guinea-pigs and humans, the placenta is permeable to free fatty acids (FFA). Changes in maternal dietary lipid intake can therefore alter fetal FFA levels and fat deposition in these species. Labelled FFA injected into the mother also appear rapidly in fetal rabbits and rats. Moreover, in the human fetus, there is a significant venous–arterial concentration difference in FFA across the umbilical circulation which widens with increases in the maternal FFA concentration. Placental transfer of maternal FFA in the human therefore appears to be dependent on the transplacental FFA gradient. In contrast, the ovine placenta is relatively impermeable to lipid. Only a very small FFA concentration difference can be detected across the umbilical circulation in the sheep fetus and manipulation of maternal dietary lipid has little, if any, effect on fetal FFA levels.

Placental nutrient production

In addition to transporting substances from the maternal nutrient pool, the placenta also produces substrates such as lactate, amino acids and FFA, which are used for fetal growth and oxidative metabolism. The amounts and type of substrate synthesized by the placenta and their distribution between the fetal and maternal circulations varies with species and gestational age. Lactate has been shown to be produced by the uteroplacental tissues in all species studied. In the sheep, its production per kilogram increases four- to fivefold between mid- and late gestation. In midgestation, the lactate is released almost entirely into the uterine circulation whereas in late gestation, it is partitioned preferentially into the umbilical circulation of the fetal lamb. The ovine placenta also deaminates and transaminates amino acids throughout the second half of gestation. The placenta is the major source of glutamine and glycine and releases more of these amino acids into the umbilical circulation than can be accounted for by the uterine uptake. Furthermore, the placenta can synthesize FFA and cholesterol in a number of species and has been shown to saturate, elongate and liberate FFA from maternal triglycerides in the human, sheep and guinea-pig. These metabolic activities of the placenta require energy and account for a significant proportion of the placental oxygen and substrate consumption. Placental oxidation of amino acids such as glutamate may also provide the NADPH needed for FFA and cholesterol synthesis. The substrate interconversions that occur in the placenta are therefore an important component of the fetal nutrient supply, particularly during adverse conditions.

Fetal nutrient production

Fetal tissues such as the liver, muscle and lung can produce nutrients either from fuel reserves or from carbon and nitrogen of maternal or placental origin. The quantity and type of nutrient produced endogenously depend on the specific tissue, gestational age and on the umbilical, or exogenous, supply of nutrients to the fetus. In normal conditions lactate is produced by the fetus at about three times the rate of umbilical supply. It is derived mainly from glucose but is also produced from fructose and amino acids in smaller amounts. In species such as the human, which have a high fat content at birth, FFA must also be synthesized by the fetal tissues as umbilical uptake of FFA can only provide 20–50% of the FFA required for fat deposition in the fetus close to term. In vitro experiments have shown that FFA can be synthesized in the fetal liver, lung, brain and adipose tissue in a number of species, the main precursor for *de novo* lipid synthesis being carbohydrate (glycogen, lactate, glucose).

Specific amino acids can also be released from the fetal tissues into the fetal circulation in certain circumstances. In fetal sheep, glutamate and serine are released from liver in normal conditions while there is a net output of two gluconeogenic amino acids, glutamine and alanine, from fetal muscle during maternal undernutrition. These effluxes of specific amino acids occur against a net uptake of amino acids into individual fetal tissues. An interorgan system of amino acid transport therefore exists between the placenta, liver and muscle that allows changes in amino acid delivery to particular tissues without an alteration in net umbilical uptake of amino nitrogen. Under normal conditions, there is little glucogenesis by the fetus as a whole, although individual tissues may release glucose into the fetal circulation. However, during adverse conditions such as placental insufficiency or undernutrition, endogenous glucose production occurs and may account for 50% or more of the actual rate of fetal glucose utilization. The main sites of fetal glucogenesis are the liver and kidneys. These tissues show no net consumption of glucose and contain all the enzymes necessary for gluconeogenesis. Fetal glucose production can occur by glycogenolysis from liver glycogen and by gluconeogenesis from precursors such as lactate and amino acids in the liver and kidney. The ability of the fetus to produce glucose in response to adverse conditions increases towards term as the hepatic glycogen content and gluconeogenic enzyme activities increase.

Fetal nutrient utilization

Nutrient utilization by the fetal tissues is dependent upon the rates of umbilical uptake and fetal production of the nutrients (Fig. 3.3). The relative contributions of the exogenous (umbilical) and endogenous (fetal) nutrient supplies to the total rate of nutrient utilization vary between substrate and with nutritional state. For instance, umbilical glucose uptake accounts for all the glucose consumed by the fetal tissues in the fed state but only 50–70% of that used during maternal undernutrition. By contrast, umbilical lactate uptake provides less than 30% of the lactate used by the fetus in fed conditions. Similarly, a significant proportion of the leucine used by the fetus comes from the breakdown of its own protein, even in well-fed conditions.

The nutrients taken up by the fetal tissues are used either for oxidation or tissue accretion (Fig. 3.3). Using labelled substrates, the partitioning of nutrients between the oxidative and nonoxidative pathways of metabolism can be determined quantitatively. These measurements show that glucose, lactate and amino acids, but not FFA, are all oxidized at significant rates by the sheep fetus during the second half of gestation. The actual rates of nutrient utilization by the whole fetus and the relative distribution of nutrients between growth and

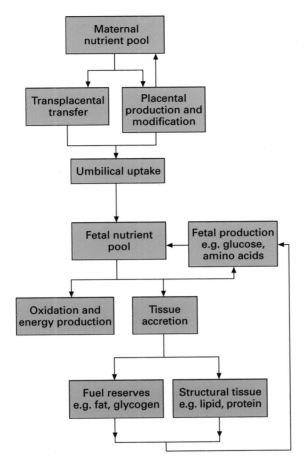

Fig. 3.3. The nutrient fluxes between the maternal, placental and fetal tissues during late gestation.

oxidation differ with species, gestational age and nutritional state. They also vary between individual fetal tissues.

In late gestation, the rate of fetal oxygen consumption is about 300 µmol/min per kilogram and shows little interspecies variation (Table 3.4). In contrast, fetal glucose utilization ranges between 20 and 50 µmol/min per kilogram depending on the species (Table 3.4). Of the glucose used by the sheep fetus as a whole, 50–60% is oxidized while the remaining 40–50% is used non-oxidatively. Glucose carbon therefore accounts for 25–30% of the total rate of fetal oxygen consumption. In fed conditions, 75% of the total fetal glucose consumption is used by the fetal carcass (skin, bone and muscle). However, during undernutrition, the fetal carcass uses proportionately less glucose while tissues such as the brain, which are obligatory glucose consumers, use proportionately more of the total glucose consumption. Less is known about fetal lactate utilization although umbilical lactate uptake has been measured in a number of species (Table 3.4). In the sheep fetus, lactate accounts for 40–50% of the total fetal oxygen consumption and is used by several individual fetal tissues. For instance, it is the main carbohydrate taken up by the liver and heart and is used by these tissues for glycogen and lipid synthesis. Together, lactate and glucose contribute about 50% of the carbon excreted as carbon dioxide when the conversion of glucose to lactate is taken into account. Carbohydrate is therefore a major, but not the sole, source of carbon for oxidative metabolism in the fetus.

Amino acids contribute the rest of the carbon required for fetal oxidative metabolism. During normal conditions, the umbilical uptake of amino acids in the sheep fetus exceeds that required for tissue accretion by about 50%. A large proportion of the fetal amino acid uptake is therefore available for catabolism and oxidative metabolism in this species. During late gestation, the sheep fetus can excrete labelled carbon dioxide derived from a variety of labelled essential and nonessential amino acids. It also produces urea, the main deamination product of amino acids. However, the fetal to maternal amino acid gradient and the rate of fetal urea production are relatively high in the sheep compared with other species (Table 3.4). Amino acids may therefore be more readily available for fetal oxidative metabolism in the sheep than in the human or other domestic animals.

Amino acids also provide carbon and nitrogen for tissue accretion. In fact, much of the net umbilical amino acid uptake is used for protein synthesis. The rate of fetal protein synthesis exceeds the rate of protein accretion as approximately 75% of the protein synthesized is subsequently degraded and resynthesized. Fetal protein turnover is therefore a quantitatively important component of the fetal energy requirement and could account for 15–20% of the total rate of oxygen consumption in the sheep fetus. Rates of protein synthesis in the fetus decline towards term as a result of reductions in both the rates of protein accretion and turnover. In individual fetal tissues, protein synthesis is highest in the gut and lowest in skeletal muscle but due to the differences in tissue mass each contributes about 20% of the total body rate of protein synthesis.

There is little evidence for lipid oxidation in the fetus although these pathways are active shortly after birth. In the fetus, FFA uptake does not exceed the requirement for growth and the enzymes for FFA oxidation have low activity until just before birth. In ruminants, volatile fatty acids such as acetate are taken up across the umbilical circulation (Table 3.4) and hind limbs. They are incorporated into FFA, steroids and membrane lipids in the sheep fetus and may be oxidized by the fetal brain in relatively small amounts, particularly during adverse conditions such as undernutrition.

Fetal metabolic balance

The total requirements for carbon, nitrogen and energy can be calculated for any given species from its oxygen consumption, growth rate, body composition and its rate of transplacental excretion of carbon and nitrogen. For example, the sheep fetus near term accumulates approximately 3.2 g carbon/kg per day as new tissue, excretes 5.2 g carbon/kg per day as carbon dioxide and loses another 0.7 g carbon/kg per day to the placenta in the form of urea and specific amino acids (Fig. 3.4). Similar calculations can be made for energy or grams of nitrogen required per day (Fig. 3.4). By comparing these requirements with the umbilical supply of nutrients, the metabolic balance of the fetus can be estimated. While the nutrient requirements for growth and oxidation are known for a number of species (Tables 3.1, 3.4), much less is known about the umbilical nutrient supply in these animals. Only in the sheep fetus are there sufficient data to assess the metabolic balance accurately (Fig. 3.4).

Quantitatively, amino acids have the most important role in fetal metabolic balance. They provide about 30–35% of the carbon, 45% of the energy and virtually all the nitrogen required by the sheep fetus each day (Fig. 3.4). After the amino acids, the next most important nutrient is glucose. It provides about 30% of the carbon and 30% of the energy requirement in the fed state (Fig. 3.4). Lactate and acetate make smaller contributions to the fetal energy and carbon balances (Fig. 3.4). When all the umbilical nutrient uptakes are summed, the total supply of energy and carbon is slightly less than the amounts required each day. There must therefore be other sources of energy and carbon in the fetus that have not yet been identified (Fig. 3.4). Given the high carbon content of fat, the most likely source of these deficits is lipid as even a small uptake of FFA represents a significant supply of substrate to the fetus.

During undernutrition, there is no change in fetal oxygen consumption. The balance between the supply and demand for nutrients is therefore maintained by reducing fetal growth rate and by changing the contributions of glucose and amino acids to the fetal energy and carbon balances. In undernourished sheep glucose accounts for a smaller proportion of oxidative metabolism and

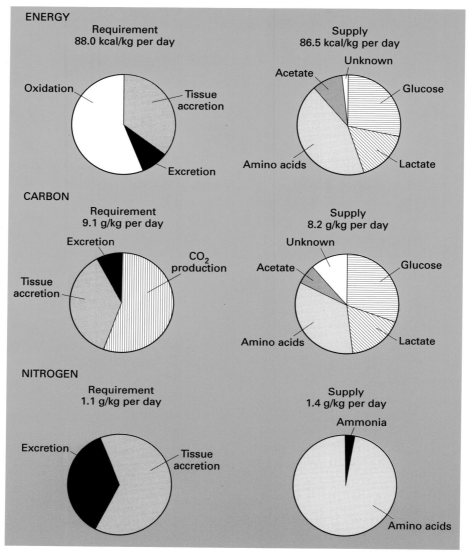

Fig. 3.4. The composition of the fetal requirements for carbon, nitrogen and energy and of the known sources of supply in sheep during late gestation. The actual values for the total fetal requirement and supply for each substance are given in grams (or kilocalories) per kilogram of fetal body weight per day.

contributes only 20% of the carbon required by the fetus each day. Conversely, amino acids contribute a greater amount of carbon to both the fetal energy (55%) and carbon (45%) requirements. Consequently, amino acids have an even more important role in maintaining the fetal metabolic balance during adverse nutritional conditions in utero.

Control of fetal metabolism

The rates of nutrient utilization and their distribution between the alternative pathways of metabolism in the fetus are controlled by the availability of the nutrients themselves and by the hormone concentrations in the fetal circulation. When availability of glucose is high, its rate of utilization and oxidation by the fetus increases and proportionately more glucose is used for oxidative metabolism. Conversely, when fetal glucose availability is limited, glucose utilization and carbon dioxide production from glucose carbon decrease and less glucose carbon is incorporated into new tissue. Fetal oxygen consumption is maintained in these circumstances by oxidizing more amino acid carbon which leads to an increased rate of urea production and a reduced rate of protein synthesis by the fetus. In contrast, lowering fetal oxygen availability reduces the fetal metabolic rate and decreases oxidation of both carbohydrate and amino acid carbon. The fractional rate of whole body protein synthesis is also reduced during fetal hypoxaemia. The rates of nutrient utilization and the relationship between glucose and amino acid oxidation are directly related to the circulating nutrient levels in the fetus but may also be influenced by the accompanying changes in the fetal endocrine environment.

A number of different hormones have been shown to affect fetal metabolism. They include insulin, thyroxine, IGF-I, cortisol, growth hormone (GH), glucagon and catecholamines. All these hormones are present in the fetal circulation from early in gestation and their concentrations in utero vary with nutritional state and oxygen availability. When nutrients are readily available, levels of insulin, IGF-I and thyroxine are high, while the concentrations of cortisol, glucagon and the catecholamines are low. Conversely, during undernutrition, fetal concentrations of insulin and IGF-I fall and the concentrations of cortisol, GH and the catecholamines rise. If hypoxaemia accompanies the nutrient restriction, there is also a fall in plasma thyroxine and an increase in plasma glucagon in the fetus. A similar endocrine milieu is observed in growth-retarded human fetuses with low insulin, thyroxine and IGF-I levels and high concentrations of cortisol and catecholamines. Concentrations of cortisol and adrenaline also rise towards term even under normal, well-fed conditions.

Insulin lowers fetal glucose and amino acid levels and stimulates their umbilical uptake. It also increases glucose utilization and carbon dioxide production from glucose carbon. In addition, fetal insulin administration enhances fat deposition and reduces protein catabolism and urea production. Insulin therefore has an anabolic effect on fetal metabolism and increases the cellular availability of nutrients for both the accretion of new structural tissue and the deposition of fuel reserves. However, once it has stimulated nutrient uptake into the cells, insulin appears to have little direct effect on the distribution of nutrients between the various pathways of intracellular metabolism. Oxidation of nutrients therefore appears to be more closely related to the glucose than insulin concentrations in the sheep fetus. Thyroxine and IGF-I also have anabolic effects in the fetus. Thyroxine stimulates oxygen consumption and oxidation of glucose and, probably also, amino acid carbon. It has little effect on fetal glucose utilization *per se* and does not appear to alter the relative contribution of different substrates to fetal oxidative metabolism. IGF-I also has little effect on glucose metabolism but does reduce protein degradation in the sheep fetus. As the concentrations of all three of these anabolic hormones rise with increased nutrient availability, they act as signals of nutrient plenty and stimulate nutrient utilization and, hence, growth of the fetus.

In contrast, hyperglycaemic hormones (e.g. cortisol, catecholamines) tend to limit whole body nutrient utilization and may even mobilize the stored fuel reserves of the fetus in certain circumstances. They enhance endogenous glucose production by the fetus although the extent to which they induce fetal hyperglycaemia varies with gestational age, nutritional state and the precise endocrine milieu. In part, they act by antagonizing the actions of insulin either at a cellular level or more directly by inhibiting insulin release in the fetus. As the concentrations of the hyperglycaemic hormones rise during adverse nutritional conditions, they act as signals of nutrient insufficiency and ensure fetal survival in these circumstances by reducing the fetal growth rate and maintaining a supply of glucose to key tissues such as the placenta and brain. In late gestation, the normal increases in fetal cortisol and adrenaline concentrations appear to be unrelated to any change in nutritional state. In these circumstances, the hormones are acting as maturational rather than nutritional signals, although they still have metabolic effects. In these circumstances cortisol and adrenaline ensure that a nutrient supply can be maintained to essential tissues during the transition from parenteral to enteral nutrition that occurs at birth.

FURTHER READING

Barker, D.J.P. (1998). *Mothers, Babies and Health in Later Life.* London: Churchill Livingstone.

Battaglia, F.C. (1997). *Placental Function and Fetal Nutrition.* Nestlé Nutrition Workshop Series 39. Philadelphia: Lippincott-Raven.

Battaglia, F.C. and Meschia, G. (1986). *An Introduction to Fetal Physiology.* New York: Academic Press.

Gluckman, P.D. and Heymann, M.A. (1996). *Pediatrics and Perinatology: The Scientific Basis,* 2nd edn, parts 3 and 5. London: Edward Arnold.

Hanson, M.A., Spencer, J.A.D. and Rodeck, C. (1995). *Fetus and the Neonate: Physiological and Clinical Applications,* vol. 3, *Growth.* Cambridge: Cambridge University Press.

Harding, R. Jenkin, G. and Grant, A. (1995). Progress in perinatal physiology. *Reprod. Fertil. Dev.,* 7, papers 7, 8, 13, 28, 29, 32.

Thorburn, G.D. and Harding, R. (1994). *Textbook of Fetal Physiology,* chapters 2, 4, 5, 6, 7. Oxford: Oxford University Press.

Cardiovascular system

Mark Hanson and Torvid Kiserud

During intrauterine life the developing cardiovascular system plays a key role in enabling the fetus to grow from only a few grams at the end of the embryonic period to reach an average weight of 3.5 kg by full term. This chapter reviews the structural and functional development of the heart and circulatory system during the fetal period. Much of the information on the structure and function of the fetal circulation presented in this chapter has been necessarily derived from animal experiments. However, the use of ultrasound techniques in recent years has provided unique insights into cardiovascular development in the human fetus and has shown it to be similar, in most respects, to cardiovascular development in experimental animals. Important differences do exist, and these are documented where relevant.

Blood volume

The blood volume in the human fetus is 10–12% of body weight whereas in the adult it is 7–8%. The reason for this difference is that, in addition to the blood contained within the body of the fetus, there is a large volume of blood in the placenta. At midgestation in fetal sheep, the fraction contained within the placenta is 50% and it falls gradually to 15% towards term (Fig. 4.1). However, the compliance of the system is large, allowing the distribution between the fetus and placenta to vary substantially. Depending on the time between birth and cord clamping (normally 0–3 min), 65–85% of the total blood volume is contained within the newborn. Reduction in blood volume (e.g. haemorrhage) is a serious threat to the fetus, but the capacity for rapid passage of water across membranes gives the fetus a powerful mechanism for restoring and regulating its blood volume (see Chapter 5).

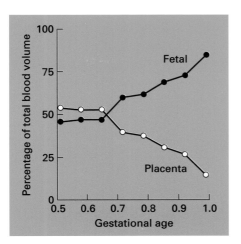

Fig. 4.1.   The distribution of blood between the fetal body and the placenta during the second half of pregnancy. Gestational age is presented as a fraction of the gestation. (Data from J. Barcroft, *Researches in Prenatal Life.* Oxford: Blackwell, 1946.)

Oxygen transport capacity

Although oxygen partial pressure (PO_2) falls both in the umbilical artery and vein during the second half of pregnancy (Fig. 4.2), the capacity of the fetal blood to transport oxygen increases due to the increase in haemoglobin concentration (Fig. 4.3A). After a short period dominated by embryonic haemoglobin, fetal haemoglobin is responsible for oxygen transport during intrauterine life. During the last weeks of pregnancy the fraction of adult haemoglobin increases and reaches 20% of total haemoglobin at term. Fetal haemoglobin has a higher affinity for oxygen and therefore its dissociation curve is shifted to the left compared with adult haemoglobin (Fig. 4.3B). This enables the fetal blood to bind more oxygen at lower PO_2 levels than maternal blood. For many species the dissociation curve shifts to the right with increasing gestational age (Fig. 4.3B) largely due to the changing composition of haemoglobin.

Typically the well-oxygenated umbilical venous blood returning from the placenta has an oxygen saturation of 80%. At 50% O_2 saturation the dissociation curve of fetal haemoglobin is steeper and more oxygen is released per millimetre of mercury reduction in PO_2 than occurs with adult haemoglobin. When oxygen content decreases, such as during anaemia or hypoxaemia, 2,3-diphosphoglycerate within the red blood cell increases, binds to the deoxygenated

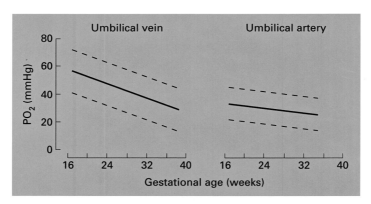

Fig. 4.2. Normal oxygen tension (PO_2) in the umbilical vein and artery expressed by the mean (solid line) and 95% confidence limits (dashed lines) during the second half of pregnancy in the human (Redrawn from Soothill *et al.* (1986), *Fetal Ther.*, **1**, 166–73.)

haemoglobin and shifts the dissociation curve to the right resulting in an increased release of oxygen to the tissues. A similar process occurs with acidaemia secondary to increased blood levels of lactate or carbon dioxide.

Arterial pressure

Arterial blood pressure is an important determinant of blood flow. Mean arterial pressure and its capacity to change depend on the size of the heart, its wall thickness and the contractile capacity of the myocardium, as well as the peripheral vascular resistance. In midpregnancy, mean arterial pressure is 15 mmHg in the human fetus, and at term it is approximately 40–50 mmHg. A similar time course for the increasing arterial pressure during gestation has been observed in the sheep fetus.

Vascular resistance to flow and viscous friction

The increase in vascularization during fetal development leads to a corresponding change in vascular cross-sectional area and a reduction in resistance to flow as pregnancy proceeds. Specific mechanisms of regulating vascular resistance exist in different organs. The adrenal gland, brain and coronary circulations, for example, have well-developed local regulatory mechanisms which ensure the delivery of arterial blood according to their needs.

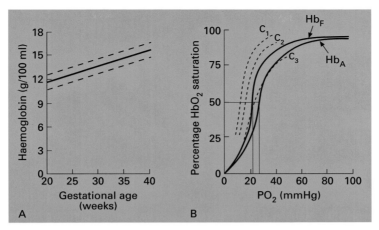

Fig. 4.3. The normal fetal haemoglobin concentration (A) increases during the second half of pregnancy, here presented as the mean and 95% confidence limits. (B) Fetal haemoglobin (Hb$_F$) has a dissociation curve to the left of that of adult haemoglobin (Hb$_A$). Accordingly, 50% saturation is reached at a PO$_2$ 4 mmHg lower than that for Hb$_A$. Typically, the dissociation curve for chicks moves to the right after the start of incubation (C$_1$, C$_2$ and C$_3$ correspond to 12, 21 and 86 days respectively). (A is redrawn from Nicolaides *et al.* (1988), *Lancet*, **i**, 1073–5.)

Resistance to flow also depends on the viscous properties of blood. Although viscous friction is low in blood of high velocity and normal haematocrit, it plays an important role in parts of the circulation with low velocity (e.g. placental and hepatic venous flow) or in situations of high haematocrit with a correspondingly high viscosity. The latter is the case in monochorionic twins with twin–twin (placental) transfusion syndrome where the recipient twin is polycythemic. Although the blood volume in the recipient twin is decreased by loss of fluid from capillaries and increased urine production, the fetus becomes haemoconcentrated with a haematocrit that may exceed 60%. This leads to a high viscosity and increased resistance to flow and myocardial hyperplasia as a result of the increased afterload on the heart.

Development and function of the heart

The embryology of the developing heart is shown diagrammatically in Fig. 4.4. The heart forms very early as a tube derived from the fusion of two

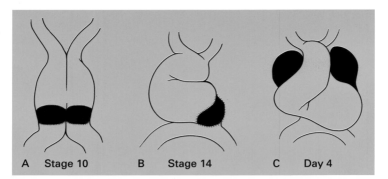

A   Stage 10   B   Stage 14   C   Day 4

Fig. 4.4.   Early development of the avian heart. A The tissue assigned for the atria (black areas) is identified as the primitive endocardial tubes fuse to form the primitive heart tube. B The tube folds to form the conotruncus (the upper portion), and the lower portion forms the ventricle, the future right and left ventricles. C A further folding moves the conus forward and an interventricular sulcus deepens. Thus the future right ventricle connected to the conus cordis and truncus arteriosus can be distinguished from the left ventricle. The presumptive auricles of the right and left atrium are now seen on both sides of the truncus arteriosus. (Redrawn after W.J. Larsen.)

mesodermal tubes and even in its early form, the heart possesses myocardial cells positioned between endo- and pericardium. The development into a four-chambered heart from a single tube is a remarkable process. Looping of the tube occurs, in the same direction in all normal embryos, due to differential growth between the left and right sides of the tube. Looping in the opposite direction results in dextrocardia, i.e. the heart is orientated towards the right side. The process of looping is followed by septation, by which interatrial and interventricular septa appear, separating the chambers (except for the foramen ovale, see below). The more common congenital abnormalities of the heart such as atrial or ventricular septal defects have their origins at this time. A simultaneous spiralling septation divides the common arterial trunk and its conical outlet into the ascending aorta and pulmonary artery, which are connected to the left and right ventricle respectively. Failure in this process leads to conditions such as the persistence of a common arterial trunk, total or partial transposition of the great arteries, or maldevelopment of one or both arterial outlets.

The development of the heart is a complicated process of interaction between molecular and cellular mechanisms as well as haemodynamic forces. Its complexity is reflected in the fact that cardiac defects represent more than a third of all congenital malformations in the human. The pressure and blood flow relationships between the cardiac compartments is delicate, and alterations in this relationship can result in malformations. The normal proportions of an early heart may develop into the disproportionate hypoplastic left heart syndrome if, for example, the left side of the heart is deprived of its blood supply due to a restriction of the foramen ovale, the left atrioventricular valve, myocardial development or the left outflow tract.

Myocytes are capable of contraction from their first appearance in the heart. As gestation proceeds they elongate, develop sarcoplasmic reticulum and t-tubules, and their myofilaments become orientated to produce increasing contractile force. In the cat, the density of myofibrils increases threefold during the second half of pregnancy, and the maximum tension per gram of muscle increases in parallel (Fig. 4.5). In addition, throughout gestation the myocytes divide, so that the heart also increases in size through hyperplasia. This growth pattern may relate to the relatively high density of adrenergic receptors that develops during the second half of pregnancy. Interestingly, just before or after birth (depending on the species) myocytes cease to divide, and any further growth throughout life must occur by hypertrophy. Thus the same cardiomyocytes that produce the heartbeat in early life must continue to do so throughout our lives!

The cardiac function curves which relate stroke volume to end-diastolic filling pressure for the left and right ventricles are shown in Fig. 4.6. Note that the curve of the right ventricle lies above that of the left. Because the venous filling pressure is, however, the same for both ventricles, the right ventricular output is greater than the left. This is a major difference from the adult, in which the output of both sides of the heart is equal as the two sides work in series. In the fetus, however, the pulmonary blood flow is low, so that the left ventricle receives much less blood from the pulmonary veins, even though it is also receiving blood from the right ventricle through the foramen ovale. Some of the difference in development of the left and right ventricle may reflect the fact that the left ventricle supplies the brain and upper body, in which vascular resistance is higher overall than in the lower body and placenta, which predominantly receive blood from the right ventricle.

It is also apparent in Fig. 4.6 that both ventricles in the fetus operate near the top of their function curves. It is sometimes said, erroneously, that the fetal heart does not show the Frank–Starling relationship, whereby stroke volume increases as the ventricles are stretched by increasing diastolic pressure, as seen in the adult heart. This idea is incorrect because it implies that the fetal heart

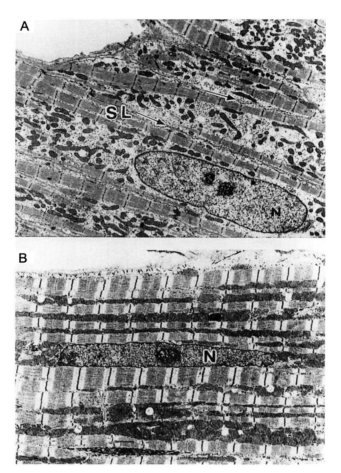

Fig. 4.5.   Electron microscopy of the heart muscle of the immature cat (A) shows less densely organized contractile elements predominantly situated at the cell periphery. In the adult cat (B), the contractile elements are densely organized and sandwiched with layers of mitochondria. SL, sarcolemma; N, nucleus. (Redrawn from J.G. Maylie (1982), *Am. J. Physiol.*, **242**, H834–43.)

cannot increase its stroke volume. However, adrenergic stimulation is known to increase cardiac output, whereby the heart then operates on a higher ventricular function curve. Nonetheless, it is true that increases in cardiac output in the fetus are achieved more by increasing heart rate than by increasing stroke volume when compared with the adult. Mechanical constraints on the ability of the fetal heart to increase its stroke volume also exist, largely due to the fluid-

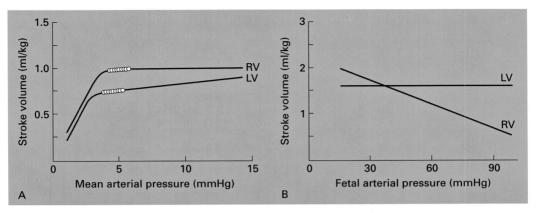

Fig. 4.6. Typical relationship between the diastolic atrial pressure and stroke volume for the left (LV) and right ventricle (RV) in fetal heart during late gestation (A). See text for details. Idealized relationship between the left (LV) and right ventricular (RV) stroke volume of the mature fetal heart at various arterial pressures (B).

filled lungs which surround it, and the effect of removal of these constraints on the heart can be seen at birth. Since the fetus relies on a high cardiac output to ensure adequate oxygen delivery to the tissues, a reduction in preload such as occurs with a decrease in venous return can rapidly result in a detrimental reduction in stroke volume.

Another difference between the left and right ventricles in the fetus is the response to increased afterload. The left ventricle maintains a stable stroke volume during experimentally increased arterial pressure, while the right ventricle reduces its stroke volume (Fig. 4.6). This pattern is evident morphologically as right ventricular hypertrophy in growth-restricted fetuses as a result of increased umbilicoplacental resistance.

Fetal heart rate falls progressively during the later part of gestation largely due to an increase in parasympathetic tone. Both animal and human studies have shown that the fetal heart rate shows normal variability, the degree of which is influenced by several factors. Changes in the patterns of heart rate, including variability, have been used to define behavioural state in the human fetus. The variability in fetal heart rate is usually greater the lower the basal level of heart rate, but analysis of the fetal heart rate now allows for this so that fetal heart rate variability can be used clinically as an index of fetal well-being. Fetal heart rate variability increases with acute hypoxaemia and this is mediated by chemoreflex mechanisms responding to the reduction in arterial PO_2 (see below). However, if hypoxaemia is prolonged, for example in association with placental insufficiency, fetal heart rate variability is reduced. Many drugs such as alcohol or opiates reduce fetal heart rate variability, as does anaesthesia. Antenatal glucocorticoid therapy, used to accelerate lung maturation in cases of threatened preterm labour, also affects fetal heart rate variability, the precise effect depending on the dose, route and the type of glucocorticoid administered. Heart rate variability may also depend on fetal gender. All of these factors make the interpretation of fetal heart rate variability complex. It is particularly important in clinical practice to monitor fetal heart rate for sufficient time to exclude behavioural state as the reason for a prolonged period of low heart rate variability. In recent years, computer programs have made the analysis of fetal heart rate more objective.

Arrangement of the fetal circulation

The blood flow distribution to various organs in the fetus is shown in Table 4.1. In considering the fetal circulation it must be remembered that the fetus possesses vascular shunts (ductus venosus, foramen ovale and ductus arteriosus) and a low-resistance vascular bed in the placenta.

Placenta

The placenta receives as much as 40% of the combined left and right cardiac output via the two umbilical arteries which arise from the left and right iliac arteries (Fig. 4.7). Resistance to flow is produced mainly by the peripheral placental vasculature, which has no neural regulation and reacts less to humoral agents than do vessels in the fetal body. This relative unresponsiveness of the placental vasculature gives the circuit a relatively stable blood flow, determined mainly by the arterial blood pressure and the degree of vascularization. Due to the extensive vascularization during normal late pregnancy, umbilical arterial blood flow has a high velocity during diastole.

Ductus venosus

This shunt is a thin trumpet-like connection between the abdominal portion of the umbilical vein (the portal sinus) and inferior vena cava (IVC) (Fig. 4.8). In midgestation the narrow entrance is 0.5 mm wide and it remains narrow for the

Table 4.1. The mean fetal combined ventricular output, distribution to organs, oxygen delivery, and vascular resistance in chronically instrumented fetal sheep at 0.9 gestation

	Blood flow (ml/min per 100 g)	% of cardiac output	Oxygen delivery (ml/min per 100 g)	Vascular resistance (mmHg/mL/min per 100 g)
Combined ventricular output	48	100		
Fetal body blood flow	32	56	2.13	0.013
Umbilical blood flow	21	44		0.016
Upper Body (total)	11	23	0.86	0.04
Brain	87	3	6.71	0.49
Heart	163	2.6	12.29	0.27
Upper carcass	22	16	1.66	1.99
Body skin	23	0.2	1.83	1.90
Lower Body (total)	14	25	0.92	0.03
Adrenals	174	0.06	10.83	0.84
Kidneys	155	2	10.61	0.28
Spleen	45	1	21.64	0.53
Small gut	41	0.3	2.78	1.04
Lower carcass	19	14	0.38	2.32
Body skin	26	0.2	1.81	1.90
Lungs	162	12	5.68	0.35

Source: Jensen *et al.* (1991). *J. Dev. Physiol.*, **15**, 309–23.

rest of gestation, rarely exceeding 2 mm. The vessel is partially embedded in the tissue of the lower surface of the liver and joins the left side of the expanded IVC near the entrance to the heart. The left and medial hepatic veins join the ductus venosus as they enter the IVC and form a functional unit. In the human fetus, these structures are found immediately below the diaphragm and a short distance from the atrial septum and the foramen ovale. In the fetal sheep, however, the intrathoracic IVC runs for several centimetres to reach the atria, but seems capable of maintaining laminar flow and streaming as in the human.

In fetal sheep at term, 50% of the oxygenated umbilical blood is shunted through the ductus venosus, but with wide variations. Recent research indicates that this fraction is less (20–30%) in the human fetus. During hypoxia or hypovolaemia the shunting increases and can reach 70% in the fetal sheep and monkey.

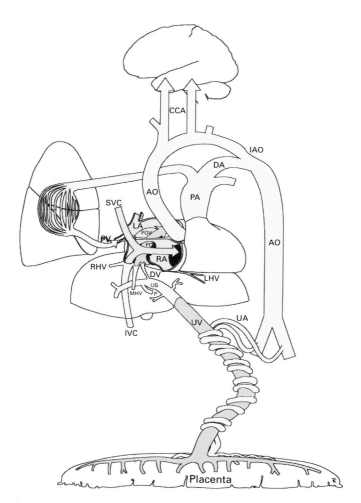

Fig. 4.7. Fetal vascular anatomy showing the three shunts: the ductus arteriosus (DA), ductus venosus (DV) and foramen ovale (FO). The left portion of the fetal liver is relatively large compared with its size in adult life. The umbilical vein (UV) is connected to the left branch of the portal system, which is usually called the intra-abdominal UV. It has a slight distension, the umbilical sinus (US), at the junction with the DV. The main stem of the portal vein (P) is a modest vessel during fetal life. In contrast to adult life, the left hepatic vein (LHV) and the medial branch (MHV) are well defined in the fetus. Note the close anatomical relationship between the DV and the FO, a detail that is commonly neglected, but important for understanding the function of the FO. AO, aorta; CCA, common carotid artery; FOV, foramen ovale valve; IAO, isthmus of the aorta; IVC, inferior vena cava; LA, left atrium; PA, pulmonary artery; PV, pulmonary vein; RA, right atrium; RHV, right hepatic vein; SVC, superior vena cava; UA, umbilical artery.

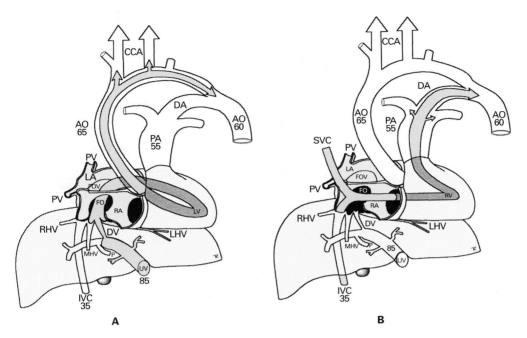

Fig. 4.8. Illustration of the two pathways of flow through the heart, the via sinistra (dark shaded) with oxygenated umbilical blood (A), and the via dextra with deoxygenated blood (B). Oxygen saturation is entered in numbers. LV, left ventricle; RV, right ventricle; other abbreviations as for Fig. 4.7.

Whether there is a sphincter, a circular arrangement of smooth muscles regulating the flow at the entrance of the ductus venosus, is not clear, although adrenergic constriction and adrenergic relaxation are believed to be part of the regulatory mechanisms. As with the ductus arteriosus, the ductus venosus seems to rely on a prostaglandin mechanism to maintain its patency. The difference between these shunts seems to be that the prostaglandin effect in the ductus venosus is weaker and that increased PO_2 is not the trigger for the postnatal obliteration of the shunt. The ductus venosus normally closes 1–2 weeks after birth.

Foramen ovale

The only intracardiac shunt during fetal life is an oval-shaped hole in the interatrial septum immediately above the inlet from the IVC (Figs. 4.7, 4.8). At the end of the embryonic period the size of the foramen ovale equals the area of the inferior vena cava, but during the fetal period, the orifice shows a relatively slow growth and is only 60% of the IVC cross-sectional area at term. The foramen ovale is partially covered by a thin valve on the left side of the septum. During most of the heart cycle, the valve is distended into the left atrium like a spinnaker, only to be closed for an instant during atrial contraction.

It is of particular importance for the function of this shunt that the fetal atrial septum is situated further to the right side than is usual for postnatal life. This permits the foramen ovale valve to act as the left wall of an extended IVC between the two atria. On the right side, the smaller IVC valve (Eustachian valve) forms the right side of the tube. The extended IVC thus conducts the blood either to the left side of the atrial septum (i.e. to the left atrium), or to the right side. Since the atrial septum divides the bloodstream to the right and left side by the edge of the foramen ovale, it is also called the 'crista dividens'. An additional effect of the shift of the atrial septum to the right side is that the foramen ovale is tilted towards the IVC to receive the bloodstream. This mechanism permits blood from the IVC to enter the left atrium directly without first entering the right atrium, thus avoiding mixing with deoxygenated blood.

In the human fetus, 34% of the combined cardiac output is believed to cross the foramen ovale at 20 weeks and 18–19% at 30–38 weeks. Animal studies indicate that the fraction which is shunted through the foramen ovale is maintained or increased during hypoxaemia or hypovolaemia. During acute hypoxaemia, oxygen content in this flow tends to increase due to an increased contribution of ductus venosus flow and a corresponding reduction of blood from the left and medial hepatic vein.

Although flow through the foramen ovale is greatly reduced immediately after birth, it takes months until the shunt has closed anatomically and, in a small percentage of the population, it stays open until adult life. The substantial increase in pulmonary blood flow after birth increases left atrial pressure in combination with the sudden disruption of umbilical venous return, and the corresponding reduction of flow through the ductus venosus and left portion of the liver, which lead to a reversal of the pressure gradient across the foramen ovale. Accordingly, the foramen ovale flap and the atrial septum approach each other to form a functional closure of the shunt. Little is known, however, of the biochemical events which slowly lead to a permanent anatomical closure.

Ductus arteriosus

This shunt connects the pulmonary arterial trunk with the descending thoracic aorta (Figs. 4.7, 4.8) and is a wide-diameter muscular vessel. The ductus arteriosus redirects a major proportion of the right ventricular output allowing it to bypass the pulmonary circulation.

The ductus arteriosus closes 1–3 days after birth, but a patent shunt is a common clinical problem in the neonatal period. The vessel is under the general influence of circulating agents as well as local paracrine control, but prostaglandin E_2 (PGE_2) is particularly important for maintaining its patency. The sensitivity of the ductus arteriosus to PGE_2 increases in the third trimester and reaches its highest level after 32 weeks of pregnancy. Fetal stress or administration of glucocorticoids enhances this sensitivity. Some of the prostaglandin effect is mediated by nitric oxide, either directly or via small nutrient vessels penetrating the muscle layer. Nitric oxide may also have a separate relaxing effect on the ductus arteriosus particularly in the immature fetus when the prostaglandin response is less. The rise in arterial PO_2 after birth is accepted to be the trigger for its closure.

Central blood distribution and oxygen saturation

In contrast to the serial arrangement of the systemic and pulmonary circulatory circuit in adult life, the fetal circulation is to a large extent arranged in parallel. Historically, the concept of the two pathways through the fetal heart, the via sinistra and the via dextra, was introduced to describe the differences from the postnatal circulation (Fig. 4.8).

The via sinistra (Fig. 4.8) provides a pathway for oxygenated blood to the left side of the heart. It starts in the intra-abdominal umbilical vein (typically, oxygen saturation of 80–85% in the fetal sheep), runs through the ductus venosus, the left side of the proximal IVC, the foramen ovale, the left atrium, left ventricle, and the aortic arch to enter the descending aorta. Thus the oxygenated blood of the umbilical vein is preferentially distributed to the left side of the heart to perfuse the coronary arteries and the brain. However, during normal pregnancy, some 70–80% of the umbilical venous return enters the liver in the human fetus. The major proportion of this blood perfuses the left half of the liver before joining the preferential streaming of the via sinistra. Since the oxygen extraction in the liver is modest (10–15%) this large volume of umbilical blood constitutes an important oxygen resource. Additionally, some mixing within the IVC and blending with the small amount of pulmonary venous return explains the oxygen saturation of 65% in the left ventricle.

The amount of umbilical blood delivered to the foramen ovale is in excess and permits a considerable spillover of oxygenated blood to the right side.

Actually, the difference in haemoglobin oxygen saturation between the left and right ventricle is only 10–12%, but this difference tends to increase during hypoxic or hypovolaemic challenges.

The via dextra (Fig. 4.8B) is supplied by the deoxygenated blood from the superior vena cava (40% saturation) and the IVC (35% saturation) and coronary venous return. The blood travels from the right atrium through the right ventricle (55% saturation), pulmonary arterial trunk and the ductus arteriosus to join the via sinistra in the descending aorta. Since only a small proportion of the right ventricular output actually enters the lungs (13–25% of the combined cardiac output in the human fetus), the proportion of flow through the ductus arteriosus is considerable (32–40% of the combined cardiac output).

Development of the peripheral circulation

Growth of fetal tissues and organs depends on their receiving an adequate blood supply allowing both tissue and vascular growth to occur simultaneously. A range of growth factors, including vascular endothelial growth factor (VEGF), promote vasculogenesis. In addition, locally produced vasoactive substances such as nitric oxide have potent effects on growth, as do some endocrine agents such as arginine vasopressin (AVP) and angiotensin (AT) II. Early in gestation, the fetal peripheral circulation becomes dominated by the placental vascular bed, which develops rapidly and is functioning in the human 7–10 weeks after conception.

Control of the fetal circulation

Considerable information is now available regarding the control of the fetal circulation, and in particular how it responds to hypoxia (Fig. 4.9) such as that produced by a reduction of umbilical blood flow (e.g. obstruction of the cord) or uterine blood flow (e.g. the contractions of labour). A decrease in fetal blood volume (e.g. fetal haemorrhage) seems to be a more serious challenge with a less favourable distributional pattern than during hypoxia leading to reduced flow to the placenta as well. An important distinction needs to be drawn between adaptation to an acute challenge, lasting a few minutes to perhaps an hour, and that to the more prolonged or chronic hypoxia which may occur with placental insufficiency (e.g. in preeclampsia). We will consider the acute

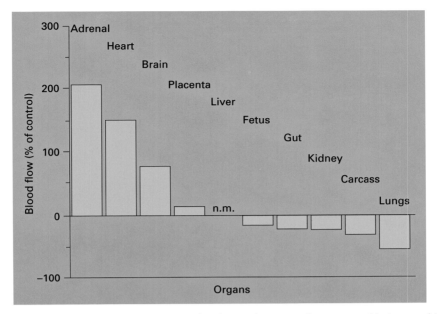

Fig. 4.9.   Cardiovascular responses to an episode of acute hypoxaemia, measured in terms of the change in blood flow to various organs during hypoxaemia in late-gestation fetal sheep. Note that blood flow to the adrenal glands, heart and liver is increased; flow to the placenta is preserved; flow to the gut, kidney, lungs and carcass (fetal body minus viscera) is reduced. n.m., not measurable. (Redrawn from Jensen and Berger, in: *Fetus and Neonate. Physiology and Clinical Application*, vol. 1. *Circulation*, ed. Hanson *et al.*, Cambridge; Cambridge University Press, 1995.)

responses first, dividing them into neural, endocrine and auto/paracrine components.

Neural reflex response

Animal studies have revealed the presence of reflex responses to acute hypoxia operating from around the beginning of the last third of pregnancy. The first line of defence is a chemoreflex initiated by the carotid bodies, and to a much lesser extent the aortic bodies. These chemoreceptors discharge spontaneously at the normal arterial PO_2 of approximately 25 mmHg in late gestation, and their activity increases briskly if PO_2 falls below this level. The efferent limb of the chemoreflex involves both parasympathetic and sympathetic nervous systems. Increased vagal activity produces a rapid fall in fetal heart rate (Fig.

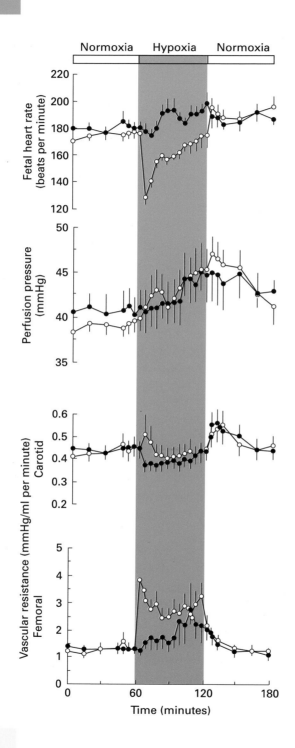

4.10), which helps to limit myocardial oxygen consumption immediately. Increased sympathetic outflow produces a rapid vasoconstriction in peripheral resistance vessels, mediated by adrenergic receptors. This is particularly pronounced in the vascular beds supplying the skin, skeletal muscle, gut, and even the kidney and lung, where a rapid fall in blood flow occurs. In contrast, blood flow to the vital organs – the heart, brain and adrenal glands – increases; however, these responses are not mediated by chemoreflexes. The advantage of the chemoreflex responses is that they convey *speed*: a rapid reduction in blood flow, and hence oxygen delivery, to nonessential organs may provide a sufficient saving of oxygen to avoid detrimental effects on the fetus if the hypoxic challenge is mild and of short duration. This is particularly valuable as it appears that fetal tissues have a pronounced ability to reduce metabolism as oxygen delivery falls. The mechanism of this process is unknown and it appears to operate over a wider range of PO_2 values than in the adult. It is likely that the release of substances such as adenosine produces an inhibition of metabolism in fetal tissues, which may be regarded as a defence mechanism in the presence of severe hypoxia.

Endocrine mechanisms

If hypoxia is maintained for more than a few minutes, the concentration of a range of hormones in the fetal plasma increases. Several of these hormones are potent vasoconstrictors, which can act to maintain the reduction in the blood flow to nonessential organs. This is demonstrated by the slow rise in mean arterial pressure during hypoxia (Fig. 4.10). Adrenaline is released from the adrenal medulla, partly as a result of increased sympathetic outflow although in the

Fig. 4.10.   Separation of the responses of late-gestation fetal sheep to acute hypoxia (stippled bar) into chemoreflex and other components by comparing the response in intact animals (open symbols) with those in which the carotid chemoreceptors have been denervated (filled symbols). Note that the rapid fall in fetal heart rate in hypoxia does not occur in denervated fetuses, although a slow rise in heart rate and in perfusion (arterial–venous) pressure does occur. The vasodilation in the brain, evident from the fall in carotid vascular resistance, occurs similarly in both groups. The rapid vasoconstriction to the carcass (rise in femoral vascular resistance) is abolished by denervation although a slower vasoconstriction occurs in both groups with the maintained hypoxia. (Redrawn from Giussani *et al.* (1993), Afferent and efferent components of the early cardiovascular response of the term sheep fetus to acute hypoxia, *J. Physiol.*, **461**, 431–49.)

fetus and neonate the adrenal gland is also directly responsive to a fall in PO_2. Along with noradrenaline, which appears in the fetal plasma after release from sympathetic nerve terminals, adrenaline has α-adrenergic effects to constrict resistance vessels and β-adrenergic effects to increase heart rate and contractility. Thus the rise in arterial pressure is usually accompanied by an increase in fetal heart rate. Reduced blood volume, β-adrenergic stimulation and tissue hypoxia also promote renin release from the kidney and this produces a rise in plasma angiotensin II concentration. This promotes vasoconstriction, although it may be selective to some vascular beds. AVP is released from the posterior lobe of the pituitary, and has effects on the kidney and lung liquid secretion as well as being a potent vasoconstrictor. Interestingly, blockade of angiotensin production by an angiotensin-converting enzyme (ACE) inhibitor, or of AVP V_1 receptors, does not substantially reduce the fetal peripheral vasoconstriction during hypoxia. It appears that reflex and adrenergic mechanisms dominate, and indeed chemoreceptor denervation and pharmacological blockade of these mechanisms in animals prevents fetal survival in acute hypoxia. The endocrine mechanisms are likely to have more important effects in response to prolonged hypoxia, including effects on growth. Finally, there are a range of other endocrine agents which increase in concentration in the plasma during hypoxaemia; these include atrial natriuretic peptide (ANP), neuropeptide Y (NPY) and adrenomedullin.

Autocrine/paracrine mechanisms

Vascular smooth muscle, which regulates the tone of resistance vessels in the circulation, is continually under the influence of factors released from smooth muscle cells themselves and from the endothelial cells. Nitric oxide is one of the best-known examples, and its powerful dilator effects on smooth muscle mediate the actions of endogenous vasodilators such as acetylcholine (ACh) or bradykinin as well as those of nitric oxide donors such as sodium nitroprusside. Nitric oxide release is promoted by increased shear-stress of the endothelial cells, for example during an increase in blood flow, and thus vascular resistance falls. Nitric oxide also acts as a growth promoter, providing a key link between the rate of tissue growth, including blood vessel growth, and its blood supply during development. Nitric oxide has also been shown to mediate the fall in cerebral vascular resistance that occurs in hypoxia and it may be involved in the mechanisms which promote brain damage during the 'reperfusion' phase which follows ischaemia. Nitric oxide-mediated dilator responses, at least in the peripheral circulation, appear to develop earlier in gestation than neural (primarily α-adrenergic) constrictor responses.

As discussed earlier, the renin–angiotensin system is a key component of neuroendocrine regulation of the circulation. Recent work has, however, drawn attention to the role of local renin–angiotensin systems at the level of the blood vessels, where all the components exist including renin and ACE as well as the angiotensin receptors. Endothelial cells are also a major source of the peptide endothelin-1. This acts via two major receptors, the endothelin-A receptor, producing constriction of vascular smooth muscle, and the endothelin-B receptor producing relaxation. Apart from paracrine actions, plasma endothelin levels increase in prolonged hypoxia or asphyxia and it may therefore act as a hormone to have effects on distant targets. Similar considerations apply to the prostaglandins and leucotrienes, which are produced in substantial amounts by many tissues including the placenta. Their actions are both local (see above) and systemic. For this reason the vascular endothelium has been said to be the largest endocrine organ in the body.

Cardiovascular control in midgestation

We know that a considerable degree of cardiovascular regulation has developed by late gestation. Precisely when this occurs is not known and it probably depends on the species. In the sheep, the animal most extensively studied, the reflex, endocrine and local mechanisms involved in the cardiovascular response to hypoxia develop after about 60% of gestation. Before this time there is little vasoconstriction in the fetal body, although some vasodilation may occur in the cerebral circulation. This may explain why placental insufficiency in early gestation produces symmetrical growth retardation whilst in late gestation growth is restricted more in the trunk and limbs than the head. It is not known whether this difference in cardiovascular response is due to immaturity of the control processes, or whether the fetus earlier in gestation can avoid mounting such responses as its metabolic requirements are less. In the llama, a species adapted to the low PO_2 of life at high altitude, potent fetal endocrine responses to hypoxaemia are well developed even at 60% of gestation.

The developing fetal circulation is a dynamic system, which responds to the demands placed upon it and which adapts to a sustained challenge. Two examples of such adaptation are now of great interest, in view of their scientific and clinical importance, and are discussed below.

Sustained hypoxia

The circulatory changes in response to acute hypoxaemia, described above, are not maintained if the hypoxaemia persists for more than a few hours. Blood pressure and heart rate return to control levels and fetal breathing and body movements return. Some components of the redistribution of cardiac output are reduced to some extent but growth of the fetal carcass also slows. There is clearly a complicated interrelationship between tissue metabolism and growth and blood supply, which varies between tissues. However, the end result from a clinical viewpoint is that it is not always possible to tell from the available non-invasive measures of the fetal circulation whether a particular fetus is healthy, or has been exposed to prolonged hypoxaemia but has adapted. This is unfortunate, as the ability of the challenged fetus to mount an effective response to a subsequent, superimposed episode of hypoxaemia, (e.g. during the contractions of labour) may be impaired. More might be learned from plasma hormone level measurements (e.g. catecholamines, AVP, angiotensin II, ACTH, cortisol) which show differences in prolonged hypoxaemia. Blood gases and pH in the umbilical cord at delivery are not always helpful, as they may have 'normalized' in the fetus which has adapted, and they will be more dependent on the immediately preceding events during delivery. More advanced methods aimed at gaining information about tissue metabolite levels and energy status, such as near infrared spectroscopy, are being developed, but they are currently expensive and can only be used intrapartum.

Cardiovascular effects of perturbed nutrition in pregnancy

Poor maternal nutrition in pregnancy inevitably constitutes a challenge to fetal development. For the first half of gestation, placental growth and size are greater than fetal, and the placenta itself has substantial nutritional requirements. However, these can change in the face of reduced food intake by the mother, so that a higher proportion of the glucose and amino acids leaving the uterine circulation crosses to the fetus rather than being utilized by the placenta. For this reason, fetal growth is not invariably impaired by reduced nutrition of the pregnant woman. Recent studies have, however, shown that the consequences of reduced nutrition in pregnancy can be far-reaching, even if during fetal and neonatal life the effects appear to be subtle. It is now known that aspects of the intrauterine environment, including nutrition, determine the risk of a range of major diseases including coronary heart disease, hypertension, stroke and type-

2 diabetes. Large epidemiological studies have shown that the risk of such diseases in adult life is correlated with reduced birthweight; however, it is unlikely that the situation is so simple, as birthweight is determined by a complex interaction of factors, and it is also known that body proportions at birth and growth and diet in childhood play important roles. Nonetheless, these studies have generated enormous interest in the field of fetal development and nutrition in pregnancy, and have caused a drastic revision of the idea that risk of cardiovascular disease is solely a combination of genetic predisposition and lifestyle in adulthood.

These ideas have led to considerable experimental work in a variety of species from rodents to nonhuman primates, aimed at determining the underlying mechanisms. In rodents, dietary restriction in pregnancy, either by giving an isocaloric reduced protein diet or by reducing total dietary intake, produces offspring in which blood pressure is higher than controls by about 3 weeks after birth and in which this pressure 'tracks' at a higher level subsequently. Reduction of uterine blood flow produces similar effects in the guinea-pig. In the rat the effect is evident at an earlier postnatal age in the male, but the mechanism for this sex difference is not known. The responses of small blood vessels in vitro, particularly nitric oxide-mediated vasodilator mechanisms, are impaired, and there are also differences in contractile responses to thromboxane analogues and noradrenaline, suggesting differences in vascular smooth muscle maturation or in receptor density.

Using sheep, attention has been focused on studying *fetal* mechanisms. This work has led to some surprising observations. First, it is possible to produce changes in fetal cardiovascular development with only mild restriction of the nutritional intake (85% of control) of the ewe for just the first half of gestation. This produces lower fetal blood pressure in late gestation and also a suppression of fetal hypothalmic-pituitary-adrenal (HPA) axis function. Fetal plasma cortisol is lower, which may account for the lower pressure. After birth a dramatic 'switch' occurs, such that by 3 months of age lambs from such nutritionally challenged ewes have a higher blood pressure and enhanced HPA axis function.

Much attention is now focused on the role which the HPA axis plays in cardiovascular development and the responses to intrauterine stress. The potential of such mechanisms, operating at a sensitive time in prenatal life, to alter the programming of cardiovascular development, is shown by experiments in which the administration of the glucocorticoid dexamethasone to pregnant sheep for only 48 hours at 30 days gestation produced offspring with higher blood pressure, from 100 to 500 days postnatally; administration of the gluco-corticoid for 48 hours at 60 days gestation did not produce such effects. The placenta normally protects the fetus from excessive exposure to endogenous maternal glucocorticoids, due to the action of the enzyme 11β HSD 2, which converts cortisol to the inactive cortisone. It is therefore possible that low activity of this enzyme at a critical period could expose the fetus to high levels of cortisol and affect HPA axis development. If nutritional restriction led to elevated maternal plasma cortisol at this time, changes in fetal developmental programming could be explained. It has been reported that placental 11β HSD activity is correlated with birthweight and inversely correlated with placental weight, and experimental inhibition of activity during pregnancy in the rat produces offspring with elevated blood pressure.

There are, however, other aspects of perturbed cardiovascular development which have to be considered, and which may or may not be related to changes in HPA axis function. One is the renin–angiotensin system (discussed above). Changes in ACE activity have been reported in rats on a low-protein diet, and inhibition of ACE activity in hypertensive pups restores blood pressure to control levels. Changes in plasma cortisol may affect fetal tissue ATI and ATII receptor expression, the former possibly producing alterations in blood pressure. Consideration of the renin-angiotensin system leads to the possibility that renal changes are involved (and of course hypertension of renal origin is well documented in the adult). Growth-restricted human fetuses have reduced numbers of nephrons and the pattern of distribution of renin-containing cells is altered. Finally, there are clear changes in the responses of resistance vessels in vitro to vasoconstrictor and vasodilator agonists. These may accompany vascular remodelling in some tissues and later the development of vascular resistance and compliance. It is clear that considerably more work is needed in this area.

Summary

In this chapter we have concentrated on some key aspects of the fetal circulation. We know that adequate fetal cardiovascular function is essential to growth, development and even to survival. Whilst the physiology of fetal cardiovascular control is complex and as yet imperfectly understood, noninvasive monitoring of aspects of its function are now widely employed in the human fetus. We need considerably more basic research, of necessity using animals, in order to improve the interpretation and diagnostic value of such monitoring. This will be particularly important in identifying fetuses which are chronically hypoxic. In addition, the striking epidemiological observations, which suggest that adult cardiovascular disease may have its origins in fetal life, demand further research on the processes which control the development of the fetal circulation under normal and abnormal conditions.

FURTHER READING

Hanson, M.A., Spencer, J.A.D. and Rodeck, C.H. (1995). *The Fetus and Neonate. Physiology and Clinical Applications*, vol. 1, *The Circulation*. Cambridge: Cambridge University Press.

Thorburn, G.D. and Harding, R. (1994). *Textbook of Fetal Physiology*. Oxford: Oxford University Press.

Long, W.A. (1990). *Fetal and Neonatal Cardiology*. Philadelphia: Saunders.

Rudolph, A.M. (1985). Distribution and regulation of blood flow in the fetal and neonatal lamb. *Circ. Res.*, **57**, 811–21.

Gluckman, P. and Heymann, M. (1986). *Pediatrics and Perinatology: The Scientific Basis*. London: Edward Arnold.

5

Fluid balance

Robert A. Brace

From many different perspectives, the fluid status of the fetus is unique in comparison with later life. The fetus is surrounded by liquid rather than air. The fetal body contains more water, as much as 95% water early in gestation, than the adult which averages 55% water. During late gestation, fluid movements within the fetal body, such as cardiac output, urinary output, swallowing, and lymph flow average 5–10 times normal adult values relative to body weight. Further, the fetal lungs are full of liquid and actively secrete large volumes of liquid each day. Finally, fluid can not only move rapidly between the fetus and mother across the placenta but water and solutes also move rapidly between the amniotic fluid and fetal blood across the fetal surface of the placenta. With so much water, such rapid fluid movements, and pathways for fluid movement unique to the fetus, it should be clear that the regulation of fluid balance in the fetus is more complex than in the adult. This chapter summarizes present knowledge about fetal fluid balance.

Ontogeny of fetal and amniotic fluids

Fetal body water

From the beginning of the fetal period (8 weeks gestation in the human), when the fetus is approximately 90–95% water, there is a continual decline in the relative amount of water within the fetal body until term, when the fetus averages 70% water. During the last month of human fetal development, when the fetus deposits a considerable amount of fat, the rate of decline in water content accelerates (Fig. 5.1). Concomitant with the decline in body water content, there is a progressive redistribution of water from the extracellular space into the intracellular space. Presumably this is due to an increase in cellularity as the fetal tissues develop in conjunction with a decline in the extracellular matrix.

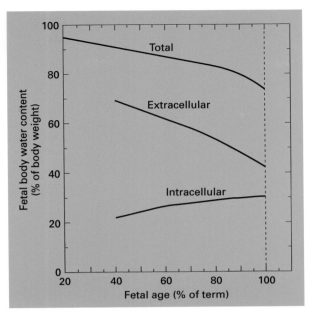

Fig. 5.1.   Body water content in the human fetus and its distribution across gestation. (Data from Friis-Hansen (1961), *Pediatrics*, **28**, 169.)

Blood, plasma and interstitial volumes

Extracellular fluid volume comprises plasma and interstitial volumes; thus the decrease in extracellular fluid volume as a fraction of body weight during gestation (Fig. 5.1) may be expected to be associated with decreases in interstitial fluid volume and plasma volume. A decrease in plasma volume would lead to a decrease in blood volume relative to fetal body weight. Recent studies, however, which determined blood volume with indicator dilution labels that do not escape from the fetal circulation, found that fetal blood volume averages 110–115 ml/kg body weight with no suggestion of a change with gestational age. In addition, approximately 30% of the blood which circulates in the fetal body is located within the umbilical cord and fetal part of the placenta. Thus, blood volume within the fetal body averages only 80 ml/kg, a value only slightly larger than the lean adult value of 75 ml/kg. Because human fetal haematocrit increases from 30% at midterm to 44% at term, there is a decrease in the plasma volume relative to body weight during gestation but this is small compared with the large decrease in interstitial fluid volume which occurs as extracellular volume decreases.

The regulation of red cell mass is under the control of the hormone

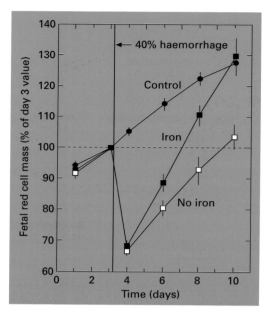

Fig. 5.2.   The effects of intra-amniotic iron supplementation of red cell production following haemorrhage in the ovine fetus. (Data are means ± SEs from Brace *et al.* (1999), *Am. J. Obstet. Gynecol.*, **180**, 214)

erythropoietin, which is produced in the kidneys, liver and placenta of the fetus, but only in the kidneys of the adult. Red cells have a circulating lifespan of 120 days in the adult and thus the daily red cell production rate is only 0.8%/day. In the fetus, red cell production rate is higher because red cells have only half the lifespan of those in the adult, and also the fetus is growing rapidly. In the ovine fetus, body growth rate is 3.5%/day and the red cell production rate is 4%/day. In the late-gestation human fetus, the growth rate slows to only 0.5%/day near term and the red cell production rate is 1%/day. When made anaemic by hae-morrhage, fetuses undergo only a mild enhancement of red cell production rate by 60%. However, if supplemental iron is provided to the fetus, red cell produc-tion is greatly enhanced to almost three times normal levels as seen in Fig. 5.2. Clearly, iron is a limiting factor in fetal red cell production.

Amniotic fluid volume

Amniotic fluid performs many important functions in the fetus. It cushions the fetus from external trauma and provides space for the developing fetus to exer-

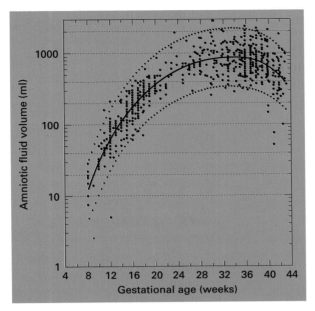

Fig. 5.3.   Amniotic fluid volume in normal fetuses as a function of gestational age showing regression line and 95% population confidence interval. (Data from Brace and Wolf (1989), *Am. J. Obstet. Gynecol.*, **161**, 382.)

cise its growing muscles. It prevents the uterus from compressing the fetus and thereby allows normal lung development. Amniotic fluid also provides a fluid reservoir from which the fetus swallows. This last activity provides several important growth factors which stimulate development of the gastrointestinal tract. Thus, in order for the fetus to develop normally it is important to have amniotic fluid volume within its normal range.

Normal amniotic fluid volume changes with gestational age are shown in Fig. 5.3. In humans, mean amniotic fluid volume increases from approximately 20 ml at 10 weeks gestation to 800 ml at 32–34 weeks. Little further change occurs until near term when volume begins to decrease. It is of particular importance to note that there is a wide normal range for amniotic fluid volume in healthy fetuses; for example, the 95% confidence interval ranges from 300 to 2000 ml at 32 weeks gestation. Further, there can be large decreases in amniotic fluid volume in pregnancies that go beyond term. Clinically, amniotic fluid volume is rarely measured directly and an ultrasound index of amniotic fluid volume is used but, to date, the correlation between ultrasonographic measurements and true amniotic fluid volume has not been made.

Abnormalities in amniotic fluid volume include oligohydramnios (too little amniotic fluid) and polyhydramnios (too much amniotic fluid, also termed hydramnios) and both are associated with increased rates of fetal and neonatal morbidity and mortality. Oligohydramnios early in gestation can have a fetal loss rate as high as 80%, whereas late in gestation it is associated with several problems including umbilical cord compression and lung hypoplasia. Polyhydramnios can lead to maternal respiratory distress as well as preterm delivery.

Placental fluid transfer

All fetal fluids are ultimately derived from maternal fluids. The term *fluid* is used to represent water along with dissolved solutes. There are two potential routes for fluid entry into the fetal compartment: (1) transfer from the uterine wall across the chorion and amnion and into the amniotic fluid, with subsequent absorption by the fetus; (2) transfer from the maternal to fetal circulation across the placenta. Early in gestation the uterine glands secrete a fluid called 'uterine milk', which may be a source of amniotic fluid during the embryonic period. However, all studies of the 'transmembranous' fluxes in the later part of gestation suggest that very little water and no solutes enter the fetal compartment from the uterine wall by crossing the membranes. In contrast, there are rapid fluxes of water and solutes across the placenta. In rapidly growing fetuses, approximately 10% of fetal body water may be derived as a normal byproduct of metabolism. In slowly growing fetuses such as the late-gestation human fetus, as much as 30% of the body water content is derived as a metabolic by-product.

In order to understand fluid balance in the fetus it is essential to distinguish between the net movement of water across the placenta and diffusional water movement. As background, recall that as blood passes through a single capillary in the adult, each water molecule diffuses back and forth across the capillary wall 100 times, whereas only 1% of the water passing through a capillary is filtered from the vascular to the interstitial compartment. This is a ratio of 10 000 to 1 and it is only that 1 part in 10 000 which affects fluid balance. Even though there have been several studies of the diffusional movement of water between mother and fetus in humans and animals, these studies yield essentially no information relevant to fetal fluid balance because the studies cannot resolve the 1 part in 10 000 needed to quantify net fluid movements.

For many years scientists have attempted to determine the transplacental forces responsible for the gradual accumulation of water in the fetal compartment as pregnancy advances. In theory, either hydrostatic pressure or osmotic forces are responsible. Several hypotheses have been offered: two of the more attractive proposals are that either the high concentration of amino acids in the fetus (due to active placental transport) or the high bicarbonate concentration relative to maternal levels (due to metabolism) are responsible for net fetal water accumulation due to their osmotic effects acting at the placenta. In species with very low placental permeabilities, leakage of sodium, with water following osmotically, has also been suggested as the force responsible for fetal water acquisition. The problem with all of these hypotheses is that, with 40 weeks to accumulate a total of perhaps 3400 ml of water in the human fetus, amniotic fluid and placenta combined, net water accumulation averages only 0.5 ml/hour or 12 ml/day. In the human placenta, a hydrostatic pressure gradient of only a small fraction of 1 mmHg would be required to move this amount of water; that is, osmotic forces generated by tiny concentration gradients would be sufficient. These hydrostatic and osmotic forces are so small that they are beyond the accuracy and limitations of present day measurement techniques. Further, these forces are probably small compared with the many fluctuations in hydrostatic and osmotic pressures which occur under normal conditions. The actual daily transplacental water gain varies depending on the species, gestational age, fetal growth rate, and body composition of the fetus. For example, a 3 kg human fetus which is 70% water and growing at 0.5%/day requires only 11 ml/day of water whereas a 3 kg ovine fetus which is 75% water and growing at 3.5%/day requires 79 ml/day of water for normal growth when amniotic fluid volume is constant.

An approach to testing the osmotic hypothesis for water accumulation in the fetal compartment is to infuse solutes into chronically catheterized animal fetuses for several days and examine any resulting fluid imbalances. Infusion of glucose has been reported to make the fetus hypoxic and acidotic due to increased metabolism without increased oxygen delivery but fluid imbalances are not usually reported. Concentrated sodium chloride infusion does not result in excess fluid within the fetal compartment and the infused sodium chloride is transferred to the mother. However, infusion of lactate into the fetal circulation produces polyhydramnios with 4–5 l of excess amniotic fluid. This clearly supports the osmotic hypothesis for fetal fluid accumulation and explains why anaemic human fetuses with elevated lactate levels may become oedematous and/or develop polyhydramnios.

Maternal factors can also be major determinants of fetal fluid balance. Maternal dehydration over a period of days causes oligohydramnios, while rapid ingestion of 2 l of water has been reported to increase amniotic fluid volume in women. Rapid increases in maternal osmolality can cause fetal fluid to be rapidly absorbed across the placenta although, unfortunately, there is little overall understanding of the long-term effects of maternal factors on fetal fluid balance.

Internal fetal fluid movements

Fluid normally filters from the plasma across the fetal capillary walls and enters the interstitial space. This capillary filtration is offset by the removal of a similar volume of interstitial fluid by the lymphatic system with return of lymph to the circulation. If capillary filtration is in excess of lymphatic removal, the interstitial space expands. The compliance of the fetal interstitial space is 45 ml/mmHg per kilogram body weight, which is 10 times the adult value; this allows interstitial absorption of considerable amounts of fluid with only small increases in interstitial fluid pressure. Fetal oedema develops when interstitial fluid accumulation becomes excessive. Gross whole-body fetal oedema is termed hydrops fetalis; the fetus can become nearly twice normal size because of such oedema.

Capillary filtration

As in the adult, the rate of fluid filtration across the capillary wall is described by the classical Starling equation:

$$J_v = CFC \times (\Delta P - \sigma \Delta \pi)$$

where CFC is the capillary filtration coefficient, and ΔP and $\Delta \pi$ are the transcapillary hydrostatic and protein osmotic pressure gradients, respectively. σ is the reflection coefficient, a factor which characterizes the effectiveness of the plasma and interstitial proteins at generating osmotic pressures. σ ranges from a value of zero for large pores which do not restrict protein movement to a value of 1 for pores which allow water but not proteins to pass through the pore. Thus, with no change in either hydrostatic pressures or protein concentrations, capillary filtration can change if either the filtration coefficient or the reflection coefficient changes. This can occur because of changes in the number of pores within the capillary wall or changes in the size of existing pores.

Fluid rapidly filters across fetal capillaries. In a 3-kg fetus, approximately 1500 ml/day of fluid filters out of the plasma and into the interstitial space. This high capillary filtration rate occurs because the whole body capillary filtration coefficient in the late gestation fetus is five times that in the adult per unit body weight and is probably even higher earlier in gestation. Furthermore, the capillary permeability surface area product for plasma proteins in the fetus averages 15 times adult values while the reflection coefficient for plasma proteins is lower in the fetus than the adult (0.7 versus 0.95 as a whole-body average).

Lymphatic function

Almost all lymphatics return fluid to the circulation in the base of the neck at the junction of the jugular and subclavian veins where the embryonic lymph sacs originated. The lymph flow rate in the left thoracic lymph duct, the body's largest lymphatic vessel, averages 0.6 ml/minute in a 3-kg ovine fetus, which is half of normal adult thoracic duct lymph flow rates (1–2 ml/minute). Because the left thoracic duct carries about two-thirds of all lymph, the total body lymph flow rate in the fetus averages 1 ml/minute (~1500 ml/day). In addition to fluid volume, the lymphatics return dissolved plasma proteins such as albumin to the circulation. By returning fluid, the lymphatics prevent excess fluid accumulation in the tissues and, by returning protein, the interstitial space concentration of protein is reduced. The net effect of this function is that interstitial protein osmotic pressure is low, which in turn reduces the amount of fluid being filtered at the capillary because of the effect on the Starling equation. Both plasma and lymph protein concentrations are about half normal adult values so the ratio of protein concentrations in thoracic duct lymph and plasma averages 0.7 in the fetus, just as in the adult. This is possible because the combination of high capillary filtration rate, high protein permeability and low protein reflection coefficient described above allows plasma proteins to move across the fetal capillaries sufficiently fast to maintain interstitial protein concentration in the presence of high lymph flow rates.

The normal functioning of the lymphatic system depends on two primary factors. One is the relationship between lymph flow rate and the outflow pressure for the lymphatic system, which equals central venous pressure at the junction of the subclavian and jugular veins. When presented graphically, this relationship is referred to as the *lymph flow function curve* (Fig. 5.4). The other primary factor which affects lymphatic function is the relationship between lymph flow rate and the hydrostatic pressure within the interstitial space

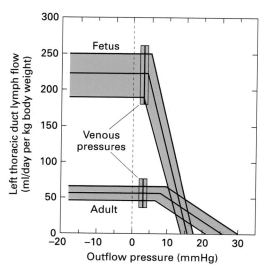

Fig. 5.4. Lymph flow function curves in ovine fetus and adult. Data are means ± 95% confidence interval. (Data from Brace (1989), *Am. J. Obstet. Gynecol.*, **160**, 494, and Brace and Valenzuela (1990), *Am. J. Physiol.*, **258**, R240.)

surrounding the initial lymphatics, i.e. interstitial fluid pressure. This, in turn, is a function of both interstitial fluid volume and interstitial compliance.

A comparison between lymph flow function curves in fetal and adult sheep is shown in Fig. 5.4. Although venous pressure in the fetus and adult is similar (2–4 mmHg), the lymph flow function curves are quite different. Under basal conditions, lymph flow rate (millilitres per minute per kilogram body weight) in the fetus is much higher than in the adult. Secondly, any increase in venous pressure causes a decrease in lymph flow rate in the fetus whereas venous pressure has to be increased to two to three times its normal value before lymph flow begins to decrease in the adult. Finally, increasing venous pressure to only 15 mmHg causes lymph flow to cease in the fetus whereas this same increment in venous pressure causes only a small reduction in lymph flow in the adult. A venous pressure of 25 mmHg is required to stop lymph from flowing in the adult, although a decrease in venous pressure does not alter lymph flow rate in either the fetus or adult. This occurs in part because the walls of the lymphatic vessels collapse when venous pressure falls below zero and therefore the negative pressure is not transmitted through the lymphatic system.

It is difficult to explore the relationship between lymph flow rate and tissue hydration in detail as it is not possible to measure an average interstitial fluid

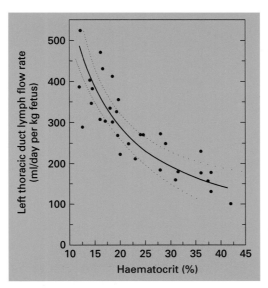

Fig. 5.5.   Lymph flow in anaemic fetuses as a function of haematocrit showing regression line and its 95% confidence interval. (Data from Davis *et al.* (1996), *Am. J. Obstet. Gynecol.*, **174**, 1469.)

pressure in the body as a whole. One approach to exploring variations in lymphatic function as tissue fluid volume changes is to infuse into the circulation equivalent amounts of fluid relative to body weight and compare the resulting changes in lymph flow rate as the infused fluid rapidly filters out of the circulation and into the interstitial space. In the late-gestation ovine fetus, large volume intravascular infusions cause left thoracic duct lymph flow rate to increase to three to four times normal as in the adult, suggesting that the responsiveness to changes in hydration is mature.

Another approach to exploring lymphatic function with changes in interstitial volume is to alter fetal haematocrit by exchange transfusion with saline. In both human and animal fetuses, severe anaemia is associated with severe fetal oedema. Fig. 5.5 shows that there is a gradual increase in thoracic duct lymph flow rate as haematocrit is reduced over a period of many days. There appears to be no maximum in lymph flow rate at the lowest haematocrit studied indicating that oedema development in the fetus is not normally due to lymphatic failure but rather to an overwhelming increase in filtration rate at the capillary wall.

Endocrine factors alter thoracic duct lymph flow rates in the fetus as in the adult; for example, atrial natriuretic factor (ANF) suppresses flow while angiotensin II stimulates it. Presently, there is no clear indication as to when sympathetic innervation of the lymphatic system becomes functional in the fetus or when this system matures.

External fetal fluid movements

In comparison with the net transplacental absorption from the mother, which averages 12 ml/day, other fluid movements into and out of the fetal body are very high. In late gestation, a 3-kg ovine fetus urinates 25–30% of its body weight per day (approximately 900 ml/day) and swallows only slightly less (~700 ml/day). The fetal lungs secrete, on average, 10% of fetal body weight per day during the last third of gestation (300 ml/day). Of this, only 1–2 ml/day are needed to expand the lungs as they grow, and the remaining volume of approximately 300 ml/day exits the lungs by the trachea. Approximately half of this fluid is swallowed as it flows out of the trachea and the rest enters the amniotic fluid. It is apparent then that the late-gestation ovine fetus swallows about 550 ml of amniotic fluid each day in addition to 150 ml of lung fluid. The fetus also swallows perhaps 12 ml/day of the potassium- and mucus-rich secretions from the fetal nasal and buccal mucosa or half of the 24 ml/day secreted in a 3-kg ovine fetus.

Intramembranous flow

Using the above values for fluid flows, swallowing and placental filtration combined provide about 725 ml/day of fluid entry into the fetal body whereas renal excretion plus lung and head secretions account for about 1225 ml/day of fluid loss from the fetal body. The difference of 500 ml/day equals the amount of fluid moving from the amniotic sac directly into the fetal blood across the fetal surface of the placenta. This movement of fluid is referred to as 'intramembranous' flow for which the anatomical details are species dependent. In many species including primates, there is a rich network of fetal capillaries just below the fetal surface of the placenta which provides the capillary surface area for intramembranous exchange of water and solutes. In some species including the ovine fetus, the chorion and outer surface of the amnion are vascularized and perfused with fetal blood. For these species, the capillaries within the membranes plus those within the fetal surface of the placenta constitute the intramembranous pathway. Even though there may be major anatomical differences between species, the high fluid movements through the intramembranous pathway appear to be common to all mammalian species.

Permeability of the intramembranous pathway, in combination with the concentration and osmotic gradients between amniotic fluid and fetal blood, determines the net water and solute movements. Studies in which the fetal oesophagus has been ligated have shown not only rapid intramembranous movements of water and solutes, but also that oesophageal ligation produces a large increase in intramembranous permeability such that water and arginine vasopressin (AVP) enter from the amniotic compartment into the fetal circulation at twice normal rates.

The concentration and osmotic gradients between fetal blood and amniotic fluid are large and therefore the intramembranous fluxes are potentially large. Amniotic fluid osmolality is 20–25 mosm/kg below that of fetal blood, thereby providing a potential osmotic pressure gradient of 400–500 mmHg for water movement out of the amniotic space. Most of the urea excreted by the fetal kidneys is reabsorbed into the fetal circulation through the intramembranous pathway. Amniotic fluid sodium concentration (Na^+) averages 20–30 mmol/l below plasma concentrations while amniotic fluid chloride concentration (Cl^-) averages 10–20 mmol/l below that of plasma. Because the fetal kidneys and lungs produce only about half of the sodium and chloride swallowed by the fetus, diffusion of sodium and chloride through the intramembranous pathway accounts for this differential.

Swallowing

The fetus begins to swallow as embryogenesis is complete (about 8 weeks in the human) and swallows an increasing volume of fluid as gestation progresses. The regulation of fetal swallowing activity is only beginning to be understood. The neurogenic regulation of swallowing activity becomes functional at least by the beginning of the third trimester. Also, classical stimuli which produce swallowing in the adult, such as increased osmolality or elevated angiotensin II levels, are effective at stimulating swallowing in the late-gestation fetus. Hypoxia is a potent stimulus for suppressing fetal swallowing activity. With the onset of acute hypoxia, fetal swallowing ceases, whereas after 24 hours of continuous hypoxia, the daily swallowed rate has returned to only half the normoxic levels.

The volume of amniotic fluid swallowed depends on the amount available as well as other factors. Reducing amniotic fluid volume does not alter the incidence or frequency of the electromechanical events associated with swallowing but the net volume swallowed is reduced and infusion of isotonic saline into the amniotic sac is associated with an increased volume of fluid which is swallowed.

A related observation is that long-term infusions of isotonic saline into the fetal circulation are associated not only with an increased production of urine but also with an increased swallowed volume. The mechanisms for these increases are not understood but may be related to an increase in amniotic fluid volume.

A variety of important growth factors are in the fluid swallowed by the fetus and these are essential for growth and development of the gastrointestinal tract as discussed in Chapter 7. In addition, because of the very large volume of fluid swallowed, it may be expected that fetal swallowing is critical to maintaining normal fetal and amniotic fluid balance. However, in human fetuses with oesophageal atresia or obstruction, and in animal fetuses with ligated oesophagi, fluid balance within the fetal body and amniotic compartment appears to be normal. This is surprising in view of the fact that the fetus continues to excrete essentially normal volumes of urine (900 ml/day) into the amniotic sac. In order to compensate for these changes, the filtration coefficient and permeabilities of the intramembranous pathway must increase markedly so that all of the increase in both excreted urine and secreted lung fluid is returned to the fetus via the intramembranous route.

Lung secretion

As discussed in Chapter 6, the lungs secrete a volume of liquid equal to approximately 10% of fetal body weight each day during the last third of gestation. This fluid is derived from the blood passing through the lung capillaries and is returned to the fetal circulation after either being swallowed or reabsorbed from the amniotic sac via the intramembranous pathway. In this process, fetal lung fluid contributes solutes to the amniotic fluid, including the phospholipids. Lung liquid also contributes chloride to the amniotic fluid as it has a high chloride concentration (150 mmol/l) relative to fetal blood (100 mmol/l) and amniotic fluid (90 mmol/l).

Kidney development and production of urine

Development of the kidneys

The development of kidneys during embryogenesis is unusual as there are actually three paired organs which develop: the pronephros, the mesonephros and the metanephros. The pronephros develop at 23–24 days in humans and contain primitive tubules which are nonfunctional. Shortly thereafter the mesonephros begin to develop and the pronephros regress except for the duct. The mesonephros contain tubules, produce urine, and are the largest intra-abdominal structures during early development in some species. In humans, the mesonephros reach maximal size at 8 weeks and complete regression occurs by 16 weeks. The metanephros arise from the ureteric bud on the mesonephric duct beginning at 5–6 weeks gestation in humans and develop into the permanent kidneys. The number of nephrons within the fetal kidneys increases with gestation until 34 weeks when nephrogenesis is complete. Thereafter, the kidneys continue to grow and mature as the loops of Henle penetrate deeper into the renal medulla.

Urine flow rate

In the human fetus, urine probably first enters the amniotic sac when the cloacal membrane degenerates at 7–8 weeks. Urine entry may be continuous at this early age and become periodic as the urinary bladder and its sphincters develop functionally. During the latter part of gestation, the bladder fills every 20–30 minutes and is emptied by active contraction of the bladder wall during micturition. Urine exits the bladder through the urethra and is excreted into the amniotic fluid. In several species, including sheep, cattle and horses, the fetal urinary bladder has a second outlet, allowing urine to pass from the bladder through a small tube within the umbilical cord (the urachus) into a second fluid filled sac (the allantois). The allantois lies between the amnion and chorion and contains approximately the same fluid volume as the amniotic sac. In other species including humans, although the urachus develops during the embryonic period, the allantoic sac does not develop and therefore fetal urine is excreted only through the urethra.

In late gestation, fetal urine production averages 0.2 ml/minute per kilogram fetal body weight or 900 ml/day near term as discussed previously. In the human fetus, urine production rate varies with fetal behavioural state and there is a 24-hour rhythm flow which may be related to maternal eating and drinking. Fetal urine production also varies with amniotic fluid volume: for example, oligohydramnios is associated with low urine production rates and polyhydramnios may be associated with high fetal urine production rates depending on the cause of the polyhydramnios.

There are a variety of stimuli which alter urine production by the fetus. Acute hypoxia elevates fetal AVP levels and reduces urine production. However, urine production returns to normal over a few hours as plasma AVP approaches near-normal levels, even though the fetus remains hypoxic. Fetal blood loss transiently reduces urine production, an effect mediated by elevated plasma AVP concentration in combination with a decrease in arterial pressure.

Composition of urine

From when it is first formed, fetal urine differs in composition from adult urine. Fetal urine osmolality is lower than blood osmolality whereas adult urine osmolality is generally considerably higher than blood osmolality. In late gestation, fetal urine osmolality usually is in the range of 100–150 mosm/kg water, and occasionally is as low as 60 mosm/kg, while blood osmolality is approximately 300 mosm/kg. Early in gestation, when the mesonephros are functional, fetal urine has a low osmolality as well as low sodium and chloride concentrations.

The low urine osmolality in the fetus occurs despite the presence of AVP in the fetal circulation at concentrations similar to those in the adult. This AVP is of fetal origin as it does not cross the human placenta. The low fetal urine osmolality is not due to a lack of sensitivity of the kidneys to AVP as only small changes in plasma AVP concentration are effective in altering fetal renal function. Rather, the low urine osmolality in the fetus occurs because the kidneys have not developed a high concentration of interstitial osmolytes and do not have the long loops of Henle which penetrate deep into the renal medulla as occurs in the adult. Fetal urine osmolality that is higher than blood osmolality is unusual but can occur late in gestation under conditions of fetal stress or exogenously produced maximal AVP antidiuresis. Induced changes in fetal urine composition with exogenous AVP administration depend strongly on the amount of AVP administered, since low doses may induce an antidiuresis whereas moderate to high plasma levels of AVP often produce a diuresis due to an elevation in vascular pressures.

Glomerular filtration rate (GFR) and renal blood flow

Renal blood flow is low in the fetus as is GFR. During the last third of gestation, renal blood flow is fairly constant relative to body weight and averages 20 ml/minute per kilogram fetal body weight in nonstressed fetuses. GFR also is steady and averages 1–1.2 ml/minute per kilogram. With the fetal haematocrit averaging approximately 30%, it can be seen that the filtration fraction averages 8–9% of renal plasma flow.

The regulation of renal blood flow in the fetus has a number of similarities and differences when compared with the adult. Renal responses to circulating vasoactive hormones develop very early in gestation, most probably during the embryonic period as the tissues are first formed. However, the renal vascular responses to renal nerve stimulation do not develop until late in gestation and mature after birth.

Glomerular–tubular balance

In the adult most of the filtered sodium (80–85%) is reabsorbed in the proximal tubule. Fine tuning of sodium reabsorption is achieved in the distal tubule under the regulation of aldosterone so that normally less than 1% of the filtered sodium is excreted. In the fetus, only 50–65% of the filtered sodium is reabsorbed proximally. The delivery of 35–50% of the filtered sodium to the distal tubule is a large sodium load which may be more than can be reabsorbed. The result is that 6–7% of the filtered sodium is excreted by the fetus. In addition, exogenous aldosterone in the fetus generally has only a modest effect on sodium excretion although it does reduce the sodium to potassium excretion ratio. The high rate of sodium excretion in the fetus and the modest effects of aldosterone can be explained from two perspectives. First, plasma sodium concentration in the fetus is totally controlled by the mother and hence any control that the fetus tried to exercise would be ineffective. Second, the high sodium excretion rate plus the high urine flow rate delivers a large volume of fluid to the amniotic sac, thereby promoting an adequate amniotic fluid volume.

Regulation of fetal blood volume

The two primary components of blood are red cells and plasma. Because total red cell volume (or mass) and plasma volume are controlled separately, regulation of these two components must be understood in order to comprehend the regulation of circulating fetal blood volume.

Basal conditions

Blood volume in the fetus is the sum of blood volumes in the fetal body, umbilical cord and fetal part of the placenta. In the healthy fetus, circulating blood volume increases exponentially as gestation proceeds. However, blood volume in the fetus averages 113 ml/kg and changes little with gestational age. In individual ovine fetuses, blood volume ranges from 94 to 128 ml/kg. These variations are not due to differences in red cell mass alone because blood volume per kilogram fetus does not vary with haematocrit. Rather, the differences are due to the combined differences in red cell mass plus plasma volume such that fetuses with high blood volume have a high red cell mass plus a high plasma volume and vice versa.

Acute changes

Under acute conditions such as hypoxia, changes in blood volume are due exclusively to changes in plasma volume because the fetus does not have a pool of releasable red cells such as occurs in the spleen of the adult. With the onset of fetal hypoxia, circulating blood volume can decrease by as much as 12–15% within 10 minutes, due to the rapid filtration of plasma into the fetal interstitial spaces. This occurs in part because the hypoxia-induced increases in both arterial and venous pressures cause an increase in capillary hydrostatic pressure. An increase in the capillary filtration coefficient mediated by increased plasma ANF concentration may also contribute to this rapid movement of plasma into the interstitial space.

With experimentally induced disturbances in blood volume, the fetus has a remarkable ability to return blood volume to near-normal levels. Following rapid intravascular infusions of physiological saline, only 6% of the infused volume remains intravascular after 30 minutes compared with 30% in the adult. Following rapid haemorrhage, the fetus replaces 50–60% of the lost volume in 30 minutes compared with only half this amount in the adult. This enhanced ability of the fetus to maintain its blood volume is due to both rapid and extensive fluid movements across capillaries. Such movements are rapid because the capillary filtration coefficient is five times adult values, and they can be extensive because the interstitial space is 10 times more compliant than in the adult.

Long-term changes

The enhanced blood volume regulation in the fetus also occurs over longer time periods. Following fetal haemorrhage over 2 hours, fetal blood volume returns to normal within a further 2 hours due to an increase in plasma volume, whereas 24–48 hours would be required in the adult. With intravascular saline

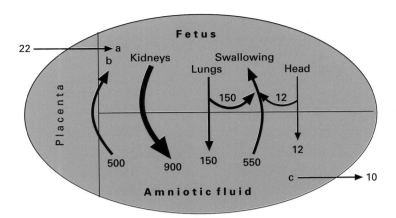

Fig. 5.6. Synthesis of normal flows into and out of the late gestation fetus and its amniotic fluid. Numbers are flow rates in millilitres per day. a, transplacental; b, intramembranous; c, transmembranous.

infusions as large as 1–4 litres over 24 hours (i.e. 0.7 to 2.8 ml/minute), fetal blood volume is elevated by only 3–5% (4–6 ml/kg), as the excess fluid is excreted by the fetal kidneys and is transplacentally transferred to the mother.

Regulation of amniotic fluid volume

Amniotic fluid was once considered to be a relatively stagnant pool of fluid surrounding the fetus. From the flow dynamics discussed previously, it is apparent that amniotic fluid is far from stagnant. Fig. 5.6 summarizes these flows for the late-gestation fetus. It is apparent from Fig. 5.6 that changes in any one of these flows could lead to alterations in amniotic fluid volume. Furthermore, over a period of weeks to months as occurs during pregnancy, the changes in amniotic fluid volume could be potentially huge. It is important to recognize also that it is not presently known whether amniotic fluid volume is regulated. For this to be so, one or more sensors with associated effector mechanisms must provide feedback to return the volume towards normal when it is too high or too low. Although no such sensor has been identified, the fetal membranes and fetal surface of the placenta are ideally situated to provide this regulatory function.

A number of studies and observations in animals have suggested that amniotic fluid volume is regulated. Amniotic fluid volume returns to near normal levels over 48 hours following drainage of two-thirds of the initial volume. Following the infusion of an isotonic saline, amniotic fluid volume returns to normal over 24 hours whereas amniotic fluid volume remains elevated 24 hours following intra-amniotic infusion of an isotonic mannitol solution. In addition, the infusion of lactate into the fetal circulation elevates plasma lactate concentration, leading to increased renal lactate excretion, and an elevation in amniotic lactate concentrations as well as a large increase in amniotic fluid volume. The results of these mannitol and lactate infusion experiments suggest that osmolytes which are larger than sodium and chloride affect amniotic fluid volume through their osmotic properties.

In contrast to amniotic fluid volume frequently being normal when the fetus cannot swallow, or when the trachea is obstructed, amniotic fluid volume is rarely normal when fetal urine does not enter the amniotic sac. Instead, severe oligohydramnios develops. Under these conditions, although the fetus continues to grow, the fetal body is distorted because uterine volume is reduced. In addition, the lungs do not grow sufficiently and the infant may die in the newborn period from pulmonary hypoplasia (Chapter 6).

Overall integration of fetal fluid balance

Fluid balance in the fetus is the integration of all fluid flows into and out of the fetal body. These fluid exchanges are necessary for normal growth and development and occur between mother and fetus as well as between fetus and amniotic fluid. That the fetus maintains a normal fluid balance and a normal amniotic fluid volume most of the time indicates that fetal and amniotic fluid volume regulatory mechanisms are highly effective. In the adult, the primary controllers of fluid homeostasis are the kidneys as they retain or shed fluid as necessary to maintain normal fluid balance. The kidneys cannot be the primary controllers in the fetus because amniotic fluid volume would be abnormal far more often than it is if they were. Thus, the primary control of fetal fluid balance must occur at the placenta. Whether fetal or maternal factors dominate and whether the primary forces are hydrostatic or osmotic has not yet been determined. An understanding of the overall regulation of fetal and amniotic fluid balance is only at its early stages, yet is an aspect directly linked to both the physiology and pathophysiology of fetal development.

FURTHER READING

Brace, R.A., Gilbert, W.M. and Moore, T.R. (ed.) (1993). Amniotic Fluid. *Semin. Perinatol.*, **17**(3).

Brace, R.A., Ross, M.G. and Robillard, J.E. (eds.) (1989). *Fetal and Neonatal Body Fluids: The Scientific Basis Underlying Clinical Practice.* Ithaca, NY: Perinatology Press.

Brace, R.A., Hanson, M.A. and Rodeck, C.H. (eds.) (1998). *Fetus and Neonate,* vol. 4, *Body Fluids and Kidney function.* Cambridge: Cambridge University Press.

Brace, R.A. (1995). Progress toward understanding the regulation of amniotic fluid volume: water and solute fluxes in and through the fetal extraplacental membranes. *Placenta*, **16**, 1–18.

6

Respiratory system

Stuart B. Hooper and
Richard Harding

During fetal life the future airways of the lung are liquid-filled and gas exchange occurs across the placenta. Thus, at birth the lung must rapidly assume a role that it has not previously performed, and in most cases the transition to an air-breathing existence is rapid and uneventful. To exchange respiratory gases successfully, the lung must be appropriately grown, have developed millions of thin-walled alveoli that are perfused by an extensive vascular network and the airways must be cleared of liquid. In addition, the lungs must be structurally and biochemically mature so that they inflate with ease and do not collapse during expiration.

Structural development of the lung

Structural development of the lung is, by convention, divided into four or five stages based on its microscopic appearance; these are the embryonic, pseudo-glandular, canalicular and saccular/alveolar stages (Table 6.1). Lung development is a continuous process that extends beyond birth in most species and, therefore, dividing it into a series of stages is somewhat arbitrary. The gestational ages which coincide with these stages of lung development are shown in Table 6.1. The stage of lung development at which birth occurs varies between species.

Embryonic stage

The primitive lung bud appears as an outgrowth from the ventral surface of the embryonic foregut at about 22 days gestation in humans and 17 days in sheep. This bud rapidly divides to form a branched tube-like structure that gives rise to the epithelial lining of the larynx, trachea, bronchioles and lower airways including the alveoli. As the epithelial cell tubes branch, they invade and become invested with the splanchnic mesoderm which forms all nonepithelial

Table 6.1. Stages of lung development in three species and the gestational ages at which they occur

Stage of lung development	Humans (weeks)	Rats (days)	Sheep (days)
Embryonic	0–6	0–13	0–40
Pseudoglandular	~6–16	~13–18	~40–80
Canalicular	~16–26	~18–20	~80–120
Saccular	~26–term	~20–term	~120–term
Alveolar	32–after birth	after birth	~120–after birth

structures such as blood vessels, fibroblasts, lymphatics and smooth muscle. The surrounding mesoderm also regulates the branching of the epithelial cell tubes as branching ceases in its absence, although airway growth continues.

Pseudoglandular stage

This stage is characterized by rapid growth and proliferation of the primitive airways caused by repeated branching at the distal ends of the epithelial tubes. The future airways are liquid-filled and are lined with tall columnar epithelial cells which give the lung a gland-like appearance. The primitive respiratory units of the lung first begin to develop although the 'airways' are surrounded by poorly vascularized mesenchyme. As gas exchange is dependent upon highly perfused gas exchange units and small diffusion distances, the structure of the lung at this stage precludes it from functioning as an organ of gas exchange. The primitive epithelial cells lining the future airways begin to differentiate into goblet cells, mucous glands and ciliated epithelial cells. This progressive maturation begins at the central zone (lung hilus) and radiates outwards towards the periphery of the lung.

Canalicular stage

During the canicular stage the 'airways' widen and lengthen, leading to a large increase in the potential air space of the lung. In particular, the complexity of the terminal airways greatly increases with further development of the terminal and respiratory bronchioles which eventually subdivide into terminal saccules. The mesenchymal tissue surrounding the terminal respiratory units thins and becomes increasingly vascularized, which reduces gas diffusing distances between capillaries and adjacent terminal airsacs; these developmental processes overlap in time with the preceding and following stages of development. Differentiated epithelial cells also first appear in the terminal airsacs during the canalicular stage. Epithelial cells destined to become type I cells elongate and form thin cytoplasmic extensions that provide a minimal barrier to gas exchange. Epithelial cells destined to become type II cells retain their spherical shape and develop cytoplasmic inclusions, called lamellar bodies, that contain surfactant. During the latter part of this stage, gas exchange becomes possible.

Alveolar/saccular stages

During the alveolar stage, which begins before birth and proceeds into early childhood, the terminal saccules progressively subdivide into individual alveoli due to remodelling of the saccule walls. This involves part of the saccule wall forming a low ridge that projects into the saccule lumen. As the ridges increase in height they form walls called secondary septa which subdivide the original saccule into individual alveoli. The laying down of elastic extracellular matrix (ECM) components in the apex of these septa is thought to be an integral part of alveolar formation. Thus, after alveolarization is complete, a ring of elastic fibres surrounds the mouth of each alveolus. The formation of the secondary septa greatly increases the complexity of the terminal airways, leading to a markedly increased surface area; the surface area of the human lung increases from 1 to $2m^2$ in the fetus to >50 m^2 in adults. Combined with the formation of alveoli, extensive capillary growth ensures that each alveolus is well vascularized. The interstitial tissue also continues to thin, which further reduces the distance between alveoli and capillaries. It is during this stage of lung development that most humans are born.

Development of the ECM

The extracellular structural component of the lung, the ECM, is comprised of collagens, elastic fibres, proteoglycans and numerous glycoproteins. This structural framework plays a key role in determining lung function as it not only provides structural support and defines the architecture of the lung, but also compartmentalizes the tissue and regulates cell behaviour. Although the cells of the lung produce the ECM, the ECM profoundly influences cell migration, proliferation, differentiation and metabolic activity.

The primary structural framework of the lung is comprised of two interconnecting fibre networks. The axial fibre network starts at the hilus and extends along the airways to the terminal respiratory units where it forms the walls of the alveolar ducts and sacs. This network is braced by the peripheral network that extends inwards from the visceral pleura, a connective tissue sac that surrounds the lungs to form incomplete septa between adjacent major segments, lobules and alveolar units. At normal lung volumes these collagen fibres are loosely folded, but they straighten and become taut as lung volume increases, thereby providing a structural limit to lung expansion. Another major structural component of the lung is the basement membrane, which forms a thin sheet-like structure that separates epithelial cells and vascular endothelial cells from other interstitial cells. Basement membranes are comprised of a mixture of collagen (type IV), glycoproteins and proteoglycans, although the individual components of the epithelial cell basement membrane vary depending upon the phenotype of the overlying epithelial cell. The significance of this variation is unclear, but it may relate to how the phenotype of individual alveolar epithelial cells (i.e. type I or type II) is determined. It is apparent that the epithelial cell basement membrane is not a rigid structure and, at the level of the alveolus, can expand as lung expansion increases, thereby increasing the gas exchange surface area.

Although the ECM is often viewed as being inert, recent research indicates that it is a highly dynamic structure which is rapidly turned over. The dynamic nature of the lung's ECM allows lung structure to be markedly remodelled during development, in response to mechanical stimuli, under pathological conditions and during the normal ageing process. Although little is known of the factors that control this remodelling, they must include a closely coordinated increase in synthesis and degradation of the principal structural components. Ultrastructural remodelling of the lung during fetal life is an integral component of the lung's development into a functional gas exchange organ.

Fetal breathing movements

Respiratory gas exchange after birth largely depends upon the ability of respiratory muscles to move air into and from the lungs. After birth, the respiratory muscles are activated in a rhythmic, coordinated manner via the activation of brainstem neuronal networks. Rhythmic contractions of respiratory muscles begin early in fetal life (11–12 weeks in humans) and are referred to as fetal breathing movements (FBMs). The neuronal processes underlying FBMs are similar to those of postnatal breathing, except that FBMs are discontinuous, particularly later in gestation. FBMs primarily result from rhythmic activation of the diaphragm, which causes small reductions in intrathoracic pressure, and the muscles which dilate the glottis are activated in phase with the diaphragm. However, despite the reduction in intrathoracic pressure and opening of the glottis, little liquid is inhaled because the fetal chest wall is very compliant and lung liquid has a high viscosity relative to air. Thus, as the diaphragm contracts, it simultaneously causes the rib cage to be drawn in and only a small change in lung volume occurs. Tidal volume is less than 0.5% of resting lung volume in the fetus whereas it is about 20% after birth.

Other inspiratory efforts made by the fetus include gasping and hiccupping, although the latter is unlikely to be respiratory in origin. Fetal gasping can be induced by severe asphyxia, caused for example by umbilical cord occlusion, and usually indicates impending fetal death. Gasping causes intense activation of most inspiratory muscles and is probably a primitive reflex response aimed at increasing pulmonary ventilation. On the other hand, hiccupping is common in healthy fetuses, particularly early in gestation. It is associated with a rapid contraction of the diaphragm thereby causing a large decrease in intra-thoracic pressure.

Factors affecting FBMs

FBMs becomes episodic after about 120 days of gestation in sheep and after about 28 weeks in humans due to the development of prolonged periods of respiratory inactivity (apnoea). This development usually coincides with the appearance of distinct sleep or activity patterns in the fetus. In the sheep, after the emergence of these sleep patterns, FBMs principally occur during periods of low-voltage electrocortical (ECoG) activity and rapid eye movements (REMs). The apnoea associated with high-voltage ECoG, non-REM periods are thought to result from inhibition of the respiratory centre by descending nerve activity from higher brain centres.

The amount of time a fetus spends making FBMs varies between fetuses and is dependent upon many factors including gestational age, time of day and maternal behaviours. Much interest has focused on factors that control FBMs, primarily because they are used clinically as an indicator of fetal health and can provide useful information on the ontogeny of respiratory control mechanisms. It is well established that FBMs are influenced by altered levels of respiratory gases, in particular hypoxia (reduced oxygen availability), hypercapnia (increased levels of carbon dioxide) and combined hypoxia and hypercapnia (asphyxia). Although hypoxia stimulates breathing after birth, it inhibits FBMs and reduces fetal body movements for up to 12 hours; this inhibition apparently results from activation of neurones in the upper lateral pontine region. It is thought that the hypoxic inhibition of fetal motor activity allows the fetus to conserve oxygen. However, during prolonged hypoxia, in the absence of acidaemia, FBMs and other body movements resume, and a chronically hypoxic fetus may have a normal incidence of FBM. The oxygen consumed by FBMs and other motor activity during prolonged hypoxia may slow some other metabolic process such as growth. In contrast to hypoxia, hypercapnia stimulates FBMs.

The role of prostaglandins (PGs) in controlling FBMs has also been closely studied, particularly in reference to the mechanisms that regulate the switch to continuous breathing postnatally. Administration of indomethacin, a PG synthase inhibitor, greatly increases the incidence of FBM, whereas PGE_2 administration inhibits FBM and causes apnoea after birth. These data suggest that FBMs are tonically suppressed by PGs. Circulating PGE_2 concentrations in the fetus markedly increase during late gestation with most of the PGE_2 coming from the placenta. At birth, separation of the fetus and placenta reduces circulating PGE_2 concentrations, which may help to allow continuous breathing in the newborn. Although a reduction in circulating PGE_2 concentrations may be involved in this process, other factors are also likely to be involved.

Fetal lung liquid

Fetal lung liquid fills the future airways from early in gestation and is present until the time of birth when it is cleared, allowing air-breathing to occur. It was once thought that lung liquid was inhaled amniotic fluid, but it is now evident that it is a secretory product of the lung itself. Obstruction of the fetal trachea causes the lungs to overexpand with accumulated liquid and the ionic composition of lung liquid is quite different from that of amniotic fluid and other fetal fluids (Table 6.2). Fetal lung liquid is a secretory product of the pulmonary epithelium and leaves the lungs by flowing from the trachea into the pharynx from where it either is swallowed or enters the amniotic sac.

Table 6.2. Composition of lung liquid, amniotic fluid, plasma and lymph in fetal sheep

	Lung liquid	Amniotic fluid	Fetal Plasma	Lymph
Chloride (mM)	140–150	90–100	100–110	~105
Sodium (mM)	140–150	115–120	~150	~150
Potassium (mM)	5–6	5–8	4–5	~5
Calcium (mM)	0.5–1.0	36161	~3	
Bicarbonate(mM)	3–4	~19	25–27	~25
Protein (g/l)	~0.4	~1.3	40–50	
pH	6.2–6.8		7.35	

Control of fetal lung liquid secretion

Fetal lung liquid is thought to be secreted across the pulmonary epithelium by an active process resulting from the net movement of Cl^- into the lung lumen which creates an osmotic gradient for water to move in the same direction (Fig. 6.1). This model is supported by the high Cl^- concentration of lung liquid relative to fetal plasma (Table 6.2) and is based upon the concept that the Na/K adenosine triphosphatase (ATPase) pump, located on the basolateral surface of pulmonary epithelial cells, establishes a transmembranous Na^+ concentration gradient by pumping it out of the cell (Fig. 6.1). This gradient promotes the passive entry of Na^+ into the cell, via a $Na^+/K^+/2Cl$ cotransporter, coupled to Cl^- which enters against its concentration gradient. Cl^- is thought to exit the cell across the apical surface through specific Cl^- channels. As a result, the flux of Cl^- across the epithelium towards the lung lumen is greater than the flux of Cl^- in the opposite direction, thereby forming an osmotic gradient for the movement of water in that direction (Fig. 6.1).

The secretion of fetal lung liquid is influenced by numerous factors. Both adrenaline and arginine vasopressin (AVP) inhibit fetal lung liquid secretion, particularly late in gestation, via specific receptors (adrenergic and V2 receptors) coupled to adenylate cyclase. Increased intracellular cyclic adenosine monophosphate (cAMP) concentrations initiate a cascade of events leading to activation of Na^+ channels, located on the apical surface, which increase Na^+ and Na^+ linked Cl^- flux from lung lumen to plasma. This reduces the osmotic gradient and, in late gestation, may reverse it leading to lung liquid reabsorption (see below). The inhibitory effect of both hormones can be blocked by amiloride, a Na^+ channel blocker, demonstrating the obligatory role of luminal Na^+ channels in this inhibitory process.

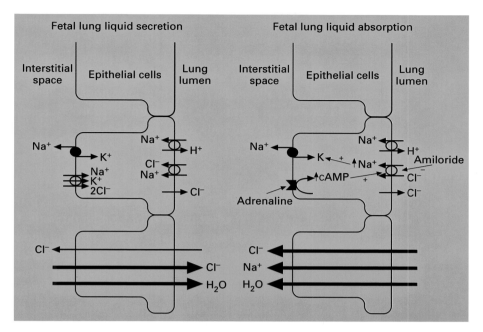

Fig. 6.1.   A currently accepted model for fetal lung liquid secretion and reabsorption. *Lung liquid secretion:* Pulmonary epithelial cells are joined by tight junctions at the apical surface which separates the lung lumen from the interstitial space. Na/K ATPase, located on the basolateral surface of epithelial cells generates the gradient for Na^+ to enter the cell linked with Cl^- and K^+. Cl^- moves out of the cell down its electrochemical gradient through specific channels located on the apical surface. The net movement of Cl^- into the lung lumen provides the osmotic gradient for the movement of water in the same direction. *Lung liquid reabsorption:* Late in gestation, stimulation of pulmonary epithelial cells by adrenaline or AVP increases intracellular cAMP concentrations which activate Na channels in the apical membrane. The resulting increase in intracellular Na^+ ions increases the activity of Na/K ATPase which promotes a net increase in Na^+ and Cl^- flux away from the lung lumen, thereby reversing the osmotic gradient across the epithelium.

Hydrostatic pressures may also influence the movement of liquid across the pulmonary epithelium. In late-gestation fetal sheep, the pressure within the trachea is 1–2 mmHg above amniotic sac pressure during apnoeic periods, indicating that lung liquid is secreted into the future airways against a small pressure head. If the intraluminal pressure is increased further, by blocking the efflux of lung liquid from the trachea, lung liquid secretion rate decreases and effectively ceases at a luminal pressure of 5–6 mmHg. It is likely that, in the presence of tracheal obstruction, the intraluminal pressure increases until it equals and opposes the osmotic pressure driving lung liquid secretion. Thus, the osmotic pressure driving lung liquid secretion probably equates to a hydrostatic pressure of 5–6 mmHg. On the other hand, prolonged reductions in the intraluminal pressure allows the rate of fetal lung liquid secretion to increase. Thus, liquid movement across the epithelium is probably regulated by two opposing forces; osmotic and hydrostatic pressures.

Control of lung liquid volume

The volume of liquid within the 'air spaces' of the fetal lung is primarily regulated by physical factors that affect the flow of lung liquid in the trachea. The liquid can flow in both directions, although it predominantly flows out of the lungs. Tracheal flow is principally controlled by the upper respiratory tract, particularly the larynx. Narrowing of the glottis during apnoeic periods slows the efflux of lung liquid and causes secreted liquid to accumulate within the future airways (Fig. 6.2). By resisting the efflux of lung liquid, the larynx is responsible for maintaining the pressure gradient (1–2 mmHg) between the lung lumen and amniotic sac. This gradient is generated by the elastic recoil properties of lung tissue which tends to cause the lungs to collapse, thereby forcing liquid out of the trachea. During FBMs the glottis rhythmically dilates, reducing its resistance to lung liquid efflux and, therefore, liquid leaves the lungs at an increased rate (Fig. 6.2), despite contractions of the diaphragm. Thus, under normal conditions, liquid flow along the trachea is largely dependent upon the presence or absence of FBMs. Lung liquid efflux is low during apnoeic periods and increases approximately fourfold during episodes of FBMs. On occasions, amniotic fluid can enter the lungs during FBM episodes, and this may allow meconium to enter the lower airways. However, this rarely occurs in the healthy fetus as fluid aspirated from the trachea is usually uncontaminated by amniotic fluid. If a shunt is experimentally created between the fetal trachea and amniotic sac, effectively bypassing the upper airway, liquid rapidly leaves the lungs causing them to collapse. This demonstrates the importance of the fetal upper airway in maintaining the volume of fetal lung liquid and its unidirectional flow along the trachea.

The volume of liquid contained within the fetal lung increases gradually from approximately 3.0 ml/kg at midgestation to approximately 45 ml/kg at term in fetal sheep (Fig. 6.3). Most of the increase occurs during the canalicular and alveolar stages of lung development when the future airways rapidly

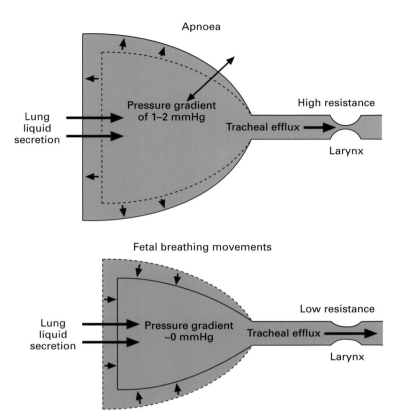

Fig. 6.2.   Summary of the factors that control the volume of fetal lung liquid during periods of fetal apnoea and episodes of fetal breathing movements (FBM). During periods of apnoea the larynx maintains a high resistance to lung liquid efflux, which promotes the accumulation of secreted liquid within the future airspaces. During episodes of FBM, the larynx dilates, which reduces its resistance to lung liquid efflux, thereby allowing liquid to escape from the lungs at an increased rate. Lung volume is dependent upon rhythmic contractions of the diaphragm which oppose the escape of lung liquid via the trachea.

expand and the terminal gas exchange units develop. Until recently, it was considered that the volume of fetal lung liquid just before birth was similar to the equivalent lung volume (functional residual capacity, FRC) after birth in air-breathing newborns. However, recent measurements of lung liquid volumes in unanaesthetized fetal sheep in utero show that it is much greater than the FRC of the air-filled lung (Fig. 6.3). It is now apparent that this high degree of lung expansion is critical for normal fetal lung growth and development.

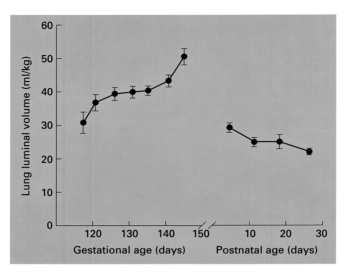

Fig. 6.3.   The volume (millilitres per kilogram) of lung liquid, measured by an indicator dilution technique, during late gestation in fetal sheep (term is 147 days). For comparison, the analogous postnatal lung volume (functional residual capacity, measured by helium dilution) is shown.

Control of fetal lung growth

The growth and structural maturation of the fetal lung are largely dependent upon the degree to which it is expanded by liquid. This dependency is highlighted by the finding that, in human fetuses, inadequate lung growth is primarily due to factors that reduce lung expansion for prolonged periods. For example, space-occupying lesions within the fetal chest cause lung hypoplasia; these can be caused by fluid accumulation, tumours or the presence of abdominal contents which enter via a diaphragmatic hernia. These and other clinical problems are considered below.

Role of lung liquid in lung growth

The strong relationship between fetal lung expansion and lung growth has been demonstrated in experiments in which the degree of lung expansion was altered for prolonged periods. For example, tracheal occlusion causes liquid to accumulate within the 'airways' thereby expanding the lungs. This is a potent stimulus of fetal lung growth, resulting in an almost doubling in total lung DNA content (i.e. cell number). The growth response diminishes with time, probably because the physical limitations imposed by the chest wall limit lung expansion and hence lung growth. Furthermore, during the period of stimulated growth, the increase in fetal lung DNA content closely parallels the increase in lung liquid volume, which indicates that volume expansion is the primary stimulus for the growth response. Because fetal tracheal obstruction is such a potent stimulus for fetal lung growth, it has been suggested that this procedure could be used therapeutically to reverse lung growth deficits in human fetuses.

Sustained deflation of the fetal lungs, caused by draining them of liquid, or by inflation of balloons within the fetal chest, essentially cause lung growth to cease. These studies highlight the requirement of the fetal lungs to be expanded with liquid for them to grow. Furthermore, fetal lung growth is not only dependent upon, but closely correlates with the degree of lung expansion. Even small (~25%) changes in lung expansion, if sustained, can cause corresponding changes in lung growth.

The mechanisms by which alterations in fetal lung expansion affect the growth and structural development of the lung are slowly being defined. The growth stimulus must act locally on the affected tissue because it is possible to induce, in the same fetus, hyperplasia and hypoplasia of the two lungs by inducing increased and decreased expansion, respectively. It is important to note that the growth induced by an increase in lung expansion is not abnormal and may simply be an acceleration of the normal growth and developmental process of the lung. Thus experiments on pulmonary responses to altered lung expansion can provide information on normal growth processes.

The synthesis and release of tissue growth factors are likely to play an important role in the growth response of the lung to increased expansion, although direct activation of cells via ECM receptors are undoubtedly involved. Candidate growth factors that have been identified include platelet-derived growth factor (PDGF) and the insulin-like growth factors (IGFs), although others are likely to be involved. The importance of growth factors may not be restricted to initiating the proliferative response, but may help to propagate and integrate the growth response. Indeed, not all cells will be stretched by increased lung expansion, as some are likely to be compressed. The evidence to date indicates that increases in fetal lung expansion cause a uniform increase in cellular proliferation of all major cell types, indicating that the stimulus is integrated throughout the affected tissue.

Role of FBMs in fetal lung growth

Several studies in vivo have shown that the abolition of FBMs impairs fetal lung growth, and these observations are supported by clinical findings and in vitro studies. In the latter, fetal lung cells in culture are stimulated to divide in response to a phasic stretch stimulus applied to the matrix they are grown on. However, as indicated above, individual FBMs are essentially isovolumic, causing a less than 0.5% change in lung volume with each breathing movement, whereas the percentage stretch required to stimulate cellular proliferation in culture is 10–20 times greater. Recent studies indicate that FBMs are important in the control of lung growth as they help to maintain lung liquid volume. Specifically, contraction of the diaphragm during FBM episodes opposes the loss of liquid from the lungs at a time when the larynx rhythmically dilates, thereby lowering its resistance to the escape of lung liquid.

Alveolar epithelial cell development

Pulmonary gas exchange occurs across the alveolar epithelium, a single layer of cells separated from adjacent tissue by a basement membrane. Early in gestation, the epithelial cells are undifferentiated, cuboidal in shape and the cytoplasm contains abundant glycogen. The epithelial cells begin to differentiate into either type I or type II cells during the canalicular stage, and this process is essentially complete by the end of gestation, particularly in humans and sheep. Type I alveolar epithelial cells (AECs) are large flattened cells that have long cytoplasmic extensions, flattened nuclei, few cytoplasmic organelles and, because of their long cytoplasmic extensions, have a large surface area (Fig. 6.4). In contrast, type II AECs are spherical with a rounded nucleus, have microvilli on their apical (luminal) surface and are characterized by the presence of abundant cytoplasmic organelles, particularly lamellar bodies which are the intracellular storage site of surfactant (Fig. 6.4). Thus, although both AEC types are derived from the same progenitor cell type, they are morphologically and functionally distinct and both play separate, yet critical roles, in respiratory physiology.

Type II AECs

In adults, type II cells constitute 40–50% of AECs and are thought to be the progenitor cell type, giving rise to type I cells by differentiation and daughter type

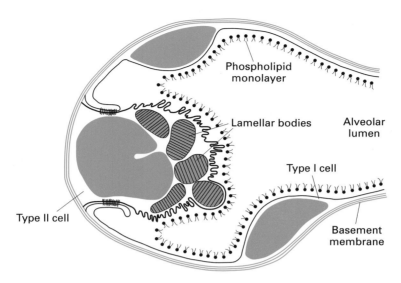

Fig. 6.4. Diagrammatic representation of the alveolar epithelium, showing the surface film surfactant monolayer, the alveolar epithelial cells (AECs) and the underlying basement membrane. The type I AECs are elongated and flattened cells that have a large surface area and make up more than 90% of the gas-exchange surface area. The type II AECs are rounded in shape and contain lamellar bodies which are the intracellular storage sites for surfactant.

II cells by division. However, during development both types of AEC must arise from undifferentiated stem cells, although the mechanisms that control differentiation into each state are largely unknown. Fully differentiated cells express a specific subset of genes that encode proteins that characterize the morphology and function of that cell; inappropriate gene expression, therefore, must be repressed. Thus, differentiation may be seen as a process that progressively limits the types of genes expressed by that cell. In some cases the repression of genes may be permanent, but in many instances it is actively maintained by some reversible process. Thus, although the mechanisms which promote differentiation of AECs are unknown, they probably lead to continuous activation and repression of specific genes. Indeed, differentiation into the type II cell phenotype is not permanent as these cells may differentiate into type I cells. An example of genes that are only expressed by type II AECs are those encoding the synthetic machinery that produces surfactant and the surfactant-associated proteins.

Surfactant

Pulmonary surfactant is a complex mixture of phospholipids, primarily dipalmitoylphosphatidylcholine (DPPC), and proteins and plays an important role by reducing surface tension at the air–liquid interface within the lung. The internal surface of the air-filled lung is lined with a film of liquid that protects epithelial cells from dehydration. Surface tension is generated at the air–liquid interface and promotes lung collapse during expiration and makes lung inflation more difficult during inspiration. Surfactant reduces these forces due to the formation of a surface film which is a monolayer of phospholipid molecules. In type II cells, surfactant exists as coiled structures within lamellar bodies whereas after its release into the alveolar space it can exist as an ordered vesicular structure called tubular myelin or as part of the surface film.

The surface-active properties of surfactant are due to its phospholipid component. Phospholipids are amphipathic molecules with a hydrophilic polar head group and a glycerol backbone to which are attached fatty acid side chains, making this part of the molecule hydrophobic. If an air–liquid interface is present, these molecules form a monolayer in which molecules orientate so that the hydrophilic polar head group is associated with the liquid and the hydrophobic tails extend into the air. This monomolecular layer causes the exclusion of water molecules from the surface layer which substantially reduces surface tension within alveoli. Thus, by reducing surface tension forces, surfactant greatly reduces the work of breathing and, importantly, stabilizes individual alveoli during the respiratory cycle allowing small and large alveoli to coexist.

Surfactant also contains proteins ($\sim$5–10%), some of which play a fundamental role in the biological function of surfactant by facilitating adsorption of the phospholipids to the surface film. Four surfactant-associated proteins have been described and are designated as surfactant protein (SP)-A, -B, -C and -D. SP-A and SP-D are large collagen-like glycoproteins that have distinctive collagen-like regions. SP-A also has a globular head region which contains carbohydrate recognition domains and its expression is not restricted to type II AECs. Recent studies indicate that it is not necessary for adsorption of the phospholipids to the surface film, but plays an important role in defending against infection, possibly by stimulating phagocytosis and activating alveolar macrophages. SP-C and SP-B are hydrophobic proteins, primarily consisting of hydrophobic amino acids, which confer their high lipid solubility and explain the colocalization of SP-C and SP-B with the phospholipids. Although SP-B expression is also not limited to type II AECs, SP-C expression is and, therefore, SP-C and its mRNA are used as cell-specific markers for type II AECs. SP-B is essential for alveolar surface film formation, and newborn infants without a functional SP-B gene die of respiratory distress shortly after birth. SP-C is thought to be of similar importance in surface film formation.

Type I AECs

Type I AECs constitute 50–60% of epithelial cells in adult lungs and are broad flattened cells with elongated cytoplasmic extensions that can extend over several adjacent alveoli (Fig. 6.4). These cells contain few cytoplasmic organelles and reduced amounts of rough endoplasmic reticulum, indicating that they have limited metabolic activity. Type I cells are derived by differentiation from type II AECs and once they reach this stage, they are considered to be terminally differentiated and are unable to divide. This implies that the processes that induce differentiation into the type I cell phenotype are irreversible and may involve the suppression of many cellular processes, including cellular division. However, the evidence supporting this concept is circumstantial and requires confirmation.

Although there is little information on the mechanisms which induce differentiation of AECs into the type I cell phenotype, it appears that physical stretch may be an important factor. Increased stretch of AECs in vitro causes type II AECs to adopt some type I cell characteristics. Similarly, increases in fetal lung expansion in vivo, which presumably increases the stretch of type II AECs, greatly decreases SP-C expression by lung tissue and reduces the proportion of type II cells (from about 35% to about 2%); the proportion of type I cells increase from about 60% to about 90%. Furthermore, the transient appearance of an intermediate cell type that has characteristics of both cell types suggests that the cells follow a specific sequence of events from type II to type I through an intermediate cell type.

Development of the air/blood barrier

The ability of oxygen and carbon dioxide to diffuse across the alveolar epithelium is determined by the tissue barrier between the alveolar space and capillaries. This barrier consists of type I AECs, the capillary endothelial cells and their respective basement membranes and any interstitial tissue or fluid between them. At midgestation the diffusion barrier is wide ($\sim$60 µm) due to the small number of capillaries and the presence of large numbers of mesenchymal cells between capillaries and adjacent alveoli. As development progresses, the capillaries penetrate further between the developing airways and the amount of interstitial tissue markedly thins, greatly reducing gas diffusion distances. Beginning during the alveolar period of development, the interstitial tissue thins to the point that the basement membranes, which underlie the capillary endothelial cells and AECs, fuse giving rise to the very small air–blood gas diffusion distances seen after birth (~0.2 µm). These points of basement membrane fusion are focal and variable in length initially but increase to cover over 50% of the epithelial surface in adults.

Type I cells, because of their large cytoplasmic extensions, occupy the majority (~95%) of the internal surface area of the lung lumen and, therefore, comprise most of the epithelial component of the air–blood gas barrier. Although the cytoplasmic extensions of type I cells are long, providing a large surface area, the cytoplasm is markedly attenuated, making the distances between the basolateral and apical surfaces very small. These characteristics make type I cells ideally suited as the primary site of gas exchange across the epithelium and maximize the gas-diffusing capacity of the lung.

Pulmonary circulation

Development of the pulmonary circulation occurs in parallel with development of the airways, as most of the arterial circulation follows the bronchial tree down to the capillary bed surrounding each alveolus. The large arteries are primarily elastic structures, but as they subsequently branch into smaller arteries, smooth muscle appears around the medial wall of the vessel. However, the presence of smooth muscle gradually diminishes as the arteries branch further and is absent in the very small arteries. At any given generation, the amount of smooth muscle surrounding pulmonary arteries is greater in fetuses than in adults and, in the fetus, the presence of smooth muscle extends further down into the smaller arteries.

Although most major arteries are formed by midgestation, over the last third of gestation, particularly in humans and sheep, the pulmonary vascular bed undergoes substantial growth resulting in an approximately eightfold increase in the number of blood vessels. Most of this increase is due to growth and extension of the capillary network which penetrates between and around developing alveoli. As a result, the cross-sectional area of the pulmonary vascular bed markedly increases, explaining the gradual decrease in pulmonary vascular resistance and the increase in pulmonary blood flow over this period. By the end of gestation, a dense capillary network closely surrounds each alveolus to maximize blood flow through the gas exchange site.

Control of blood flow through the fetal lungs

In contrast to adults, only a small proportion of the blood returning to the fetal heart passes through the lungs (about 8% versus 100% in adults), as most of it bypasses the lungs via specialized shunts. Blood returning to the fetal heart can bypass the right heart and lungs by flowing through the foramen ovale directly into the left atrium. In addition, blood leaving the right ventricle can bypass the lungs and flow directly from the pulmonary artery into the descending aorta through the ductus arteriosus. Indeed, only 12% of right ventricular output passes through the fetal lungs, compared with 100% in adults. The very low pulmonary blood flow in the fetus is primarily due to a high resistance in the pulmonary vascular bed. This maintains pulmonary arterial pressure 4–5 mmHg above systemic arterial pressure, which promotes the flow of blood from the pulmonary into the systemic circulation through the ductus arteriosus.

The mechanisms responsible for the high pulmonary vascular resistance in the fetus are not clear, but are unlikely to be structural as the resistance rapidly decreases after birth, indicating that the vascular bed can rapidly dilate. Many mechanisms have been suggested, including the relatively low oxygen tension in fetal blood and the release of vasoconstrictors (e.g. leucotrienes) or the inhibition of release of vasodilators such as bradykinins or PGI_2. The recent recognition that the baseline level of lung expansion is greater before birth than after birth has led to the suggestion that the high degree of fetal lung expansion may contribute to the high pulmonary vascular resistance. Indeed, pulmonary vascular resistance is closely and directly related to the degree of lung expansion in the fetus, newborn and adult. With increased lung expansion the smaller blood vessels and capillaries close, presumably due to compression between adjacent alveoli, although it could also cause the release of vasoconstrictor agents.

Changes in the lung at birth

The successful transition from fetus to air-breathing newborn is largely dependent upon the ability of the lungs to rapidly take over the role of gas exchange from the placenta. If the lungs are appropriately developed, this transition relies upon the clearance of liquid from the future airways to facilitate the entry of air, as well as a greatly increased pulmonary blood flow. Although these events appear unrelated, they maybe linked as the clearance of lung liquid will necessarily cause a reduction in lung volume which may contribute to the reduction in pulmonary vascular resistance.

Clearance of liquid from the future airways

It is now evident that most, if not all, lung liquid is cleared during labour. During labour, lung liquid is reabsorbed by the pulmonary epithelium due to the reversal of the osmotic gradient that drives lung liquid secretion during fetal life (Fig. 6.1). The reversal of this gradient is caused by the release of stress-related hormones (e.g. adrenaline and AVP) during labour. These hormones act via adenylate cyclase-linked receptors which lead to the activation of Na^+ channels (amiloride inhibitable) located on the apical surface of epithelial cells. This increases Na^+ and Na^+ linked Cl^- movement away from the lung lumen, which reverses the osmotic gradient for liquid movement across the epithelium causing lung liquid reabsorption. The abilities of these hormones to inhibit lung liquid secretion and stimulate reabsorption are dependent upon fetal maturity, indicating that this process matures late in gestation and, therefore, may not be functional in preterm infants. Indeed, the progressive maturation of the reabsorptive process is thought to be regulated by the large increase in circulating corticosteroids, and perhaps thyroid hormones, which precedes the onset of labour.

Although reabsorption may be responsible for some lung liquid clearance, calculations of maximum reabsorption rates and the volumes to be cleared indicate that the majority of lung liquid leaves via some other mechanism. Indeed, much of the liquid can be cleared before the second stage of labour, which is when the reabsorption mechanisms are most active. It is possible that, during the early stages of labour, large amounts of liquid are lost due to changes in fetal posture imposed by uterine contractions. The gradual shortening of the myometrium is likely to cause marked flexion of the fetal trunk, particularly if little amniotic fluid is present. This would increase fetal abdominal pressure, elevate the diaphragm and increase transthoracic pressure thereby causing liquid to leave the lungs via the trachea.

After birth, the replacement of liquid with air within the airways and the development of surface forces within the alveoli cause the lungs to increase their recoil (Fig. 6.3). Changes in intrapleural pressure at birth are consistent with a reduction in lung volume at this time. Before birth intrapleural pressures are negligible whereas after birth they become negative with respect to atmospheric pressure due to the tendency of the lung to collapse away from the chest wall. Thus, at birth, the forces which oppose lung collapse change from internal distending forces, due to the presence of lung liquid, to external forces due to the structural integrity of the chest wall. Indeed, the stiffness of the chest wall increases markedly within the first days of extrauterine life, which may be in response to the structural load imposed by the lung's tendency to collapse.

Changes in the pulmonary circulation at birth

One of the most striking changes to occur in the lung at birth is the decrease in pulmonary vascular resistance. When the lungs take over the role of gas exchange at birth, pulmonary blood flow markedly increases so that all blood leaving the right ventricle passes through the lungs for oxygenation. This increase in blood flow is primarily achieved due to a large (approximately eight-fold) decrease in pulmonary vascular resistance and, following closure of the ductus arteriosus, coincides with a marked decrease in pulmonary arterial pressure (to 10–15 mmHg). Thus, the pulmonary circulation changes from a high-pressure, low-flow circulation to a high-flow, low-pressure circulation as in adults.

The mechanisms leading to the decrease in pulmonary vascular resistance at birth are unclear, although they probably relate to the factors that maintain the high resistance during fetal life. Increased blood oxygen levels, the onset of gaseous ventilation and the decrease in lung volume associated with the entry of air into the lungs have all been implicated. As indicated above, it is possible that the decrease in pulmonary vascular resistance caused by the onset of ventilation is largely mediated by the decrease in lung volume associated with this event. Thus, a reduction in lung volume and an increase in oxygenation are likely candidates for inducing the decrease in pulmonary vascular resistance at birth. Both of these factors may operate independently of each other and could be mediated by the local release of vasodilators (e.g. nitric oxide, bradykinins or specific PGs). Reduced lung volumes may also decrease pulmonary vascular resistance via a mechanical effect. By late gestation the pulmonary capillaries have penetrated between the very thin interalveolar walls and septa and, therefore, they may be readily affected by changes in alveolar volume.

Clinical complications related to fetal lung development

The inability of an infant's lungs to exchange respiratory gases after birth results in respiratory insufficiency that can be fatal. Respiratory insufficiency, whether it is caused by immature lungs due to preterm birth or to undergrown lungs, is the primary cause of neonatal morbidity and mortality, affecting up to 7% of all pregnancies.

Lung immaturity and respiratory distress syndrome (RDS)

Preterm birth is one the greatest problems facing modern obstetrics. While the problems faced by preterm infants are numerous, lung immaturity usually provides the greatest threat to their survival, leading to hyaline membrane disease and in some instances to broncho-pulmonary dysplasia (BPD) and permanent lung injury. In particular, in very young preterm infants (<30 weeks gestation), the lungs are structurally immature with little penetration of capillaries between the terminal air sacs (alveoli have not yet formed), the epithelial cells lining the terminal air sacs have not begun to differentiate and the lungs have a limited ability to reabsorb lung liquid. Thus, the lungs may only be partially aerated, perhaps due to the persistence of luminal liquid, are difficult to inflate due their structure and to the absence of surfactant; the air–blood barrier is thick, which restricts gas diffusion, and the terminal air sacs tend to collapse, which requires the generation of high pressures to reopen them. Collectively, these problems present considerable difficulty in the clinical management of preterm infants.

One of the greatest advances in the treatment of preterm infants is the maternal administration of glucocorticoids at least 48 hours before delivery. This has greatly reduced the incidence and/or the severity of RDS in preterm infants. While the ability of glucocorticoids to increase the production and secretion of surfactant is controversial, they have a profound maturational effect on lung architecture. This includes thinning of interalveolar walls, induction of epithelial cell differentiation and increased tissue compliance.

The administration of natural and/or artificial surfactant preparations to infants via the trachea has also been successful in reducing the severity of RDS in preterm infants. While surfactant treatment can alleviate many of the ventilatory problems associated with lung immaturity, the immature lung is more than simply surfactant deficient and, therefore, a permanent solution will only be achieved following significant development of the lung postnatally.

Pulmonary hypoplasia

Pulmonary hypoplasia in the newborn results from inadequate lung growth during fetal life and is a major cause of respiratory insufficiency in fetuses born at or near term (about 1.1 per 1000 live births). Many, seemingly diverse, conditions are causally associated with pulmonary hypoplasia and include oligohydramnios (a lack of amniotic fluid due to reduced fetal urine production or to premature rupture of the membranes); congenital diaphragmatic hernias (CDH), in which the diaphragm fails to close allowing abdominal contents to enter the chest; space-occupying lesions in the chest due to the accumulation of liquid within the pleural space or the presence of intrathoracic cysts or tumours; and some skeletal and neuromuscular defects. Although they are diverse in nature, it is now apparent that all of these conditions result in impaired fetal lung growth by causing prolonged reductions in the degree of lung expansion. In some instances (e.g. CDH) the extent of the lung hypoplasia is so severe that it is lethal in 70–80% of cases. These conditions highlight the necessity of adequate lung expansion for the normal growth and development of the fetal lung.

The experimental finding that increased fetal lung expansion, induced by tracheal obstruction, stimulates lung growth has led to the suggestion that tracheal obstruction may be used therapeutically to treat human fetuses with severe lung hypoplasia in utero.

This has been trialled in human fetuses with CDH as the induced lung expansion has the capacity to both induce lung growth and to displace the abdominal contents from the chest. However, the initial success of this treatment has been limited, primarily due to preterm labour, the induction of fetal fluid accumulation and, in some cases, the failure to stimulate lung growth. In particular, more needs to be known about mechanisms whereby alterations in lung expansion affect fetal lung development so that treatment protocols may be optimized to avoid detrimental effects. For example, the increase in lung expansion induced by tracheal occlusion inhibits surfactant protein gene expression and reduces the number of type II AECs.

Summary

During fetal life, the future airways of the lung are liquid-filled and gas exchange occurs across the placenta. The luminal liquid within the fetal lung plays a critical role in fetal lung growth and structural maturation by regulating the degree of lung expansion and hence tissue stretch. It is clear that increases in fetal lung expansion that occur during development, or in response to tracheal obstruction, have a profound effect on tissue and vascular growth, structural development, ECM deposition and cellular differentiation. It is now evident that inadequate lung growth is primarily due to factors that cause the lungs to deflate for prolonged periods of time. To function successfully as the sole organ of gas exchange at birth, the lung must be appropriately grown, have developed thin-walled alveoli that are perfused by an extensive vascular network and the airways must be cleared of liquid; in addition, the lung must be structurally and biochemically mature. It is apparent that for these maturational processes to occur, the endocrine and physical environment of the lungs are vitally important.

FURTHER READING

Chambers, R.C. and Laurent, G.J. (1996). The lung. In: *Extracellular Matrix: Tissue Function*, ed. W.D. Comper, pp. 378–409. Amsterdam: Harwood Academic.

Harding, R. (1994). Development of the respiratory system. In: *Textbook of Fetal Physiology*, ed. R. Harding and G.D. Thorburn, pp. 140–67. Oxford: Oxford University Press.

Harding, R. and Hooper, S.B. (1996). Regulation of lung expansion and lung growth before birth. *J. Appl. Physiol.*, **81**, 209–24.

Hawgood, S. (1997). Surfactant: composition, structure, and metabolism. In: *The Lung: Scientific Foundations*, ed. R.G. Crystal, J.B. West, E.R. Weibel and P.J. Barnes, pp. 557–71. New York: Lippincott-Raven.

Hooper, S.B. and Harding, R. (1995). Fetal lung liquid: a major determinant of the growth and functional development of the fetal lung. *Clin. Exp. Pharmacol. Physiol.*, **22**, 235–47.

Mason, R.J. and Shannon, J.M. (1997). Alveolar type II cells. In: *The Lung: Scientific Foundations*, ed. R.G. Crystal, J.B. West, E.R. Weibel and P.J. Barnes, pp. 543–55. New York: Lippincott-Raven.

McDonald, J. A. (ed.) (1997). *Lung Growth and Development.* New York: Marcel Dekker.

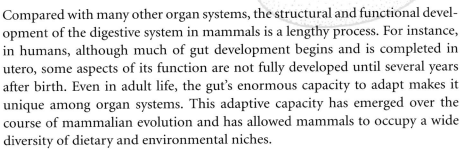

Digestive system

Jeffrey Trahair

Compared with many other organ systems, the structural and functional development of the digestive system in mammals is a lengthy process. For instance, in humans, although much of gut development begins and is completed in utero, some aspects of its function are not fully developed until several years after birth. Even in adult life, the gut's enormous capacity to adapt makes it unique among organ systems. This adaptive capacity has emerged over the course of mammalian evolution and has allowed mammals to occupy a wide diversity of dietary and environmental niches.

Events around the time of birth are particularly critical for gut development. Because cessation of placental (parenteral) nutrient supply occurs at birth, the digestive tract must be sufficiently mature to digest and transport substrates derived from colostrum and milk (enteral nutrition). The immunological function of the gut must be prepared to adapt to changes at birth, particularly the presentation of a significant burden of foreign antigen. The gut's endocrine system must also be ready to maintain functional homeostasis. All of these functional capacities are acquired during development in the intrauterine environment.

Region-specific development

Early gut tube formation

In humans, at about 22 days after conception, the embryonic disc undergoes head and tail flexion and lateral folding. During this process, the dorsal portion of the yolk sac endoderm, supported by somatic and splanchnic mesoderm, is incorporated into the embryo, forming a tube, the primitive gut tube (Fig. 7.1). Over the next few days the gut tube rapidly elongates and can be divided into foregut, midgut and hindgut. These divisions, together with various contributions of mesenchymal tissues, each give rise to their own group of gut (and other)

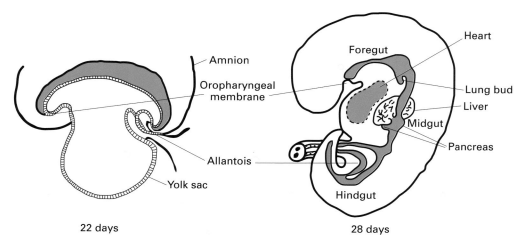

Fig. 7.1. At 22 days the primitive gut is formed as the dorsal yolk sac is incorporated as the embryo flexes and folds. Within a few days, the gut tube (fore, mid and hind) has formed. Lung, liver and pancreas begin to develop.

organs (Fig. 7.1). The foregut, supplied by the coeliac artery, gives rise to the pharynx, thyroid, thymus, parathyroid, respiratory tract, oesophagus, stomach, upper duodenum, liver and pancreas. The midgut, supplied by the superior mesenteric artery produces the lower duodenum and small and large intestine (to the distal third of the transverse colon). The hindgut, supplied by the inferior mesenteric artery, gives rise to the remainder of the large intestine. The major landmarks of human gastrointestinal organogenesis are summarized in Table 7.1.

Differentiation of the tissue elements of the gut wall

Soon after the gut tube is formed, high rates of proliferation of the endodermal cells facilitate its rapid growth (particularly in length). There is a rudimentary lumen in the gut tube at this stage (Fig. 7.2). The production of new cells (the highest rate of cell proliferation occurs during this phase) is apparently in excess of the requirements for elongation, causing the lining epithelium to appear stratified. The endodermal tube is surrounded by mesenchyme, and, depending on the region, either continuous with other mesodermal tissues or covered with a mesothelium. In most regions, development of the accessory coats of the gut tube (muscularis mucosa, submucosa, muscularis externa) and their innervation is initiated at the same time as the period of rapid proliferation of the lining endoderm.

Table 7.1. Major landmarks in regional development of the human gastrointestinal tract

Age (weeks postconception)	Feature
3	Formation of endodermal tube as a result of flexion and folding of embryonic disc. Gut is still joined to the yolk sac
3.5	Formation of distinct tube, elongation and regional (fore, mid, hindgut) differentiation. Buds of lung, liver, pancreas are present
4	Foregut and mouth structures develop from brachial arch and cleft structures. Buccopharyngeal membrane has ruptured
4.5	Stomach and caecal swelling forms
5	Proximal portions of the intestine rapidly elongate into a U-shaped loop
6	Stomach rotates and duodenum and splenic flexure of the colon is fixed. Ventral diverticulum in the hindgut develops into the allantois. Division of the cloaca into rectum (dorsal) and urogenital sinus (ventral)
7	Liver grows rapidly and takes up most of the abdomen. Intestine herniates outside the abdomen. Elongates further and begins series of rotations. Pancreas anlagen fuse. Stomach position fixed. Recanalization of the gut tube
8	Differentiation of small intestinal tissues begins (muscle, nerves, epithelium, previllus ridges, rudimentary villi). Cloacal membrane ruptures
10	Midgut is retracted back into the abdomen, which has now grown large enough to accommodate it. Differentiation of specific cell types in the epithelium begins. Lymphoid cells present in gut wall and epithelium. Swallowing begins
11	Villi appear in the small intestine. Enterocytes differentiate (including formation of apical endocytic complex). Goblet cells appear
12	Colon enlarges
13	Stomach, duodenum and small intestine growth now at full-grown fetal proportions. Further growth of ascending colon causes the caecum to move to right iliac fossa
16	Whole length of the intestine (including colon) has villi. Apical endocytic complex disappearing
20	Peyer's patches (jejunum and ileum). By 20 weeks all major tissue components of the mature gut are present. Accessory structures (e.g. glands) continue to develop throughout fetal life (and beyond)

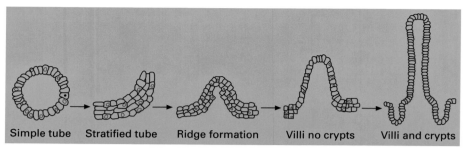

Simple tube   Stratified tube   Ridge formation   Villi no crypts   Villi and crypts

Fig. 7.2.   The gut tube first forms as a simple endodermal tube which rapidly stratifies. Ridges form as the underlying mesenchyme develops. The epithelium becomes a single layer of columnar cells and the tissue quickly differentiates into region-specific architectural units (glands, villi, crypts).(Redrawn from J.F. Trahair and R. Harding, in: *Animal Models in Fetal Medicine*. VI. *Metabolism*, ed. P.W. Nathanielsz. Ithaca, NY: Perinatology Press, 1987.)

A marked polarity of development is present throughout the various regions of the gut tube. In the stomach, the lesser curvature is the first to develop the secretory units (gastric pits and glands). In the small intestine and colon, proximal regions develop first, and more rapidly, compared with distal regions. Because the gut tube developed from a common precursor, the architecture of the mature gut follows a similar pattern throughout its entire length (Fig. 7.3). Despite this generic background, the pattern of gene expression is highly specific, resulting in the establishment of significant regional specializations (Fig. 7.3). The triggers which regulate the highly specific patterns of gene expression are areas of considerable current research interest.

The lining epithelial cells also undergo extremely region-specific pathways of differentiation with the result that the progenitor cells that persist have been programmed to 'know' which region of the gut they come from. While ultimately all of this program is written in the genetic code, studies in transgenic and chimeric animals, tissue transplant or explant, and tissue recombinant models reveal that there are many factors involved in this programming. These include the age of the endoderm, the region of the endoderm, the age and region of the surrounding mesenchyme, as well as blood borne and lumenal factors (see later).

Oesophagus

In the human fetus a patent lumen lined by a stratified ciliated columnar epithelium is present from about 10 weeks. Swallowing has been observed as early

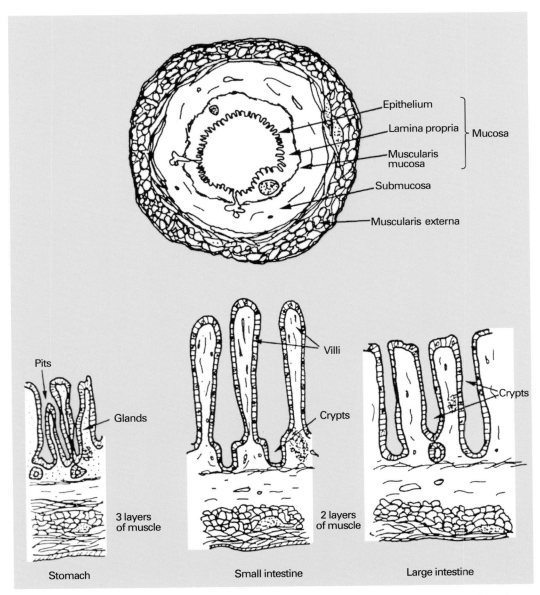

Fig. 7.3.   Overall, the structure of the gastrointestinal tube is similar throughout its entire length (mucosa – epithelium, lamina propria, musclaris mucosa – submucosa, muscularis externa). The mucosa of each region exhibits highly specific tissue features (glands, villi, crypts) and many specialized cell types.

as 10 weeks (see below). By 5 months, a noncornified stratified squamous lining has developed. It is well innervated by 13 weeks, by which time the muscularis mucosa (longitudinal, which is an exception to the general circular orientation) has developed. In the human, the upper portion of the oesophagus has voluntary (skeletal) muscle, the lower third has smooth muscle and the middle third contains both. Oesophageal and cardial mucous glands develop by week 28.

Stomach

By 18 weeks tubular glands have already appeared in the human gastric mucosa. The glands increase in number by division more rapidly than their openings to the lumen (gastric pits). The gland–pit ratio is still only half the adult value at birth. Parietal cells are present from 10–11 weeks, but are not ultrastructurally mature until 4–5 months. Although there are fewer parietal cells in the immature gastric mucosa, their number relative to the tissue volume is actually much higher in children than in adults. Although hydrochloric acid can be produced in the human fetal stomach by late gestation, little is produced. The absence of acid production seems anomalous because, at least in the sheep, blood levels of gastrin are high and exogenous gastrin does stimulate acid production. Since acid production is relatively low and the buffering capacity of milk (and amnionic fluid) is relatively high, digestion of protein in the immature gut must occur almost entirely at near neutral pH or via other pathways for protein uptake and digestion (see below).

Zymogen granules (protein granules, presumably enzymes) are present in the glandular cells of the human fetal stomach from 11 weeks. In some species these granules also have a mucous component that disappears with development. Pepsinogen is secreted well before term in the human but does not reach adult levels until some years after birth.

Well-differentiated mucous cells are present in the human fetal stomach by 11 weeks, first appearing in the fundus. Endocrine cells (e.g. gastrin-secreting cells) develop as early as 8 weeks.

Exocrine pancreas

In the human fetus, the exocrine (secretory) acini develop from the blind ends of the tubules that have branched and proliferated from the pancreatic diverticula; this process begins at 12 weeks. The epithelial cells develop a pyramidal morphology and zymogen granules appear by 20 weeks. Development of the secretory capacity of the pancreas includes increases in the enzyme content, fluid production, and cell responsiveness to secretagogues. There is considerable variability in the activity of the pancreas in the late fetal and newborn period. This is coordinated with the period of transfer of passive immunity from the mother to offspring (see below). In some species milk contains powerful trypsin inhibitors which inhibit the proteolytic activity of pancreatic secretions thus preventing digestion of the colostral immunoglobulins. In other species, low levels of intestinal enterokinase prevent activation of pancreatic enzymes.

Small intestine

As the endodermal tube proliferates and stratifies, the specific cell types of the epithelium (enterocytes, goblet cells, endocrine cells and 'M' cells) begin to appear. The tube 'mounds up' to produce ridges and furrows along its length (Fig. 7.2); these ridges then separate to form villi. It is thought that these non-symmetrical structures provide the first gradients to 'cue' differentiation. Thus, cells that lose the capacity to divide become terminally differentiated and accumulate over the surfaces of the developing villi. At this stage the gut lumen becomes patent and filled with fluid derived either from gut secretions or swallowing (which begin as early as 10–11 weeks). The cells which retain the capacity to continue dividing remain at the base of the lengthening villi, still in stratified clusters. Lengthening of the gut tube and increasing diameter are important stimuli for the formation of new villi, which continue to be produced from the stratified areas of undifferentiated cells. Eventually the stratified areas become a simple epithelium at the same time as the crypts form. Throughout this whole process the production of new cells is in excess of the requirements of villus and crypt growth resulting in cell migration along the length of the villus, with cell shedding at the tip. However, for the whole of fetal life the rate of migration is extremely slow. Both cell division and cell migration rates increase towards birth partly under the control of cortisol, which is increasingly produced by the fetal adrenal gland. In some species this occurs after birth but prior to weaning. As a result, the epithelial lining is 'flushed' of fetal cells. In some species the crypts become 'monoclonal'; that is, they are comprised of the progeny of just a single stem cell as a result of 'flushing'.

As soon as the gut tube endodormal cells begin to proliferate, the accessory coats also develop. Ingrowth and migration of neuroblasts (derived from the vagal neural crest) occur at the same time. By 7 weeks, nerve cells appear in the midgut and development proceeds in a caudal direction, reaching the rectum by 12 weeks. There is some evidence that neuroblasts from the sacral neural crest also give rise to nerves in the distal gut. Between 9 and 13 weeks the nerves develop into the ganglia of the two major plexuses: Auerbach's plexus, between the inner and outer coats of the muscularis externa, and Meissner's plexus, in the submucosa. Auerbach's plexus is responsible for the powerful coordinated contraction and relaxation of the muscularis externa (peristalsis) which propels material along the length of the gut (see below). Meissner's plexus also contributes to the process of peristalsis and, additionally, innervates the muscularis mucosa to stimulate mixing movements, as well as innervating the lamina propria and epithelium.

Uptake and transport of macromolecules in the small intestine

When patency of the lumen is established, the newly differentiated enterocytes towards the tips of the villi are significantly different from their adult counterparts. These 'fetal' enterocytes are found in all species, at some stage during development, either during the fetal or early newborn period. The fetal enterocytes have highly developed intracellular machinery for the uptake and transport of material taken up from the intestinal lumen (Fig. 7.4). Between adjacent microvilli, small pits and channels take up material from the lumen by endocytosis. In the apical region of the cell, there is an extensive network of tubules and vesicles called the apical endocytic complex. Below this is a region where vesicles coalesce to form larger vacuoles. The supranuclear region of the enterocyte is dominated by an extremely large single vacuole which contains lysosomal enzymes. The vacuoles are easily seen at the light microscopic level, hence the name 'vacuolated epithelium' is often used to refer to the immature small intestinal surface. In distal regions of the small intestine meconium is often taken into these cells (these droplets are called meconium corpuscles). In suckling rats, receptors for immunoglobulin G (IgG) are present on the lumenal surface of the membranes lining the endocytic compartment. It has been suggested that in the ileum, receptors for other molecules could also be present, for instance, for growth factors and hormones. Most of the material taken up into the fetal enterocytes is transported to the large vacuole, where it is degraded, providing substrates particularly for growth of the gut tissues themselves. Thus, growth of the gut tissues is adversely affected in the absence of swallowing. In addition, some molecules (including immunoglobulins) are sorted in the endosomal compartment and avoid entering the late endosomal/early lysoso-

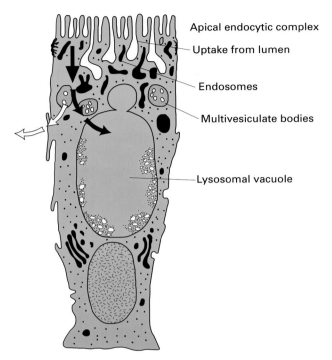

Apical endocytic complex

Uptake from lumen

Endosomes

Multivesiculate bodies

Lysosomal vacuole

Fig. 7.4. Fetal enterocytes are specialized for the uptake of macromolecules from the lumen. Lumenal contents enter the cells via endocytosis into the apical endocytic complex. After passing through the apical network of vesicular and tubular endosomes, it is sorted into a pathway directed either to the supranuclear vacuole, where it is degraded (black arrows), or to the lateral cell wall, where it is released intact into the intercellular spaces (white arrows), and enters the circulation.

mal compartment. They are instead transported in vesicles to the lateral cell membrane and released undegraded into the interstitium, from where they eventually enter the bloodstream.

After birth, passive immunity to disease is provided by ingestion of immunoglobulins from maternal milk until the offspring's own active immunity develops. Although normal full term human infants transport only minute quantities of immunoglobulins, the recent finding of mRNA for an epithelial IgG receptor in human fetal small intestinal tissue suggests that, like the suckling rat, this capacity may be present before birth. There are many hormones, growth factors and immunomodulatory agents present in the fluids ingested by the immature gut (milk, colostrum, amniotic fluid, buccal secretions and lung liquid). These may also cross the gut at various stages during development via the transporting systems of the immature gut epithelium and thereby exert their effects locally or systemically. For example, the timing of eyelid opening and tooth eruption in suckling mice is cued by the epidermal growth factor taken up from milk.

Underlying this structural and functional capacity for intact macromolecular transport is the coordinated regulation of digestive function. Throughout the period of macromolecular uptake, intrinsic and/or extrinsic mechanisms ensure that lumenal proteolysis is either suppressed or absent altogether. The digestive capacity of the intestine throughout this period is essentially the result of the intracellular (lysosomal) digestive enzymes. This is not to suggest that brush border hydrolases are not present. Disaccharidases and alkaline phosphatases are present from early in gestation (10–14 weeks in humans). Enterokinase, which is necessary for activation of pancreatic enzymes, appears only late in gestation and still remains at relatively low levels in children.

Pancreatic and gastric lipases are low in abundance in the neonate. Intraluminal bile salt concentration is also low. However, salivary lipase is produced in large amounts and is essential for adequate digestion of milk fats. In higher primates, bile salt-stimulated lipases secreted in milk also are important for lipolysis, especially in the first feeds. Thus, feeding pasteurized milk or the milk of other species may severely limit fat absorption in the neonate, particularly if preterm.

Adaptation to diet: the change from cellular to luminal digestion

Throughout the whole of life the gut is one of the most adaptable organs in the body. Its entire surface is constantly being shed and replaced, a process which takes 3–5 days, depending on the region. After surgery or trauma the gut can massively upregulate its structure and function. It dynamically responds to the daily input of diverse antigens and allergens. It actively maintains a highly specific milieu of flora and fauna within the lumen. In certain regards, it is helpful to consider the gut to be growing *all* the time. Whether or not its structural and functional state changes really depends on the sum total of the many processes of differentiation constantly at work.

In species in which the fetus swallows for significant periods in utero, for example the human, 60–70% of the protein in amniotic fluid is turned over every day. This occurs in the gut, via the process of intracellular digestion (see above). When the rates of synthesis of protein per day are calculated for the whole fetus, studies in the sheep suggest that the input of protein from amniotic fluid alone could account for 15–20% of total body protein deposition. In the adult, it is known that the gut tissues derive a significant part of their nutrition from locally absorbed substances, hence it is also likely that the fetal gut tissues benefit directly from swallowed input. Consistent with this, studies in fetal sheep have shown that gut tissues are severely growth retarded and develop abnormally in the absence of swallowed fluid input. Such studies suggest that many aspects of ingestion might be important for gut development, including the composition of swallowed fluid, the volume and frequency of ingestion, and the presence of specific factors: hormones, growth factors, immunomodulatory factors.

Towards the end of gestation, the gut must be prepared to face the change in diet that begins with milk ingestion. In some species maturation of features necessary for the digestion of milk are regulated by the same hormonal and metabolic changes which initiate labour. Important amongst these, especially for lung maturation, is the activation of the pituitary–adrenal axis. What is curious from the perspective of gut maturation is that in some species this critical window occurs in utero (e.g. precocial species such as humans) while in others it occurs prior to weaning (e.g. altricial species such as rats and mice).

Large intestine

Like the small intestine, the large intestine also develops villi. Villi are prominent in the proximal colon and reach their maximum development during the fourth or fifth month of gestation in the human. A vacuolated epithelium is present, suggesting that the immature colon also possesses the capacity to transport macromolecules. However, it seems unlikely that very little ingested material would normally reach the distal colon during the second half of gestation, except for a low turnover rate of the accumulating meconium which forms a semi solid plug. The villi disappear after the fifth month and are replaced by crypts, with increasing numbers of goblet cells as development proceeds. In some species the villi disappear very rapidly through a process called 'villus deletion', by which the tips of the villi are rapidly lost.

Hormones and growth factors as regulators of growth

In addition to their adult homeostatic functions, hormones and growth factors in the fetus also appear to play a role in developmental processes. Some of these substances are produced by the mother and some cross the placenta or are secreted in milk. Others are produced by fetal tissues. In many cases how and why they alter growth rates of the digestive tissues is not known, although experiments in animals are beginning to identify the mechanisms involved.

Cortisol is a hormone used clinically prior to birth to stimulate lung maturation and its administration is thought to mimic the effects of the prelabour endogenous surge in fetal cortisol production. In the gut, cortisol also has marked effects on epithelial cell proliferation and differentiation. In suckling rats, the biochemical and structural changes in the gut associated with weaning are dependent (in part) on corticosteroids. In humans, in which weaning is not an abrupt process, as well as in other long-gestation species, elevated cortisol levels do not coincide with weaning. Rather, adrenal activity is stimulated prior to birth and to the beginning of suckling, at the transition from fetal ingestion to the establishment of enteral feeding. This is a critical time for gut development and evidence suggests that the prenatal cortisol surge might be at least permissive in achieving normal gut function at birth. In some species cortisol is involved in the timing of gut epithelial 'closure' to macromolecular transport (e.g. cows, sheep, pigs) via changes in cell differentiation, increase in cell renewal and alterations in enterocyte physiology.

Gastrointestinal motility

Swallowing, the role of amniotic fluid, and suckling

It is likely that fluid taken into the fetal gut by ingestion distends the gut tube causing it to become patent and fetal enterocytes first appear at the same time. The human fetus swallows large volumes of fluid, estimated at 300–1000 ml/day. Swallowed fluid contains contributions from amniotic fluid (which includes fetal urine), lung liquid and buccal secretions. Within the gut, further secretions are added from the gut wall itself and the accessory organs (pancreas, liver). In fetal sheep, about 2–7 swallowing episodes occur per day; however, it is not clear how well regulated fetal swallowing actually is. Thus it is not known whether the daily volume or the volume per bout of swallowing, or both, is critical; nor is it known what provides the physiological drive for fetal ingestion. In late-gestation fetal sheep, swallowing episodes are associated with the aroused behavioural state and fetal breathing movements. This may explain why swallowed fluid contains lung liquid, although it should be noted that fetal swallowing still continues even if the tracheal flow is prevented.

Studies in fetal sheep have shown that when swallowing has been prevented, gut development (chiefly the small intestine) is impaired and that some of these defects are reversible if swallowing is resumed. The capacity for epithelial uptake and digestion of proteins from colostrum and milk is also present in utero and the regulation of these processes is the subject of current research.

The small intestine has, second to the liver, the highest turnover rate of protein in the fetus. The input of swallowed material appears to be critical in the local development of the gut wall tissues. In its absence the growing gut relies solely on placental delivery to provide adequate substrates, thereby competing with all the other fetal tissues and organs. Studies in sheep confirm this because small intestinal growth correlates well with liver growth when the fetal oesophagus is ligated. The correlation shifts to favour more intestinal growth when swallowing is either normal or restored after oesophageal ligation. Perhaps more surprising is the finding that when the composition of swallowed fluid is altered, the body allometry is also changed. This suggests that fetal or neonatal organ growth is a highly coordinated process, exhibiting an extremely high degree of whole body cooperation and communication.

While fetal swallowing begins early in development, the critical sucking reflexes do not appear until some time later. In the human fetus, nonnutritive sucking movements have been observed by 18 weeks. Coordinated sucking develops at about 35 to 40 weeks, but is not fully developed until after birth. This coincides with the acquisition of mature patterns (cyclic fasting, migratory motor complexes and continuous postprandial pattern) of gastric antral and small intestinal motor activity. Development of effective sucking, and later oral pharyngeal motor activity is necessary to ensure adequate nutrition. There are many behavioural and social cues, as well as underlying anatomical and physiological (endocrine, neural and motility) factors involved in this process.

Gastric emptying and intestinal motility

Peristalsis in the human fetal stomach has been observed as early as 14 weeks, but coordinated gastric emptying does not develop until 30–35 weeks. Small intestinal peristalsis has been observed a few weeks earlier, at around 11 weeks. Migrating motor complexes increasingly appear in the small intestine after 34 weeks in humans. By this age radio-opaque material injected into the amniotic sac is present in the small intestine within 1 hour and in the proximal colon by 8 hours, indicating effective (rapid) intestinal transport.

Meconium accumulates in the distal gut of the fetus and is eliminated soon after birth. Generally the presence of meconium in the amniotic liquor is thought to indicate fetal stress, but the stimuli for in utero meconium expulsion are not known. However, the presence of measurable levels (albeit low) of highly specific gut enzymes in amniotic fluid in the absence of overt meconium contamination suggests that there may be a low level of intestinal throughput in utero, especially earlier in gestation. The role of meconium in gut development is not known, but it is curious that it contains high levels of some hormones (e.g. oxytocin).

Gastrointestinal immune system

The epithelium as a barrier to infection

The epithelium of the gastrointestinal tract is essentially an exterior surface of the body. Like all surfaces it has its own mechanisms for defence and protection. While this is easy to achieve in some regions, for example the oral cavity, oesophagus and anal canal, which have a relatively robust stratified squamous epithelium, in other regions where absorption and digestion takes place a thinner and diversified cellular layer is required. At the stage when the proliferating stratified epithelium begins to develop precursors to the final tissue units (glands, crypts, villi), the columnar epithelial cells begin to develop polarity in their morphology. With the exception of the endocrine cells, a common feature of this polarity is the development of the junctional complex at the level of the terminal web. As cells mature the complexity of this junction increases. The development and dynamic maintenance of the junctional complex is the structural basis for the relative impermeability and high electrical resistance of the gut epithelium.

Mucosal immunity

All moist mucosal (epithelial) surfaces have a specialized division of the immune system, known as the mucosal-associated lymphoid tissue (MALT), which is involved in surface defence and response to external antigens. In the gut, the gastrointestinal-associated lymphoid tissue (GALT) includes the intra-epithelial lymphocytes (IEL), lamina propria, lymphoid follicles, and Peyer's patches. These cells and tissues interact with the other immune organs of the body, including the thymus, spleen and peripheral lymph nodes.

In the adult, enzymes and IgA present in saliva begin to neutralize antigens as they are ingested into the oral cavity. IgA production is markedly reduced, or even absent in the fetus and newborn. In the absence of active immunity to produce antibodies, the immunoglobulin profile of colostrum and milk reflects the need of the neonate for mucosal protection. Human newborns have relatively normal IgG serum titres, having already received significant transfer of IgG across the placenta, however, they are IgA deficient. Colostrum has high levels of IgA; it is produced in the mammary gland and is secreted across the acinar epithelium together with secretory components of milk which are vital for IgA to exert its protective effects. The secretory component of milk also inhibits proteolysis of IgA. In other species, usually those with little placental transfer of antibodies, the IgG titre of mammary secretions is extremely high. IgG is taken up by the gut and transported to the circulation where it imparts so-called passive immunity.

The transfer of specific antibodies into breast milk may be an important feature of the protective circuit between mother and infant. For instance, in the newborn rat, defecation occurs as a reflex response to the dam licking the anus. In this way she samples the flora and fauna of the pup's gut. Specific antibodies can be produced in response to this sampling, which then in turn are transferred into the milk which the pup ingests, with protective benefits.

M cells and antigen sampling

The lymphoid tissues of the lamina propria aggregate into organized follicles (as clusters of T and B lymphocytes) throughout the whole of the gut. In the adult, these are usually transient, however in some sites in the small intestine they form aggregates known as Peyer's patches. They are present by 14 weeks in the human fetus. Although they are initially also present in the duodenum and jejunum, they are more frequent in the ileum, which is the site at which they are found in the adult.

The Peyer's patches are covered with mucosal epithelium called the dome, or follicle associated, epithelium. So-called M cells are found in this epithelium as early as 14 weeks in the human. M cells are similar to the absorptive enterocytes of the small intestine, but do not possess a well-developed brush border or microvilli. Instead they have microfolds (hence their name). Within the cytoplasm is a network of transport vesicles that can transfer material from the lumen to the intercellular spaces. In these spaces, or clefts, are found clusters of intraepithelial lymphocytes. Thus, the M cells function to present antigens to the underlying lymphoid tissues.

Intraepithelial lymphocytes

In the human fetus, at 10–11 weeks intraepithelial lymphocytes appear in the small intestine. Some of these are $CD4^+$ and some are $CD8^+$. Unusually, about 50% of the $CD3^+$ cells are $CD4^-$ and $CD8^-$ (cells of this phenotype make up only about 6% in the postnatal gut). T cell receptor (TcR) expression increases with fetal age. By 18 weeks 30% of the $CD3^+$ cells are of the $\gamma\delta$TcR type. As early as 11 weeks, macrophages and dendritic cells are present in the lamina propria.

Summary

The digestive system, with its extensive epithelial, neural, endocrine and immune components, is one of the most complex systems in the body. Although it forms from a single continuous tube, its embryonic portions (fore, mid, hind) contain the necessary genetic programming to develop into its highly specific parts. All parts of the gastrointestinal tract are based on a common wall structure. From very early in their development the gut tissues are extremely sensitive to external stimuli, including nutrition, hormones and growth factors and functional drives such as swallowing and digestion. This labile quality is retained in the adult and is an important element in survival and adaptation of the species to its environment, and its maladaptation and dysfunction in disease. The initial 'goal' of gut development is to adapt successfully to the fetal environment. Thus, by birth, the fetal gut has already passed through this unique period of adaptation as a precursor or prerequisite for adequate function at birth and beyond. The differentiation of the vacuolated enterocyte and the phase of macromolecule uptake and cellular, as opposed to luminal digestion, is a unique feature of the immature gut. The ubiquity across species of biochemical markers and anatomical features of the vacuolated or immature epithelial cells indicates a strongly conserved function throughout evolution. How the renewing epithelium alters the programming for its daughter cells throughout life is one of the great challenges of future research because these issues underlie the mechanisms of altered differentiation in health and disease.

FURTHER READING

Baintner, K. (1984). *Intestinal Absorption of Macromolecules and Immune Transfer from Mother to Young*. Boca Raton, Fl.: CRC Press.

Heinz-Erian, P., Deutsch, J. and Granditsch, G. (ed.) (1992). *Regulatory Gut Peptides in Paediatric Gastroenterology and Nutrition*. Frontiers of Gastrointestinal Research, vol. 21, Basel: Karger.

Mestecky, J., Blain, C. and Ogra, P.L. (ed.) (1991). *Immunology of Milk and the Neonate*. Advances in Experimental Medicine and Biology, vol. 310. New York: Plenum Press.

Ogra, P., Mestecky, J., Lamm, M., Strober, W., Bienenstock, J. and McGhee, J.R. (ed.) (1998). *Mucosal Immunology*, 2nd edn. San Diego: Academic Press.

Trahair, J.F. and Harding, R. (1994). Development of the gastrointestinal tract. In: *Textbook of Fetal Physiology*, ed. G.D. Thorburn and R. Harding, pp. 219–235. Oxford: Oxford University Press.

Walker, W.A., Durie, P.R., Hamilton, J.R., Walker-Smith, J.A. and Watkins, J.B. (ed.) (1996). *Pediatric Gastrointestinal Disease: Pathophysiology, Diagnosis, Management*. St Louis: Mosby.

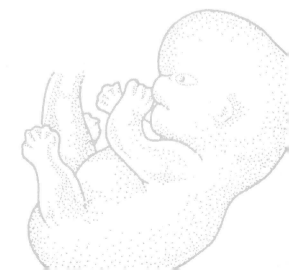

8

Nervous and neuromuscular systems

Sandra Rees and David Walker

The human nervous system is composed of billions of nerve cells (10^{11}–10^{12}) each with many processes which must make highly specific synaptic connections with target cells. In addition, the nervous system contains at least twice this number of neuroglial cells which carry out vital roles to support the function of neurones. Understanding the events which lead to the formation of this highly complex structure from a single sheet of ectodermal cells in the embryo is one of the greatest challenges in neurobiology today.

Embryonic origins of the nervous system

The development of the nervous system begins at the end of the gastrula stage of embryogenesis when the embryo is composed of three layers of germ cells surrounding a primitive gut. The outer layer, the ectoderm, forms the skin and nervous system. In the human, this stage is reached during the third week of embryonic development. Neurulation begins when a sheet of ectodermal cells (neural plate) on the dorsal surface is transformed into the specialized tissue from which the entire nervous system develops (Fig. 8.1). The critical event in this process, neural induction, is an interaction between the ectoderm and the underlying mesoderm. A distinct cylinder of mesodermal cells,the notochord, which extends along the midline of the embryo, underlies the portion of the plate which will eventually become the midbrain, hindbrain and spinal cord. Rostral to this is the prechordal mesoderm which underlies the region of the plate that will give rise to the forebrain. Inductive signals are sent from the mesoderm to the overlying ectoderm resulting in a subset of cells differentiating into neural precursors.

During neurulation, the neural plate buckles at the midline, and the edges of the plate elevate and fuse at the dorsal midline to form the neural tube which then separates from the overlying ectoderm (Fig. 8.1). Fusion occurs first in the region of the future hindbrain and progresses rostrally and caudally from this

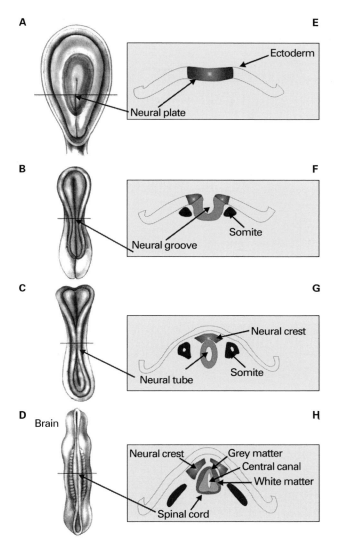

Fig. 8.1.   A–D. Dorsal views of the frog embryo showing the morphological changes that occur during neurulation. E–H. Cross-sectional views of the ectoderm and notochord at the corresponding stages. A,E. The nervous system develops from the neural plate, a flat plate of cells on the dorsal surface. B,F. The neural plate buckles at the midline to form the neural tube (C,G), which then separates from the overlying ectoderm. D,H. Neural crest cells arise from the neural folds and migrate away from the closing tube to differentiate into the cells of the peripheral nervous system and other structures.

point. Defective closure of the neural tube is a frequent cause of congenital malformations. When closure fails at rostral levels, anencephaly occurs in which the overall structure of the brain is grossly disturbed. When the caudal portion fails to close, spina bifida results. In this condition, the spinal cord is not confined by the vertebral column and the functions subserved by the lumbar and sacral cord are disrupted.

The neural tube eventually gives rise to all the cells of the central nervous system (CNS); that is, the brain and spinal cord. The peripheral nervous system (PNS) originates from a distinct group of cells, the neural crest (Fig. 8.1), a transient structure that arises from the dorsolateral margins of the closing neural tube. Epithelial–mesenchymal transition (EMT) occurs and neural crest cells migrate extensively throughout the body and differentiate into a variety of cells including the spinal (sensory) and autonomic ganglia, Schwann cells and melanocytes. EMT is associated with a decrease in cell–cell adhesion, and particularly with the loss of the cell adhesion molecule, N-cadherin from the surface of neural crest cells. Cell migration is influenced by the interaction of cell surface receptors (integrins) with extracellular matrix (ECM) molecules, particularly fibronectin, laminin and collagen I and IV. It is not yet known what causes neural crest cells to stop migrating and to aggregate into ganglia.

Cell generation and migration

Cell generation

At the time of neural tube closure there is only a single, or at most, double layer of columnar epithelial cells (neuroepithelium). Once the tube has closed rapid cell division occurs. Assuming that the fully developed human brain contains 10^{11} neurones, cells must be formed at an average rate of 250 000/minute. Olfactory neurones continue to be formed throughout life, but neurogenesis in the adult brain has been difficult to demonstrate. New evidence indicates low levels of neurogenesis in some brain regions (e.g. hippocampus) in rats, monkeys and even humans. During development, most of the proliferation occurs at the inner surface of the neural tube, the ventricular zone (Fig. 8.2A), so called because it lies adjacent to the cavity that will become the ventricular system of the brain and the central canal of the spinal cord. Initially, the neuroepithelial cells put out long processes which span the entire wall of the neural tube. The cell nucleus then migrates up the process towards the outer or mar-

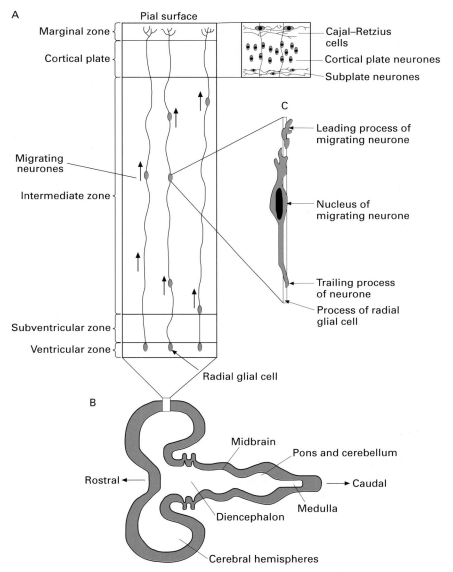

Fig. 8.2.   A. Cross-section of the neural tube in the region of the forebrain. Cell proliferation occurs in the ventricular and subventricular zones; cells then migrate through the intermediate zone towards the marginal zone where the first cells to arrive form the cortical plate. B. As cell proliferation increases, vesicles form at the rostral end of the tube; these are the forebrain vesicle which gives rise to the cerebral hemispheres and the diencephalon, the midbrain vesicle and the hindbrain vesicle, which gives rise to the medulla, pons and cerebellum. C. Radial glial processes along which immature neurones migrate.

ginal zone where it undergoes replication (synthetic phase). The nucleus then migrates back to the ventricular surface, retracts its processes and divides to produce two daughter cells. Early in the process of cell genesis, both daughter cells will remain in the mitotic cycle. However, after several divisions a precursor cell will lose its ability to divide and will begin to migrate away from the germinal zone to its appropriate position in the developing nervous system. This process marks the birthdate of the cell and determines its fate.

Formation of specific neuronal populations

As cells begin to migrate (as discussed below), the neural tube expands and an intermediate zone forms between the ventricular and marginal zones. By the fourth to fifth weeks of human embryonic development, this process results in the formation of three distinct swellings or vesicles at the rostral end of the tube, in the regions of the future brain. These are called the forebrain vesicle, which gives rise to the cerebral hemispheres and diencephalon, the midbrain vesicle, which gives rise to the adult midbrain and the hindbrain vesicle, which gives rise to the pons, medulla and cerebellum (Fig. 8.2B).

The birthdate of populations of cells can be determined by pulse labelling with tritiated thymidine. When injected into a pregnant animal it crosses the placenta and is incorporated into DNA by all cells in the synthetic phase of the mitotic cycle. Those cells that cease dividing after incorporation of the thymidine (and can therefore be considered to be 'born' at that time) will retain a strong radioactive signal which can be detected at a later stage when the tissue is analysed by autoradiography.

From such studies we can make some generalizations:

1 The larger neurones (e.g. Purkinje cells in the cerebellum) are produced before smaller neurones (e.g. cerebellar granule cells).
2 In the cerebral cortex, hippocampus and optic tectum, the cells that form the deepest layers are produced first while those that are generated at successively later times form the progressively more superficial layers. Once a neurone has completed the synthetic phase of neurogenesis it is committed to migrate to a particular lamina.
3 There appear to be two distinct periods of cell proliferation: the first relates to the major period of neurogenesis (10–18 weeks of gestation in the human) and the second with gliogenesis (midgestation to 18–24 months after birth in the human) although glial precursors and radial glial cells are present from very early in development.

4 There is a ventral-to-dorsal progression of cell proliferation in the developing nervous system (e.g. in the spinal cord, proliferation of ventrally located motor neurones is completed before that of sensory neurones in the dorsal horn).

Cell lineage commitments

Of considerable interest is the question of whether neurones and glia are produced by the same progenitor cells. The application of lineage tracers to individual progenitors has yielded clones of neurones and glia indicating that progenitors can exhibit a range of capabilities. It is possible, however, that in some regions there are no multipotential cells or that cells are committed to a particular lineage very early in development.

Neuronal migration

In the developing nervous system, immature, postmitotic neurones must migrate from the germinal zone to their definitive location. In several, but not all parts of the CNS, processes of specialized supporting cells called radial glia form a scaffold along which immature neurones migrate. These glial processes, which are formed early in development, have very different lengths and trajectories in different regions of the CNS. For example, in the cerebral cortex, neurones follow very long glial processes from the ventricular surface, through the intermediate zone, to the emerging cortical plate (the first cells to arrive in the developing cortex). Neurones form a specialized junction with the glial fibre along the length of the neuronal soma and extend a motile, leading process in the direction of migration (Fig. 8.2C). Recently it has been proposed that the molecule *reelin* (an ECM-related protein) secreted by transient cells called Cajal–Retzius cells located in the marginal zone of the cerebral cortex (and hippocampus and cerebellum) during development, arrests the progress of neurones along radial glia. A second molecule called *derailin* appears to be involved in breaking the bonds between a glial cell and neurone, thereby 'derailing' the neurone. The neurone will then take up its definitive position within a cellular layer or nucleus. Although the glial fibre system provides the primary guidance system for radial migration in the developing neocortex, some neurones undergo tangential migration to reach their final destination.

Many neurones migrate, without the benefit of glial guides, both within the CNS and in the PNS from the neural crest. These immature neurones rely on cellular and extracellular molecules in the matrix through which they move and the cues are probably similar to those used in axonal guidance described below.

Neuronal differentiation

A remarkable feature of vertebrate development is that the proliferating cells of the neural tube ultimately produce an enormous variety of neuronal phenotypes. At some point during development each of these young neurones must acquire a specific identity that defines the pattern and type of connections it should form with other neurones. For cortical neurones, the birthdate of a neurone will predict its laminar fate; for example the first formed neurones form the deepest layers (V and IV). Some cortical neurones will become projection neurones with a range of targets (e.g. corticospinal, corticobulbar), and others, interneurones. What controls this cellular differentiation? It is likely that it will involve an interplay between the cell's lineage history and environmental signals. For example, all pyramidal cells in layer V throughout the cerebral cortex in the rodent initially extend an axon down the pyramidal tract to the spinal cord. However, during development, cells of the visual cortex retract this axon collateral and develop stable connections with the regions of the visual system known as the tectum; in contrast, cells of the motor cortex retain the projection, the fibres ultimately forming the corticospinal tract. Thus, projection neurones from cortical layer V do not carry information about their specific set of targets and it is likely that the appropriate destination is determined by guidance molecules emanating from the target.

Neuroglial cells

There are two major classes of glial cells in the vertebrate nervous system: macroglia – oligodendrocytes and astrocytes – and microglia. The macroglia originate from neuroepthelial cells with their production extending well into the second postnatal year in the human. In addition, they are continuously renewed by a process of cell death and cell proliferation throughout life. Microglia on the other hand, originate from a specific population of mononuclear leucocytes which penetrate the blood–brain barrier and enter the CNS during late fetal to early postnatal periods and transform into microglial cells.

In addition, to their roles in structural support in the CNS, neuroglia play many important active roles in brain development and function. Astrocytes buffer the K^+ ion concentration in the extracellular space and some take up and remove chemical transmitters released by neurones during synaptic transmission. They also produce growth factors such as glial cell line-derived growth factor (GDNF) and insulin-like growth factor (IGF), contribute to the formation of the blood–brain barrier, and some play a role in neuronal and axonal guidance during development. The main function of oligodendrocytes is to form and maintain a myelin sheath around axons of certain cells in the CNS. In the PNS this role is carried out by Schwann cells which originate from the neural crest. Microglia are the resident immune cells in the brain and play an important role in phagocytosis of cellular debris.

Development of neural processes

Having migrated to the appropriate position in the nervous system the young neurone now faces the challenging task of forming precise connections with targets which range from micrometres to centimetres away. The initial outgrowth of the axon and its orientation appear to be genetically determined. However, the genome probably contains only the instructions for general directions for axonal pathfinding and more specific cues must be sought from the environment.

The growth cone

At the tip of most growing neurites (axons and dendrites) is a distinctive structure called a growth cone (Fig. 8.3A). This consists of a flattened region (lamellipodium) from which extend finger-like processes (filopodia) which are typically 5–30 μm long and 0.1 μm in diameter. The filopodia and the leading edge of the lamellipodia are filled with fibrillar actin (Figs. 8.3B, C). The proximal region of the growth cone is packed with cellular organelles. When growth cones are observed in vitro they are highly motile, dynamic structures constantly moving and exploring the environment by extension and retraction of their leading edge and filopodia. Once the leading edge has extended, an appropriate substratum onto which it can attach and become stabilized must be present for forward movement to occur. Once attached, an inherent traction-generating mechanism within the growth cone causes tension to develop. Unattached or poorly attached processes are withdrawn while tension exerted against attached processes might help to draw the growth cone forward.

By what intrinsic mechanism is the leading edge advanced? One proposal is

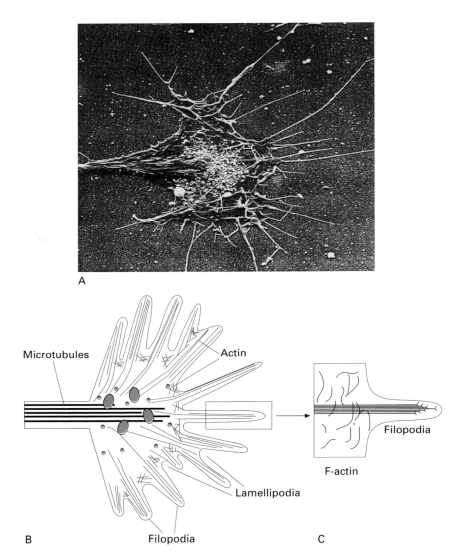

Microtubules

Actin

Filopodia

F-actin

Lamellipodia

B   Filopodia   C

Fig. 8.3. A. Scanning electron micrograph of a growth cone in tissue culture (redrawn from N.K. Wessels and R.P. Nuttal (1978), *Exp. Cell Res.*, **115**, 111–22). B,C. The distribution of the microtubules and actin in the growth cone. Actin is highly concentrated within the filopodia and leading edge. Many fibrils are orientated with their growing tips pointed distally, although some are orientated randomly forming a dense network.

that actin monomers are polymerized at the leading edge of the growth cone, swept rearward where they are depolymerized and then recycled to the leading edge where they are repolymerized. This continuous cycling of actin generates a kind of 'caterpillar' tread within the interior of the growth cone. If the actin meshwork is linked to cell surface receptors (integrins, N-CAMs, cadherins) which bind to permissive substrate molecules (e.g. ECM molecules, laminin and fibronectin) the meshwork remains in place and newly polymerized actin helps to advance the leading edge.

Axonal path finding

Growing axons use many guidance cues operating over different segments of the trajectory; the cues are likely to direct growth by altering the location or rate of actin polymerization. Such a mechanism requires the presence of receptors on the growth cone surface linked to intracellular signalling mechanisms. Axons tend to grow in a straight line unless directed otherwise by these cues or if they encounter a specific 'guide post' cell which will instruct them to change course. The first pioneer axons that develop in an embryo navigate through a relatively axon-free environment. Many of the later developing axons use these preexisting axon tracts as guides. It is now believed that axonal guidance involves the coordinated action of four main types of cues: short-range (or local) cues and long-range cues, each of which can be either positive (attraction) or negative (repulsion).

Short-range contact attraction

As indicated above, when the receptor molecules on a growth cone find a permissive substrate with which to bind, forward movement of the growth cone and neurite occurs. Growth of the neurite plasma membrane will occur at the growth cone by local insertion of membrane components. These have been transported to the growing tip by fast axoplasmic transport along microtubules.

Short-range contact repulsion

Studies on the topographical specificity of connections in the retinotectal system have indicated that nerve cells recognize each other by means of complementary surface marker molecules. In this system, it is considered that molecules are arranged in gradients across the retina and tectum to encode positional information. The marker molecules have only recently been identified and it appears that they have repulsive rather than attractive interactions. Eph receptors (the largest known family of tyrosine kinase receptors) are expressed on retinal axons and bind with ligands, called ephrins, on the surface of tectal neurones. The binding of receptor and ligand results in the axon being repelled rather than attracted. The receptors and their ligands are arranged in counter gradients across the retina and tectum and would thus encode the positional information required. Other examples of repulsive interactions have been reported whereby axons are channelled down specific pathways hemmed in by repellent molecules.

Long-range chemoattraction

In addition to short range gradients in which the molecular cues are displayed on the surface of cells or the surrounding extracellular matrix, there is now evidence that guidance can also be by diffusible molecules. These cues are referred to as chemotropic. For example, commissural axons in the CNS have been shown to be attracted by molecules called *netrins* secreted by intermediate targets, floor plate cells in both spinal cord and brainstem.

Long-range chemorepulsion

Growth cones can also be repelled by diffusible factors secreted from a distance, a process termed chemorepulsion. For example, during development the ventral spinal cord secretes a diffusible repellent for sensory axons; the action of this molecule is thought to prevent subclasses of sensory axons that enter the spinal cord from projecting too far ventrally.

Formation of connections

Synaptogenesis

On reaching the target, axonal elongation ceases and the formation of a synapse is initiated. It is possible that target-derived signals induce a cessation in motility and the transformation of the growth cone into a synaptic bouton. The sequence of events in synaptogenesis appears to be similar whether an axon forms a synapse on a muscle fibre or on a neurone. In tissue culture, growing mammalian axons have been observed by phase contrast microscopy and fixed at different stages of synapse formation. In this instance, when one or more filipodia made contact with a postsynaptic cell, there was cessation of all filopodial activity for up to 30 minutes. One of the filopodia eventually broadened and a postsynaptic specialization began to form within 6 hours. In the growth cone, presynaptic dense projections developed and synaptic vesicles appeared 18 hours after first contact. In the eutherian nervous system, synaptogenesis reaches a peak in the immediate postnatal period, although some of the synapses are eliminated as the mature nervous system is shaped. The mature human brain contains approximately 10^{13} synapses.

Specificity of connections

Synaptogenesis is shaped by two mechanisms: synapses are initially formed without neural activity but they then require activation to refine their distribution. When an axon courses through the developing brain it does not innervate everything along its path but is highly selective in where it forms a synapse; this selectivity can be manifest in several ways. Specific types of neurones will invariably be attracted to make connections with each other, presumably due to the presence of specific marker molecules; this is called *cell specificity* (e.g. retinal ganglion cells with tectal cells). In addition, in systems where it is necessary to preserve a topographical map of the peripheral input, for example in the visual system, the axons of retinal ganglion cells must connect with their target cells in a highly ordered manner; this is called topographic specificity (as discussed above in relation to the retinotectal system). This requires a gradient of signalling molecules to encode positional information. A third form of specificity is called *synaptic site specificity* where an axon synapses on a particular region of the soma or dendritic field of a cell. These restricted sites might depend on the timing of the arrival of a particular afferent fibre, but they could also result from afferent fibres competing for specific cellular and/or molecular markers.

Regressive events during development

So far we have described cell proliferation and the growth of neural processes; that is progressive developmental effects. There is now considerable evidence that regressive phenomena also play an important role in determining the form of the mature nervous system.

Neuronal death

It is now known that programmed or physiological cell death is a major feature of normal development in the nervous system. This form of cell death appears to be due to the cell 'committing suicide' by upregulating cytoplasmic proteases and endonucleases that degrade the DNA. The signal for the expression or activity of these proteins produced by 'cell death genes' might be the failure of arrival of a retrogradely transported neurotrophic factor from the target tissue (see below). In contrast, necrotic cell death results from the inhibition of cellular activities by toxic agents and ischaemia, for example. Programmed cell death has now been described for many regions of the nervous system with the extent of death ranging from 15 to 75% of the neuronal population (most typically 50%). Cell death is usually confined to a specific period that is distinct for each neuronal population.

What is the purpose of this overproduction of neurones followed by the subsequent elimination of considerable numbers of cells? The major purpose is presumed to be matching the size of innervating populations of neurones to the capacity of their targets. In addition, cell death corrects for errors of migration (mislocation) and projection (misprojection).

Target dependent cell death

In most neuronal populations cell death occurs at the time of synaptogenesis in the target tissue. This temporal coincidence, together with the demonstration that manipulation of the availability of putative synaptic targets alters the numbers of surviving neurones, has led to the concept that the target cells are instrumental in defining the final population of innervating cells. For example, experiments performed on amphibian larvae have shown that removal or addition of a limb bud could respectively deplete or increase the number of motor and sensory neurones in the related innervating neuronal populations (Fig. 8.4). No given cell therefore is destined to die. It appears that neurones compete for a sustaining neurotrophic factor produced by the target cells in limited amounts, sufficient to support the survival of only a proportion of all neurones. Trophic support may also be derived from autocrine (secretions from neighbouring cells) or paracrine sources (self-secreting or stimulating).

Nerve growth factor (NGF) was the first molecule to qualify as a specific neurotrophic factor involved in regulating the survival of some classes of neurones (mammalian and avian sensory and sympathetic ganglion cells). Many

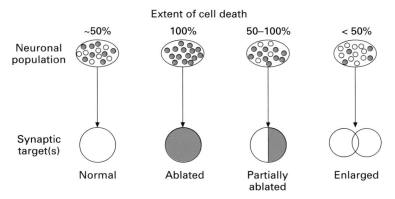

Fig. 8.4.   Target-dependent cell death. In most normal neuronal populations approximately 50% of cells die at about the time of synaptogenesis in the target tissue. If the tissue is partially or totally ablated neurones are lost in proportion to the amount of tissue removed. Adding additional target tissue or providing growth factors rescues some of the neurones that would otherwise have died.

other growth factors have now been identified and shown to be important for the survival of various neuronal populations in vitro; their role in vivo is being determined. For example, brain-derived neurotrophic factor (BDNF) increases the survival and growth of hippocampal and cortical neurones and cilliary neurotrophic factor (CNTF) promotes the survival of chick sympathetic cilliary ganglion cells in culture and enhances chick spinal motor neurone survival in vivo.

Hormone-dependent neuronal death

Neuronal death during development can also be related directly or indirectly to the action of circulating hormones. For example, in the spinal nucleus of the bulbocavernosus (SNB) of the rat, a nucleus which innervates the penile and anal musculature, there are more motor neurones in the mature male than female. This sexual dimorphism arises primarily because motor neurone loss is greater in the female than male during the period of naturally occurring cell death. It is not yet certain whether androgens rescue these SNB neurones in the male by saving the muscle to which they project or by acting as direct trophic agents for neurones. Penile musculature is initially present in the female but atrophies during the first postnatal weeks. Whatever the locus of action of the sex steroids, the result is a developmental difference in the nervous system.

Elimination of neuronal processes

After the phase of cell death there is an exuberant growth of synaptic connections between surviving cells; selective elimination of some of these neuronal processes will then occur without the death of that cell. Initially, evidence for the elimination of processes during development came from studies on the neuromuscular junction and has now been demonstrated in the PNS and in the CNS. This form of process elimination involves the removal of axons and their synapses over relatively short distances and occurs in the early postnatal period, appreciably later than cell death in the same neuronal system. Its purpose appears to be to sharpen and refine the initial exuberant growth of synaptic connections and, as with cell death, possibly involves a competitive mechanism resulting in the death of some processes and the survival of others.

There is evidence to suggest that one factor that might give some fibres a competitive edge over others is their state of functional activity. This has been shown most strikingly in the mammalian visual system. In layer IV of the visual cortex of cats and monkeys, the neural inputs from the relevant layers of the lateral geniculate nucleus, which are connected with the two eyes, overlap extensively at first, but become progressively separated into distinct eye (ocular) dominance columns or stripes (Fig. 8.5A, B). In normal animals the stripes connected with each eye are of the same width but if, during a critical period in early postnatal life, one eye is deprived of form vision by suturing the eyelids closed, the stripes in layer IV associated with the deprived eye become significantly reduced in width whilst those connected to the nondeprived eye are correspondingly enlarged. This suggests that the relative absence of activity in the deprived eye places it at a competitive disadvantage. It is not known how neural activity alters neuronal arbour size and distribution, but it appears that the activity of neurones is correlated with their response to trophic molecules; N-methyl-D-aspartate (NMDA) receptors might also be important in this process.

Development of the neuromuscular system

Many of the principles outlined for the CNS also apply to the PNS, and to the innervation of skeletal muscles. Thus, as in the brain, muscle fibres are initially innervated by several nerve fibres and connections are refined through an activity-dependent process. Muscles are also dependent on trophic factors, some of which are derived from the newly arrived nerve fibres, or from the muscle itself.

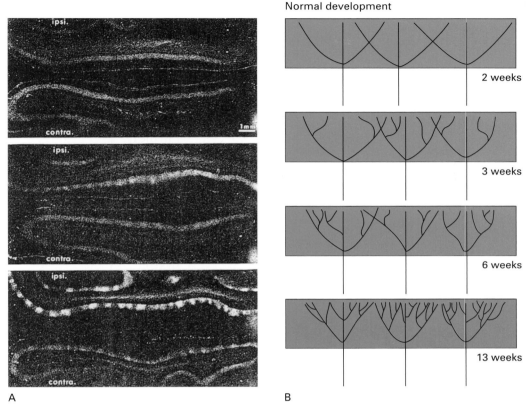

Fig. 8.5. A. Radioactively labelled afferent fibre terminations in the visual cortex; label injected into the left eye at 2, 3, 6 and 13 weeks after birth. Inputs initially overlap with the right eye but are progressively separated into distinctive eye (ocular) dominance columns. (From S. LeVay *et al.* (1978), *J.Comp.Neurol.*, **179**, 223–44.) B. Diagrammatic representation of fibre terminations illustrating the elimination of some axonal branches to form the columns.

Furthermore, the contractile properties of muscle fibres initially are similar between muscles, but they become different and highly specialized as the fetus and then the newborn develops a repertoire of motor behaviours.

Development of muscle fibres

Despite the very different environmental conditions that exist for those species born at an immature stage of development (e.g. mouse, rat, cat) or at a more mature stage (e.g. sheep, cow, horse), the course of skeletal muscle differentiation is similar. Early muscle development is regulated by myogenic factors. Skeletal muscle is derived from mesodermal stem cells located on either side of the notocord. The paired somites that give rise to aggregations of myoblasts are formed by segmentation of this mesoderm into parallel blocks on either side of the neural tube. This segmentation proceeds in an anterior to posterior direction, and within the somites there is a separation into lateral and ventral compartments, to ultimately form the lateral and ventral myotomes. The commitment of these cells to develop as muscle cells probably occurs at the time of somite formation. There appears to be at least four myogenic regulatory factors. Myf-5 and MyoD are expressed first, probably under the influence of signals arising from the overlying ectoderm, and these are required for the initial commitment and survival of cells as myoblasts. Continued expression of the *MyoD* gene may be under neural influence. Myogenin and MRF4 are proteins expressed after myoblast formation and appear to be important in further differentiation and the fusion of myoblasts into multinucleated myotubes. Not all of the cells in a somite become muscle cells, indicating that expression of myogenic determining factors must also be repressed by other transcription factors expressed locally in some cells.

Myotubes have the capacity to transcribe the muscle-specific contractile proteins and assemble them into arrays of thick and thin filaments that slide along one another, the basis of muscle fibre contraction. Thin filaments are formed by the coordinated accumulation of troponin, tropomysin and actin. Thick filaments are formed by the polymerization of myosin, and both the heavy and light chains exist as variants so that a large number of combinations can arise. The myosin isoforms differ in the rate at which they promote the splitting of adenosine triphosphate (ATP) to release energy, so that the rate at which a muscle fibre contracts is determined by the type of myosin it contains.

Muscles in adults are classified as either fast- or slow-twitch, based upon the difference in the rate at which they develop maximum force and then relax following the arrival of a single nerve impulse; this property correlates with the possession of 'fast' or 'slow' myosin. This characteristic, together with their oxidative capacity and resistance to fatigue, is the basis for the classification of muscle fibre types in the adult.

Innervation of muscle fibres

The nerve fibres which grow out from the ventral horn of the developing spinal cord, or from the dorsal root ganglia, must be directed towards the primordial

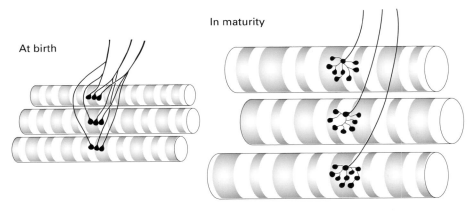

Fig. 8.6.   Illustration of the initial hyperinnervation of a muscle in a young mammal, and the changes which occur involving elimination of nerve fibres to yield uni-neuronal contact with the postsynaptic target. Note that the terminal arborization of the surviving contact becomes more complex. (Redrawn from D. Purves, *Body and Brain: a Trophic Theory of Neural Connections.* Cambridge, MA: Harvard University Press, 1988.)

clumps of mesodermal cells which will differentiate into the definitive muscles. The tips of growing nerve fibres are specialized (the growth cone) and possess receptors responsive to substances found in the ECM. The growing neurites use cues to navigate through the tissue mass in much the same way as fibres negotiate through the developing nervous system. But while it might be thought that the nerve fibre must navigate through complex structures to find the distant muscle target, it should be remembered that both the nerve fibre and the primordial muscle cells are both migrating centrifugally at approximately the same time.

As in other parts of the nervous system, there is an excess of nerve fibres which invade the primitive muscle, but a fraction of these will not survive beyond the embryonic/early fetal period. Skeletal muscle fibres are hyperinnervated at this early stage. This is evident by the fact that nerve fibres contact the myofibre at many points along its length, and also that more than one nerve fibre can be present at each point of contact on the myofibre (Fig. 8.6). This 'polyneuronal' innervation is gradually reduced by the withdrawal of all but one axon from the site of synapse formation. Each muscle fibre is then in contact with just one nerve fibre arising from one neurone whose cell body is situated in the ventral horn of the spinal cord. Each neurone has axons which may have several or many branches, so that within a muscle a neurone eventually makes contact with a group of muscle fibres. Such a group of fibres contract synchronously, and is known as a contractile muscle unit. All of the fibres within the muscle unit are the same with respect to their contractile properties. The individual fibres of the muscle unit may be close to one another or dispersed across the whole muscle. The gradual 'pruning' of the excess neuronal contacts results in the formation of unineuronal motor units. The sequential activation of these separate motor units is the basis of the ability of a muscle to perform graded contractions.

Nerve fibres grow outwards from both the ventral horn of the spinal cord and from the dorsal root ganglia, almost always following the same path so that nerve trunks contain both motor and sensory fibres. The contact between motor nerves and muscle usually occurs at the stage of muscle development when myoblasts have fused to form multinucleated myotubes (Fig. 8.7). At this stage gene expression in these mesodermally derived cells has committed the cell to develop along the myofibre line. There is evidence that expression of these 'muscle-determining' genes is influenced by the arrival of nerve fibres into the myoblast cell mass. Hence, one explanation for the hyperinnervation of muscle fibres in early development is that nerve processes promote the commitment of cells as muscle cells at this stage; subsequently, excess fibres are eliminated so that a single nerve fibre establishes control over a significant number of the muscle cells within each muscle.

Formation of the neuromuscular junction

The points of contact between the growth cone of the advancing nerve fibre and the cell membrane of the myotube soon become highly specialized. Acetylcholine receptor protein is initially spread over the entire surface of the myotube, but this disappears at sites remote from the point of neural contact, or migrates to the region where the cell membrane becomes modified as the motor endplate is formed (Fig. 8.8). Muscle nuclei near this region become associated with the expression of the acetylcholine receptor protein and other proteins associated with the synapse, and with the high density of ion channels which are now localized to this structure. Some of the endplates may be multiply innervated, and some myotubes may have more than one endplate, but both are eliminated so that each myofibre possesses a single endplate contacted by a single motor fibre. Within the whole muscle the endplates are restricted to a zone, usually near to the middle of the muscle, but the processes which control this spatial restriction are not well understood. As in other parts of the CNS,

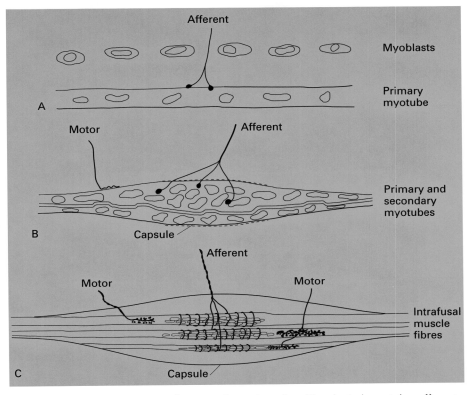

Fig. 8.7.   Development of the muscle spindle. A. On formation of multinucleated myotube, afferent
fibres from dorsal root ganglia make contact. B. Several myoblasts are incorporated within
a structure which begins to be encapsulated, and which now receives a motor innervation.
C. Afferent and motor (gamma) nerve fibres develop specialized endings on these
'intrafusal' myofibres, which are smaller than extrafusal fibres and are tightly coupled
along their length within the encapsulated structure. Both the sensory (afferent) and
motor nerve endings are probably responsible for inducing the changes in the myotubes
which distinguish them from the normal, extrafusal muscle fibres. (Redrawn from D.
Barker, *Handbook of Sensory Physiology*, 1974.)

the neuromuscular junction is probably stabilized and strengthened by an
activity-dependent process, as well as by trophic substances released from
muscle fibres, taken up by the nerve terminal, and then transported retrogradely to the cell body of the motor neurone. Muscle-derived substances with
neurotrophic effects include the well-characterized neurotrophins, BDNF and
NT-3, the cell-to-cell signalling agents nitric oxide and ATP, and the peptide
growth factor IGF-1.

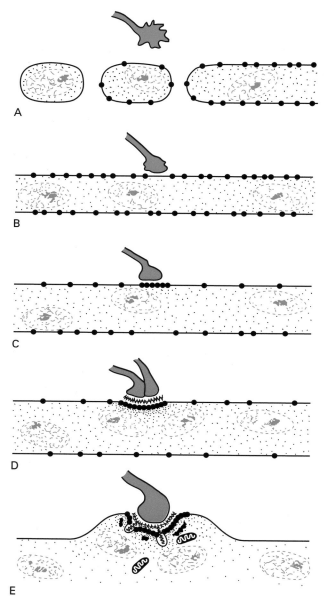

A

B

C

D

E

Fig. 8.8.   Illustration of the formation of the neuromuscular junction. A. The nerve fibre arrives at
the surface of the myoblast; note the specialized growth cone at the advancing tip of the
nerve fibre. At this stage myoblasts express acetylcholine receptor (AChR) protein (dots)
over most of their surface. B. Mononucleated myoblasts have fused to form multinucleated
myotubes; dispersed expression of the AChR protein continues. C. The nerve ending is

Sensory innervation of muscle

Nerve fibres originating from the dorsal root ganglia also make contact with muscle fibres, but a series of changes in both nerve fibre and myotube result in the development of stretch- and pressure-sensitive structures from which essential information is provided to the CNS about the contractile performance and mechanical load on the muscle. Fibres from sensory axons arrive in the muscle at about the same time as the primitive motor fibres, and at about the time myoblasts are fusing to become multinucleated myotubes. It is not known whether sensory fibres contact myotubes randomly, seek out a particular class of myotube already destined to become the specialized 'intrafusal' muscle fibre, or whether sensory axons induce changes in myotubes which set them apart from the bulk of the normal 'extrafusal' muscle fibres. The intrafusal fibres also receive a motor innervation, and it is perhaps significant that this arrives just after the arrival of the sensory nerve. The motor neurones which innervate the intrafusal muscle fibres are termed 'gamma' motor neurones, and they come to be distinguishable in terms of their smaller size from the 'alpha' motor neurones which innervate the extrafusal muscle fibres. The point of contact of the sensory fibre and myotube becomes encapsulated by fibrous tissue derived from the perineural epithelium (Fig. 8.7B). Within the capsule the sensory fibres form one of several highly specialized structures (bag1, bag2, chain) from which action potentials are generated in response to changes of muscle length. Sensory fibres also penetrate to the tendon region of the developing muscle where an encapsulated structure is also formed that becomes sensitive to the load, or strain on the muscle. Again, the sensory fibre induces changes in the myotube so that fibrillary development in the muscle fibre recedes from the region where the nerve fibre touches the tendon fibrils; the nerve fibre then arborizes and becomes encapsulated in fibrous and elastic material produced from nearby Schwann cells.

Although muscle spindles and tendon organs begin to develop early in fetal life it is not known if sensory information arising from muscles is important in the subsequent development of the neuromuscular system. Sensory fibres are

Fig. 8.8.
(cont.)

associated with the accumulation of AChR protein. D. Sites of nerve–muscle contact may include several nerve fibres at the same point. E. Multiple innervation is eliminated. There is an accumulation of muscle nuclei near to motor endplate, which becomes increasingly complex in structure. Genes encoding AChR proteins are now restricted to the nuclei adjacent to the endplate. (Redrawn from J.P. Changeux.)

important in inducing the changes in muscle fibres which result in the development of muscle spindles and tendon organs, but sensory denervation of a muscle during development, although it causes atrophy of these specialized structures, does not otherwise prevent the normal development of the extrafusal fibres.

Changes in muscle fibres with development

Skeletal muscle development is critically dependent upon its innervation. More precisely, the motor nerves to a muscle provide an essential growth stimulus that allows the muscle to mature and that also sustains it, even in the adult. Selective denervation of a muscle, to remove the sensory fibre that passes from the muscle into the spinal cord, does not affect muscle growth and differentiation, or its ability to contract. On the other hand, severing the motor nerves which pass from the ventral horn of the spinal cord to the muscles not only prevents growth and maturation of the muscle, but also results in atrophy to the point where the remaining muscle is severely compromised in its ability to contract when stimulated directly (Fig. 8.9). Thus, the motor nerve is thought to release a trophic substance essential for maintaining the normal growth and metabolic processes in muscle, in addition to the release of acetylcholine, the neurotransmitter which acts at receptors of the motor endplate causing the muscle to contract. These skeletal muscle 'neurotrophic factors' are not yet as fully described and characterized as other neurotrophic factors known to be important in the development of the nervous system. There could be at least two skeletal muscle trophic factors associated with the fast- and slow-twitch muscle fibres, or perhaps a single trophic factor whose action is modified as the fast- or slow-twitch phenotype emerges with development. As for other neurotrophic factors, the substance(s) is probably a small, diffusible polypeptide acting on a specific receptor on the myoblast, myotube or muscle fibre. Such trophic factors are likely to be produced in the neuronal cell body and to pass down the axon by one of the many transport systems associated with the microtubular system within the axon.

During development, embryonic and fetal myotubes appear to possess slow myosins, and all fetal and neonatal muscle fibres initially contract slowly. The embryonic form of myosin is slowly replaced by a fetal (or neonatal, depending on the species and length of gestation) myosin which is immunologically distinct but shares similarities in ATPase properties with the embryonic and adult slow myosins which precede and follow it. In some fibres the myosin is replaced with a neonatal and then an adult isoform which is 'fast'.

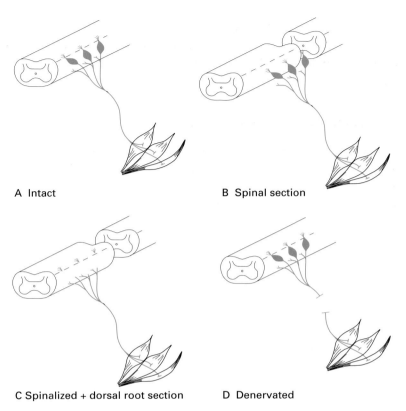

A Intact   B Spinal section

C Spinalized + dorsal root section   D Denervated

Fig. 8.9.   A. The complete motor and sensory innervation of a muscle is derived from the ventral and dorsal roots (respectively) of the spinal cord. B. Separating the spinal cord so that information can no longer pass from higher centres does not prevent full functional development of muscles. C. Removal of sensory control by section of the dorsal roots does not affect development of the extrafusal muscle fibres. D. Section of the whole nerve results in muscle atrophy, indicating the essential role of the motor nerves in sustaining muscle growth and differentiation. (Redrawn from D. Walker and A. Luff (1995), *Reprod. Fertil. Dev.*, **7**, 391–8.)

The factors which control this sequential expression of myosin genes are not fully understood. Myosin gene expression is influenced by hormones (especially thyroid hormone), and by stretch and load; in some way muscle growth occurs in register with bone growth. The most important influence on the expression of genes which determine muscle fibre type is probably the pattern of activity in the motor nerves. This is because, in those species born at an early stage of development where much muscle development occurs after birth (e.g.

rats, rabbits), all muscles initially contract slowly, and individual muscles are developed by the particular type of activity to which they are subjected as the animal develops its behavioural repertoire.

Compelling evidence that muscle fibre phenotype is under neural control comes from 'cross-innervation' experiments. When a slow muscle is innervated by a foreign 'fast' nerve, the muscle fibres express fast myosins and physiologically become fast-twitch muscles. Conversely, fast-twitch muscles innervated by slow nerves increase the expression of 'slow' myosins and contract more slowly. Furthermore, motor nerves to fast- and slow-twitch muscles have different patterns of activity due probably to the different excitatory and inhibitory inputs delivered to their cell bodies in the spinal cord from higher levels of the central nervous system. Thus, in the newborn and even in the adult it is possible to change the biochemical and biophysical phenotype of a muscle by experimentally imposing upon it a pattern of neural activity different from that which it normally receives. Against the evidence for the importance of neural activity is the observation that fast- and slow-twitch muscles develop normally even if the spinal cord is transected so that information from the CNS cannot reach the muscles concerned. This suggests that the expression of particular myosin isoforms may depend on interactions between the muscle and nerve other than that associated with centrally generated activity, or with activity associated with exercise of the muscle in a particular motor function.

Role of muscle activity in the fetus

Spontaneous activity is a feature of the developing CNS, and it probably has a crucial role in establishing and refining specific connections between nerve cells. In the spinal cord spontaneous activity is present in the embryo and fetus. Bursts of activity occur in dispersed groups of motor neurones, and can occur simultaneously in the groups of cells that innervate separate muscles that will be functional antagonists of each other (e.g. flexor and extensor muscles). This accounts for the many stretching movements that can be seen by ultrasound in the human fetus. In the developing spinal cord, adjacent motor neurones appear to be coupled to each other by gap junctions; this is particularly evident for the group of motor neurones innervating homonymous muscles.

The pattern of activity in nerves has an important influence on the functional characteristics of muscle fibres during development. Slow-twitch muscles normally receive a nearly continuous pattern of neural discharge and develop rather prolonged and maintained contractions, consistent with their role as postural, or antigravity muscles. Fast-twitch muscles receive bursts of nerve discharge at high frequencies, and therefore contract briefly and often, which is consistent with their major role in performing short, fast motor actions. As most muscles have to perform in both ways from time to time, slow and fast motor units are interdigitated within the muscle, or distributed across the muscle in such a way as to increase the efficiency of each function.

Specific patterns of nerve activity have been shown to be important in determining the contractile characteristics of muscle fibres. For species that are immature at birth, such as mice and rats, it is assumed that the gradual development of the motor patterns associated with crawling and walking allow the muscles to develop in concert with the neural activity they are receiving. But for those species that are more highly developed when born (e.g. sheep, horses) the means by which the muscles are brought to almost complete functional development is not fully understood. The movements that occur in utero may be more intricate than we suppose, or specific trophic factors may be delivered to each type of muscle so that they differentiate appropriately for their eventual postnatal use. Some muscles do experience activity during fetal life which is consistent with postnatal function (e.g. the diaphragm, chest wall and laryngeal muscles are 'exercised' by fetal breathing movement), but it is difficult to envisage how the limb muscles are subjected to activity in utero that is anything like that imposed on them after birth.

Environmental conditions which influence development of the brain and neuromuscular systems

The developing mammalian nervous system is vulnerable to many agents and conditions both before and after birth, including viruses, radiation, hyperthermia, hypoxia, malnutrition, growth factors and changes in circulating hormone levels, particularly thyroid hormone. The effects which these factors have on the brain depend on the developmental processes which are most active at the time the insult is imposed. At birth the human brain is approximately 25% of its adult weight, the rat 15%, guinea-pig 62% and monkey 72%. As few new neurones are produced after birth in the human, the increase in brain weight is accounted for by an increase in cell size, proliferation of axonal and dendritic processes, synaptogenesis, multiplication of glial cells and myelination of axons. These processes are all vulnerable to environmental influences.

Undernutrition

One of the most extensively studied factors to influence brain development is malnutrition (maternal and neonatal) particularly in rats. Several parameters are affected, depending on the time of insult. In undernutrition there is a reduction in glial numbers, in myelination, in growth of axonal and dendritic processes and perhaps most importantly a reduction in the number of synapses per neurone. Restoration of normal nutrition allows for the reversal of most but not all of these effects. Maternal malnutrition can result in placental insufficiency causing premature birth, which carries a risk of mental retardation. When children are subjected to chronic malnutrition from birth to 18 months of age severe enough to result in growth restriction, they have been shown to suffer from permanent deficits in emotional, cognitive and intellectual function. It is possible that the structural deficits underlying these problems are similar to those described for malnourished rats. Nutritional therapy and enriched social and educational conditions from birth to 18 months can reverse this situation. If therapy is delayed beyond 2 years, the deficit is only partially reversed.

Intrauterine growth restriction (IUGR) is characterized by a reduction in muscle mass which is often proportionally greater than the reduction in growth overall. The individual muscle fibres are smaller, and the amount of glycogen laid down in the muscle is reduced. However, the gross and microscopic structure of the muscle is not altered, and observations on growth-restricted newborn animals suggests that there is no functional impairment of skeletal muscle. Indeed, some observations suggest that muscle development may be speeded up in growth-restricted animals, and that the diaphragm and limb muscles are more resistant to fatigue.

Hypoxia

Severe, acute hypoxia in late gestation can result in gross lesions in the fetal white matter (myelinated axons) adjacent to the ventricles in the forebrain and also to cell death in the cerebral cortex and forebrain nuclei. Brief episodes of hypoxia in midgestation can result in damage to the white matter, cell death in the hippocampus, cerebellum and cerebral cortex and can significantly affect the long-term growth of neural processes in regions (such as the cerebellum) which are immature at the time of the insult. Chronic hypoxia, which is usually due to placental insufficiency and associated with fetal undernutrition/

hypoglycaemia, can result in IUGR. Growth-restricted children have a higher than normal incidence of neurological deficits. The effects of prenatal hypoxia on brain development are of considerable interest as hypoxia is thought to be an important antecedent of neurological impairment in human infants and might underlie conditions such as cerebral palsy, sudden infant death syndrome, minimal brain dysfunction and schizophrenia.

Altered hormones and growth factor levels

Thyroid hormones play an important role in stimulating neural development. For example, they increase cell proliferation, myelination and the assembly of microtubules which are a component of axons and dendrites and essential for their elongation. Hypothyroidism in experimental animals results in a marked reduction of brain development particularly in the growth of neural processes and synapse formation in the cerebral and cerebellar cortices. Children with congenital hypothyroidism have a high incidence of congenital mental deficiency. Severe deficiency of iodine, an essential component of thyroid hormone, affects fetal brain development and is associated with endemic cretinism and mental retardation. Thyroid hormone and growth hormone act synergistically to promote muscle growth; the reduction in muscle development seen in IUGR may be a combination of the effects of low hormone levels and reduced activity in the CNS, spinal cord and motor neurones. Androgens are now known to be essential for neuronal survival and growth of neural processes in specific spinal cord and hypothalamic nuclei; it is likely that other sex steroids will also play an important role in brain development. Growth factors such as nerve growth factor as mentioned above are essential for the appropriate development of specific cell populations during development. IGF is important for oligodendrocyte proliferation and myelination. In experimental IUGR, IGF-I levels are reduced and this could affect myelination and consequently axonal conduction and nerve formation. IGF-I is initially produced at a high level by developing muscle but production is suppressed when innervation is completed. It has been suggested that IGF-I is a retrograde trophic factor that is produced in increased amounts when there is nerve injury, or nerve activity is decreased.

Emergence of functional systems during development

Somatosensory system

The somatosensory system deals with information from a variety of sensory receptors that are located in the skin, muscle, joints and other deeper tissues. It enables us to experience touch, pain and temperature and to sense the position and movement of our bodies. Observations of the human fetus with ultrasound have shown that the first discernible movements are detected at 7–8 weeks of postmenstrual age.

Movement of individual limbs occurs at about 9–10 weeks with more complex movements such as sucking and swallowing evident at 12–14 weeks. Episodes of movements involving simultaneous extensions of the leg, trunk and neck also occur at intervals in both the human and sheep fetus. In aborted fetuses it has been possible to evoke movements from light stimulation of the perioral region from 6–7 weeks (gestational age). This indicates that low-threshold mechanoreceptors are operative by this age and have established functional connections with motor neurones.

Within the uterus, stimulation of low-threshold cutaneous mechanoreceptors in the fetus could occur with movement of the amniotic fluid, contractions of the uterus or from self-stimulation as limbs touch the body and the fingers touch the face. This could then result in reflex contraction of muscles and activation of Golgi tendon organs and muscle spindles. Muscle spindles would also be activated by changes in limb position and these receptors also generate resting or background activity as they develop. Ultrasound studies have demonstrated that there is a marked increase in the rate of change in position of the fetus from about 10 weeks onwards peaking at 15 weeks after which time there are spatial restrictions on fetal movement.

Whether a fetus can 'feel' pain in utero is controversial. Some definitions of pain imply that the brain must achieve a certain level of neural functioning as well as having prior experience before pain can be understood. Such a definition would clearly exclude the fetus from 'feeling' pain. It is clear, however, that the fetal nervous system can respond to potentially damaging stimuli at the beginning of the last trimester. At about 26 weeks of gestation, premature infants show a measurable flexion withdrawal reflex to noxious cutaneous stimulation and coordinated facial actions indicative of pain to a heel prick, suggesting that the nociceptive afferent input to the spinal cord is present and can function at this age. It is reasonable to assume that such responses could also occur in utero although it is difficult to envisage nociceptor activation occurring during fetal life except, perhaps, during fetal surgery. It is still not certain whether nociceptor activation in the premature infant, or in the fetus, would be perceived as pain at this early age given the observations that sensory impulses do not evoke a mature cortical response until 29 weeks of gestation. Any assessment of pain in the neonate must also take into account that the infant nervous system has a very low threshold for excitation. In the case of the cutaneous withdrawal reflex, features of the response evoked preferentially or specifically by noxious stimuli in the adult can be evoked by non-noxious stimuli in the neonate.

Vision

The highly ordered projections from the retina in the eyes to the lateral geniculate nucleus in the brain form in utero before the retina can respond to light but at a time when retinal ganglion cells spontaneously generate highly correlated bursts of action potentials. Blockade of the endogenous activity, or biasing the competition in favour of one eye, results in severe disruption to the pattern of retinogeniculate connections. After birth, competition between the projections from the neurones in the lateral geniculate nucleus to the visual cortex, shapes eye-specific connections from an initially diffuse projection, into ocular dominance columns. When the competition is altered during a critical period for changes (up to about 12 weeks in the cat and 6 months in humans) by depriving one eye of vision, the normal pattern of ocular dominance is disrupted and vision is significantly compromised. Clearly, an equal input from both eyes in this period is vital for the appropriate connections to be made in the visual cortex in order that the system can function normally. After birth there are also further improvements in the optics and accommodation of the eye and changes in shape of the lens.

Auditory system

In humans, hearing is thought to begin in utero. The fetus responds with movement to tones (500 Hz) delivered via a loudspeaker placed on the maternal abdomen. For all frequencies, there is a large decrease (20–30 dB) in the intensity required to elicit a response as the fetus matures. Furthermore, it is possible at birth to elicit electrical responses to sound from the auditory brainstem of very premature infants. These responses to sound have been used to argue that the fetus can hear during fetal life perhaps as early as 19 weeks of gestation. It seems likely though, that through a combination of sound attenuation to the inner ear as a result of the fluid in the ear and the amniotic sac, and the immaturity of the auditory system, the hearing of external sounds is likely to be poor unless those sounds are intense and of a low frequency. Nevertheless, infants are born with a preference for the sound of their mother's voice, indicating either that the auditory system responds preferentially to specific sound cues present during the time of fetal development, or that the fetus has 'learnt' to recognize key features of its mother's voice.

Sleep/wake activity and behavioural states in fetuses

Towards the end of gestation, complicated patterns of breathing, oculomotor and trunk muscle activities emerge suggestive of the establishment of sleep states. Observations of the human fetus in utero and of sheep fetuses show that the CNS is able to generate sophisticated programmes of motor behaviour that must involve changes of both excitatory and inhibitory activity in the spinal cord. There is some evidence that the fetus is occasionally 'awake', or is somewhat more responsive to external stimuli for short periods of time, but other evidence suggests that the activity of the fetal CNS is suppressed by substances such as adenosine, prostaglandins and pregnancy steroids released from the placenta. Respiratory movements are present from early in fetal life in many species, and apart from the demonstrated importance of these for lung development, this prenatal exercise may also be important for development of the diaphragm and chest wall muscles. The intensity of fetal activity varies between day and night, but it is not known if such rhythms are merely 'diurnal' changes that occur in response to changes of maternal activity and nutrition, or that they are determined by activity of the fetus's own 'circadian' pacemakers, particularly the suprachiasmatic nuclei.

Summary

The major events to occur during development of the brain and the neuromuscular system are neurogenesis, neuronal migration, growth of neuronal processes (axons and dendrites), programmed cell death, synaptogenesis, and refinement of connections between neurones, and between motor neurones and muscle fibres. Neurones gradually lose their ability for self-sustenance and become dependent on target-derived trophic factors for survival. Neural activity is critical for sculpting the intricate circuits of the nervous system from initially diffuse connections in the brain itself, the spinal cord, and at the neuromuscular junction. As development of the brain and neuromuscular system is not entirely genetically programmed, pre- and postnatal environmental factors such as malnutrition, hypoxia and an altered endocrine status can significantly influence development. The impact of developmental delays and perturbations has implications not only for the immediate survival of the fetus and its ability to withstand the rigours of birth, but also for the development of the individual's full potential.

FURTHER READING

Anton, E.S., Marchionni, M.A., Lee, K.F. and Rakic, P. (1997). Role of GGF/neuregulin signalling in interactions between migrating neurones and radial glia in the developing cerebral cortex. *Development*, **124**, 3501–10.

Hatton, M.E. (1999). Central nervous system neuronal migration. *Ann. Rev. Neurosci.* **22**, 511–39.

Hoh, J.F.Y. (1991). Myogenic regulation of mammalian skeletal muscle fibers. *News Physiol. Sci.*, **6**, 1–6.

Jansen, J.K. and Fladby, T. (1990). The perinatal reorganization of the innervation of skeletal muscle in mammals. *Prog. Neurobiol.*, **34**, 39–90.

Lin, C.-H., Thompson, C.A. and Forscher, P. (1994). Cytoskeletal reorganisation underlying growth cone motility. *Curr. Opin. Neurobiol.*, **4**, 640–7.

Lloyd-Thomas, A.R. and Fitzgerald, M. (1996). Do fetuses feel pain? Reflex responses do not necessarily signify pain. *BMJ*, **313**, 797–8.

Lumsden, A. and Krumlauf, R. (1996). Patterning the vertebrate neuraxis. *Science*, **274**, 1109–15.

McConnell, S. (1995). Constructing the cerebral cortex: neurogenesis and fate determination in developing neocortex. *Science*, **254**, 282–5.

McKoy, G., Leger, M.E., Bacou F. and Goldspink, G. (1998). Differential expression of myosin heavy chain mRNA and protein isoforms in four functionally diverse rabbit skeletal muscles during pre- and postnatal development. *Dev. Dyn.*, **211**, 193–203.

Megeney, L.A. and Rudnicki, M.A. (1995). Determination versus differentiation and the MyoD family of transcription factors. *Biochem. Cell Biol.*, **73**, 723–32.

Oppenheim, R.W. (1996). The concept of uptake and retrograde transport of neurotrophic molecules during development: history and present status. *Neurochem. Res.*, **21**, 769–77.

Penn, A.A. and Shatz, C.J. (1999). Brain waves and brain wiring: the role of endogenous and sensory-driven neural activity in development. *Pediatr. Res.*, **45**, 447–58.

Sanes, D.H., Reh, T.A. and Harris, W.A. (2000). *Development of the Nervous System*, San Diego: Academic Press.

9

Endocrine functions

Charles E. Wood

The focus of this chapter will be the major endocrine axes of the fetus, including oestrogen biosynthesis and hypothalamic and pituitary control of adrenal, gonad and thyroid function. Special emphasis will be placed on the roles that these endocrine axes play in the development of the fetus and its preparation for extrauterine life. The endocrine systems of the fetus might be thought of as the modulators of the more classical physiological organ systems. For example, the basic components of the cardiovascular system work together to affect the transport of nutrients and waste products and to perfuse the tissues with blood. However, the blood volume and osmolality are controlled via the actions of endocrine feedback mechanisms, and the distribution of combined ventricular output is affected by several hormones which are released in response to fetal stress. The fetal lung makes lung liquid prior to birth, and serves as an organ of gas exchange after birth. However, the reabsorption of lung liquid is coordinated by several hormones which are secreted around the time of birth. Owing to the nature of research in the field of fetal endocrinology, much of the data have been obtained from experiments involving fetal sheep. However, some of the more interesting topics in fetal endocrinology relate to the differences among species. It is, perhaps, the differences among the species which allow us to identify the truly basic principles of endocrine control in fetuses. This chapter is not intended to be a comprehensive review of the literature in this field, but rather a summary of the current knowledge of several aspects of this large subject.

Introduction to endocrine interactions

As in adult endocrinology, fetal endocrinology involves the molecular interplay of hormones, paracrine substances and autocrine substances, which ultimately aid or maintain fetal homeostasis. All of fetal endocrinology can ultimately be described as a collection of control systems. Most hormonal systems are controlled by negative feedback (Fig. 9.1). The concentration of a hormone is

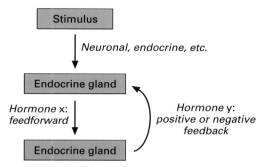

Fig. 9.1. A general overview of endocrine feedforward and feedback relationships.

controlled within limits: the secretion of the hormone is increased by a stimulus to secretion and generally inhibited by the negative feedback inhibition from itself, by another hormone which it stimulates, or by a change in metabolic activity. An excellent example of negative feedback is the inhibition of adrenocorticotrophic hormone (ACTH) secretion by cortisol. Plasma cortisol concentrations are maintained within normal limits, appropriate for gestational age, via changes in the rate of secretion of ACTH. When plasma cortisol concentrations are below the so-called set-point for the gestational age, ACTH secretion is increased until plasma cortisol concentrations rise to appropriate levels. Conversely, when plasma cortisol concentrations are higher than the set-point for that gestational age, ACTH secretion is reduced until plasma cortisol concentrations fall to within normal limits.

Another important interaction among hormones is positive feed forward. In this interaction, one hormone stimulates the release of another (Fig. 9.1). Trophic hormones secreted by the fetal anterior pituitary all stimulate the release of other hormones, such as thyroxine and tri-iodothyronine from the thyroid, androgens from the testes, oestrogens from the ovaries, and cortisol from the adrenal cortices. This concept is also illustrated by the release of anterior pituitary hormones by specific releasing factors.

Fetal pituitary hormones

The fetal pituitary contains and secretes trophic hormones which control the secretory activity and growth of the adrenal cortex, the gonad and the thyroid. The fetal pituitary also secretes growth hormone and prolactin. The hormones of the anterior pituitary are controlled, in turn, by hypothalamic-releasing hormones (Fig. 9.2). ACTH secretion is stimulated by corticotrophin-releasing hormone (CRH) and arginine vasopressin (AVP) which are synthesized in the parvocellular cells of the paraventricular nuclei of the hypothalamus, and released into hypothalamo-hypophyseal portal blood at the median eminence. Thyroid-stimulating hormone (thyrotrophin, TSH) release from the thyrotropes of the anterior pituitary is stimulated by thyrotrophin-releasing hormone (TRH), a releasing hormone synthesized in the paraventricular nuclei in cells which are similar to those which contain CRH. Gonadotrophin-releasing hormone (GnRH), which is responsible for the release of luteinizing hormone (LH) and follicle-stimulating hormone (FSH) from gonadotropes in the anterior pituitary, is synthesized in the medial preoptic area. Growth hormone (somatotropin, GH) release from somatotropes is stimulated by growth hormone-releasing hormone (GHRH), synthesized in the arcuate nuclei, and inhibited by somatostatin, synthesized in the paraventricular nuclei. Prolactin (PRL) release from lactrotropes is primarily under negative control, being inhibited by dopamine synthesized in neurones in the arcuate nuclei.

Hypothalamus–pituitary–gonadal (HPG) axis

The structure of the fetal HPG axis is similar to that of the adult: GnRH, released into the hypophyseal-portal blood at the median eminence, stimulates the release of both LH and FSH from gonadotropes in the anterior pituitary. In the fetus of the sheep, a species which is relatively mature at birth, the proteins and the mRNA for LH and FSH appear in gonadotropes and the protein and mRNA for GnRH appear in the hypothalamus at midgestation or before. The abundance of both the protein and the mRNA for these hormones is sex-related. Female fetuses tend to have higher concentrations than males. Circulating concentrations of LH and FSH are pulsatile in the sheep fetus, as they are postnatally. Plasma concentrations of both these hormones increase to reach a maximum at about 30–40% gestation, then decrease until the time of birth. In the fetus of the rat, a species which is relatively immature at birth, the tissue concentrations of protein and mRNA for GnRH, LH, and FSH, increase continuously until birth. Indeed, the highest concentrations are reached postnatally in this late-developing species. Within the hypothalamus, GnRH neurones are located in the region of the organum vasculosum of the lamina terminalis (OVLT), specifically in the medial preoptic nucleus and in the nucleus of the diagonal band of Broca.

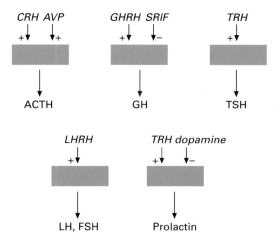

Fig. 9.2. Anterior pituitary hormones and their respective releasing hormones (see text).

Interestingly, in the sheep, GnRH does not appear to be stored significantly in terminals in the median eminence, as in older fetuses or postnatal animals.

Circulating plasma concentrations of androgens and oestrogens in the fetus originate both in the fetal gonads and in the placenta. Gonadal testosterone, for example, peaks at about the same time as the peak in plasma concentrations of gonadotrophins, about 30–40% of gestation. However, later in gestation, the fetus is exposed to several androgens and oestrogens of placental origin, secretion of which is regulated either by fetal pituitary–adrenal activity or by induction of critical steroidogenic enzymes in the placenta itself (placental steroidogenesis is discussed below). The midgestational peak in gonadal steroid hormone secretion is associated with gonadal growth and differentiation. The concentrations of androgens and oestrogens later in gestation do not appear to be sex-related, but might be important in terms of other endocrine functions (e.g. the control of parturition). In early fetal life, the development of both internal and external genitalia is determined endocrinologically. For a more detailed description of the development of the reproductive organs see Chapter 10.

Fetal oestrogen and androgen biosynthesis

In the adult mammal, androgen and oestrogen biosynthesis is mostly accomplished by the gonads, with more minor amounts originating from the adrenal cortices. The fetus, however, is dramatically different. The fetal gonads are

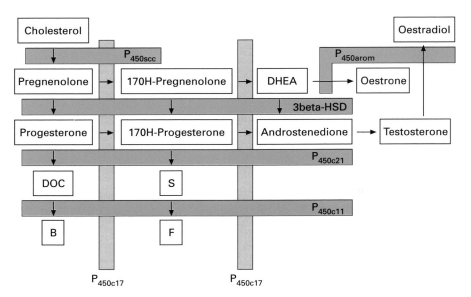

Fig. 9.3. The biosynthesis of adrenal and gonadal steroids. The activities of the steroidogenic enzymes (cytochromes P_{450scc}, P_{450c11}, P_{450c17} and $P_{450arom}$ and 3-hydroxysteroid dehydrogenase) are represented by shaded boxes. DOC, 11-deoxycorticosterone; B, corticosterone; S, 11-deoxycortisol; F, cortisol; DHEA, dehydroepiandrosterone.

relatively immature and secrete small amounts of androgen and oestrogen. The major source of sex steroids in the fetus is the placenta. The high rate of production of androgens, oestrogens and progesterone by the placenta is an important feature of pregnancy: alterations in the balance among these hormones dramatically affect the activity of the myometrium and therefore the integrity of the pregnancy.

In the sheep, progesterone, oestrogens, and androgens are synthesized *de novo* by the placenta. The relative proportions of the oestrogens and androgens to progesterone is dependent upon the relative activity of placental 17-hydroxylase (cytochrome P_{450c17}), a key step in the conversion of progesterone ultimately to androgen and oestrogen (Fig. 9.3). The activity of this enzyme is induced by increased fetal plasma concentrations of cortisol. It is in this way that a normal increase in fetal plasma cortisol concentration at the end of gestation leads to the initiation of parturition. The increased abundance of oestrogen relative to progesterone at the myometrium increases the contractile activity of the smooth muscle and therefore initiates labour. This process is discussed in Chapter 12.

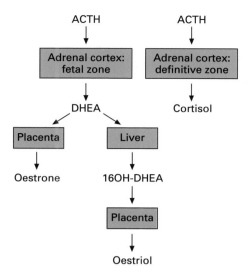

The biosynthesis of oestrogens, androgens, and glucocorticoids by the adrenal glands and placenta of the fetal primate. DHEA, dehydroepiandrosterone; 16OH-DHEA, 16-hydroxy-dehydroepiandrosterone.

In primates (including the human), the biosynthesis of oestrogen and androgen is somewhat more complicated. In these species, the placenta lacks cytochrome P_{450c17}, and the abundance of this enzyme cannot be induced by cortisol. Nevertheless, the placenta synthesizes large amounts of oestrogen with the help of the fetus. The fetus supplies, from the *fetal zone* of the fetal adrenal cortex, a steroid precursor for oestrogen biosynthesis, dehydroepiandrosterone (DHEA) and dehydroepiandrosterone sulfate (DHEAS). The fetal zone of the fetal adrenal cortex differs from the so-called *adult zone* or *definitive zone* because it lacks the enzyme 3-hydroxysteroid dehydrogenase (Fig. 9.4). It is this enzyme which catalyses the formation of pregnenolone from progesterone and from 17-hydroxypregnenolone to 17-hydroxyprogesterone, and is therefore a requisite step in the pathway to oestrogen biosynthesis. In combination, however, the fetal zone of the fetal adrenal cortex and the placenta have all of the enzymatic activity needed for oestrogen biosynthesis. This combined activity of fetal adrenal and placenta has been termed the *fetoplacental unit*. The activity of the fetoplacental unit is influenced strongly by the fetal pituitary secretion of ACTH. In primate fetuses, infusion of ACTH into the fetal blood has been shown to increase the circulating concentrations of oestrogen in maternal plasma, and negative feedback inhibition of fetal ACTH secretion by infusion of glucocorticoid reduces maternal plasma oestrogen concentrations.

Hypothalamus–pituitary–adrenal (HPA) axis

The HPA axis is critically important in the fetus for homeostasis and, at least in ruminants, for the initiation of parturition. In the adult, the HPA axis is thought of as the endocrine axis of *stress*. The term *stress* was first used in physiology to describe the response to various apparently nonspecific stimuli which were potentially harmful. However, it has been noted that apparently diverse stimuli, including, for example, chronic restraint, or pain, produce a so-called *general adaptation syndrome* in which experimental animals develop peptic ulcers, adrenal enlargement and thymic involution. In later years, these effects were found to be related to the elevation in plasma glucocorticoid concentration. A more modern view of the HPA axis is that it responds not to stimuli which are nonspecific, but rather to specific physiological or psychological stimuli. In accordance with this view, the response of the HPA axis (and the neuronal pathways mediating these responses) to specific stimuli, such as hypoxia, hypercapnia, acidaemia, hypotension, have been extensively studied in the fetus. Because of the fundamental importance of the HPA axis to the maintenance and termination of pregnancy, understanding the mechanism of HPA responses to what is often termed *stress* is one of the most important aspects of fetal endocrinology.

The structure of the fetal HPA axis is similar to that of the adult (Fig. 9.5). ACTH is synthesized and secreted by the corticotropes of the anterior pituitary in response to two hypothalamic-releasing factors: AVP and CRH. The two releasing hormones work in concert: each increases the sensitivity of the corticotrope to the other. The control of the fetal HPA axis appears to be integrated at the paraventricular nuclei (PVN). Ablation of the PVN or implantation of dexamethasone crystals in the PVN disrupts the function of the axis with respect to both generation of responses to 'stress' and the initiation of parturition.

ACTH stimulates the release of glucocorticoid hormones (i.e. cortisol in the human, primate, and sheep, and corticosterone in rodents). In primate and human fetuses, the majority of the adrenal cortex in the fetus is the *fetal zone* which lacks 3β-hydroxysteroid dehydrogenase. The fetal zone of the adrenal is responsive to ACTH, and provides precursors for placental oestrogen biosyn-

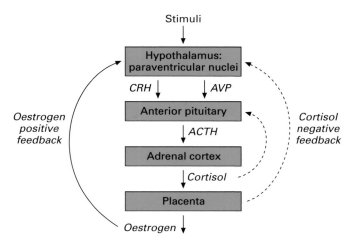

Fig. 9.5.   The ovine fetal hypothalamus-pituitary-adrenal axis.

thesis, as discussed above. The mass of the fetal zone increases as a function of fetal gestational age, reaching a peak at the time of birth and regressing thereafter. The *definitive zone*, or the remainder of the fetal adrenal of the primate and human, contains the full complement of steroidogenic enzymes which are found in the adult adrenal cortex. The definitive zone responds to ACTH with an increase in cortisol secretion and responds to angiotensin II and K^+ with an increase in aldosterone secretion. In the fetal sheep, perhaps the best-studied mammalian fetus, the entire adrenal cortex is similar to that of the adult, capable of responding to both ACTH and angiotensin II, and capable of secreting both cortisol and aldosterone. In the sheep, the fetal adrenal also increases in size as a function of gestational age, with both the relative mass and responsiveness to ACTH highest at the time of spontaneous parturition.

The fetal HPA axis is activated progressively throughout the latter part of gestation as a normal consequence of ontogenetic development. Throughout the last 10–15% of gestation, fetal ACTH and cortisol concentrations increase progressively in a semilogarithmic pattern (Fig. 9.6). The increase in fetal ACTH secretion is accompanied by an increase in the protein and mRNA encoding for CRH and AVP in the paraventricular nuclei. In the anterior pituitary, the corticotropes appear to undergo a maturation, with a switch from so-called fetal-type to adult-type corticotropes. Within the corticotropes, there is increased synthesis of pro-opiomelanocortin, the precursor protein for ACTH, as well as an increased proportion of fully processed ACTH. The increase in fetal plasma

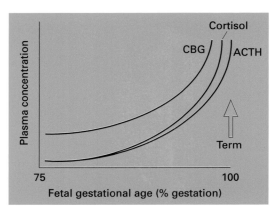

Fig. 9.6. A schematic representation of the ontogenetic changes in fetal plasma concentrations of adrenocorticotrophic hormone (ACTH), cortisol, and corticosteroid-binding globulin (CBG) in the last 25% of gestation.

cortisol concentration is dependent upon the rising plasma ACTH concentration and an ontogenetic increase in the sensitivity of the fetal adrenal cortex to ACTH. In sheep, there is also an increase in the binding capacity for cortisol near the end of gestation which exaggerates the increase in fetal plasma cortisol concentration. The increase in adrenal sensitivity is, in part, dependent upon the growth and subsequent increase in mass of the adrenal cortex. Other variables, such as adrenal blood flow, also influence adrenal sensitivity to ACTH. It has been proposed that adrenal nerves play a role in producing acute (and possibly chronic) changes in adrenal sensitivity to ACTH; however, the relative roles of efferent nerves and/or humoral factors are as yet unknown.

The ontogenetic increase in fetal ACTH secretion is essential for the initiation of parturition in sheep, and might play as important a role in primates. In sheep, ontogenetic increases in fetal plasma cortisol induce the synthesis of cytochrome P_{450c17} in the placenta, increasing oestrogen production relative to progesterone production, and ultimately increasing myometrial contractility. In primates, including humans, increases in fetal ACTH secretion might accomplish the same thing by increasing DHEA and DHEAS production by the fetal zone of the fetal adrenal cortex, thereby increasing oestrogen production by the placenta, and ultimately increasing myometrial contractility. The mechanism of the ontogenetic increase in fetal ACTH secretion is unknown, but an understanding of this mechanism is of obvious importance because it might provide the key to understanding the aetiology of idiopathic preterm labour.

It appears that several events occur simultaneously to allow fetal ACTH secretion to rise at the end of gestation. First, there is a decrease in sensitivity of cortisol-negative feedback control of fetal ACTH secretion. Prior to term, cortisol very potently inhibits fetal ACTH secretion. However, near term, the negative feedback system is desensitized so that even supraphysiological plasma concentrations of cortisol do not inhibit fetal ACTH responses to stimuli. Also occurring at term is a rising plasma concentration of oestrogen (in part because of increasing plasma cortisol-inducing cytochrome P_{450c17}). The oestrogen has a potent effect on fetal ACTH secretion, increasing both basal and stimulated rates of secretion of ACTH. Oestrogen has long been known to augment HPA axis activity in adult animals; the effect of oestrogen on ACTH is much greater in the fetus than in the adult. Thus, cortisol, oestrogen and ACTH form a type of positive feedback loop at the end of gestation: cortisol induces the enzyme which synthesizes oestrogen, oestrogen augments ACTH secretion, and ACTH further increases cortisol secretion (Fig. 9.5).

Interestingly, the decrease in cortisol-negative feedback sensitivity might also be under hormonal control. Concomitant with the increase in fetal plasma oestrogen concentration at the end of gestation is an increase in fetal plasma concentrations of androstenedione, a weak androgen which serves as a precursor for oestrogen biosynthesis. Modest increases in fetal plasma concentrations of androstenedione, along with the increases in oestrogen concentration, have been shown to decrease negative feedback sensitivity. Thus, the ontogenetic activation of the fetal HPA axis which triggers parturition might occur as a result of hormonal interactions between the placenta (oestrogens and androgens) and the HPA axis. On the other hand, the mechanisms controlling the ontogenetic increase in fetal ACTH secretion are probably multifactorial and may be influenced (or even driven by) other factors such as neuronal maturation within the fetal hypothalamus. It is likely that an answer to this question will ultimately provide the key to understanding the onset of parturition.

An important feature of this endocrine axis in the fetus is that it operates in parallel with the HPA axis of the mother. ACTH is a peptide hormone which does not cross the placenta. For this reason the ACTH measured in the maternal plasma originates from maternal sources and the ACTH measured in the fetal plasma originates from fetal sources. However, cortisol does cross the placenta to some degree. In sheep, about 1–2 % of the total maternal adrenal production rate of cortisol crosses the placenta into the fetus. Throughout most of gestation, before the occurrence of any significant activation of the fetal HPA axis near the time of spontaneous parturition, most of the cortisol (and aldosterone) in the fetal circulation is derived from maternal sources. This can be thought of as beneficial to the fetus. Before the time that the fetal adrenal is mature enough to maintain 'physiological' levels of cortisol in plasma, either under basal or stimulated conditions, cortisol is essentially infused into the fetal circulation from the mother. This supply of cortisol is essential for maintenance of fetal homeostasis and, indeed, for maintenance of fetal life. The fetus therefore has access to maternal cortisol under both basal and stimulated conditions. Because the fetal hypothalamus cannot distinguish maternal from fetal cortisol, the transplacental transfer of cortisol allows communication between the two axes. Increases in maternal plasma cortisol concentration, to levels which are similar to those produced by maternal hypoxia, haemorrhage or psychological stimuli, inhibit fetal ACTH secretion and reduce the fetal ACTH response to subsequent stimulation.

In the human the placenta contains the enzyme 11β-hydroxysteroid dehydrogenase (HSD), which converts cortisol to cortisone (biologically inactive at the glucocorticoid receptor). It is the presence of this enzyme that primarily 'protects' the fetus from the cortisol in the maternal circulation. As the fetus matures, the activity of 11β-HSD is increased, theoretically allowing less maternal cortisol into the fetal circulation. It has been proposed that the reduction in cortisol transfer from mother to fetus activates the fetal HPA axis by reducing the cortisol-negative feedback inhibition of fetal ACTH secretion. If this hypothesis is correct, it could provide a mechanism by which the human placenta participates in the timing of parturition.

Neurointermediate lobe of the pituitary

Situated between the anterior and posterior pituitary is the neurointermediate lobe. The histological appearance of the neurointermediate lobe differs somewhat between species. The cells of the neurointermediate lobe synthesize and contain pro-opiomelanocortin (POMC). However, these cells process the POMC somewhat more completely than the corticotropes of the anterior pituitary in that they secrete MSH and γMSH. Liberation of both of these peptides from POMC requires further cleavage of fully processed ACTH and further cleavage of the N-terminal fragment of POMC (Fig. 9.7). While the neurointermediate lobe of the pituitary appears to be quite active in the fetal sheep, its function is not fully appreciated at the present time. It is not clear that its function is an integral part of the fetal stress response, nor is it clear that it partici-

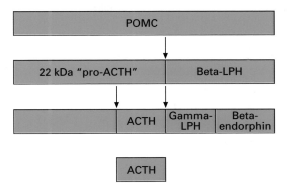

Fig. 9.7. A schematic representation of the posttranslational processing of pro-opiomelanocortin (POMC) in the fetal corticotrope.

pates in the initiation of parturition. One recent report suggests that neuro-intermediate lobe cells in fetal sheep respond to CRH and/or AVP with increased secretion of immunoreactive ACTH, whereas neurointermediate lobe cells from neonatal sheep did not respond to CRH and/or AVP. The responsiveness of the cells to CRH and/or AVP was altered by prior adrenalectomy. The authors suggest that neurointermediate lobe cells mature in late gestation, perhaps in response to cortisol in fetal plasma.

Adrenal medulla

The adrenal medulla develops in concordance with the other components of the sympathetic nervous system. In the late-gestation fetus, the adrenal medulla plays a relatively important role in cardiovascular adaptations to stress and in regulating fetal metabolism.

The adrenal medulla secretes both adrenaline and noradrenaline. The adrenal medullary biosynthesis of adrenaline is dependent upon the expression of phenylethanolamine-N-methyltransferase (PNMT) which is, in turn, induced by the secretion of cortisol by the adrenal cortex. For this reason, the secretory capacity of the adrenal medulla for adrenaline increases late in gestation. In fetal sheep, the adrenal medulla gains its innervation relatively late (~0.8) in gestation.

During periods of fetal stress, adrenal medullary secretion of adrenaline and noradrenaline acts together with the remainder of the sympathetic nervous system to maintain homeostasis. Among the best-studied stimuli to adrenal medullary secretion are haemorrhage, hypotension and hypoxia. It is generally agreed that the increases in plasma concentrations of catecholamines, as well as the increase in vasomotor and cardioacceleratory tone which occurs during periods of hypovolaemia or hypotension, are important components of the overall mechanism by which the fetus defends arterial pressure. Increases in sympathoadrenal activity during hypoxia are thought to be important for producing the vasoconstriction which redistributes the combined ventricular output of the fetus towards the umbilicoplacental circulation. Interestingly, the fetal adrenal medulla increases its activity in response to hypoxia even before substantial innervation has occurred. Finally, the adrenal medulla plays an important role in terms of fetal glucose homeostasis. Physiological increases in fetal plasma adrenaline concentration stimulate increases in fetal plasma glucose concentration, in part because of hepatic release of glucose into the fetal blood. It is because of this endocrine interaction that fetal plasma glucose concentrations increase during and following periods of fetal distress.

Hypothalamus–pituitary–thyroid (HPT) axis

The ontogeny of the HPT axis is only partially understood in the human. Thyrotrophin (TSH) is present in the fetal pituitary and in fetal plasma at midgestation, approximately the time of hypothalamo-hypophyseal portal system development. In the first trimester of human pregnancy the abundance of TRH in extrahypothalamic tissue is greater than in the fetal hypothalamus, suggesting a role for extrahypothalamic TRH in the stimulation of TSH secretion from the developing anterior pituitary. In the sheep fetus, the development of the thyrotrope occurs starting at about 30% of gestation, followed by the development of the thyroid gland starting at about 40% of gestation, followed by the development of hypothalamic TRH, starting at about 50% of gestation (Fig. 9.8). Plasma concentrations of TSH in the sheep fetus increase from about 30% of gestation, again suggesting the possible importance of extrahypothalamic TRH synthesis and release. True neuroendocrine control of the HPT axis develops near the end of human and ovine pregnancy.

The maternal and fetal HPT axes operate somewhat independently. The placenta is relatively impermeable to thyroxine (T_4) and 3,5,3′ triiodothyronine (T_3) because of the presence of a deiodinase which converts T_4 to 3,5,5′ triiodothyronine, reverse T_3 (rT_3). The placenta is, of course, also impermeable to the

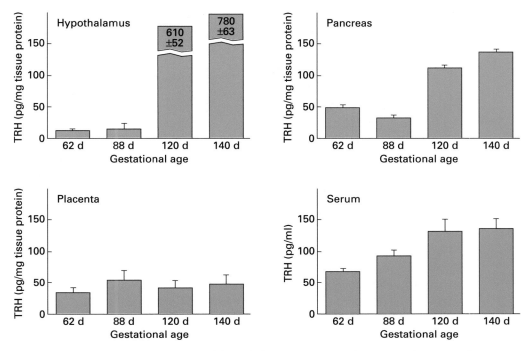

Fig. 9.8. Immunoreactive TRH in fetal hypothalamus, pancreas, placenta, and serum at four stages of ovine fetal development. At 62 and 88 days gestation, the concentration of TRH in pancreas and placenta exceed the concentration in hypothalamus. The concentration in hypothalamus increases in relatively late gestation. (Redrawn from Polk *et al.* (1982), *Am. J. Physiol.*, **260**, E53–8.)

relatively large TSH- and thyroid-binding globulins. On the other hand, the placenta of the human is relatively permeable to TRH, a relatively small molecule (the ovine placenta is impermeable to TRH). For this reason, there is usually a gradient from maternal to fetal plasma in terms of both T_4 and T_3.

Development of the HPT axis of the fetus is critically important for differentiation of the nervous system, but also plays a role in the adaptation to extrauterine life. Congenital hypothyroidism causes mental retardation in human infants. The infant can be treated with some success after birth, although the infant will tend to be less responsive if the mother was also hypothyroid during the pregnancy. The role of the HPT axis in the adaptation to extrauterine life has been illustrated in sheep. When thyroidectomy is performed days before birth, severe neonatal hypothermia occurs, in part because of a failure of thermogenesis in the brown adipose tissue. The effect of thyroid hormones in this process is to accelerate development of the brown adipose tissue in the last few days of gestation.

Posterior pituitary

The posterior pituitary of the fetus secretes vasopressin and oxytocin, as it does in the adult. Both of these hormones are synthesized in the supraoptic nucleus and the magnocellular portion of the paraventricular nucleus. Both peptides are controlled separately, but can be released together during conditions of hypotension and hypoxia.

AVP is a hormone with at least three biological activities. The vasopressor action of this hormone is mediated by the V_{1a} vasopressin receptor in the peripheral vasculature. The corticotrophin-releasing activity is mediated by the V_{1b} receptor (the role of vasopressin as a releasing factor for ACTH is discussed above). The antidiuretic activity is mediated by the V_2 vasopressin receptor. Although the fetal kidney is less sensitive to AVP than the adult kidney, maximal antidiuretic effects in the fetus are usually achieved with circulating concentrations of less than 15 pg/ml, and concentrations greater than this have a significant effect on vasoconstriction in the fetal cardiovascular system. The renal actions of vasopressin in the fetus appear to be somewhat less potent than in the adult animal. The fetal sheep, for example, excretes a relatively large volume of dilute urine. Physiological increases in plasma vasopressin concentrations lead to concentration of the urine. In part because of the immaturity of the renal concentrating mechanisms, however, the increase in urine osmolality after exposure to vasopressin is not as dramatic as in the adult animal. Vasopressin plays a substantial role in fetal cardiovascular regulation. After haemorrhage or during periods of hypotension, high plasma concentrations of vasopressin have been measured. Infusion of antagonists of the V_{1a} receptor significantly impair the control of blood pressure, demonstrating that these increases in plasma vasopressin concentration are physiologically relevant. Interestingly, the vasoconstrictor actions of vasopressin are not evenly distributed throughout the fetal cardiovascular system. Increases in plasma vasopressin concentration appear to promote a redistribution of fetal combined ventricular output towards the umbilicoplacental circulation, maintaining transfer of oxygen from the maternal to the fetal circulation. The effect of vasopressin in redistributing combined ventricular output is observed during acute hypoxia, during which plasma vasopressin concentrations are increased.

Oxytocin, secreted by the fetal posterior pituitary, circulates in fetal plasma in concentrations which generally exceed those in maternal plasma. The literature is somewhat divided on the issue of whether fetal plasma oxytocin concentrations increase at the end of gestation, although some reports indicate that these are increased in the human during active labour. Immunoreactive oxytocin which circulates in fetal plasma is a mixture of both processed and unprocessed forms. As the fetus matures, the proportion of processed oxytocin increases in fetal plasma. The function of oxytocin in the fetus is not known. Because oxytocin does not cross the placental barrier into the maternal circulation, fetal oxytocin is not thought to play a role in altering myometrial tone. However, high concentrations of oxytocin in the plasma perfusing the anterior pituitary are known to stimulate the release of ACTH from corticotropes, probably via an interaction with the V_{1b} receptor. It is possible that, in some circumstances, oxytocin acts as a releasing factor for ACTH.

Fetal and maternal plasma concentrations of oxytocin are independently regulated. In the rhesus monkey, for example, maternal plasma concentrations of oxytocin transiently increase at night. The average concentrations of oxytocin also increase in maternal plasma during labour and delivery. In contrast, the fetal plasma concentrations do not change throughout the 24-hour day, and do not increase during labour or delivery.

Finally, it should be noted that both human and ovine fetal plasma contains arginine vasotocin. The function of the vasotocin in fetal plasma is unknown.

Placental hormones and hormones of ectopic synthesis

The placenta synthesizes and secretes a large number of steroid and peptide hormones. The peptide hormones which are secreted into the maternal circulation (e.g. chorionic gonadotrophin and chorionic somatomammotrophin) are discussed in Chapter 2. Placental biosynthesis of oestrogen is discussed elsewhere in this chapter. However, there are several hormones synthesized within the placenta which have been proposed as having significant actions within the fetus, both in respect of facilitating fetal development and initiating parturition.

The placenta has long been recognized as an important site of prostanoid biosynthesis. Prostanoids, or eicosanoids, are derivatives of arachidonic acid (Fig. 9.9). Arachidonic acid is liberated from phospholipid through the action of phospholipase A_2. Arachidonic acid is then available for conversion to the

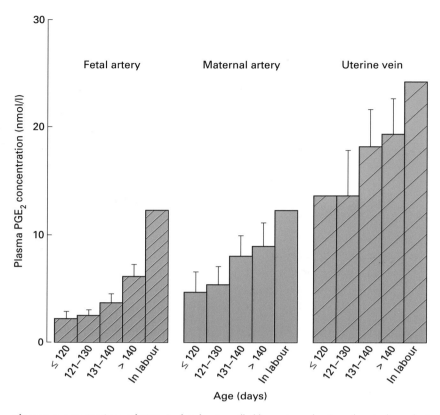

Fig. 9.9. Plasma concentrations of PGE$_2$ in fetal artery (left), maternal artery (centre), and uterine vein (right) in ovine pregnancies. These data demonstrate that there is significant release of PGE$_2$ into the circulation by the uteroplacental circulation in the sheep. (Redrawn from G.D. Thorburn (1991), *Reprod. Fertil. Dev.*, **3**, 277–94.)

so-called leucotrienes, through the action of lipoxygenase, or available for conversion to prostaglandins and thromboxane A$_2$, through the action of prostaglandin endoperoxide synthase (PGHS). This enzyme contains both cyclooxygenase and peroxidase activities. PGH$_2$, the product of PGHS action on arachidonic acid, is converted to primary prostaglandins. The most notable of these prostanoids is prostaglandin E$_2$ (PGE$_2$). Large quantities of PGE$_2$ and other prostanoids (such as PGF$_2$) are synthesized within the placenta and released into the fetal umbilical blood and into the maternal uterine venous blood. In early pregnancy, the increased concentrations of PGF$_2$ in the uterine vein causes luteolysis. The high plasma concentrations in the uterine vein produce locally high plasma concentrations of PGF_2 in the ovarian artery by the process of countercurrent exchange (from vein to adjacent artery).

The PGE_2 released into the fetal circulation has attracted a great deal of interest because of the myriad actions of this prostanoid in the fetus and because of the ontogenetic pattern of PGE_2 synthesis and secretion by the placenta. Increases in plasma concentrations of PGE_2 are known to increase the secretion of ACTH from the fetal pituitary and, perhaps, from extrapituitary sites such as the lung or placenta. The striking similarity between the ontogenetic pattern of plasma PGE_2 and plasma ACTH concentrations has led some investigators to propose that PGE_2 secreted by the placenta is the stimulus to the preparturient increase in fetal ACTH secretion which ultimately stimulates parturition in sheep. This idea has been challenged on the basis that the circulating concentrations of PGE_2 produced by placental secretion are not high enough to stimulate the secretion of ACTH. Nevertheless, it is possible that the placenta secretes an endocrine signal which communicates readiness for birth to the fetal neuroendocrine apparatus controlling the fetal HPA axis. PGE_2 is also known to inhibit fetal breathing movements. It has been proposed that the secretion of PGE_2 by the placenta tonically suppresses fetal breathing activity, and that the interruption of the supply of PGE_2 at birth allows the initiation of continuous breathing of air. However, this idea has been challenged, partially with respect to the sufficiency of plasma concentrations of PGE_2 to inhibit fetal breathing movements. While the potential hormonal actions of placental PGE_2 have been questioned, there is no doubt that the locally high concentrations of PGE_2 within the uteroplacental and umbilicoplacental circulations have important physiological actions, including alterations in vascular and myometrial tone.

The placenta synthesizes and releases several peptide hormones. It is interesting that the placenta often makes several of the hormones of an endocrine axis, hormones which are otherwise synthesized in separate endocrine glands. Perhaps relevant to the maintenance and termination of pregnancy, the peptide hormones of the HPA axis are found within the placenta. For example, the primate placenta contains significant amounts of ACTH and CRH. It has been proposed that the release of ACTH and/or CRH into the fetal blood might be a physiologically important mechanism by which the placenta affects the timing of parturition in these species.

Plasma concentrations of CRH are high in both fetal and maternal plasma in primates. However, the biological activity of the circulating CRH is limited by the secretion of a CRH-binding protein by the placental tissue. The function of the binding protein is not known; the presence of the binding protein in plasma suggests that the high circulating concentrations of CRH in plasma are due to spillover from sites of production and (paracrine or autocrine) action in the placenta and other sites within the peripheral circulation. Ovine placenta contains measurable amounts of immunoreactive ACTH but little CRH. Neither peptide appears to be secreted into either the fetal or maternal bloodstream. It has been proposed that placental ACTH or CRH might play a significant role in the timing of parturition. In human placenta, for example, CRH causes the release of ACTH locally, followed by an alteration in placental steroidogenesis. It has also been proposed that the release of CRH from the human placenta into the fetal umbilical venous blood stimulates the activity of the fetal HPA axis at the end of gestation which ultimately might initiate parturition. As for the arguments concerning hormonal actions of placental PGE$_2$, the plasma concentrations of ACTH and *unbound* plasma CRH which arise from placental secretion appear to be too low to play a hormonal function. Nevertheless, there are many questions which need answers. Is there a functioning hypothalamopituitary unit in the human placenta that ultimately determines the timing of birth? Alternatively, do ACTH and CRH play other roles within the placenta of the human? For example, CRH is known to alter vascular tone within the umbilicoplacental circulation, and it is possible that POMC is primarily processed to endorphin or MSH which might have other functions within the placental tissue.

The placenta secretes other peptide hormones. Several of these, including chorionic gonadotrophin and placental lactogen play a role in maternal adaptations to pregnancy (see Chapter 11). There are many other peptide hormones, the functions of which are not completely understood. For example, GnRH and inhibin are synthesized within the human placenta. It has been proposed that these hormones act locally in a paracrine fashion to influence the release of human chorionic gonadotrophin (hCG). The human placenta also contains prorenin, although the function of this hormone in the placenta is not known.

In addition to the placenta, 'pituitary' hormones are synthesized and released from other tissues in the fetal body (Fig. 9.10). One example of this phenomenon is the synthesis and release of POMC and POMC-related peptides by the neuroendocrine cells of the fetal lung. It has been proposed that POMC secreted by the lung might play a role in the timing of parturition by altering adrenal sensitivity to circulating ACTH. It is perhaps interesting that these cells, after transformation, form the basis of small-cell carcinoma of the lung in the adult, a disease in which significant secretion of POMC and ACTH can produce symptoms of hyperadrenocorticism. The neuroendocrine cells of the lung syn-

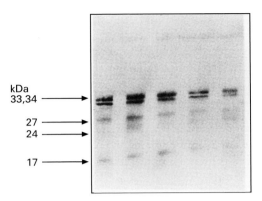

Fig. 9.10.   Molecular weight profile of immunoreactive ACTH in five samples of fetal lung. Immunoprecipitated peptide was observed in five molecular weights. A doublet band at 33 and 34 kDa was accompanied by bands at 27, 24, and 17 kDa. These peptides are similar in molecular weight to POMC and posttranslational products which are produced by the action of adrenal chromaffin cell aspartyl protease on POMC. (Reproduced with permission from Wood *et al.* (1998), *Regul. Peptides*, **73**, 191–6.)

thesize many hormones in addition to POMC, such as vasoactive intestinal polypeptide (VIP) and serotonin. While truly endocrine functions of the lung have been proposed, the physiological roles played by the pulmonary hormones have not been defined. Do pulmonary neuroendocrine cells play a role in parturition, do they play a role in the reabsorption of lung liquid prior to the first breath of life, or do they play a role in the endocrine adjustments to hypoxia in the fetus? Answers to these questions await further research.

Summary

The endocrinology of the fetus is, in some respects, similar or analogous to the endocrinology of the postnatal animal. The endocrine axes of the fetus are recognizable as the same axes which maintain life or homeostasis in the adult. Nevertheless, it would be a mistake to view the fetus as a small adult. The endocrine relationships in the fetus influence or control processes irrelevant in the postnatal animal (e.g. the initiation of parturition) or qualitatively and quantitatively different than in the postnatal animal (e.g. influences on the frequency of breathing movements). Perhaps the pathological endocrinology of the adult (e.g. the hyperadrenocorticism observed in some patients with small-cell carcinoma of the lung) can point to normal function in the fetus (e.g. does the lung normally function as an endocrine organ in the fetus?). Finally, an important player in the endocrinology of the fetus might be an organ which is lacking in the postnatal animal, the placenta. A better understanding of the mechanisms which maintain fetal well-being and homeostasis, the mechanisms which initiate parturition, and the mechanisms which defend the fetus during periods of fetal distress will involve a better understanding of fetal endocrine function.

FURTHER READING

Albrecht, E.D. and Pepe, G.J. (1990). Placental steroid hormone biosynthesis in primate pregnancy. *Endocr. Rev.*, 11, 124–50.

Challis, J.R., Lye, S.J. and Gibb, W. (1997). Prostaglandins and parturition. *Ann. N.Y. Acad. Sci.*, **828**, 254–67.

Gunn, T.R. and Gluckman, P.D. (1995). Perinatal thermogenesis. *Early Hum. Devel.*, **42**, 169–83.

McMillen, I.C., Phillips, I.D., Ross, J.T., Robinson, J.S. and Owens, J.A. (1995). Chronic stress – the key to parturition? *Reprod. Fertil. Dev.*, **7**, 499–507.

Pepe, G.J. and Albrecht, E.D. (1990). Regulation of the primate fetal adrenal cortex. *Endocr. Rev.*, **11**, 151–76.

Pepe, G.J. and Albrecht, E.D. (1995). Actions of placental and fetal adrenal steroid hormones in primate pregnancy. *Endocr. Rev.*, **16**, 608–48.

Polk, D.H. (1995). Thyroid hormone metabolism during development. *Reprod. Fertil. Dev.*, **7**, 469–77.

Wood, C.E. (1995). Baroreflex and chemoreflex control of fetal hormone secretion. *Reprod. Fertil. Dev.*, **7**, 479–89.

Wood, C.E. and Cudd, T.A. (1997). Development of the hypothalamus–pituitary–adrenal axis of the equine fetus: a comparative review. *Equine Vet. J. Suppl.*, **24**, 74–82.

10

Sexual differentiation and development of the reproductive organs

A. Nigel Brooks

In eutherian mammals sex determination is defined as the initiation of testis development, whereas sexual differentiation encompasses all processes that occur thereafter and are dependent on this initial event. Sex determination and the development of the reproductive organs is a complex process which can occur by a number of different mechanisms in different species. Some species have an identical genetic makeup between sexes but rely on external signals to direct the male or female pathway. For instance in alligators (and other reptiles) the sexual phenotype depends on the temperature at which the eggs are incubated, with only small variations of a few degrees centigrade causing complete sex reversal. In contrast in eutherian mammals, the development of the reproductive organs is a sequential process, beginning with the establishment of genetic sex, which is dependent on whether an embryo is fertilized by an X- or Y-bearing sperm. This is followed by the development of gonadal sex in which the fate of bipotential gonad is determined by the presence of the Y-chromosome in XY embryos, and ends with the formation of sexual phenotypes as a result of hormonal secretions from the developing testis. The aim of this chapter is to describe some of these complex processes which result in sexual differentiation and development of the reproductive organs in eutherian mammals.

Sex determination

A series of experiments performed by Alfred Jost in the 1950s demonstrated that the fetal testis is necessary for male development to occur and that in the absence of gonads a female urogenital tract develops, irrespective of chromosomal sex. Because of these experiments, we often refer to the female developmental route as the default pathway.

Jost's pioneering work demonstrated that hormones secreted from the testes are responsible for the differentiation of the male secondary sexual organs. But what actually causes sex determination and allows testes to form in the first place? During early embryogenesis the gonad is bipotential; it has the capacity to develop into either an ovary or a testis. The development of the bipotential gonad is thought to be regulated by two important genes. The first is an orphan member of the nuclear hormone receptor superfamily (an orphan receptor is one for which there is no known ligand) called SF1, and the second, Wilms Tumour 1 (*WT1*) is a gene encoding a tumour suppressor protein (Fig. 10.1). Point mutations of *WT1* in humans lead to childhood kidney cancer (Wilm's Tumours) and varying degrees of gonadal abnormalities and targeted disruption of *WT1* and *SF1* (steroidogenic factor 1) in mice leads to the failure of gonadal development. Once the bipotential gonad has formed the development of the testis is regulated by a specific gene located on the Y-chromosome, called the sex-determining region of the Y-chromosome (*SRY* in humans, *Sry* in mice). There is no evidence for an equivalent ovary-determining gene. *SRY* was discovered in 1990, and shown to be necessary for male development. Targeted disruption of *Sry* in transgenic mice leads to female development, whereas addition of *Sry* in transgenic XX mice leads to testicular development and sex reversal.

The *Sry* gene is expressed in the mouse urogenital ridge between embryonic day 10.5 and 12, in a region which will ultimately form either the ovary or the testis. An *Sry* transcript has also been identified in adult mouse testis but here it is initiated from a different start site on the promoter than is the case in the urogenital ridge. This results in formation of a longer transcript, which adopts a circular conformation and is not transcribed. The function of this different form of *Sry* remains to be determined. In humans the *SRY* gene is expressed over a much longer period and there is no evidence for alternative forms of the gene. In fact, humans with mutations of the *SRY* gene have no observable defects other than sex reversal. A number of experiments have suggested that it is the level of *Sry/SRY* expression, rather than its presence *per se*, which dictates its function. However, the molecular basis for transcriptional regulation, and thus regulation of expression of *Sry/SRY* remains unknown.

The mechanisms by which *SRY* acts to trigger the formation of the testis, has been the subject of intense investigation. The *SRY* gene encodes a protein which is thought to regulate transcription of other downstream genes. The *SRY* protein does this by virtue of a specialized region contained within the protein, which is called a high-mobility group (HMG) box DNA-binding domain and is highly conserved across species. SRY appears to work by causing DNA to bend as a result of the interaction between the HMG box and specific DNA sequences located in the minor groove of the DNA of target genes. DNA bending allows

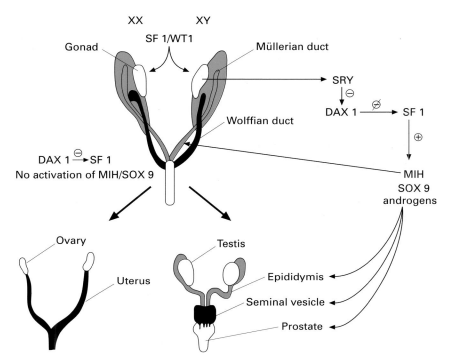

Fig. 10.1. Current model for mammalian sex determination and differentiation. The formation of the bipotential gonads (irrespective of genetic sex) is dependent on SF1 and WT1. In XY individuals SRY suppresses the activity of DAX1 thus removing its repressive effect on SF1. Increased expression of SF1 leads to activation of target genes such as müllerian-inhibiting hormone (MIH), SOX9 and enzymes involved in androgen synthesis. MIH causes regression of the müllerian ducts which would normally form the female reproductive tract. Testosterone masculinizes the wolffian duct to form the male reproductive tract. In XX individuals, the lack of SRY means that DAX1 continues to suppress SF1 and there is no activation of MIH or androgen synthesis. In the absence of MIH, the müllerian ducts differentiate into the female reproductive tract.

contact to be made between the various components of the transcriptional complex and gene activation occurs. Recently another gene product, SOX9 has been implicated in the early events leading to sex determination. SOX9, like SRY, is a member of the HMG box family of DNA-binding proteins, and has a similar DNA-binding domain structure to SRY. Mutation in the SOX9 gene is associated with the skeletal malformation syndrome, campomelic dysplasia (CD), and is sometimes associated with genital defects. The mechanism by which SOX9 causes altered sex differentiation is unknown but is thought to be via an interaction with SRY to modify chromatin structure leading to a change in DNA architecture which allows other transcription factors to exert their action.

The identification of genes which are regulated by SRY has proved an immensely difficult task, mainly because of the lack of suitable in vitro culture systems to serve as a screen for SRY activation. However, a strong contender for SRY action is müllerian-inhibiting hormone which is responsible for müllerian duct regression and is an important factor in the male developmental pathway. SRY has been shown to induce the expression of müllerian inhibiting hormone, although surprisingly this can still occur after mutation of the SRY-binding region in the gene. This suggests that activation of müllerian-inhibiting hormone by SRY is indirect and may be mediated by other SRY-regulated proteins. The leading candidate for this intermediary role is SF1 which, apart from regulating müllerian-inhibiting hormone, is an important transcription factor for the regulation of p450 enzymes involved in androgen production in the testis.

DAX1 is another orphan nuclear hormone receptor which has been shown to play a crucial role in the pathway of sex determination. Mutations of DAX1 lead to adrenal hypoplasia congenita (AHC) an X-linked disorder in which the adrenals fail to develop normally. This condition is often associated with impaired maturation of the reproductive axis, a condition known as hypogonadotrophic hypogonadism (HHG). DAX1 and SF1 are thought to act through a common pathway since their expression is colocalized in many cell types, including the adrenal cortex, gonads and gonadotrophs of the pituitary gland. The interaction between SF1 and DAX1 in the gonad is thought to be antagonistic since after their first appearance in the gonad, DAX1 continues to be expressed in the ovary but is switched off in the testis, whereas SF1 increases in the testis but decreases in the ovary. DAX1 is thought to act predominantly as an antitestis factor by causing repression of SF1, thus preventing the normal activation of müllerian-inhibiting hormone. In XY embryos, SRY suppresses DAX1 which in turn removes the repression of SF1, leading to activation of müllerian-inhibiting hormone and androgen synthesis (Fig. 10.1).

Sex differentiation

Gonadal sex differentiation

The mammalian gonad develops from the urogenital ridge around the fourth week of gestation in humans. Most of the cells of the gonad are derived from the mesoderm of the urogenital region, but the germ cells originate outside the area of the presumptive gonad and actually migrate from the yolk sac wall into the gonadal ridge. The formation of the indifferent gonad is complete by the fifth week of gestation and consists of germ cells, supporting cells of the coelomic epithelium of the gonadal ridge, which give rise to either Sertoli cells of the testis or granulosa cells of the ovary, and stromal cells derived from the mesenchyme of the gonadal ridge. The first histological sign of sexual dimorphism of the gonads is the development of the primordial Sertoli cells and their organization into seminiferous cords in the male. The primordial germ cells have taken up residence in the seminiferous cords. Leydig cells differentiate from mesenchymal cells of the testicular interstitium at about 8 weeks of human gestation. In contrast, the onset of ovarian differentiation is difficult to observe histologically and identification is made by the absence of observed testicular features rather than the appearance of ovarian structures. The primitive ovary consists mainly of mesonephric cells with clusters of germ cells (oogonia) found at the periphery. Meoisis occurs in oogonia but is arrested in late prophase of the first meiotic phase, and does not proceed until puberty. After meiotic arrest, the oogonia become surrounded by follicular cells known as primordial follicles.

The previously discussed experiments by Jost established that two hormones from the fetal testis are essential for development of the male urogenital tract: müllerian-inhibiting hormone, which causes regression of the müllerian duct, and testosterone, which masculinizes the wolffian duct (Fig. 10.1). Müllerian-inhibiting hormone (also known as antimüllerian hormone) is a dimeric glycoprotein synthesized in the Sertoli cells of the fetal and newborn testis, and is thought to act locally rather than as a circulating hormone. Experiments which show that müllerian duct regression can be prevented by treating animals with specific antibodies raised against müllerian-inhibiting hormone, have provided definitive evidence for the role that this hormone plays in male urogenital tract development. However, müllerian-inhibiting hormone may play another important role in fetal development. Researchers have produced transgenic female mice which have the müllerian-inhibiting hormone gene introduced into the genome (a technique known as gene addition). These genetically female mice develop gonads with seminiferous cord structures in addition to having regressed müllerian ducts. The development of these cord-like structures can also be induced by adding müllerian inhibiting hormone to cultured fetal ovaries in vitro. Collectively these experiments provide good evidence that müllerian-inhibiting hormone plays an active role in promoting testis differentiation and development, in addition to its classical role of causing müllerian duct regression.

Testosterone is the other testicular hormone necessary for full male phenotypic development. Testosterone is produced by the fetal testis soon after the appearance of the seminiferous cords, at the time when Leydig cells first differentiate. Evidence for the critical role that this hormone plays in the development of the male urogenital tract has been provided by experiments showing that testosterone administration to female embryos causes development of male genitalia, whereas pharmacological blockade of testosterone synthesis in males prevents male genital development. Humans with genetic defects which result in impaired testosterone production often develop with a female phenotype, again pointing to the pivotal role that testosterone plays in the development of the male phenotype.

Differentiation of the endocrine ovary is characterized by its ability to produce oestrogen, and this takes place at a similar time as the testis becomes steroidogenically active. Oestrogen action is mediated by two oestrogen receptors, ERα and ERβ. Experiments in transgenic female mice which lack a functional ERα have a normal female phenotype, but have altered reproductive function in adulthood. This suggests that oestrogen is not essential for the development of the female phenotype itself, but instead may play a role in the development of the ovary. However, it is also possible that the second oestrogen receptor, ER may be responsible for mediating oestrogenic effects on sexual differentiation. Transgenic experiments in which both these receptors are knocked out either individually or together will be necessary before we have a complete understanding of the role of oestrogen in female sexual differentiation.

Differentiation of the central nervous system

Sexual differentiation of the central nervous system is mainly affected by steroids which come from the developing gonads, and induce irreversible changes in the structure and function of specific regions in the brain. Because these changes are permanent, they are referred to as organizational effects. The organizational effects of sex steroids can only occur at specific times during development; exposure of the brain to steroids outside these critical windows does not cause sexual differentiation. The critical window for sexual differentiation of the brain varies between species (rats, 18–27 days postconception; mouse, postnatal; guinea-pig, 30–37 days postconception). It is now known that it is testosterone secreted from the developing fetal testis which causes these structural changes. However, a surprising finding was that oestrogens were able to mimic the effects of androgens and this led to the development of the so called 'aromatization hypothesis'. The brain during fetal and neonatal development possesses an enzyme called aromatase which is capable of converting testosterone into oestradiol. It is this local production of oestrogen, rather than testosterone which actually leads to sexual differentiation in the specific brain regions.

There are many aspects of brain function which are sexually differentiated, of which the most important for reproduction are differences between males and females in patterns of gonadotrophin secretion and aspects of sexual behaviour. When female rat fetuses are exposed to androgens during development, this results in the abolition of the normal cyclical female patterns of gonadotrophin secretion (these animals can no longer display the luteinizing hormone surge which is characteristic of ovulation in females), and a reduction in a display of sexual behaviour known as lordosis, in which a female rat stands rigid to allow copulation to occur. The regions in the brain responsible for these sexually differentiated reproductive characteristics are contained with the hypothalamus; the sexually dimorphic nucleus of the preoptic area (SDN-POA) is involved in the control of sexual behaviour and the anteroventricular periventricular nucleus (AVPV) is involved in patterns of gonadotrophin secretion. Morphologically these regions differ in size; the SDN-POA is bigger, and the AVPV is smaller, in males compared with females. During normal fetal development, the testes produce androgens from an early age which are converted locally into oestrogens within the brain. Through mechanisms which are largely unknown, oestrogen alters the rate of programmed cell death (apoptosis), which is responsible for the normal demise of a large percentage of neural cells during fetal life. Oestrogen also induces the expression of a number of neural-specific growth factors called neurotrophins, which promote cell survival. The interaction between mechanisms of cell survival and apoptosis is thought to lead to the differences in the size of the sexually dimorphic nuclei in the hypothalamus with consequent effects on reproductive function.

Development of the hypothalamus and pituitary gland

The fetal hypothalamus and pituitary gland are organs of different embryological origin, yet exhibit coordinated development to yield an integrated biological system which regulates endocrine function. Recent characterization of a number of tissue-specific transcription factors, and the application of molecular transgenic techniques, have enabled researchers to begin to unravel some of the complex mechanisms underlying this intriguing developmental process. The primordium of the pituitary gland is a structure called Rathke's pouch, which arises as an invagination of an ectodermal layer of cells beneath the diencephalon. However, even before the appearance of Rathke's pouch, cell compartments in the neural ridge are already committed to form either nonneural structures such as the anterior pituitary and olfactory placode, or neural structures such as the hypothalamus and posterior pituitary. Certain homeobox genes have been identified during this early stage of commitment, which are thought to be responsible for the formation of the anterior pituitary, namely *Pax6*, *Rpx* (Rathke's pouch homeobox) and *Six3*. The anterior pituitary gland synthesizes and secretes six individual hormones, adrenocorticotrophin (ACTH), growth hormone (GH), prolactin (PRL), thyroid-stimulating hormone (TSH), luteinizing hormone (LH) and follicle-stimulating hormone (FSH). LH and FSH are found within one cell type, the gonadotroph, whereas the remaining hormones are synthesized within individual cells; ACTH in corticotrophs, GH in somatotrophs, PRL in lactotrophs and TSH in thyrotrophs. During early embryogenesis the five specialized cell types of the anterior pituitary gland are derived from a common progenitor cell, but there is a spatial and temporal pattern to the appearance of each of these. Corticotrophs are the first cell type to appear, followed by thyrotrophs, gonadotrophs and finally lactotrophs and somatotrophs. A number of homeodomain factors have recently been described which specify the appearance of these different cell types (Fig. 10.2). For instance Lhx3 is required for commitment of gonadotrophs, thyrotrophs, somatotrophs and lactotrophs in the anterior pituitary, whereas Ptx1(pituitary homeobox 1, also called P-OTX; pituitary OTX-related factor) is expressed in most cells of the Rathke's pouch but becomes restricted to corticotrophs in the adult anterior pituitary. The final steps in the differentiation of the individual hormone-secreting cell types, involves two genes, *Pit1* and *SF1*. *Pit1* has an essential role in the determination and differentiation of thyrotrophs, somatotrophs and lactotrophs whereas *SF1* may play a role in the differentiation of gonadotrophs although other factors are likely to be involved.

Several pieces of evidence suggest that there are inductive interactions between the developing pituitary gland and diencephalon which ensure their cooperative development. Targeted disruption of a gene which encodes a protein called the thyroid-specific enhancer-binding protein (T/EBP), which is found in the hypothalamus and not Rathke's pouch, leads to the absence of

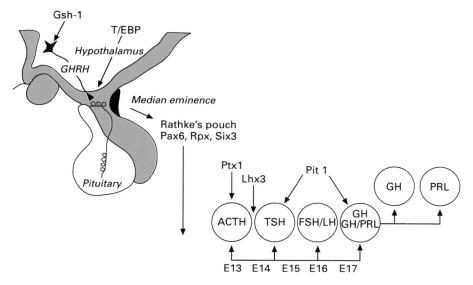

Fig. 10.2. Current model for the development of the hypothalamus and anterior pituitary gland. The temporal appearance of the five hormone secreting cell types in the anterior pituitary gland is shown alongside the appearance of the homeodomain transcription factors Ptx1, Lhx3 and Pit1, during mouse development. Targeted disruption of these genes leads to inappropriate development of the pituitary cell types (see text for detail). Development of Rathke's pouch is regulated by a further three homeodomain factors, Pax6, Rpx and Six3. T/EBP is expressed in the hypothalamus but not the pituitary gland. Targeted disruption of this gene leads to absence of many hypothalamic structures and absence of a pituitary gland. Gsh-1 disruption leads to a reduced number of somatotrophs and lactotrophs, which appears to result from the absence of GHRH in the hypothalamus. These findings suggest that signals from the hypothalamus are crucial for normal pituitary gland development.

many nuclei within the hypothalamus and a complete absence of a pituitary gland. The factors that cause the inductive interaction between the diencephalon and the cells which give rise to the Rathke's pouch remain to be determined. Another homeobox gene called *Gsh-1* is found in high abundance in the hypothalamus immediately adjacent to Rathke's pouch. Transgenic mice with targeted disruption of *Gsh-1* have a pituitary gland with a reduced number of somatotrophs and lactotrophs, which appears to result from the absence of growth hormone-releasing hormone (GHRH) in the hypothalamus. *Gsh-1* is therefore intimately involved in the development of the hypothalamus, which in turn leads to inappropriate development of pituitary hormone-secreting cells (Fig. 10.2). The development of the posterior pituitary gland appears to be dependent on the Pou homeodomain factor, Brn-2, since transgenic mice lacking this factor have no expression of arginine vasopressin (AVP), oxytocin and corticotrophin-releasing hormone (CRH) in the paraventricular nuclei, and supraoptic nuclei, and a complete lack of axonal projections in the posterior pituitary which arise from these two nuclei. Collectively these findings demonstrate the complex interactions which take place between the developing hypothalamus and pituitary gland, which although of differing embryonic origin, must be able to function as a coordinated unit during adult life to regulate hormonal homeostasis.

Many of the cell bodies of neurones within the hypothalamus are found in specific nuclei. For instance, neurones containing corticotrophin-releasing factor (CRF) which stimulates the secretion of ACTH from the pituitary gland, are found within a specialized structure called the paraventricular nucleus. In contrast, neurones containing gonadotrophin-releasing hormone (GnRH) have a much more diffuse distribution throughout a larger hypothalamic region called the preoptic area. Studies in the mouse, rhesus monkey and human have shown that GnRH neurones do not begin their life in the central nervous system. Instead, they arise during early embryogenesis from the olfactory placode and migrate along the pathway of the nervus terminalis–vomeronasal complex to their resting place in the preoptic area. In mice, GnRH neurones are first detected in the olfactory placode by embryonic day 9.5 (e9.5), after which time there is a period of rapid mitosis with all cells that make up the postnatal population being present by e12.5. Migration into the central nervous system takes place after e12.5 and is complete by e16.5.

In humans with Kallman syndrome (hypogonadotrophic hypogonadism coupled with anosmia), there are no detectable GnRH neurones in the hypothalamus. Instead GnRH neurones remain in their embryonic birthplace in the olfactory placode. This lack of migration appears to result from a deficiency in a substance called neural cell adhesion molecule, which has been shown to form a scaffold-like pathway through which the GnRH neurones pass. Once GnRH cell bodies have migrated to the preoptic area, nerve fibres originating from these cell bodies grow specifically to the lateral median eminence, which is located at the base of the hypothalamus and is the anatomical link between the neural and endocrine systems. Neurones projecting to this region form terminal connections with a capillary plexus which feeds into the hypothalamo-hypophyseal portal blood supply. This blood supply consists of portal vessels which course down the pituitary stalk and provide the humoral link between the hypothalamus and the pituitary gland. The mechanisms responsible for directing the growth of these neurones to ensure that they contact the median eminence are poorly understood, but it is thought that specialized growth factors called neurotrophins, produced locally in the median eminence, may be responsible for neural survival and target cell recognition. Once the GnRH neurones have targeted the median eminence, they then begin to stimulate the pituitary gland to synthesize and secrete the gonadotrophic hormones, and another component of the complex reproductive endocrine system has reached functional status.

Ontogeny and physiological role of fetal gonadotrophins

The attainment of a fully functional reproductive system takes place as a continuous maturational process from early fetal life through to puberty. In many species including man the fetal period represents a time of heightened activity in this sequence of events. For instance, plasma gonadotrophin concentrations reach a peak at midgestation to levels which are equivalent to those seen in castrated adults. There is also a sex difference in fetal gonadotrophins with lower LH and FSH concentrations in males compared with females (Fig. 10.3). This difference results from the negative feedback effects of elevated fetal testosterone concentrations in males. During the last third of gestation fetal gonadotrophins decline, but temporarily rise again after birth in the first few months of life before declining again until the onset of puberty.

There is now good evidence that the high level of gonadotrophic activity in utero is important for normal gonadal maturation. This was first suspected on the basis of observations made in human fetuses with anencephaly (severe abnormality of central nervous system development). Anencephalic fetuses have hypoplastic external genitalia and hypoplastic and undescended testes, while female anencephalic fetuses have hypoplastic ovaries with reduced numbers of primordial and primary follicles. These observations provide evidence that the central nervous system and pituitary gland are involved in some way in controlling the development of the reproductive organs during fetal life. An experimental approach has been used to determine more specifically the role of the pituitary gland in the process of gonadal development. This approach involves the surgical removal of the pituitary gland (hypophysectomy) from the developing fetus, which when performed in the rhesus monkey or in sheep, results in a marked reduction in male infant testis weight, a decrease in the proportion of Leydig cells, and a reduced number of spermatogonia. In

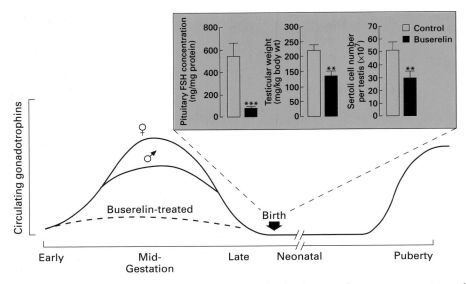

Fig. 10.3. Fetal gonadotrophins are crucial for maturation of the fetal testis. Plasma concentrations of gonadotrophins reach a peak at midgestation compared with low levels observed in early gestation and just before birth. Concentrations are lower in males compared with females, because of the negative feedback effects of testosterone. Suppression of the fetal gonadotrophins in sheep, by treatment with the GnRH agonist buserelin, leads to reduced testis size and Sertoli cell number at birth.

the female infant hypophysectomy decreases ovarian weight and the total number of germ cells.

Whilst these experiments demonstrate an important role for the fetal pituitary in gonadal development they do not tell us which hormones may actually be involved. This has recently been addressed by pharmacologically inhibiting gonadotrophin secretion during fetal and/or neonatal development and examining the consequences for gonadal development. A series of experiments have been conducted in sheep, in which fetal lambs receive small biodegradable implants that continuously release a potent GnRH agonist called buserelin. After a short period of time the continuous release of this hormone from the implant switches off gonadotrophin secretion by a process known as receptor desensitization. This results in a significant reduction in the expression of mRNA encoding pituitary LH and FSHβ and, consequent to this, LH pulses are absent and the midgestation surge in gonadotrophins is abolished. Male lambs born after this treatment were found to have considerably smaller testes than their untreated counterparts (Fig. 10.3). Histological examination of these small testes revealed that the reduction in testis weight was due to a significant reduction in the number of Sertoli cells. When gonadotrophins were blocked for only a limited period in midgestation there were no effects on testis development, suggesting that the period during which gonadotrophins influence gonadal maturation extends throughout the last half of gestation. In fact, it has been shown that the ability of gonadotrophins (in particular FSH) to regulate Sertoli cell numbers, and hence testis size, is restricted to critical windows during fetal and neonatal development and that these windows of time vary between species. For instance, in sheep Sertoli cell replication ceases at around 8–10 weeks of postnatal life, whereas in the rat it stops at around postnatal day 15. In humans, Sertoli cell replication is thought to take place throughout the prepubertal period. Inhibition of gonadotrophin secretion or treatment with FSH outside these critical windows have no effect on the number of Sertoli cells. The Sertoli cell acts as a nurse cell for the developing spermatogonia and the number of Sertoli cells in the testis determines its capacity to produce sperm in adult life. This critical number is fixed at the end of the period of Sertoli cell replication and as we have seen, this is controlled by the amount of gonadotrophins secreted from the pituitary gland. Thus, any change in the pattern of gonadotrophin secretion during this critical window may lead to impaired testicular development (reduced Sertoli cell number and reduced sperm production), which could have adverse consequences for reproductive ability in adulthood.

In female lambs treated with buserelin, there were no effects on ovarian weight, or morphological development. This lack of an effect on ovarian development contrasts with the findings from experiments in which the pituitary gland was removed, and may result from the inability of buserelin to completely suppress FSH secretion. Low levels of FSH are known to be sufficient to sustain ovarian development. Alternatively, pituitary hormones other than LH and FSH may be important determinants for ovarian development during fetal life.

Control of prenatal gonadotrophins

We have seen how the pattern of gonadotrophin secretion during fetal and early neonatal development is important for normal gonadal maturation and that impaired development can lead to longlasting detrimental effects on reproductive function (at least in the male). It is therefore important to understand the normal control mechanisms that determine this pattern and consider any external factors which may disrupt it.

Internal control mechanisms

We now know that GnRH is a key factor responsible for regulating gonadotrophin synthesis and secretion during fetal life. However, a variety of internal control mechanisms alter the pattern of GnRH secretion and the way in which the pituitary gland responds to GnRH. During late gestation there is a decline in gonadotrophin concentrations in the fetal circulation which is thought to result from an interplay between the development of inhibitory mechanisms within the central nervous system and the development of sex steroid-negative feedback pathways (Fig. 10.4).

The mechanisms by which the central nervous system controls GnRH neuronal activity during fetal development are poorly understood. Because of this it is tempting to assume that mechanisms active in adult life are also active in the fetus, but this is certainly not always the case. A number of potential candidates have been implicated, as important inhibitory and stimulatory effectors of GnRH secretion, including the endogenous opioid peptides and neuroactive amino acids, respectively. However, the ability of these inhibitory and stimulatory neurotransmitter systems to alter the pattern of GnRH secretion is influenced by the amount of circulating sex steroids.

If the gonads are removed from sheep fetuses at midgestation there is an increase in LH secretion in males but not in females. These findings tell us that the testis, but not the ovary, exerts negative feedback effects to cause a sex difference in gonadotrophin concentrations. However, when LH concentrations are measured in the same male fetuses during late gestation, just before birth, the peak concentrations and frequency of LH pulses are reduced to values similar to females and intact males. Therefore, at midgestation, testosterone from the fetal testis inhibits LH secretion, but in addition there are probably factors other than testosterone which become important inhibitors of LH secretion during late gestation. One possibility is that steroids that come from the placenta, rather than the gonads, take over during late gestation to cause suppression of gonadotrophin secretion. Certainly, in fetuses which have no gonads, there are still high levels of sex steroids such as progesterone and oestrogen in the fetal circulation, and these steroids are known to have inhibitory effects on gonadotrophins in adults. Administration of a progesterone receptor antagonist has little effect on the secretion of LH in male or female gonadecto-

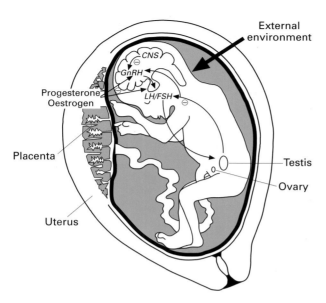

Fig. 10.4. Control of prenatal gonadotrophins. Gonadotrophin releasing hormone (GnRH) occupies a pivotal position in the control of gonadotrophin synthesis and secretion. The fetal testis is very active during fetal life and has negative feedback effects on the hypothalamus and pituitary resulting in lower gonadotrophin concentrations in male compared with female fetuses. During late gestation gonadotrophin concentrations decline and this is thought to result from the interplay between the development of inhibitory mechanisms within the central nervous system (CNS) and the development of sex-steroid negative feedback, with steroids originating from the placenta having a predominant role. In addition, a variety of external signals, such as light, nutrition and environmental chemicals, can alter the activity of the fetal hypothalamo-pituitary-gonadal axis.

mized fetal sheep, whereas an oestrogen receptor antagonist given to gonadec-tomized fetal lambs increases the number of LH pulses secreted from the fetal pituitary gland. These findings suggest that in the fetus, placentally derived oestrogens may serve as the inhibitory factor responsible for regulating the late gestation decline in gonadotrophin secretion.

Removal of the gonads from sheep fetuses during midgestation results in elevated plasma concentrations of FSH in males but not in females. Plasma concentrations of the gonadal hormone, inhibin are higher in male compared with female fetuses and inhibin has been detected in the fetal testis, but not in the ovary. In adult animals, FSH is controlled primarily by inhibin, and these data suggest that the same is the case in the fetus.

External influences

A number of signals external to the fetus could potentially alter fetal gonadotrophin secretion, and therefore have the potential to impair gonadal development. These include day length, nutrition and environmental pollutants. We know that information about day length is relayed to the fetus via the transplacental passage of melatonin from the mother. Day length in the adult is an important regulator of gonadotrophin secretion in photoperiodic species such as sheep, so it is possible the fetus responds in a similar manner to the adult in this respect. Nutrition is also known to have effects on reproduction in adults, and some of these effects are due to changes in gonadotrophin secretion. In the fetus undernutrition has been shown to retard ovarian development, although the mechanism by which this occurs is unknown. Recently, concerns have been raised that certain chemicals in the environment mimic the actions of oestrogen and can have adverse effects on reproductive health. These so called environmental oestrogens have been linked to many reproductive disorders, such as testicular cancer, hypospadias and cryptorchidism, as well as recent reports of declining sperm counts in men. Environmental oestrogens mimic the actions of endogenous oestrogens by binding to oestrogen receptors, and may act in the fetus to disrupt normal reproductive development. For example, when pregnant animals are exposed to a chemical called octylphenol, a breakdown product of a group of chemicals used in the manufacture of some detergents and paints, the secretion of FSH in the fetus is reduced. If exposure to this chemical were to take place for long enough during the period when FSH influences Sertoli cell replication, then this could lead to smaller testes and reduced sperm counts.

Summary

In recent years, there have been major advances in our understanding of the mechanism of sex determination and the subsequent development of the reproductive organs, which have largely been derived from the application of new molecular techniques such as targeted gene disruption in transgenic mice. For instance, these techniques have revealed hitherto unknown roles for the two orphan nuclear hormone receptors, SF1 and DAX1 as crucial components in the molecular pathway leading to sex determination. Similarly, it has recently been determined that several homoeodomain transcription factors organize the development of the five distinct hormone-secreting cell types in the pituitary gland. These different systems have in common a cascade of molecular events with a temporal as well as spatial component, which ultimately leads to coordinated development of related organ systems. Subsequent functional maturation of the reproductive organs is also a highly coordinated event mediated predominantly by the developing neuroendocrine system. What is now becoming increasingly clear is that during development these systems may be particularly vulnerable to external influences such as environmental toxins, to which exposure may result in long-term adverse reproductive health effects.

FURTHER READING

Brooks, A.N., Hagan, D.M., Sheng, C., McNeilly, A.S. and Sweeney, T. (1996). Prenatal gonadotrophins in sheep. *Anim. Reprod. Sci.*, **42**, 471–81.

Capel, B. (1998). Sex in the 90s: SRY and the switch to the male pathway. *Ann. Rev. Physiol.*, **60**, 497–523.

George, F.W. and Wilson, J.D. (1994). Sex determination and differentiation. In: *The Physiology of Reproduction*, ed. E. Knobil and J.D. Neill, pp. 3–28. New York: Raven Press.

Jimenez, R. and Burgos, M. (1998). Mammalian sex determination: joining pieces of the genetic puzzle. *Bioessays*, **20**, 696–9.

Simmerley, R.B. (1998). Organization and regulation of sexually dimorphic neuroendocrine pathways. *Behav. Brain Res.*, **92**, 195–203.

Treier, M. and Rosenfeld, M.G. (19960. The hypothalamic–pituitary axis: co-development of two organs. *Curr. Opin. Cell Biol.*, **8**, 833–43.

11

Maternal adaptation to pregnancy

Alan D. Bocking

The maternal physiological adaptations to pregnancy are profound and vital for successful fetal growth and development. Many of these adaptations are mediated through hormones produced by the placenta and others are due to the mechanical effect of the gravid uterus. This chapter will review some of the changes that occur within the maternal cardiovascular, renal, haematological, respiratory, gastrointestinal, endocrine and metabolic systems in order to promote and allow the normal growth and development of the fetus. In many occasions when these changes do not take place, fetal growth and development may be compromised.

Cardiovascular system

Total circulating blood volume in the mother increases during pregnancy as a result of an increase in both red blood cell mass and plasma volume. The increase in plasma volume, however, is greater than the increase in red cell mass and the resultant relative decrease in haemoglobin content and haematocrit gives rise to what has been called the 'physiological' anaemia of pregnancy.

In human pregnancy plasma volume begins to rise as early as 6–8 weeks of gestation and has increased by about 45% by 30 weeks A similar increase in plasma volume has been noted over the last 30 days of gestation in pregnant sheep (term about 147days). It is of interest that the failure of plasma volume to increase during human pregnancy is associated with an increased incidence of pregnancy complications such as maternal hypertension and/or intrauterine growth restriction indicating that this increase in circulating volume is important for optimal fetal outcomes.

It has been suggested that the effects of pregnancy on maternal plasma volume and blood pressure are mediated by the increase in circulating oestrogen concentrations. Support for this hypothesis is provided by studies in non-pregnant sheep which showed that infusion of 17β-oestradiol for 3 weeks (to mimic the endocrine changes during pregnancy) led to a 27% increase in plasma volume. Acute injections of oestrogens into the uterine artery of non-pregnant sheep have also been shown to cause a significant increase in uterine blood flow, supporting a direct dilator effect of this hormone on the uterine vessels. There are a number of additional endocrine changes which affect maternal blood volume by influencing the renal excretion and reabsorption of sodium (including increased progesterone, antidiuretic hormone, aldosterone, cortisol, placental lactogen and prolactin). The overall effect of these factors in combination with the increased glomerular filtration rate is to decrease the excretion of sodium relative to the amount which is filtered by the glomeruli. The observed increase in red blood cell mass during pregnancy occurs as a result of an increase in red cell production, not prolongation of the lifespan of the cells.

In addition to the increase in blood volume, pregnancy is accompanied by an increase in maternal cardiac output of 30–40% from early in the first trimester. This increase in cardiac output occurs initially as a result of an increase in stroke volume and subsequently an increase in heart rate as well. The increase in stroke volume parallels the increase in blood volume described above. Systemic vascular resistance in healthy pregnant women at term, measured using invasive techniques, has been shown to be decreased by 20% in the same women when compared with the nonpregnant state (at approximately 12 weeks postpartum) as shown in Fig. 11.1.

Recent studies have shown that up to 50% of the increase in cardiac output observed during pregnancy is present by 8 weeks of gestation. This suggests that a considerable portion of the increase in cardiac output that occurs in association with a fall in systemic vascular resistance early in pregnancy is due to endocrine alterations. Many of these cardiovascular adaptations persist during the postpartum period and are even greater during subsequent pregnancies (Fig. 11.2). This suggests that the vascular remodelling which takes place during pregnancy persists for prolonged periods of time. It has been shown that the mesenteric arteries of pregnant rats have decreased stiffness as well as a reduction in their contractile ability, both of which would contribute to the decrease in systemic vascular resistance. Pulmonary vascular resistance is also decreased during pregnancy, whereas pulmonary capillary wedge pressure and central venous pressure are unchanged.

Measurements of haemodynamic alterations in pregnancy are dependent on maternal posture, as studies carried out with women in the supine position are associated with a decrease in central venous return due to compression of the

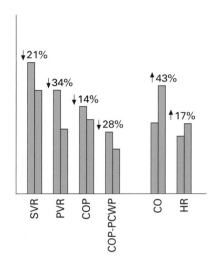

Fig. 11.1. Relative haemodynamic changes in pregnancy: nonpregnant versus late phase of third trimester. SVR, systemic vascular resistance; PVR, pulmonary vascular resistance; COP, colloid osmotic pressure; COP−PCWP, colloid osmotic pressure minus pulmonary capillary wedge pressure; CO, cardiac output; HR, heart rate. (Redrawn from S.L Clark *et al.* (1989), *Am. J. Obstet. Gynecol.*, **161**, 1439–42.)

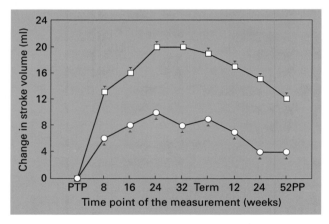

Fig. 11.2. Change in stroke volume during normal pregnancy and the first year postpartum in nulliparous (circles) and parous (squares) women. The rate of change is significantly different in the two groups up to the 24th week and the magnitude of the change is significantly greater in the parous group at all time points other than prior to pregnancy (PTP). PP, post partum. (Redrawn from J.F. Clapp and E. Capeless (1997), *Am. J. Cardiol.*, **80**, 1469–73.)

inferior vena cava by the pregnant uterus. This, in turn, gives rise to a fall in stroke volume and therefore cardiac output. It is important, then, in interpreting studies of maternal cardiovascular physiology during pregnancy, that the posture of the women during the study be taken into account. It is not only unwise but often impossible for pregnant women, particularly during the latter part of gestation, to lie on their back for a prolonged period of time due to the development of hypotension, and underperfusion of vital organs including the gravid uterus.

Maternal heart rate increases during the first 16 weeks of gestation reaching a plateau level approximately 11% greater than preconceptual rates. Mean arterial blood pressure decreases initially during the first trimester and then returns to prepregnancy values. There is little information regarding the regional distribution of blood flow during human pregnancy. However, in pregnant sheep at term uterine blood flow constitutes approximately 15% of cardiac output, compared with 2% during the nonpregnant state. The mammary gland also receives a significantly greater proportion of cardiac output during pregnancy compared with the nonpregnant state (2% versus 0.2%).

An important result, therefore, of the increase in cardiac output during pregnancy is the increase in uterine blood flow which provides nutrients and oxygen to the fetus via the placenta. In addition to oestrogen, nitric oxide has also been implicated in this increase in uteroplacental blood flow. The biosynthesis of nitric oxide is increased during pregnancy in some species, as is cyclic guanosine 3,5′-monophosphate (cGMP) which is the second messenger for the action of nitric oxide. Although both plasma levels and urinary excretion of cGMP are known to be increased in human pregnancy, their role in mediating both the early decrease in systemic vascular resistance and the increase in uterine blood flow are still under investigation.

As a consequence of the increase in cardiac output during pregnancy, renal blood flow increases by about 40% by 20 weeks of gestation, with a further 10% increase during the latter half of gestation. Glomerular filtration rate increases in a parallel fashion to renal blood flow. It is quite common for pregnant women to have glucose in their urine (glycosuria) as a consequence of the increase in glucose filtered by the glomerulus exceeding the amount that can be reabsorbed by the renal tubule. Overall, tubular reabsorption of glucose is unchanged in pregnancy and, therefore, glycosuria occurs in those pregnant women with a relatively low tubular maximum threshold for glucose reabsorption. Postural changes during pregnancy will also give rise to significant changes in sodium homeostasis with sodium excretion being decreased in the supine position along with the previously described fall in cardiac output and presumably renal blood flow.

Plasma concentrations of aldosterone increase from very early during pregnancy. There are also increases in circulating concentrations of renin substrate and angiotensin I and II. Renin substrate production by the liver is known to be increased by oestrogen, providing further evidence that the rise in plasma renin activity (PRA), observed from as early as 8 weeks of gestation, is mediated by the increase in circulating oestrogen concentrations. It has been estimated that half of this increase in PRA occurs as a result of an increase in the concentration of active renin, the enzyme produced within the juxta-glomerular apparatus of the kidney that releases angiotensin. The remaining 50% increase in PRA during pregnancy occurs as a result of the increase in plasma angiotensin itself. Although angiotensin II levels are increased, pregnancy is characterized by a decrease in vascular responsiveness to exogenously infused angiotensin, the explanation for which is not known. In women who subsequently develop pregnancy-induced hypertension or preeclampsia, however, the refractoriness to infused angiotensin is observed to decrease with advancing gestation.

Respiratory system

The alterations that occur within the respiratory system during pregnancy can be placed within two broad categories: (1) those occurring due to the mechanical effects of the enlarging uterus, and (2) those that are secondary to the endocrine changes. The increasing abdominal volume with advancing gestation gives rise to an elevation in the resting position of the diaphragm but does not significantly alter diaphragmatic function.

The major effect of pregnancy on respiratory function is one of hyperventilation. This occurs largely due to an increase in tidal volume with only a slight increase in respiratory rate. The increase in tidal volume begins during the first trimester and by term the increase is approximately 50%. There is also a 20% decrease, during the last third of pregnancy, in functional residual capacity (FRC), which is the lung volume at rest after a normal respiration. Expiratory reserve volume and residual volume also decrease progressively with advancing gestation, whereas vital capacity remains unchanged (Fig. 11.3). The cause of the increase in tidal volume during pregnancy is probably the increase in circulating progesterone concentrations. Progesterone is a well-known respiratory stimulant, acting possibly by increasing the sensitivity of central respiratory

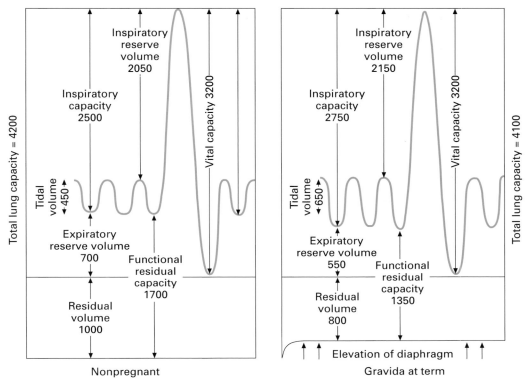

Fig. 11.3.   Lung volume changes (mL) in pregnancy. (Redrawn from J. Bonica and J.S. Macdonald, eds., *Principles and Practice of Obstetric Analgesia and Anesthesia*, 2nd edn. Malvern, PA: Williams and Wilkins, 1995.)

neurones to fluctuations in PCO_2. The role of oestrogens in mediating the respiratory changes during pregnancy is less certain.

As a consequence of the increased ventilation during pregnancy, maternal alveolar and arterial PCO_2 are consistently lower than in nonpregnant women, giving rise to a respiratory alkalosis and a compensatory metabolic acidosis. As a consequence of the decrease in PCO_2, alveolar and arterial PO_2 are increased during pregnancy by about 5 mmHg. Airway function, as determined by measurements of the forced expiratory volume in 1 second (FEV_1), is not altered during pregnancy. The effect of pregnancy on small-airway function is less certain, with conflicting results, probably reflecting the fact that this aspect of pulmonary function is more difficult to study. The diffusing capacity of the lung is altered only slightly during pregnancy, with an initial increase during the first trimester followed by a decrease during the remainder of pregnancy. Even though normal maternal respiratory function is maintained during pregnancy, it is quite common for pregnant women to experience a subjective sensation of shortness of breath particularly as they enter the third trimester. This is known as 'dyspnoea of pregnancy' and is thought to be due to the action of progesterone on the respiratory centres in the brain although the exact mechanism is not known.

Genitourinary tract

Dilatation of components of the urinary collecting system including the renal calices, pelves, and ureters is generally present by 20 weeks of gestation and occurs in virtually all pregnant women by term. The increased circulating concentrations of progesterone, may inhibit ureteral smooth muscle function giving rise to dilatation, although there is some evidence that ureteral contractile pressure, frequency and tone are not altered in human pregnancy. Second, there is a relative obstruction to drainage of the ureters above the bony pelvic inlet that is probably due to compression by the enlarging uterus. This physiological obstruction is greater on the right side than the left, as a result of the normal dextrorotation of the uterus during human pregnancy.

As a consequence of these alterations in the urinary collecting system, there is an increase in the 'dead space' or amount of urine remaining in the ureters and bladder at any given time during pregnancy, which predisposes pregnant women to urinary tract infections. Clinicians must also be aware of these normal changes during pregnancy when interpreting radiological or ultrasonic investigations of the urinary tract during pregnancy.

Gastrointestinal tract

During pregnancy, there is a decrease in the contractility of the gall bladder as a result of the inhibitory effect of progesterone on baseline smooth muscle contractility as well as a decrease in cholecystokinin-induced contraction of the gall bladder. This decrease in biliary contractility leads to biliary stasis, which predisposes pregnant women to the formation of bile stones. It is also known that nonpregnant women who have been exposed to increased oestrogen concentrations have a decrease in the proportion of chenodeoxycholic acid in their bile, which decreases the bile salt pool causing a further predisposition to the formation of bile stones. Whether this same alteration occurs in pregnant women is unknown, although it is highly likely given the large increase in circulating oestrogen concentrations during pregnancy. It has been well documented using ultrasound, that there is an increase in the incidence of gallstones or cholelithiasis during pregnancy as a consequence of these changes.

The inhibitory effect of progesterone on gastrointestinal smooth muscle contractility also affects the lower oesophageal sphincter. The administration of oestrogen and progesterone to animals giving rise to a condition known as pseudopregnancy has been shown to cause a decrease in lower oesophageal sphincter pressure in keeping with observations in humans. This results in many pregnant women experiencing 'heartburn' due to reflux of gastric contents. Reflux can generally be relieved by antacids and/or maintained elevation of the head during sleep. Gastric emptying time is also reduced during pregnancy, particularly during labour. Extra precautions are therefore required to prevent the aspiration of gastric contents in pregnant women who require general anaesthesia.

As a result of the enlarging uterus with advancing gestation, the small and large intestines are displaced upwards, with traditional abdominal landmarks being altered. The appendix, which is normally present in the right lower quadrant of the abdomen in the nonpregnant state, is displaced to the right upper quadrant during late pregnancy. This change in the position of the appendix can, on occasion, make the diagnosis of appendicitis difficult since the pain may not be present in the usual location for nonpregnant individuals.

Liver size remains unchanged during pregnancy as do the serological tests of liver function with the exception of alkaline phosphatase. Alkaline phosphatase is an enzyme that is produced by the placenta as well as the liver, and therefore its concentration in blood may increase as much as twofold or more during pregnancy. Placental alkaline phosphatase may be differentiated from that from hepatic sources by gel electrophoresis as well as by its stability on heating.

Serum protein and albumin concentrations decrease during pregnancy as a dilutional effect of the increase in plasma volume. In contrast, a number of proteins produced by the liver, such as fibrinogen, globulins and caeruloplasmin, increase during pregnancy, probably as a result of the increased circulating concentrations of oestrogen. Changes in plasma concentrations of fibrinogen, albumin and globulins similar to those occurring in human pregnancy have been induced in nonpregnant sheep exposed to high concentrations of 17β-oestradiol for 3 weeks. These observations strengthen the belief that these alterations are mediated by increased oestrogen concentrations.

Endocrine changes

Pituitary

During pregnancy, the maternal pituitary gland increases in volume by two- to threefold due primarily to hyperplasia and hypertrophy of the lactotrophs. The increase in number and size of lactotrophs is probably a result of the increased circulating concentrations of oestrogen and progesterone, which are known to stimulate prolactin secretion. This leads to an increase in maternal plasma concentrations of prolactin with advancing gestational age which then prepares the mammary gland for lactation.

Maternal serum concentrations of the pituitary gonadotrophins, follicle-stimulating hormone (FSH), and luteinizing hormone (LH) are lower during pregnancy than in the nonpregnant condition, as a result of increased negative feedback exerted by increased concentrations of oestrogen and progesterone. Concentrations of thyroid-stimulating hormone (TSH) are unchanged during pregnancy in keeping with the lack of a change in the normal negative feedback relationship between thyroid hormones and TSH. Baseline concentrations of growth hormone (GH) are also unchanged, although the pituitary responsiveness to stimulation tests of GH release, such as insulin-induced hypoglycaemia, appears to be reduced during pregnancy. This alteration in GH release during pregnancy is possibly related to the increased concentrations of progesterone, cortisol and human placental lactogen (hPL). In addition, during the second half of pregnancy, there is a decrease in pituitary secretion of GH which is accompanied by an increase in placental production of a GH variant.

It is of interest that plasma adrenocorticotrophin (ACTH) concentrations are elevated during pregnancy despite an increase in plasma cortisol concentrations. This suggests that there may be other factors that regulate ACTH production by the pituitary during pregnancy. Alternatively, there may be other sources of ACTH during pregnancy such as the placenta, which is known to produce a variety of peptides. Administration of glucocorticoids to pregnant women at risk of giving birth prematurely does not completely suppress maternal ACTH concentrations, in keeping with a nonpituitary source of ACTH such as the placenta. In contrast, maternal cortisol concentrations are decreased to near undetectable levels for up to 7 days following the commonly used clinical dose of glucocorticoids given to pregnant women to enhance fetal pulmonary maturation. Plasma concentrations of corticotrophin-releasing-hormone (CRH) also increase progressively during the last two-thirds of pregnancy and fall immediately after birth, in keeping with placental production. Recently it has been shown that maternal CRH concentrations are higher in women destined to give birth prematurely, supporting a role for placental CRH production in the pathogenesis of premature labour in some women. Interestingly, glucocorticoids increase placental production of CRH, which contrasts with the normally occurring negative feedback effect of cortisol on hypothalamic CRH production.

Plasma concentrations of vasopressin, which is produced by the posterior pituitary, are unchanged during pregnancy. This is of particular interest owing to the 5–10% decrease in plasma osmolality during normal pregnancy compared with the nonpregnant state, in addition to a decrease in plasma sodium concentrations. This would suggest that, during normal pregnancy, there is a downwards shift in the osmotic threshold for vasopressin release. The effect of this is that pregnant women experience thirst at a lower plasma osmolality than nonpregnant women.

Oxytocin is also synthesized and released from the posterior pituitary during pregnancy and is important in the process of parturition through its regulation of uterine contractility during and following delivery. Oxytocin is also important in lactation as it causes contraction of the myoepithelial cells within the mammary gland as well as contraction of the smooth muscle in the mammary duct leading to ejection of milk from the gland. This is mediated through a neurohumoral reflex, with neural impulses in response to suckling being transmitted through the intercostal nerves and dorsal roots of the spinal cord and terminating in the supraoptic and paraventricular nuclei of the hypothalamus. Oxytocin is thereby released in a pulsatile fashion during lactation.

Adrenal function

Plasma cortisol concentrations increase approximately threefold during pregnancy, largely due to an increase in plasma cortisol-binding-globulin (CBG) which is produced by the liver. The plasma concentration of free cortisol also increases during pregnancy, this being due to a decrease in clearance and metabolism with no increase in cortisol production. The diurnal rhythm in plasma cortisol concentrations normally present in nonpregnant individuals persists during pregnancy but can be abolished by daily use of glucocorticoids when taken by pregnant women with particular medical conditions. The changes in clearance and metabolism of CBG and cortisol observed during normal pregnancy may be reproduced in nonpregnant women by administering oestrogen over 1–2 weeks further implicating this hormone in a normal physiological adaptation to pregnancy.

As discussed previously, plasma renin activity as well as angiotensin and aldosterone concentrations all increase in the mother during normal pregnancy. Concentrations of deoxycorticosterone (DOC), a mineralocorticoid produced by the adrenal cortex, increase markedly during pregnancy, although its role in regulating fluid balance remains uncertain. Plasma concentrations of testosterone increase significantly due to the increase in sex hormone-binding globulin (SHBG). SHBG is increased due to the elevation in oestrogen concentrations during pregnancy and this increase in SHBG gives rise to an increase in bound testosterone but a decrease in free testosterone.

Thyroid Function

The major change in thyroid hormone physiology during pregnancy is an increase in thyroid-binding globulin (TBG) produced by the liver in response to the elevation in oestrogen concentrations. This gives rise to an increase in total thyroxine (T_4) concentrations with a minimal increase in free T_4. Although the basal metabolic rate increases during pregnancy by about 25%, this is not due to changes in thyroid hormone function but is a result of the addition of the fetus, placenta and increased myometrial mass to the maternal organism. Underlying abnormalities of thyroid function are common in women in the reproductive age group and therefore also in pregnant women. Hypothyroidism in pregnancy is treated with thyroid hormone replacement and hyperthyroidism is treated with medications which block the synthesis and release of thyroxine. It is important to monitor the fetus carefully during pregnancies in which the mother has either treated or untreated Grave's disease (hyperthyroidism); in this disease the thyroid-stimulating antibodies which were the cause of maternal hyperthyroidism, and remain in the maternal circulation despite treatment, can cross the placenta and give rise to fetal hyperthyroidism.

Calcium metabolism

The absorption of calcium across the gastrointestinal tract of the mother is increased during pregnancy in order to meet the substantial requirements of the fetus for its skeletal development. In addition, urinary excretion of calcium by pregnant women is increased as a result of the increased renal glomerular filtration rate described previously. The increase in maternal intestinal calcium absorption is mediated by an increase in parathyroid hormone (PTH) bioactivity as well as an increase in 1,25-dihydroxyvitamin D (1,25(OH)$_2$D) synthesis. Maternal 1,25(OH)$_2$D levels are two- to threefold greater than nonpregnant levels. Possible sources of these increased levels include the placenta and the maternal kidney. PTH regulates short-term fluctuations in maternal calcium levels through its actions on renal calcium reabsorption as well as calcium fluxes to and from bone. In the long term, however, PTH influences intestinal absorption of calcium through its action on renal and possibly placental production of 1,25(OH)$_2$D. It is of interest that, although PTH bioactivity increases during pregnancy, assays of intact PTH actually demonstrate a decrease in its concentration. One possible explanation for this apparent anomaly is that the fetus and placenta produce a PTH-related peptide (PTHrP), which acts on the same receptors as PTH itself in bone and the kidney. Circulating concentrations of calcitonin, which increases production of 1,25(OH)$_2$D, appear to be unchanged during pregnancy. Although total serum calcium concentrations decrease in the mother due to the dilutional decrease in serum albumin concentrations, there is no change in the maternal levels of ionized calcium. Thus the maternal–placental–fetal unit is uniquely suited to meet the large demands for calcium required by the fetus and yet avoids depletion of skeletal reserves within the mother.

Carbohydrate metabolism

The major alterations in carbohydrate metabolism during early pregnancy are directed at augmenting tissue storage of nutrients in preparation for later fetal growth. The increase in maternal concentrations of oestrogen and progesterone gives rise to pancreatic B cell hyperplasia and increased insulin secretion. As a consequence, tissue glycogen deposition and peripheral glucose utilization are increased, while hepatic glucose production and plasma glucose concentrations decrease (Table 11.1).

With advancing gestation, there is a progressive rise in circulating concentrations of human placental chorionic somatomammotrophin (hCS), or human placental lactogen, as well as prolactin, cortisol and glucagon. The net effect of these hormonal changes is to promote a state of insulin resistance and to increase hepatic production of glucose by decreasing stores of hepatic glycogen. hCS increases circulating concentrations of insulin and the normal fluctuations

Table 11.1. Carbohydrate metabolism during human pregnancy

Hormonal change		Effect	
Early (to 20 weeks)			
↑	Oestrogen	↑	Tissue glycogen storage
	and		
↑	Progesterone	↓	Hepatic glucose production
	↓		
	Beta cell hyperplasia	↑	Peripheral glucose utilization
	and		
↑	Insulin secretion	↓	Fasting plasma glucose
Late (20–40 weeks)			
↑	hCS		'Diabetogenic'
		↓	Glucose tolerance
↑	Prolactin		Insulin resistance
↑	Bound and free cortisol	↓	Hepatic glycogen stores
		↓	Hepatic glucose production

Notes:
hCS, human placental chorionic somatomammotrophin.
Source: Adapted from Moore ,T.R. (1994). Diabetes in pregnancy. In: *Maternal Fetal Medicine: Principles and Practice*, ed. R.K. Creasy and R. Resnik, pp. 934–78. Philadelphia: W.B. Saunders Co.

in insulin concentrations around meals increase with advancing gestation. Thus, although fasting plasma glucose concentrations decrease with advancing gestation, oscillations in glucose concentrations around meals are accentuated (Fig. 11.4).

There are similar increases in the magnitude of oscillations in the utilization and production of most fuels (glucose, free fatty acids, and triglyceride) during the transition between the fed and fasted state. The terms 'accelerated starvation' alternating with 'facilitated anabolism' have been used to characterize the metabolic fluctuations that occur with meals in later gestation. The effect of these changes is to ensure a constant supply of nutrients to the fetus and placenta through their rapid mobilization and ready transfer at a time when fetal growth is maximal. The importance of these metabolic adjustments in regulating fetal growth is illustrated further in Fig. 11.5.

Fasting plasma concentrations of amino acids tend to be lower in late gestation compared with those in nonpregnant women although, in contrast to most

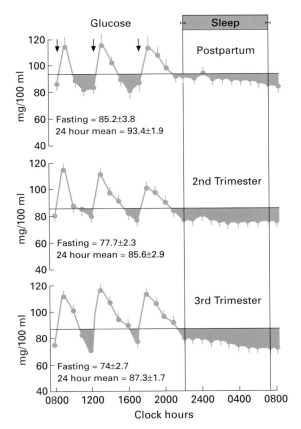

Fig. 11.4. Profile of blood glucose over 24 hours in postpartum women and during the second and third trimesters of pregnancy. Horizontal lines show daily mean values, and arrows indicate meals. (Redrawn from Cousins *et al.* (1980), *Am. J. Obstet. Gynecol.*, **136**, 483–8.)

other fuels, postprandial increases tend to be greater in the nonpregnant state than in the pregnant. The explanation for this variation among metabolic fuels is unknown.

Immune system

The effect of pregnancy on the maternal immune system has been a subject of great interest as well as controversy. The reason for this is the fascinating ability of the fetus to survive as what is essentially a 'semiallograft' within the maternal environment. It was originally suggested that one possible explanation for

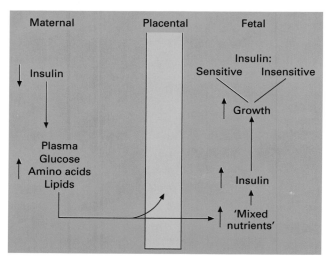

Fig. 11.5. Major metabolic and endocrine changes during fetal development according to the modified Pedersen hypothesis. (Redrawn from N. Freinkel (1980), *Diabetes*, **29**, 1023–35.)

this was a generalized suppression of the maternal immune response. Recent studies, however, have refuted this hypothesis. The total number of circulating white blood cells increases slightly in human pregnancy and this increase is largely due to a greater number of polymorphonuclear leucocytes with no change in the number of lymphocytes. B cell function is maintained during pregnancy and normal concentrations of IgG, IgM, IgA and complement are present in the sera of pregnant women. This indicates that systemic antibody-mediated immunity is not different from that during the nonpregnant state. In addition, total T cell numbers and percentages of their subsets in the peripheral blood, as measured using flow cytometry in pregnant women with specific monoclonal antibodies, are either increased or unchanged compared with those in nonpregnant women. The number of circulating natural killer (NK) cells is also unchanged during pregnancy. Although there are conflicting reports regarding systemic T cell function during pregnancy, most suggest that maternal cell-mediated immunity is unchanged during pregnancy.

Of greater importance is an understanding of the immune events occurring at the maternal–fetal interface as it is apparent that these are the mechanisms most probably responsible for the ability of the fetus to survive within the maternal organism. A variety of maternal antibodies directed against fetal epitopes (or antigenic determinants), have been detected including leucocytotoxic antibodies, anti-FcR antibodies, and antibodies to oncofetal and trophoblastic antigens. These have been collectively termed 'blocking' antibodies as they may protect the fetus by preventing further immune processing by maternal cells. The exact importance of these antibodies in the maintenance of pregnancy is yet to be confirmed.

Syncytiotrophoblast, which comprises the majority of placental tissue in contact with the maternal circulation, does not exhibit the major histocompatibility complex (MHC) antigens required for T cells to exert their cytotoxic action. In addition, syncytiotrophoblast cells are covered by a highly charged sialomucin coating that provides protection from immune surveillance. In contrast, the extravillous cytotrophoblast does express a type of MHC antigen which is an immunoreactive HLA antigen. This nonclassical, truncated, nonpolymorphic class 1 antigen is often referred to as HLA-G. In addition, there is an overall low density of potential immunogens on the surface of the extravillous cytotrophoblast which may act to limit the antigenic challenge to the maternal immune system. It is known that, overall, trophoblast cells have a reduced susceptibility to both specific and nonspecific cell lysis.

Large numbers of white blood cells are present within the decidua in early pregnancy, these cells having the histological appearance of large granular lymphocytes (LGL). The role of these cells is unknown although they are most abundant during early and midpregnancy. They have the ability to secrete a number of cytokines including interleukin-1 and 2, interferon, tumour-necrosis factor-alpha and colony-stimulating factors. This would be in keeping with LGLs playing a role in trophoblast cell invasion of the decidua rather than a traditional immunological role. Another important consideration in local immune responses at the fetoplacental–maternal interface is the presence of immunoregulatory substances such as progesterone, corticosteroids, eicosanoids, α-fetoprotein and others. Some of these compounds are present in large concentrations systemically in the mother and may exert their effect locally while others are present in high concentrations within the placenta and decidua, and they may all have an effect in suppressing the immune response in a paracrine fashion. In addition to the presence of immunoregulators, it is known that there are natural suppressor cells present in the decidual bed which are thought to release a factor similar to transforming growth factor-$\beta2$ (TGF-$\beta2$), which in turn inhibits both cytotoxic T and NK cells.

Thus, during pregnancy, there appears to be very little change in the maternal systemic immune system. In contrast, there are very important immune mechanisms present within the decidua and placenta that are critical to the growth and development of fetal and placental tissues.

Summary

The numerous maternal physiological adaptations to pregnancy described in this chapter are essential in order to achieve optimal fetal outcome. They are designed to minimize any long-term adverse consequences for the mother, although clearly some of the changes such as vascular remodelling can persist for years. In addition, some of the changes which occur in the mother, such as smooth muscle relaxation, can give rise to unpleasant side-effects involving the genitourinary and gastrointestinal tracts (heartburn, constipation, urinary frequency) during pregnancy. Finally, it is important for clinicians to be aware of the normal physiological changes which occur during pregnancy in order to understand the reported symptoms of pregnant women, to interpret investigations appropriately and to develop management strategies for pregnant women with underlying medical conditions, some of which can be influenced adversely by pregnancy.

FURTHER READING

Clapp, J.F. and Capeless, E. (1997). Cardiovascular function before, during and after the first and subsequent pregnancies. *Am. J. Cardiol.*, **80**, 1469–73.

Clark, S.L., *et al.* (1989). Central hemodynamic assessment of normal term pregnancy. *Am. J. Obstet. Gynecol.*, **161**, 1439–42.

Hollingsworth, D. (1983). Alterations of maternal metabolism in normal and diabetic pregnancies: differences in insulin-dependent, non-insulin-dependent and gestational diabetes. *Am. J. Obstet. Gynecol.*, **146**, 417–29.

Hollingsworth, D. (1989). Endocrine disorders of pregnancy. In: *Maternal Fetal Medicine: Principles and Practice*, ed. R.K. Creasy and R. Resnik, pp. 989–1031. Philadelphia: W.B. Saunders Co.

Hosking, D.J. (1996). Calcium homeostasis in pregnancy. *Clin. Endocrinol.*, **45**, 1–6.

O'Day, M.P. (1997) Cardio-respiratory physiological adaptation of pregnancy. *Semin. Perinatol.*, **21**, 268–75.

Sladek, S.M., *et al.* (1997). Nitric oxide and pregnancy. *Am. J. Physiol.*, **272**, R441–63.

Ware Branch, D. and Scott, J.R. (1994). The immunology of pregnancy. In: *Maternal Fetal Medicine: Principles and Practice*, ed. R.K. Creasy and R. Resnik, pp. 115–27. Philadelphia: W.B. Saunders Co.

Weinberger, S.E., *et al.* (1980). Pregnancy and the lung. *Am. Rev. Respir. Dis.*, **121**, 559–81.

12

Parturition

Stephen J. Lye and John R. G. Challis

Preterm birth occurs in 5–10% of all pregnancies but is associated with 70% of all neonatal deaths and up to 75% of neonatal morbidity. In the neonatal period preterm infants are 40 times more likely to die than are term infants. Not only is preterm birth associated with considerable neonatal mortality, premature infants are also at increased risk of cerebral palsy, blindness, deafness, respiratory illness and complications of neonatal intensive care. These complications result in tremendous costs to health care systems. It is estimated that neonatal care alone for preterm infants approaches $5–6 billion in the USA. Perhaps even more disturbing are reports that children born preterm display signs of learning and behavioural difficulties as they reach school age Unfortunately, despite decades of research directed to the development of drugs to inhibit myometrial contractile activity, there has been no reduction in the incidence of preterm birth. Present therapies cannot prevent preterm delivery, but at best provide sufficient delay to allow for transfer to tertiary centres where treatments to ameliorate the consequences of preterm birth can be attempted. While there are many reasons for the failure to prevent preterm birth, a primary factor is our failure to recognize the complexities of the labour process and develop treatment therapies based on sound biological data. In this chapter we will explore the pathways that lead to the onset of labour in animals and humans. Where appropriate we will discuss how such pathways may be activated prematurely in preterm labour.

The contribution of the fetus to the initiation of labour

It is now clear that the signals that initiate labour originate in the fetus. These signals represent the expression of the fetal genome acting through endocrine pathways involving the fetal brain, adrenal gland and placenta as well as mechanical signals acting directly on the myometrium as a result of the growth of the fetus. Together, these fetal signals contribute to the timely, safe and effective delivery of the fetus at term. Inappropriate expression of these signals, or their bypass under pathological conditions, probably makes a major contribution to preterm labour.

Fetal endocrine signals

Non-primate studies

Although the original clues to the role of the fetus in parturition were gained from studies in cattle, it was a series of studies in sheep that led to our current understanding of the initiation of labour. In 1963 it was observed that ingestion of the skunk cabbage (*Veratrum californicum*) by ewes during pregnancy was associated with prolonged pregnancy. Examination of the fetus revealed cyclopian-type malformations associated with an absence or abnormality of neural connections to the pituitary gland. It was also noted that the fetal adrenal glands, which normally are comparatively large at birth, were atrophied. In 1965 G.C. Liggins developed techniques for ablating the pituitary gland of the fetus in utero and, together with others, investigated the role of the fetal brain in the initiation of labour. These studies revealed that activation of the fetal hypothalamic–pituitary–adrenal (HPA) axis and increased output of cortisol from the fetal adrenal gland were central to the endocrine events leading to the initiation of labour (Fig. 12.1). Thus, lesions in the paraventricular region of the hypothalamus, hypophysectomy or adrenalectomy of the fetus in utero led to prolonged gestation, whereas infusion of adrenocorticotrophic hormone (ACTH) or glucocorticoid into the fetus resulted in premature parturition. Fetal cortisol acts on the placenta, resulting in increased expression of the enzyme P450 C17. This results in decreased output of progesterone, a rise in oestrogen levels, and later increase in the production of prostaglandin $F_{2\alpha}$ ($PGF_{2\alpha}$) by intrauterine tissues.

Evidence in support of these concepts includes the demonstration of progressive rises in levels of mRNA encoding corticotrophin-releasing hormone (CRH) in the parvocellular region of the paraventricular nucleus (PVN) of the fetal hypothalamus, and of pro-opiomelanocortin (POMC), the precursor for ACTH, in the pars distalis of the fetal pituitary. The rise in fetal pituitary POMC mRNA levels corresponds to increases in immunoreactive (ir)-ACTH staining in the pituitary gland and to the prepartum increase in ir-$ACTH_{1-39}$ in plasma. The concurrent increase in ACTH and cortisol in the fetal circulation occurs

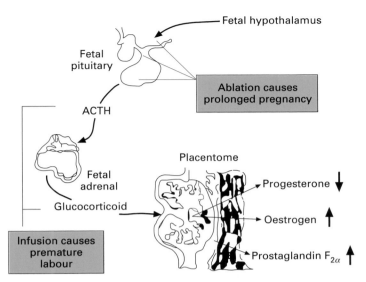

Fig. 12.1.   Summary of endocrine events classically associated with the onset of parturition in sheep. (Modified from various publications of Sir Graham (Mont) Liggins and Geoffrey Thorburn.)

despite the potential for negative feedback of cortisol at the level of the hypothalamus and pituitary. The ovine fetus appears to have evolved mechanisms to prevent negative feedback. These include the ability of fetal cortisol to stimulate synthesis and secretion in the liver of its own high-affinity binding protein, corticosteroid-binding globulin (CBG). Although glucocorticoid receptors (GR) are abundant in the fetal pituitary, they are decreased at the level of the PVN thereby reducing the potential for negative feedback. Finally, the fetal pituitary in late gestation expresses increased amounts of the enzyme 11-β hydroxysteroid dehydrogenase (11-β–HSD)-1, and has the ability to inactivate circulating cortisol by oxidation to cortisone.

ACTH acts on the fetal adrenal to increase the number of ACTH receptors, adenylate cyclase activity (potential for cyclic AMP generation), and expression of key steroidogenic enzymes, especially P450 C17. Induction of this enzyme is essential to allow C21 steroids to proceed through the 17-hydroxy pathway leading to cortisol synthesis. An obligatory role for an increase in ACTH drive to the adrenal has, however, been challenged recently. When hypophysectomized fetal sheep were infused with a constant, low level of ACTH, there was a normal rise in fetal cortisol concentrations, decrease in maternal progesterone levels, and birth occurred at about the expected time. The molecular mechanisms underlying this result clearly require elucidation. The importance of this observation to our understanding of birth of human anencephalic fetuses, with low pituitary ACTH output, remains unclear.

Fetal cortisol acts on the placenta to change the pattern of steroidogenesis such that progesterone output falls, and oestrogen rises. Prostaglandin output increases sharply at term, although increased secretion of prostaglandin E_2 (PGE_2) into the fetal circulation occurs throughout the last 2–3 weeks of ovine pregnancy. Current evidence suggests that cortisol upregulates P450 C17 in the sheep placenta, allowing metabolism of C21 steroids through the $\Delta 5$ pathway to form C19 oestrogen precursors. However, it is equally possible that fetal cortisol directly upregulates prostaglandin synthesis in placental tissue, in a manner similar to that in human amnion and chorion. In that case, increased output of PGE_2 may act directly to increase placental P450 C17, as it does in the adrenal, giving rise to the altered pattern of placental steroid secretion.

Activation of the fetal HPA axis can take place in response to an adverse intrauterine environment, for example hypoxaemia. With hypoxaemia, there is increased expression of CRH in the fetal hypothalamus, and increased levels of POMC mRNA in the fetal pituitary. Levels of steroidogenic enzymes in the fetal adrenal increase, and cortisol output rises. This elevation of cortisol, in addition to promoting organ maturation and premature delivery, may also be inhibitory to the growth of many fetal organs, in part by suppressing the expression of insulin-like growth factors. In this case, birth may be considered as a necessary escape for the fetus from a stressful environment, characterized by fetal hypercortisolaemia.

Primate studies

The role of the human fetus in initiating labour is less well defined than in the sheep. In human anencephaly, the mean length of pregnancy is similar to that of a normal population, after exclusion of patients with polyhydramnios. There is a marked increase, however, in the distribution of both premature and postmature births, similar to that reported for the rhesus monkey after experimental fetal exencephaly. In the monkey it is now clear that the length of 'placental pregnancy' is considerably prolonged after removal of the fetus. Levels of C19 oestrogen precursors rise in the circulation of the intact fetal monkey in late gestation, mimicking the rise of cortisol in the circulation of the fetal sheep. Infusion of androstenedione in pregnant rhesus monkeys at 0.8 of gestation increases maternal plasma oestrogen levels and leads to preterm birth. Importantly, this effect is blocked by the coinfusion of the aromatase inhibitor 4-hydroxy-androstenedione. This compound prevents the maternal endocrine changes, the fetal membrane changes, and inhibits the patterns of uterine myometrial contractility induced with androstenedione. However, infusion of systemic oestrogen into the mother increases myometrial activity, but does not produce premature delivery or fetal membrane changes. This suggests that in the primate, as in the sheep, oestrogen is important for normal processes of parturition. These findings also suggest that the bioactive oestrogen must be generated close to the site of its paracrine/autocrine action to be effective as this response cannot be reproduced by systemic oestrogen administration.

There are data which also support a role for oestrogen in the initiation of human labour. Maternal oestrogen concentrations rise progressively through the latter half of human gestation, and oestriol measurements, particularly in saliva, have been advocated as a clinically useful method for identifying women at increased risk of preterm labour and birth. There is also some indication of increased oestrogen synthesis within the intrauterine tissues themselves at term and with the onset of labour. For example, the activity of oestrone sulphohydrolase (which can convert sulphated oestrogen precursors to oestrogen) is increased in fetal membranes of women in labour.

Another critical difference in the endocrine events surrounding labour in the human is that, in contrast to virtually all other species, there is no indication of a fall in progesterone (or of an acute rise in oestrogen) either in the plasma or within intrauterine tissues. These major differences have led to suggestions that different mechanisms exist in the human to induce a progesterone withdrawal prior to labour. We know that progesterone is normally required for the maintenance of pregnancy since blockade of progesterone action (through the administration of progesterone receptor antagonists such as RU486) leads to the onset of labour. While some investigators have suggested that progesterone may not be the active 'progestagen' in the human, studies have failed to find any decrease in other C21 steroids or progesterone metabolites. A new model for the involvement of progesterone is now emerging suggesting that the maintenance of elevated levels of progesterone may actually benefit the labour process by supporting relaxation of the lower uterine segment and that progesterone withdrawal may be effected functionally through blockade of progesterone receptor action at the level of the genome.

Myometrial quiescence during pregnancy

During pregnancy in virtually all species the uterus is essentially quiescent, that is the muscle layer (myometrium) is relatively inexcitable and has little spontaneous activity. Those contractions that do occur are of low frequency and only capable of developing small increases in uterine pressure. In addition, the myometrium is relatively unresponsive to uterotonic stimulants (e.g. oxytocin, prostaglandins) and the muscle cells are not well coordinated, significantly reducing the ability of the uterus to develop propagated contractions. The maintenance of this inhibitory state probably involves both the action of myometrial inhibitors and the active blockade of the expression of genes that increase myometrial contractility.

Inhibitory agents include progesterone, relaxin, prostacyclin (PGI_2), parathyroid hormone-related protein (PTHrP) and nitric oxide (Fig. 12.2). As its name implies, progesterone is a critical component of the mechanisms which act to maintain uterine quiescence and the 'gestational state' during pregnancy. Progesterone inhibits myometrial contractility, cell–cell coupling and responsiveness to endogenous stimulants such as oxytocin and stimulatory prostaglandins. For the most part, progesterone acts at the level of the genome to directly or indirectly block the expression of proteins (e.g. gap junctions, receptors for prostaglandins and oxytocin) that contribute to the activation of the myometrium. However, progesterone and some of its metabolites have recently been demonstrated to interact directly with the oxytocin receptor at the cell membrane, blocking its ability to bind oxytocin.

PTHrP is produced by the pregnant myometrium; its mRNA levels are increased by progesterone and transforming growth factor-beta (TGF-β), and PTHrP-receptor mRNA is present in myometrial tissue. PTHrP synthesized in human myometrium may therefore act in an autocrine/paracrine fashion through specific receptors to activate the $G_{\alpha s}$ subunit of G-proteins, and increase levels of intracellular cyclic AMP. In the rat PTHrP expression is increased by myometrial stretch so it may contribute to maintaining myometrial quiescence during the period of sustained fetal growth during the third trimester. Whether this activity is altered at term remains unclear at the present time. Nitric oxide is a potent endogenous muscle relaxant which acts through cyclic GMP and on Ca^{2+} channels. Nitric oxide synthase (NOS) isoforms have been detected using reverse transcriptase-polymerase chain reaction (RT-PCR) in human fetal membranes and choriodecidua. Levels of mRNA encoding inducible NOS (iNOS) are highest in human myometrium of late-gestation,

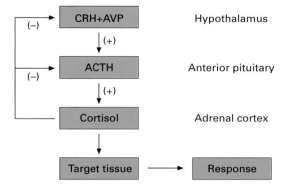

Fig. 12.2. Diagram of the fetal hypothalamic-pituitary-adrenal (HPA) axis. The hypothalamus secretes corticotrophin-releasing hormone (CRH) and arginine vasopressin (AVP) in response to inputs from the hippocampus and other regions. CRH and AVP act on the anterior pituitary to promote increased synthesis of pro-opiomelanocortin (POMC), and its processing to adrenocorticotrophic hormone (ACTH). ACTH then drives steroidogenesis within the fetal adrenal cortex, particularly production of cortisol. In adults, cortisol exerts negative feedback on this pathway at the level of the hypothalamus and pituitary. In the fetus, various mechanisms have developed by which, in late gestation, the negative feedback actions of cortisol on pituitary ACTH output are no longer functional.

but nonlabouring women, and decrease, with a corresponding fall in iNOS protein, in myometrium collected at term. Several authors have therefore suggested that nitric oxide acts in a paracrine manner, potentially in conjunction with progesterone to effect myometrial quiescence during pregnancy. There appears to be a progressive decrease in NOS activity of decidua and myometrium in a variety of species before parturition, in a manner that would presumably diminish its inhibitory influence on the uterus. Studies in the rat at term have shown that there is a corresponding increase in nitric oxide production by inflammatory cells in the cervix. This suggests a role for nitric oxide in cervical effacement and relaxation, as the influence of NOS on the myometrium is diminished.

Relaxin might also have a dual role in inhibition of myometrial contractility and in regulating connective tissue changes in the cervix. The inhibitory effect of relaxin on the myometrium is well established from animal studies, and is primarily one of frequency modulation. Many years ago Porter, amongst others, showed that relaxin suppressed spontaneous uterine contractility in the rat and guinea-pig, but sensitivity to oxytocin was preserved. Relaxin acts by elevating myometrial cyclic AMP, and inhibits oxytocin-induced turnover of phosphoinositide (PI) by the action of cyclic AMP-dependent protein kinase. In the cervix, relaxin also upregulates MMP-1 and MMP-3 expression, and inhibits activity of the tissue inhibitor of metalloproteinase (TIMP-1). This action of relaxin may therefore contribute to normal mechanisms of remodelling cervical connective tissue at term, and suggests a mechanism by which hyperrelaxinaemia is associated with prematurity.

Myometrial activation

In contrast to the state of quiescence during pregnancy, the initiation of labour is associated with a remarkable change in the phenotype of the myometrium. The myocytes become highly excitable and develop spontaneous contractile activity. High-frequency, high-amplitude contractions are generated that spread rapidly across the surface of the uterus due to a high degree of cell–cell coordination. The myometrium also becomes very responsive to stimulation from endogenous agents (e.g. oxytocin, stimulatory prostaglandins) at this time. This transformation in phenotype of the myometrium is termed 'activation'. Once activated the myometrium can respond effectively to endogenous stimulants (eg oxytocin, prostaglandins) to produce labour contractions that aid in the expulsion of the fetus (Fig. 12.3).

Biochemically, the process of *activation* can be defined as an increase in the expression of a cassette of genes encoding proteins (which we have termed contraction-associated proteins or CAPs), which confer the change in phenotype of the myometrium. These CAPs would include ion channels, including sodium channels, which regulate resting membrane potential and hence excitability of the cells, and Ca^{2+} channels which facilitate influx of Ca^{2+} and activate the contractile machinery. Agonist receptors (e.g. for oxytocin and stimulatory prostaglandins) would increase the responsiveness of the myometrium to endogenous stimulant, while an increase in the expression of gap junction proteins would facilitate cell–cell coupling and permit synchronization of the contraction wave (Fig. 12.3). The mechanisms that activate the CAP genes are thus central to the events that control the onset of labour.

The contribution of endocrine signals

Recently it has been shown that the expression of putative CAP genes is relatively low during pregnancy but increases dramatically at term with the onset

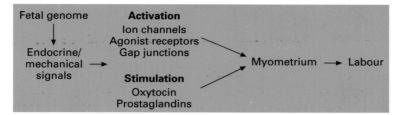

Fig. 12.3. Onset of labour. Myometrial *activation* can be described biochemically by the activation of a cassette of 'contraction-associated' (CAP) genes encoding proteins such as uterotonic receptors, ion channels and gap junctions; these CAPs enable the myometrium to respond more effectively to the increased *stimulation* afforded by the increased production of uterotonic stimulants such as oxytocin and stimulatory prostaglandins.

of labour in association with the increase in oestrogen and decrease in progesterone levels (i.e. increase in E:P ratio) in the plasma. It has also been shown that oestrogen positively regulates the expression of several CAPs including the gap junction protein, connexin43, the oxytocin receptor (OTR) and the prostaglandin F receptor (FP). The action of oestrogen in increased CAP gene transcription does not appear to be direct because, at least for connexin43, blockade of new protein synthesis blocks the oestrogen-induced increase in their expression. Moreover, analysis of the connexin43 promoter reveals that there are no palindromic oestrogen response elements that typically confer responsiveness of genes to this steroid. Thus it appears that one or more transcription factors (possibly acting as master control genes) might modulate oestrogen- (and possibly labour-) induced CAP gene expression in the myometrium. Identification of these transcription factors is important as they may provide novel targets for pharmacological intervention in the treatment of preterm labour.

While these transcription factors have yet to be identified, there is evidence to suggest that members of the Fos and Jun family may contribute to the transcription regulation of CAP genes. Not only are there putative Fos/Jun binding sites (AP-1 sites) within the promoters of CAP genes (e.g. connexin43, OTR) but the expression of c-*fos* (one of the Fos family members) increases dramatically at the time of labour. As with the CAP genes, expression of c-*fos* is regulated positively by oestrogen and negatively by progesterone. Moreover, treatment of near-term rats with exogenous progesterone (to block the normal fall in levels of this steroid) inhibits the increased expression of c-*fos* and the CAP genes and prevents the onset of labour.

Data from other systems suggest that the oestrogen receptor may also associate with the Fos and Jun at the AP-1 site providing an additional potential mechanism for this steroid to regulate CAP expression. In addition other regulatory elements have been demonstrated in the connexin43 promoter which might contribute to the regulation of this CAP gene. However, regulation of CAP gene expression is unlikely to be limited to the level of transcription. Recent data suggest that the expression of connexin43 may also be mediated by changes in mRNA stability through elements in the 3′untranslated region of the transcript. Furthermore, it has been shown that metabolites of progesterone can directly modulate the ability of oxytocin to bind and activate its receptor through interactions of the steroid with the ligand-binding domain of the receptor.

The contribution of mechanical signals to the initiation of labour

The data described above support the concept of endocrine regulation of the onset of labour. However, it has been recently shown that, while the endocrine changes were necessary, they were not alone sufficient for *activation*. These studies showed no increase in CAP gene (connexin43, OTR) expression in the nongravid horn of a unilaterally pregnant rat even though this horn was exposed to the same changes in oestrogen and progesterone as the gravid horn. However, if the nongravid horn was subjected to mechanical stretch, through the placement of a polyvinyl tube, CAP gene expression increased to similar levels to that found in the gravid horn. Importantly, this same mechanical stretch did not lead to increased CAP gene expression during late pregnancy (prior to the increase in the E:P ratio), suggesting that some factor operating during pregnancy normally inhibits stretch-induced *myometrial activation*. Since in nonpregnant rats progesterone was able to block stretch-induced expression of connexin43 mRNA it is likely that this steroid acts to prevent mechanical stretch from increasing CAP gene expression during pregnancy.

These data thus suggest that there are two parallel pathways by which the fetus can induce myometrial activation and the onset of labour: (a) the classical endocrine pathway, involving activation of the fetal hypothalamic–pituitary–adrenal–placental axis, and (b) a mechanical pathway by which fetal growth induces tension in the uterine wall, which in turn contributes to the increased expression of CAPs and the onset of labour. We speculate that this mechanical pathway may explain the increased incidence of preterm labour found in twin and multifetal pregnancies. In these pregnancies the amniotic fluid pressure is similar to that in singleton pregnancies despite the increased uterine volume. According to the law of LaPlace (which states that wall tension must increase in proportion to the diameter in order to maintain a constant pressure within a vessel) this would suggest that there is an increased myometrial wall tension in multifetal pregnancies. This increased tension in the myometrium might predispose to premature activation of CAP gene expression and therefore be responsible for the increased incidence of preterm labour in multiple gestations.

The mechanisms by which physical stretch increases CAP gene expression remain to be determined. In other smooth muscles (e.g. vascular smooth muscle), stretch has been shown to activate multiple intracellular signalling pathways. It has been shown that stretch of vascular smooth muscle cells in vitro increases the transcription rate and protein synthesis of connexin43, although this has yet to be shown in myometrial cells. It is known, however, that growth of the uterus during pregnancy can attenuate any increase in myometrial tension that would otherwise be induced by fetal growth. Thus myometrial growth impacts indirectly on the mechanisms that lead to myometrial *activation*. Studies have shown that there are distinct phases of myometrial growth during pregnancy: an initial phase of hyperplasia, which in rats occurs during the first trimester (up to day 12), and a later phase of hypertrophy which parallels fetal growth during the third trimester. It also appears that there is a final phase at the end of pregnancy when myometrial growth reaches a plateau whereas fetal growth continues. The early phase of myometrial hyperplasia appears to be due to endocrine regulation, possibly involving oestrogen and IGF-1 as shown in nonpregnant rats. Myometrial hypertrophy in the third trimester in rats occurs only in the gravid horn and not the nongravid horn of unilaterally pregnant animals. This is consistent with the hypothesis that the hypertrophy is induced in response to tension on the myometrium as a result of fetal growth. There is some evidence to suggest that the hypertrophy requires the presence of progesterone. Thus there are reports that myometrial growth reaches a plateau at term when progesterone levels fall, but is maintained after term if exogenous progesterone is administered. In addition to the myometrial hypertrophy there is evidence of considerable remodelling of the extracellular matrix and induction of matrix-degrading enzymes during this period.

The data outlined above suggest that mechanical signals can induce quite distinct responses in the myometrium, namely the activation of CAP genes as well as the induction of growth. How might the myocytes sense these mechanical

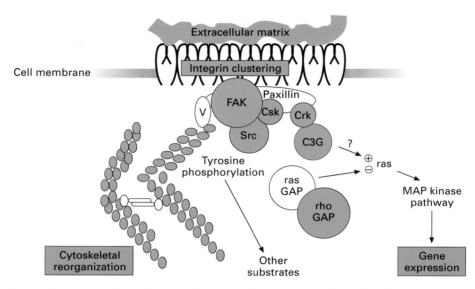

Fig. 12.4. Focal adhesions are formed from a clustering of integrin molecules within the cell membrane, which form a link between the extracellular matrix and the cellular cytoskeleton. Binding of integrins to the matrix is through an RGD domain in their extracellular surface. The cytoplasmic surface of the integrins supports binding of a complex of cytoplasmic proteins that enable binding to the actin cytoskeleton as well as cytoplasmic proteins involved in a series of intracellular signalling pathways. Focal adhesion kinase (FAK) is a critical component of focal adhesions. Through vinculin (V), FAK modulates binding to the actin cytoskeleton. FAK association with Src, Csk and paxillin contributes to activation of intracellular signalling pathways. (From Richardson, A. and Parsons, J.T. (1995), *Bioessays*, **17**, 229–36, and Juliano, R. (1996), *Bioessays*, **18**, 911–17.)

signals and how would such diverse responses be generated? While stretch has been reported to activate multiple intracellular signalling pathways, structures called focal adhesions have been widely reported to contribute to mechano-transduction. Focal adhesions are the cell's 'spot welds' to its surrounding matrix. Focal adhesions are formed from an aggregation of integrin molecules which traverse the cell membrane (Fig. 12.4). The extracellular domain of the integrin molecules bind to components of the extracellular matrix (e.g. colla-gen, fibronectin, laminin) while the intracellular domain forms a platform to which a number of 'adaptor proteins' bind which, in turn, anchor the integrin to the actin cytoskeleton. Some of these adaptor proteins also contribute to the activation of intracellular signalling pathways (e.g. the MAPkinase pathway), which in turn regulate gene expression. Focal adhesions thus offer the potential to transmit a mechanical signal from the extracellular environment to the cellular cytoskeleton as well as transduce the mechanical signal to a biochemical one.

A key molecule in the formation and turnover of focal adhesions is focal adhesion kinase or FAK. Null mutations in the *fak* gene lead to embryonic death and fibroblast cells from these embryos form very large focal adhesions that disrupt normal cell functions (e.g. cell migration and proliferation). Studies of the expression and activity of FAK and other focal adhesion proteins in the rat myometrium during late pregnancy and at labour have shown that FAK activity is low at midpregnancy but increases markedly during late pregnancy (day 20–22) at a time when fetal growth and myometrial hypertrophy are maximal. Most interestingly, FAK activity falls dramatically at the onset of labour on day 23. These changes in FAK activity appear to induce cellular signalling as phosphorylation of paxillin, another focal adhesion protein and a substrate of FAK, follows a similar temporal pattern to that of FAK. Interestingly, treatment of rats with progesterone at term (to block the endogenous fall in this steroid) results in maintenance of elevated FAK activity, continued myometrial growth, inhibition of CAP gene expression and inhibition of labour onset. As shown in Fig. 12.5, it is likely that, during late pregnancy (i.e. day 18 onwards), as the rate of fetal growth becomes maximal, tension is placed on the uterine wall. In the presence of progesterone FAK activity is increased and this permits remodelling of focal adhesions, allowing hypertrophy of myocytes within the myometrium. As long as myometrial growth keeps pace with fetal growth, CAP gene expression is not activated. However, once progesterone levels start to fall at term, FAK activity falls and focal adhesion remodelling ceases. This results in the formation of large focal adhesions which anchor the cell firmly to the extracellular matrix. This impedes myocyte hypertrophy and with continued fetal growth increased tension is placed on the myocyte. This increased tension (possibly transmitted through the focal adhesion) induces the activation of CAP genes and the onset of labour.

Myometrial activation and relaxation of the human myometrium

This model of myometrial activation requires withdrawal of the actions of progesterone. In virtually all species this is accomplished by a fall in the plasma levels of this steroid. However, in the human there is no such fall, leading investigators to question whether the onset of labour in the human is

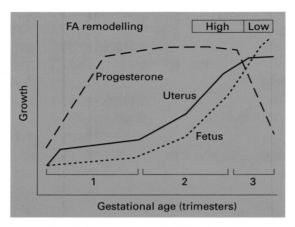

Fig. 12.5. A model for linkage between fetal/uterine growth and the onset of labour. During the first trimester embryonic growth is minimal and uterine growth is due to hyperplasia and is controlled by endocrine mechanisms. During the second and third trimesters fetal growth (through tension placed on the uterine wall) induces myometrial growth through cell hypertrophy. This requires the presence of progesterone and focal adhesion (FA) remodelling which is modulated by activated focal adhesion kinase (FAK). At term the fall in progesterone leads to reduced FAK activity and turnover of focal adhesions and hence termination of myometrial growth. In this context, continued fetal growth results in increased tension within the myometrium, which in turn leads to increased expression of CAP genes, *activation* of the myometrium and the onset of labour.

quite different from other species. Recent studies indicate that, as with plasma levels, there is no local withdrawal of progesterone within intrauterine tissues, there is no fall in progesterone metabolites (e.g. allopregnenolone) that might provide progestational activities and there is no change in progesterone-binding sites or in the A or B isoforms of the progesterone receptor in myometrial samples. These studies suggest, therefore, that the progesterone signalling pathway is fully functional within human uterine tissues.

Other data may help explain the apparent discrepancy between humans and other species. In contrast to animal data in which there is no significant increase in the expression of CAP genes during labour, in the human there is no increase in mRNA encoding the gap junction protein (connexin43), the oxytocin receptor or stimulatory prostaglandin receptors. There is increased expression of connexin26, CRH receptor II, and the EP4 receptor; however, these genes probably encode proteins that would promote relaxation rather than contraction. Importantly, myometrial samples for these (and most other studies of the human myometrium) were collected at the time of caesarian section from the lower uterine segment. Studies of myometrial contractions in vitro have demonstrated that, at labour, the lower segment shows a marked change in its responsiveness to prostaglandins. Before labour prostaglandin E (PGE) caused contraction of both fundal and lower segment myometrium in response to PGE whereas during labour PGE caused contraction of the fundus but relaxation of the lower segment. Taken together these data suggest a regionalization of the human myometrium during labour. While the fundus remains contractile the lower segment activates genes that induce myometrial relaxation, which may aid the descent of the fetus into the birth canal. In the rat, it has been found that at least one of these 'relaxation' genes is positively regulated by progesterone. It is possible, therefore, that the elevated progesterone levels during labour in the human may actually be needed to increase the expression of these genes. Presumably some mechanism must therefore exist to induce a 'functional withdrawal' of progesterone in the fundal region. Clearly more investigation of myometrial gene expression in the human myometrium is required to fully resolve these issues.

Myometrial stimulation

Once the myometrium has been activated it is capable of responding optimally to the stimulants generated within the maternal and fetal compartments that 'drive' the uterine contractions of labour. However, while numerous agonists (including endothelin and α-adrenergic agonists) are able to stimulate uterine contractions, only stimulatory prostaglandins and oxytocin have been convincingly shown to contribute to the generation of labour contractions.

Prostaglandins

There is now strong evidence that stimulatory prostaglandins are critically important for the process of labour. Supporting data include the dramatic rise in prostaglandin levels with the progression of labour, the ability to induce labour with exogenous prostaglandins and the ability of nonsteroidal anti-inflammatory drugs (NSAIDs), as prostaglandin synthesis inhibitors, to effectively inhibit labour. Primary prostaglandins, including PGE_2 and $PGF_{2\alpha}$ are formed from the precursor arachidonic acid (Fig. 12.6), liberated from

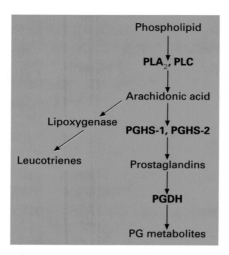

Fig. 12.6. Metabolic pathway for generation and metabolism of prostaglandins (PGs) within intrauterine tissues.

membrane phospholipids such as phosphatidyl ethanolamine and phosphatidyl inositol probably through the action of cytosolic phospholipase A$_2$ (PLA$_2$) which is increased during labour in intrauterine tissues. Formation of primary prostaglandins from arachidonic acid requires the action of prostaglandin H synthase (PGHS) and the specific primary prostaglandin isomerases. Two forms of PGHS have been recently identified, cloned and characterized. The constitutive form of PGHS (PGHS-1) and the inducible form (PGHS-2) are separate gene products, although they have considerable sequence homology; cDNAs for the two PGHS isoforms are 60–65% homologous. Studies now clearly indicate that it is the PGHS-2 gene product that is increased in expression in uterine tissues during labour. Metabolism of the primary prostaglandins to inactive metabolites is achieved through the action of prostaglandin dehydrogenase (PGDH).

In women, prostaglandin production is discretely compartmentalized within the fetal membranes. In amnion, PGHS activity predominates; PGE$_2$ is the principal prostaglandin formed, and there is an increase in prostaglandin synthesis and levels of PGHS-2, but not PGHS-1, mRNA at preterm and term labour. Decidua has been reported to produce increased amounts of prostaglandin at the time of labour, but this is not a consistent observation. The chorion, interposed between amnion and decidua, has both PGHS and PGDH activities, but metabolism predominates. Output of prostaglandins, and PGHS-2 activity, is higher in chorion obtained from patients at spontaneous labour than at elective term caesarean section, although in chorion obtained at preterm labour both PGHS-1 and PGHS-2 mRNA levels are increased. It has been suggested that, for much of pregnancy, chorionic PGDH forms a relative metabolic barrier that prevents the passage of prostaglandins generated in amnion or chorion from reaching the underlying decidua and/or myometrium. This suggests that, unless the synthetic activity of amnion/chorion exceeds the metabolic potential of chorion, those prostaglandins which drive myometrial activity would have to be generated within the decidua or the myometrium itself. Preliminary results suggest that labour may be associated with increased expression of PGHS-2, but not PGHS-1, in the myometrium. However, the relative importance of autocrine control of myometrial contractility versus paracrine control by prostaglandins from amnion or chorion in relation to labour onset remains unclear.

In the human, glucocorticoids may act as primary stimulators of PGHS-2 expression in the amnion. The glucocorticoids may act directly on fibroblasts within the amnion or indirectly through the increased expression of CRH by amnion epithelial cells; the CRH in turn acts on the fibroblasts to induce PGHS-2 expression. Several other pathways have been shown to lead to increased prostaglandin synthesis including elevation of intracellular Ca^{2+} concentrations ($[Ca^{2+}]_i$), epidermal growth factor, platelet activating factor and catecholamines, though their role in the generation of prostaglandins during labour remains to be determined.

Prostaglandins have been implicated as critical mediators in the onset of infection-associated preterm labour, which has been estimated by some studies to comprise up to 30% of all preterm labour. Prostaglandins levels in amniotic fluid and prostaglandin production by amnion and choriodecidua are markedly elevated in patients in preterm labour with evidence of infection. In the amniotic fluid of these patients there are also increased concentrations of cytokines including interleukin-1β, interleukin-6 (IL-6) and tumour necrosis factor (TNF), factors that have been shown to be potent stimulators of prostaglandin synthesis in intrauterine tissues. Administration of cytokines such as IL-1, or of bacterial endotoxin, (lipopolysaccharide; LPS) to pregnant mice provokes premature delivery, and provides a convenient animal model to study, in a precise temporal sequence, the events of cytokine-induced premature labour.

Prostaglandins act through specific receptors including the four main subtypes, EP_1, EP_2, EP_3 and EP_4 for PGE_2, and FP for $PGF_{2\alpha}$. EP_1 and EP_3 receptors mediate contractions of smooth muscle in a number of tissues through mechanisms that include increased Ca^{2+} utilization and inhibition of intracellular cyclic AMP. EP_3 receptors exist as a number of isoforms produced after alternative splicing of a single gene product. EP_2 and EP_4 receptors act through increased cyclic AMP formation and relax smooth muscle. These receptor subtypes are expressed in human myometrium in late pregnancy; EP_2 expression is higher late in gestation, regardless of the presence or absence of labour, but FP is unchanged. In the rat, it has been shown that parturition is associated with upregulation of myometrial FP receptors, and downregulation of EP receptor subtypes – effectively a switch from inhibition to stimulation of contractility.

The major metabolizing enzyme for prostaglandins, NAD^+-dependent 15-hydroxy PGDH, catalyses oxidation of 15 hydroxy groups of E and F series prostaglandins. This initial step results in the formation of 15-keto and 13,14-dihydro-15-keto metabolites which have reduced biological activity. In intrauterine tissues PGDH is localized in trophoblast cells within the chorion and may thus act as a barrier preventing biologically active prostaglandin derived from amnion and/or chorion from reaching the underlying decidua and myometrium during most of pregnancy. Recently, a group of patients in idiopathic preterm labour was identified with a deficiency of PGDH in chorion trophoblast cells. There was a further reduction of ir-PGDH and PGDH activity in the chorion of patients in preterm labour with diagnosed infection; this was accounted for by the loss of trophoblast cells that accompanies the infective process. These results have led to the speculation that in full-term pregnancy the activity of PGDH in the chorion is normally sufficient to prevent transmembrane passage of most of the prostaglandin generated in the amnion or chorion. The likely source of the prostaglandin that stimulates myometrial contractility is therefore decidua and/or myometrium. In idiopathic preterm delivery, in the absence of infection, PGDH expression is reduced, and so is the number of chorionic trophoblast cells. In the presence of an inflammatory response with loss of trophoblast cells, PGDH activity in chorion is dramatically reduced. In these circumstances, if prostaglandin production is stimulated in amnion or chorion, those prostaglandins will not be metabolized and can easily reach the myometrium to provoke preterm birth (Fig. 12.7).

Oxytocin

Our understanding of the physiological role of oxytocin (OT) in the regulation of labour has been clarified in recent years. While there has been no question

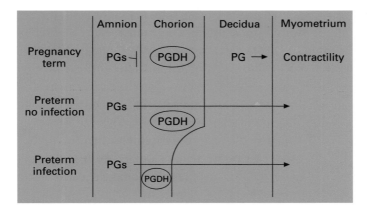

	Amnion	Chorion	Decidua	Myometrium
Pregnancy term	PGs⊣	(PGDH)	PG →	Contractility
Preterm no infection	PGs	(PGDH)		
Preterm infection	PGs	(PGDH)		

Fig. 12.7.   Prostaglandin metabolism at term and preterm: role of chorionic prostaglandin dehydrogenase (PGDH) in regulating transfer of primary prostaglandins (PGs) across human fetal membranes. In normal term pregnancy, PGDH activity in chorion is high, and we suggest there is little transfer of primary PG generated within amnion and chorion across the membranes. In some patients in idiopathic preterm delivery with a relative deficiency of chorionic PGDH, PGE_2 generated in response to a variety of potential stimulants in amnion and chorion, can partially escape metabolism. With infection, the chorionic trophoblast cells are destroyed, PGDH activity is therefore very low in chorion, and PGs generated within amniochorion are able to reach decidua and myometrium.

that OT is a potent myometrial stimulant, few studies showed increases in plasma OT with the initiation of labour. This led some to propose that the major role of OT was restricted to the second stages during passage of the fetus through the birth canal, when there is a reflex release of OT from the posterior pituitary. However, the finding that human intrauterine tissues (excluding the placenta) can synthesize OT and that there is a significant increase in OT expression in the choriodecidua with the onset of labour, has re-established OT as a major endogenous regulator of labour contractions. While the mechanisms controlling OT expression in intrauterine tissues are not fully understood, expression can be increased *in vitro* by treatment with oestrogen.

While a number of other hormonal agents (CRH, endothelin, bradykinin, platelet activating factor) can stimulate myometrial activity under various circumstances, their precise role, if any, in the generation of labour contractions remains to be determined.

In addition to their individual uterotonic actions, there is evidence to suggest that myometrial stimulants might interact to regulate the expression and action of other agonists. Oxytocin has been shown to stimulate the production of PGE$_2$ and PGF$_{2\alpha}$ from human and rat decidua, an effect blocked by OT antagonists. Inhibitors of prostaglandin synthesis or antagonists of prostaglandin action have been reported to block OT-stimulated contractions of uterine strips in rabbits, although part of this effect may have been due to nonspecific effects of the blocking agents used. In rats, blockade of prostaglandin synthesis did not prevent OT-stimulated myometrial contraction nor was the number or affinity of OT receptors affected by infusions of indomethacin or PGF$_{2\alpha}$. Oxytocin may also interact with other uterine stimulants to regulate contractility. A synergistic effect of oxytocin and CRH to increase myometrial contractions in human myometrium has been reported; this may also act through effects on prostaglandins. In addition, OT has been reported to stimulate endothelin-1 release from endometrial cells in culture.

Myometrial contraction

Up to this point, we have discussed the endocrine changes that are associated with the initiation of labour as well as the effects these changes may have on the pattern of uterine activity. We now consider the pathways within the myometrial cell that result in contraction.

The biochemical pathways that result in the interaction of actin and myosin leading to a contraction are shown in Fig. 12.8. The myosin molecule is a hexamer, approximately 160 nm in length, and is composed of two heavy chains (200 kDa each) and two pairs of light chains (one pair around 17 kDa and one around 20 kDa). The heavy chain components form α helices (130 nm in length). Towards the NH$_2$ terminal these chains unfold to form two globular heads. Each globular head contains: (1) ATPase activity (localized only on the heavy chain component); (2) an actin-binding site; (3) one light chain (20 kDa) that can bind Ca^{2+} and Mg^{2+} and can be phosphorylated, and another (17 kDa) the functional role of which is unknown. The helical tail of the myosin molecule acts to transmit tension during shortening. The globular actin molecules (45 kDa) polymerize into long filaments, 6–9 nm in diameter. In smooth muscles there are 11–15 thin filaments per myosin (thick) filament.

Interaction of actin and myosin occurs following the development of ATPase activity on the myosin head (Fig. 12.9). This then allows the formation of cross-links with the actin molecules. The myosin head then rotates as a result of conformational changes in the protein structure, leading to a pulling on the actin

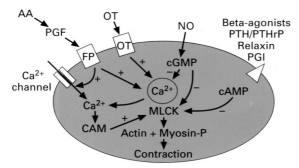

Fig. 12.8.   Simplified biochemical pathway leading to actin–myosin interaction and myometrial contraction showing the multiple parallel pathways which can increase/reduce intracellular calcium levels or raise levels of cyclic nucleotides and hence regulate myometrial contractility. AA, arachidonic acid; PGF, prostaglandin $F_{2\alpha}$; FP, PGF receptor; OT, oxytocin and OT receptor; NO, nitric oxide; PTH, parathyroid hormone; PTHrP, parathyroid hormone-related protein; PGI, prostacyclin; CAM, calmodulin; MLCK, myosin light chain kinase; myosin-P, phosphorylated myosin.

filament to create tension and produce a relative spatial displacement. The energy required for these changes is believed to result from the phosphorylation of the 20 kDa light chains of myosin (MLC20) by the enzyme myosin light chain kinase (MLCK). Other contractile proteins, such as caldesmon, which interact with myosin to increase the efficiency of actin–myosin coupling, may also play a role in regulating myometrial contraction.

MLCK can be considered a pivotal point in regulating smooth muscle contraction. Most information on MLCK comes from enzyme isolated from the turkey gizzard, although more recently we have gained information on MLCK from the sheep myometrium. These data can be summarized as follows. MLCK has an absolute requirement for Ca^{2+}-calmodulin (Ca-CaM). In the presence of activating levels of Ca^{2+} ($>10^{-6}$ M) the Ca-CaM complex binds to a site on MLCK which in turn (presumably by some conformational change in MLCK) opens up the kinase site to enable the enzyme to phosphorylate MLC20 and hence initiate contraction.

Relaxation of smooth muscle, as a result of reduction in the phosphorylation of MLC20, can occur due to a decrease in MLCK activity with the subsequent dephosphorylation of the light chains by MLC phosphatase. The reduction in MLCK activity can either be as a result of a fall in intracellular Ca^{2+} concentrations leading to a decrease in Ca-CaM levels or possibly due to phosphorylation of MLCK itself by a cyclic AMP-dependent protein kinase (A-kinase) (Fig.

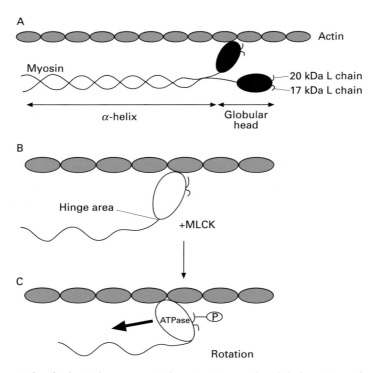

Fig. 12.9. Molecular basis for myometrial contraction. A. The globular actin molecules polymerize to form long filaments of F-actin to which the globular myosin head of myosin filament attaches. B. Myometrial contraction involves interactions between actin and myosin myofilaments. Phosphorylation (P) of the 20-kDa myosin light chain on the myosin head by MLCK induces (C) an ATPase activity that supports a rotation in the myosin head relative to actin and consequently the sliding of the actin and myosin filaments in apposition to each other.

12.9). In this phosphorylated state the affinity of this regulatory protein for Ca-CaM is reduced. Thus the contractile state of the cell can, in large part, be represented as a balance between the actions of Ca^{2+} through calmodulin, and cyclic AMP through A-kinase on the activity of the enzyme MLCK. Cyclic AMP can also affect contractility by reducing intracellular Ca^{2+} levels either by increasing intracellular uptake of free Ca^{2+} or by increasing Ca^{2+} efflux from the myocyte.

The resting intracellular Ca^{2+} concentration is 10^{-7}–10^{-8} M and this must increase to at least 10^{-6} M for MLCK to be activated and for contraction to occur. Under normal resting conditions the extracellular Ca^{2+} concentration is around

10^{-3} M and in order to maintain this electrical imbalance, ATP-dependent (Ca/Mg-ATPase) and ATP-independent (Na exchange) cell membrane Ca^{2+} pumps have been developed.

An increase in intracellular Ca^{2+} to initiate contraction within the myometrial cell can occur through several mechanisms (Fig. 12.9): (1) release of Ca^{2+} from intracellular (sarcoplasmic reticulum, mitochondria, inner cell membrane bound) stores; (2) inhibition of Ca^{2+} efflux; (3) increase in Ca^{2+} influx from extracellular sources. Depending on the stimulus one or more of these events may occur during contraction. The entry of Ca^{2+} from extracellular sources may occur via voltage-sensitive (during discharge of action potentials) or receptor-operated mechanisms. Mechanisms may also operate to link cell membrane receptors to the intracellular Ca^{2+} stores. Thus agonist-receptor activation of phospholipase C (via the prostaglandin or OT receptors) can lead to the hydrolysis of inositol phosphates leading to the release of inositol-1,4,5,-triphosphate (IP_3). IP_3, in turn, can cause the release of Ca^{2+} from intracellular stores. Diacyl glycerol generated during inositol hydrolysis can also interact with intracellular signalling pathways as well as be a substrate for prostaglandin synthesis. Alpha-adrenergic agonists and OT operate through the inositol phosphate pathway. Stimulatory prostaglandins can also act to increase the influx of Ca^{2+} through cell membrane channels, while OT and prostaglandins have been reported to inhibit Ca^{2+} efflux. $PGF_{2\alpha}$ may also stimulate the hydrolysis of arachidonic acid from phospholipids and this arachidonic acid, in turn, could act as a mediator for the release of intracellular Ca^{2+}. Hence prostaglandins can have multiple actions to cause an elevation of intracellular Ca^{2+}. Agents which inhibit myometrial activity (progesterone, β-agonists, relaxin) may operate to increase intracellular uptake or efflux of Ca^{2+} which, by reducing the affinity of calmodulin for Ca^{2+}, would effectively reduce the activity of MLCK and hence inhibit contractile activity.

Cyclic AMP levels are regulated by adenylate cyclase (cyclic AMP synthesis) and phosphodiesterase (cyclic AMP degradation). Inhibitors of myometrial activity, such as β-adrenergic agonists, relaxin and prostacyclin are known to increase cyclic AMP probably through an increase in adenylate cyclase activity. Recently it has been suggested that nitric oxide may act as an endogenous inhibitor of myometrial contractile activity. The mechanism by which nitric oxide might inhibit myometrial contractions is unclear, however, in other smooth muscles it has been shown to increase intracellular cyclic GMP levels which in turn reduce intracellular Ca^{2+} levels and hence contractile activity.

Cervical maturation

The three basic components of the human cervix are smooth muscle, collagen (together with the connective tissue matrix composed of glycosaminoglycans including dermatan sulphate, heparin sulphate and hyaluronic acid) and elastin. Collagen is a rigid, rod-shaped molecule of 300 kDa which imparts the tensile strength to the cervix. Elastin, which provides for tissue elasticity, is observed in connective tissue along with collagen and proteoglycans (glycosaminoglycans linked to a protein core). The glycosaminoglycans heparin and dermatin are highly polar due to sulphation and together with hyaluronic acid are linked to collagen and each other to form a complex matrix.

The degradation of collagen occurs as an action of the enzymes collagenase and leucocyte elastase, levels of which have been shown to increase in cervical tissue during late pregnancy and labour. Collagenase may be the principal enzyme in the regulated control of collagen degradation, whereas elastase, which is located in the azurophil granules of polymorphonuclear leucocytes, may be more associated with collagen degradation in granulocyte-dependent inflammatory reactions. Other proteolytic enzymes in addition to collagenase and elastase are found in the cervix, which may also be involved with collagen remodelling and cervical maturation at term.

Although the cervix contains contractile smooth muscle, its role in the changes that occur at term is unknown. Similarly the precise role of uterine contractions in eliciting cervical changes is unclear. There is little correlation between these two events and, in sheep, surgical isolation of the cervix from the uterus does not prevent cervical maturation. Taken together, the data suggest that cervical maturation is not caused by a muscular contribution from the cervix or myometrium. Rather, biochemical changes begin to occur long before there is any indication of labour onset. These events involve more than a mere degradation of collagen and dermatan sulphate; rather, they include a remodelling of the cervical matrix with new collagen and proteoglycan synthesis.

Many studies have shown that oestrogen, relaxin and prostaglandins have a major impact on the processes of cervical softening described above. In one study, a monoclonal antibody against rat relaxin was used to passively immunize pregnant rats and demonstrated the critical role of this hormone in the cervical changes necessary for successful delivery. Amongst other actions, relaxin upregulates the expression of matrix metalloproteinases (MMP-1 and MMP-3), and inhibits the activity of tissue inhibitor of metalloproteinase (TIMP-1). Prostaglandins produced within the cervix and by intrauterine tissues are also believed to have a major impact in regulating changes in collagen and cervical remodelling at term. These data have led to their extensive use to produce a more favourable cervix when clinical induction of labour is required. In the rat at term, there is an increase in nitric oxide production by inflammatory cells in the cervix, suggesting a role for nitric oxide in cervical effacement and relaxation.

Summary

In this chapter we have shown how fetal endocrine pathways are activated during late pregnancy leading to changes in placental endocrine systems that result in a fall in progesterone and an increase in oestrogen in maternal plasma. This switch in the E:P ratio supports the increased expression of myometrial genes that activate the myometrium and enable this muscle to respond optimally to the endogenous stimulation provided by uterotonic agonists such as OT and stimulatory prostaglandins. In the human, where there is no fall in progesterone levels, it is likely that there are changes in the ability of the progesterone receptor to modulate myometrial genes, thus effecting a functional withdrawal of progesterone. While these endocrine changes are necessary for the onset of labour, recent data suggest that they are not, of themselves, sufficient to induce myometrial activation and that mechanical tension on the myometrium is also required. The successful completion of labour is critical to the survival of mammalian species. It is not surprising therefore that multiple and redundant mechanisms have been developed to initiate labour and to drive labour contractions. It thus follows that there are multiple opportunities for this system to break down and lead to preterm labour. The development of effective and safe means of preventing preterm labour require that new therapies be based on a thorough understanding of the biological basis of parturition.

FURTHER READING

Challis, J.R.G, Lye, S.J. and Gibb, W. (1997). Prostaglandins and parturition. *Ann. N.Y. Acad. Sci.*, **26**, 254–67.

Challis, J.R.G. and Lye, S.J. (1994). Parturition. In: *The Physiology of Reproduction*, vol. 2, ed. E. Knobil and J.D. Neill, pp. 985–1031. New York: Raven Press.

Smith, R. (1999). The timing of birth. *Sci. Am.*, **280**, 68–75.

Hansen, W.R., Keelan, J.A., Skinner, S.J. and Mitchell, M.D. (1999). Key enzymes of prostaglandin biosynthesis and metabolism. Coordinate regulation of expression by cytokines in gestational tissues: a review. *Prostaglandins Other Lipid Mediat.*, **57**, 243–57.

Bryant-Greenwood, G.D. (1998). The extracellular matrix of human fetal membranes: structure and function. *Placenta*, **19**, 1–11.

Winkler, M. and Rath, W. (1999). Changes in the cervical extracellular matrix during pregnancy and parturition. *J. Perinat. Med.*, **27**, 45–60.

Nathanielsz, P.W. (1998). Comparative studies on the initiation of labor. *Eur. J. Obstet. Gynecol. Reprod. Biol.*, **78**, 127–32.

Challis, J.R.G. and Lye, S.J. (1998). In: *Estrogen and Progesterone During Pregnancy and Parturition*, ed. I. Fraser, R. Jansen, R. Lobo and M. Whitehead, pp. 243–54. Edinburgh: Churchill Livingstone.

Lye, S. (1994). The initiation and inhibition of labour: toward a molecular understanding. In: *Semin. Reprod. Endocrinol.*, **12**, 284–94.

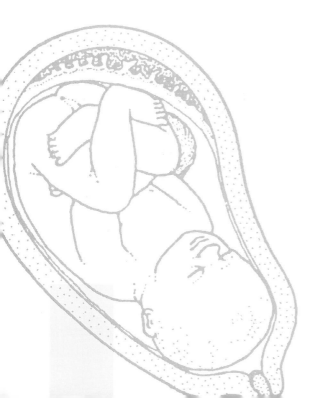

Index

Note: page numbers in *italics* refer to figures and tables